T0075919

Advanced BlackBerry 6 Development

Chris King

Apress®

Advanced BlackBerry 6 Development

Copyright © 2011 by Chris King

All rights reserved. No part of this work may be reproduced or transmitted in any form or by any means, electronic or mechanical, including photocopying, recording, or by any information storage or retrieval system, without the prior written permission of the copyright owner and the publisher.

ISBN-13 (pbk): 978-1-4302-3210-0

ISBN-13 (electronic): 978-1-4302-3211-7

Printed and bound in the United States of America (POD)

Trademarked names, logos, and images may appear in this book. Rather than use a trademark symbol with every occurrence of a trademarked name, logo, or image we use the names, logos, and images only in an editorial fashion and to the benefit of the trademark owner, with no intention of infringement of the trademark.

The use in this publication of trade names, trademarks, service marks, and similar terms, even if they are not identified as such, is not to be taken as an expression of opinion as to whether or not they are subject to proprietary rights.

President and Publisher: Paul Manning
Lead Editor: Steve Anglin
Development Editor: Matthew Moodie
Technical Reviewer: Kunal Mittal
Editorial Board: Steve Anglin, Mark Beckner, Ewan Buckingham, Gary Cornell, Jonathan Gennick, Jonathan Hassell, Michelle Lowman, James Markham, Matthew Moodie, Jeff Olson, Jeffrey Pepper, Frank Pohlmann, Douglas Pundick, Ben Renow-Clarke, Dominic Shakeshaft, Matt Wade, Tom Welsh
Coordinating Editor: Laurin Becker
Copy Editor: Mary Ann Fugate
Compositor: MacPS, LLC
Indexer: John Collins
Artist: April Milne
Cover Designer: Anna Ishchenko

Distributed to the book trade worldwide by Springer Science+Business Media, LLC., 233 Spring Street, 6th Floor, New York, NY 10013. Phone 1-800-SPRINGER, fax (201) 348-4505, e-mail orders-ny@springer-sbm.com, or visit www.springeronline.com.

For information on translations, please e-mail rights@apress.com, or visit www.apress.com.

Apress and friends of ED books may be purchased in bulk for academic, corporate, or promotional use. eBook versions and licenses are also available for most titles. For more information, reference our Special Bulk Sales–eBook Licensing web page at www.apress.com/info/bulksales.

The information in this book is distributed on an "as is" basis, without warranty. Although every precaution has been taken in the preparation of this work, neither the author(s) nor Apress shall have any liability to any person or entity with respect to any loss or damage caused or alleged to be caused directly or indirectly by the information contained in this work.

The source code for this book is available to readers at www.apress.com.

For Patrick, Kathryn, and Andrew

Contents at a Glance

Contents

v

■ Chapter 7: Browser with Web Apps...................................... 233

About the Author

 **Chris King** is a software engineer specializing in mobile development. He has written a wide variety of embedded and downloadable apps and libraries, including wireless messaging, lifestyle, shopping, music, and video applications. His software has been pre-loaded on tens of millions of phones in the United States. Chris develops applications for BlackBerry, Android, Java ME, BREW, and Windows Phone devices. Chris has also written *Advanced BlackBerry Development* (Apress, 2009) and *Android in Action, Second Edition* (Manning, 2011). He is the author of several articles on mobile development, and was the technical reviewer for the books *Android Essentials*, by Chris Haseman (Apress, 2008), and *Beginning Java ME Platform*, by Ray Rischpater (Apress, 2008). He currently serves as a senior engineer for Gravity Mobile in San Francisco.

Chris graduated summa cum laude from Washington University in St. Louis with majors in computer science and English literature. When he isn't programming or writing for fun or profit, Chris can be found reading, baking, cycling, or hiking throughout the San Francisco Bay Area.

About the Technical Reviewer

 **Kunal Mittal** serves as an Executive Director of Technology at Sony Pictures Entertainment, where he is responsible for the SOA, Identity Management, and Content Management programs. He provides a centralized engineering service to different lines of business, and he leads efforts to introduce new platforms and technologies into the Sony Pictures Enterprise IT environment.

Kunal is an entrepreneur who helps startups defining their technology strategy, product roadmap, and development plans. With his strong relations with several development partners worldwide, he is able to help startups and even large companies build appropriate development partnerships. He generally works in an Advisor or Consulting CTO capacity, and he serves actively in the Project Management and Technical Architect functions.

He has authored and edited several books and articles on J2EE, cloud computing, and mobile technologies. He holds a Master's degree in Software Engineering and is an instrument-rated private pilot.

Acknowledgments

This book never would have happened without the original *Advanced BlackBerry Development*, and so I owe a particular debt to everyone who helped with that book. I'm particularly grateful for Steve Anglin, who has been relentless in championing both of these books. Big thanks as well to Ray Rischpater, who opened doors for me at Apress and provided rare insight into his craft.

Once again I've been humbled by the skill and dedication shown by everyone at Apress. Laurin Becker has brought good cheer, organization, and grace to her role as my coordinating editor. Editor Matt Moodie provided welcome feedback at every stage of the project, from the table of contents to the last dangling note. Technical reviewer Kunal Mittal tenaciously chased down every undefined acronym in the book. My two copy editors, Mary Ann Fugate and Mary Behr, brought great style to the text while preserving my voice. I'm certain that many other people at Apress have contributed in ways I cannot see, and I thank all of them.

I consider myself profoundly fortunate in many ways, not the least of which is the support of the whole crew at Gravity Mobile. Noah Hurwitz, Chris Lyon, and Young Yoon have built a wonderful team of talented and fun folks, and provide an enthusiastic environment for us to produce great work. Sam Trychin combines a frightening intelligence with a calming demeanor, setting a great example for all of us to follow. All of the guys challenge and inspire one another to be better; the last few years have been the most rewarding of my life.

No book or person exists in a vacuum, and I feel extremely grateful for all the people who have supported me throughout my career and made software development so satisfying. I'm particularly thankful for Frank Ableson, Jim Alisago, Richard Aplin, Erik Browne, Levon Dolbakian, Chris Haseman, Graham Darcey, Cathy Donovan, Dr. Chris Gill, Dr. Ken Goldman, Jonathan Jackson, Craig Kawahara, Glen Kunene, Mike Ma, Chad Moats, Troy Mott, Sasha Parry, Greg Peters, Ian Peters-Campbell, Brian Pridham, Rajiv Ramanasankaran, Dave Robaska, Jason Salge, Tom Seago, Charles Stearns, and Wayne Yurtin. My apologies for anyone whose name I may have forgotten; I consider myself fortunate to have met a surplus of talented and generous people in my career.

Introduction

Carrying a BlackBerry used to speak volumes about a person. When you saw someone tapping at that wide keyboard with both thumbs, you could safely assume that the owner was a businessperson, and that the person's time was so valuable that he or she couldn't afford to be out of touch from the office for even a moment. Today, you can no longer make that assumption. BlackBerry 6 and other recent releases have played up the devices' power, connectivity, and media capabilities. Now these devices are carried by teenagers, surfers, knitters—seemingly everyone. Anyone who has experienced that large screen, that expansive keyboard, and that powerful processor will not contentedly return to a crammed phone with a multi-tap dial pad.

The explosion in the number of BlackBerry devices has raised people's expectations, and also created a tempting marketplace for programmers everywhere. BlackBerry 6 applications offer a rich and expressive interface for a mobile device, and people will pay for the best apps available. Developers sell their applications on BlackBerry App World, through off-deck stores like Handango, and through wireless carrier stores. Many more people program for fun and load their applications on their own devices or those of friends. And, because BlackBerry still has dominated the enterprise marketplace, many programmers write applications particularly for their internal business customers.

This book will show you how to make the most of your BlackBerry applications. It focuses on the most fun, the most impressive, and the most rewarding aspects of development. By the time you finish, you should be able to write professional-quality applications that run on the latest devices.

The Book's Anatomy

Advanced BlackBerry 6 Development is divided into four parts. Each part concentrates on a particular theme. The book was designed to be read in sequence, as each chapter builds on the chapters that come before, but veteran developers can easily move to the parts that interest them the most.

Part 1, "Advanced APIs"

This first part of the book focuses on the rich feature set offered by BlackBerry 6 devices. By examining individual topics, you can gain a great depth of knowledge about the material.

- **Chapter 1**, "Getting Started": Provides a quick introduction to BlackBerry development. You'll see how to set up your programming environment and learn the fundamentals of Java development for BlackBerry.

■ **Chapter 2**, "Media Capture": Shows how to record audio, photos, and video from within your application or other applications on the device.

■ **Chapter 3**, "Media Playback": Describes the vast range of media types supported by BlackBerry 6 and how to include each one within an application.

■ **Chapter 4**, "Wireless Messaging": Introduces the technologies used to send and receive various types of messages including SMS, e-mail, and BlackBerry PIN.

■ **Chapter 5**, "Cryptography": Offers a quick primer on security, including how to obscure information, determine authenticity, and prevent tampering. Discusses the various toolkits available for cryptography, their advantages, and how to use each.

Part 2, "Device Integration"

This part of the book turns toward leveraging existing functions on the device. Canny programmers will take advantage of the resources built into each BlackBerry, and learn how to make their app indispensible to the user.

■ **Chapter 6**, "Personal Information": Examines the various repositories of personal data on the phone, such as the address book and calendar. Shows how to read, update, and create new records from within your application.

■ **Chapter 7**, "Browser with Web Apps": Explores the trade-offs between web app, widget, and application development. Describes the various types of browsers and how they impact your development. Covers browser APIs for embedding browsers within apps or apps within browsers.

■ **Chapter 8**, "Integrating with the BlackBerry OS": Covers several useful techniques such as providing customized icons, communicating between applications, and adding options to the device's native menus.

Part 3, "Going Pro"

While the first two parts of the book primarily focus on adding features to your applications, this part focuses on technique: how to improve your software in ways that may not be visible to the user, but that make it more robust and improve your efficiency.

■ **Chapter 9**, "RIM Security": Deciphers the occasionally baffling security model that constrains the behavior of BlackBerry applications. This chapter explains the critical issues that may come up as you develop your application or that emerge only after it has been released. In the process, you'll learn what tools are available to get the permissions you need, and how to deal with cases where your app is forbidden from doing certain things.

■ **Chapter 10**, "Porting Your App": Provides an overview of the many issues to face when you make your application available for multiple devices or multiple countries. By learning these lessons early, you can make the inevitable porting process much quicker and more enjoyable.

■ **Chapter 11**, "Advanced Build Techniques": Shows how to move from a one-person operation to a more professional and organized approach. Introduces the many tools available for use, including build scripts, debug logging, release packages, and more.

Part 4, "The New Frontier"

This final part describes the latest additions to the BlackBerry 6 OS, which will help differentiate your app and provide maximum impact.

- ▨ **Chapter 12**, "Push Services": Explains how to hook your client application into an end-to-end push solution, which can dramatically transform the user experience and improve efficiency. Use the latest APIs to significantly ease push app development.
- ▨ **Chapter 13**, "BlackBerry 6 UI": Covers the latest and most complex additions to the BlackBerry UI toolkit, including building complex tables, crafting arbitrary layouts based on absolute coordinates, using native pickers, and displaying standardized progress indicators.
- ▨ **Chapter 14**, "Cross-Platform Libraries": Provides an introduction to several popular open source libraries that RIM has recently added to the OS, including OpenGL ES for 3D graphics, OpenVG for accelerated 2D graphics, SQLite for relational databases, and ZXing for barcode scanning.

What's Changed?

If you have previously read *Advanced BlackBerry Development*, you'll find that the content has been updated throughout the book to reflect the latest capabilities and the best current practices. I have also removed material that has grown obsolete. Some areas, like personal information, have remained very similar, while others, like the browser, have drastically changed. The final part of the book contains three all-new chapters covering push services, advanced UI topics, and a variety of cross-platform libraries.

Keep in mind that BlackBerry devices are backward-compatible, so any app you wrote for previous versions of the OS should continue to work properly on OS 6. However, the latest devices have the newest and most compelling features, so over time you may want to upgrade those old apps to use BlackBerry 6 APIs. You may want to review the chapters covering features used by your apps to see what has changed and whether any of the new features appeal to you.

How to Read This Book

Depending on your background and goals, you might approach this book in different ways. The chapters are designed to be read in order, as later chapters may reference content from earlier chapters. However, such references are made explicit in the text, and you might find it more useful to approach the book in another order according to your interests or most pressing deadlines.

Novice

If you are new to BlackBerry development, you should start with Chapter 1, which offers an accelerated introduction to the platform. Spend as much time here as you need, and continue once you are comfortable with all the material. You can continue reading the remainder of the book in sequence, working through all the examples and reading the notes.

Apprentice

If you have previously written basic BlackBerry apps, you can skim Chapter 1, reading any unfamiliar topics. From here, you can proceed through the book in sequence, focusing on the chapters that offer new material.

Journeyman

Veteran Java ME developers will notice that many of the BlackBerry APIs, particularly those related to media, personal information, and wireless messaging, are similar or identical to their Java ME counterparts. I point out the important differences within the text. These developers should particularly focus on Chapter 1 for setting up their BlackBerry environment and Chapter 9 to learn about the critical differences between Java ME and BlackBerry security.

Master

Finally, BlackBerry experts can largely skip Chapter 1, and refer to individual chapters to learn about particular topics of interest. Veterans will recognize the importance of BlackBerry device software versions, and will pay particular attention to the tables that show the significant differences between versions.

Notes on Conventions

One of my personal pet peeves is that most programming books today are written as if it were still 1990. Thanks to the ubiquitous availability of Javadocs, we can easily look up the details about individual methods. Thanks to modern IDEs, we can easily discover available APIs and find out how to use them properly.

In writing this book, I've focused on the things that you can't easily see in the Javadocs: the meaning behind methods, when to call particular APIs, and the trade-offs between various solutions. To avoid distraction, I generally omit parameters when I name a method. I generally omit the package name when I name a class. In Eclipse, Ctrl+Space is your friend. Of course, in situations where usage is ambiguous, I provide the details explaining which item to use.

Similarly, exception handling is a great tool for writing robust software, but tends to muddy even the simplest examples. I generally omit exception handling when introducing a new method unless its exceptions are particularly unusual.

The end of each chapter contains a longer set of sample code that runs as a stand-alone application. Here, I fully handle all exceptions, include full package names, and do everything else to show how a real-world application should look and perform.

Your Media App

Each chapter contains numerous small snippets of code designed to help illustrate particular points. The end of each chapter shows how to create a useful, stand-alone application that incorporates concepts from throughout the chapter. In order to provide the experience of writing a realistic, feature-rich application, you will build a single media-sharing application throughout the course of the book. Each chapter from Chapter 2 onward will contribute a new section to it, gradually improving it from a skeleton of an app to a robust platform for media communication.

Complete source code for this media app is provided at the Apress web site, www.apress.com. You can download the sample for each chapter, along with any other listings provided within the main body of the chapter. I encourage you to use the source code as a reference, not an answer key. You will learn the most by working through the sample yourself, adding sections gradually, then running and observing the code. If you skip chapters while reading, you might want to download the previous chapter's source code solution, and then make the modifications for the current chapter on your own.

The Trailhead

I go hiking in the mountains almost every weekend. I love the sensations you get in a good hike. You feel invigorated by the sense of mystery and possibility. As you climb higher and higher, the ground drops away below you. You start to gain perspective, with your visual range extending to yards and then miles. As you continue to ascend, you see even more of the landscape, but it isn't static: every curve brings an unexpected new sight, every switchback a fresh vista. No matter how challenging a hike is, once you reach the summit, you feel that it's all worthwhile, and feel a sense of ownership as you survey the land below you.

I find that learning a new technology is a great deal like that sort of hike. When you start, you can see only the things right in front of you: the editor, the syntax, the tools. As you continue to progress, you begin to catch sight of the wide range of features that the technology offers. You gain more and more mastery, and with that experience comes perspective, as you begin to see how the technology's pieces all work together. But as with a hike, you can always keep going a little further, always learn something new. I've found BlackBerry programming to be a particularly fun trail, and hope you will enjoy the journey too. Keep striving, keep moving upward, and appreciate the view.

Part I

Advanced APIs

The best BlackBerry apps take advantage of the rich set of advanced APIs available on this platform. The chapters in Part 1 describe some of the most exciting and compelling features available to you. Chapter 1 provides a crash course in building a variety of RIM applications that can access the local filesystem and the Internet. From there, learn how to use the device to shoot photos, record sound and video, and use the captured data in your app. Next, see the wide variety of options available for playing video, animations, and audio content. Connect the BlackBerry to the rest of the mobile world with wireless messaging and email technologies. Finally, incorporate today's techniques for safeguarding data into your own applications.

Chapter 1

Getting Started

Welcome to the wonderful world of BlackBerry app development! Chapter 1 aims to get you up to speed as quickly as possible, so you can get right into the good stuff, and it assumes no previous knowledge other than a basic grasp of Java. This chapter will walk you through downloading software and setting up your environment, and then it will give you a quick tour through the basics of BlackBerry app development. You may linger, skim, or skip ahead as your patience demands.

Initial Setup

As with any new language or platform, you will need to install some new software and set up your computer appropriately. You have many different options for creating a successful BlackBerry project. Research In Motion (RIM) historically supported only Windows development, but it has done a good job of releasing tools that enable development on a variety of configurations. The following section will focus on what I have found to be the simplest and most effective setup for independent development, with occasional notes for alternative choices you might consider.

Getting Java

You will develop in Java for the BlackBerry, but before we get that far, we need to make sure Java on your desktop is running properly. RIM uses Java for its *toolchain*—the set of programs that will convert your application source files into a format that can run on the mobile device. Additionally, our Eclipse IDE requires a Java runtime environment.

To see if Java is installed, open a command prompt. You can do this by clicking Start ➤ Run, typing cmd, and pressing enter. A black-and-white command prompt window will appear. Type java -version. You should see something like the following:

```
java version "1.6.0_14"
Java(TM) SE Runtime Environment (build 1.6.0_14-b08)
Java HotSpot(TM) Client VM (build 14.0-b16, mixed mode, sharing)
```

As long as you get a response and see a version of at least 1.6, your system is set. If Java is not installed or is not configured correctly, you will see an error like the following:

```
'java' is not recognized as an internal or external command,
operable program or batch file.
```

To install Java, go to http://java.sun.com and look for the Java SE download. You only need to install the Java Runtime Environment (JRE). However, if you plan on doing other Java development besides BlackBerry, you can download the full Java Development Kit (JDK), which also includes the JRE.

> **TIP:** When installing any development software, I suggest you pick an install path that has no spaces in it. For example, instead of installing to c:\Program Files\Java, install to c:\dev\java. This will save you time in the future, as some Java programs and other useful utilities have a hard time working with paths that have spaces in their names. Follow this rule for all the other downloads in this chapter as well.

Once you have downloaded and installed the JRE, try opening another command prompt and typing java -version again. If it still doesn't recognize the command, you probably need to add Java to your PATH environment variable. In recent versions of Windows, you can access this by right-clicking Computer, selecting Properties, clicking "Advanced system settings," checking that the Advanced tab is selected, and then clicking Environment Variables. Make sure the PATH includes the location of your installed java.exe directory. This will probably be something like c:\dev\java\jre1.6.0_14\bin.

Goldilocks and the Three IDEs

Once upon a time, a developer was evaluating which IDE to use when writing BlackBerry apps. First she tried the RIM JDE. "Oh my!" she exclaimed. "This IDE is much too ugly!" Then she tried NetBeans. "This IDE doesn't understand BlackBerry," she complained. Finally, she installed Eclipse with the BlackBerry Plug-in. "Ahhh," she smiled. "This IDE is just right!"

You can develop in any IDE that you want. The question is how much time and effort you will invest in getting everything to work right. I've found that Eclipse is the best platform for doing serious development, and it has only gotten better and easier since RIM released its official plug-in. I use Eclipse for my examples in the rest of this book, and I recommend installing it unless you are already doing BlackBerry development in another environment.

To get started, go to www.eclipse.org/downloads/packages/release/galileo/sr2. Download Eclipse Classic 3.5.2 for your platform.

NOTE: As of this writing, more recent versions of Eclipse are available, but the BlackBerry Java Plug-in does not run properly on those. This situation may change in the future, in which case you can find updated installation instructions on the official BlackBerry developer site at `http://na.blackberry.com/eng/developers/`.

Eclipse doesn't have a standard Windows installer. Instead, you simply unzip it to a folder on your computer. You could put it somewhere like `c:\dev\eclipse`. To make it easier to launch, you can right-click and drag the `eclipse.exe` icon to your desktop or task bar in order to create a shortcut.

When you first launch Eclipse, it will ask you to choose a workspace. You can create one wherever you like. Do not check the option for "Use this as the default and do not ask me again."

CAUTION: Depending on your environment, you may have difficulty running a 64-bit version of Eclipse with the proper runtime of Java. If you experience launch problems, consider switching to a 32-bit version instead.

Plugged In

I have been a fan of Eclipse for many years now, in large part because of its very flexible and powerful plug-in system. Plug-ins allow developers to tune their workspace for their specific tasks, without requiring the bother of relearning a new tool for each new task.

To install the BlackBerry Plug-in, do the following:

1. Open Eclipse, click the Help menu, and then click Install New Software....

2. Click Add. Enter any name that you like, and for the location, enter `http://www.blackberry.com/go/eclipseUpdate/3.5/java`. Click OK.

3. Expand the BlackBerry Java Plug-in category. You will see several options. At a minimum, you will need to select the BlackBerry Java Plug-in and at least one BlackBerry Java SDK.

NOTE: Eclipse may prompt you to enter a username and password. You can register for a free developer account on the BlackBerry developer web site if you have not already done so. This prompt may appear multiple times, so continue entering the account name and password until it goes away. The servers hosting the plug-in are sometimes temperamental and will fail with unhelpful messages; other times, the installation may appear to hang when it is actually progressing, especially on slower connections. If you experience problems, you can try again later.

If you have a particular BlackBerry device in mind, pick the Java SDK that matches the software version of that device. All these files are very large, so you should probably start with only a few, even if you know you will eventually want more. For the rest of this book, we will use the version 6.0 Java SDK.

> **TIP:** You can find the software version on your BlackBerry by selecting Options and then About. It should be a value like "6.0.0.141". When selecting a component pack, only the first two numbers are important. The rest will be used to select an appropriate simulator.

You should restart Eclipse once the install is complete. After it restarts, you will see a new BlackBerry menu option in the Project menu. You will also have access to three new debug configurations: BlackBerry Device, BlackBerry Simulator, and Running BlackBerry Simulator. Figure 1–1 shows what your Eclipse environment should look like once you have installed the plug-in and started a new project.

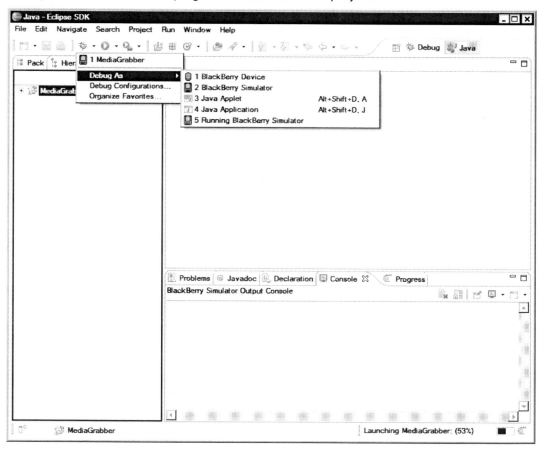

Figure 1–1. Eclipse configured for BlackBerry development

TIP: Some users have problems installing through the BlackBerry Eclipse Plug-in site. Depending on your physical location, you may have trouble connecting to the servers, and if there is a high load or they are down for maintenance, you will only receive cryptic error messages. If all else fails, try to download the plug-in installer directly from the BlackBerry developer web site. This should allow you to use the plug-in, although it will require you to manually download and install any updates RIM releases in the future.

BlackBerry Programs

If you are developing for a personal BlackBerry device, you probably already have the BlackBerry Desktop Software and the BlackBerry Device Manager installed. If not, you can easily install them; the tools will come in handy for loading different firmware versions on your devices and transferring files between the device and computer. Go to www.blackberry.com and look for the "Desktop Software" download. Run the downloaded setup file. You may be prompted to install additional software, such as the .NET Framework runtime. Once it's complete, reboot your computer if prompted. The next time you connect your BlackBerry device to the computer, Windows should automatically install the drivers to access it.

You can launch the BlackBerry Desktop Manager by going to your Start menu and looking under BlackBerry. Depending on your installation choices, the manager may automatically start when you log in to Windows. Figure 1–2 shows the BlackBerry Desktop Manager running.

Figure 1–2. BlackBerry Desktop Software

NOTE: BlackBerry Desktop Software is not specifically a tool for developers. Every BlackBerry user can install it, and most do. I include it in this setup process because the Desktop Manager lets you easily test certain methods of app distribution like cable-loaded ALX files, upgrade or downgrade your device firmware, and explore content on the device.

Simulator Files

You will need to download the proper simulator files for the devices you plan to run on, because different types of devices will have different screen sizes and input modes. Even if you have two devices with the same model number, they will behave differently depending on their software versions. Simulators are not just important for testing on the computer, though. They also contain essential information for debugging on the actual device.

If you have the physical device you will use, find the device software version. Depending on your device, you may find it by opening Options ➤ About, or by selecting Options ➤ Device ➤ About Device Versions. You will be looking for a version that matches all parts of the version number. For example, if your device has version 6.0.0.141, use only 6.0.0.141, not another version that starts with 6.0.0. You can download simulator packs from the BlackBerry web site. The exact location will change, so your best bet is to visit the Developers page and look around for the BlackBerry Smartphone Simulators. You will see many, many choices. Pick the one that matches your exact version number, device model, and, if applicable, carrier. Unfortunately, RIM requires you to click through yet another web form—get used to it. As it does not provide any way to save your information, you will need to repeat these steps with each simulator. Download the simulator file, and then run it to install. You can install to any directory you like.

1. To switch to a new simulator in Eclipse, follow these steps. From the top Eclipse menu, click Run, and then click Debug Configurations.

2. Create a new BlackBerry Simulator configuration.

3. Click the Simulator tab.

4. From the Device drop-down, select the item that corresponds to the simulator you installed.

You can now use your device's proper simulator, and you will have access to high-quality on-device debugging.

The Keys to Development

So far, you have installed everything you need to get started writing BlackBerry software. There's a catch, though: RIM has marked some of its APIs as restricted, and if your program uses any of these APIs, it will not run on the device unless it has been code signed. For example, you won't be able to access cryptographic functions, the web browser, or certain geolocation APIs.

We will cover code signing in more detail in Chapter 9. For now, just know that this is often a necessary step in development. It can take anywhere from a few days to a few weeks to receive code signing keys, so request them early.

You apply for the keys from the BlackBerry developer web site. Once again, you will need to fill out a form with your information. Part of the form asks you for an e-mail address. Be aware that RIM will send multiple e-mails to this address every time you sign an application. Also, keep in mind that you must sign an application *every* time you make a change and load it on the device. It isn't unusual for a large RIM app to generate 50 or more e-mails on a single signing. Therefore, I strongly urge you to enter an unmonitored e-mail address here, or one where you can automatically delete e-mails from the signing server. If you use your personal e-mail address instead, it will make your life miserable.

The form also includes a question about Certicom cryptography keys. We cover Certicom cryptography in more detail in Chapter 5; for now, you can just say "No" here. You should also pick a unique ten-digit PIN. RIM charges a nominal fee for generating code signing keys, currently $20. You will need one set of keys for each computer you will use for development. The RIM servers sometimes have problems; if you aren't able to complete your order online, you can choose to fax it in instead.

Eventually, you should receive an e-mail from RIM with three key files and instruction on installation. Follow the e-mail instructions. If you run into problems during your installation, follow the links in the e-mail for more support. Once you have installed and registered the keys, you will be all set. You have a limited number of signatures, but the limit is absurdly high, so you don't need to worry about ever running out. Within Eclipse, you can manage your signing keys by clicking Window ➤ Preferences ➤ BlackBerry Java Plug-in ➤ Signature Tool. From this screen, you can install new code signing keys or remove previously installed keys. This screen also allows you to import keys that you may have acquired previously. The latest version of the plug-in offers much smoother integrated support for signing, so once you have set up your keys, you can easily sign builds for testing or release.

That's it for setup! You now have all the tools you will need to write, debug, and install your own BlackBerry apps.

Application Types

Early in your development cycle, you will face an important decision—what kind of application architecture you should use. BlackBerry supports three very different types of programs, and each offers a unique set of advantages and style of development. This section will provide a quick tour and critique of the available options.

MIDlets

A MIDlet is a Java ME application. Java ME, previously known as J2ME, was developed by Sun Microsystems in the 1990s as an early way to write Java applications for extremely limited devices. The ME stands for Micro Edition, and the initial requirements were very micro indeed: devices could have as little as 192 kilobytes of RAM. Over the years, Java ME has expanded and matured along with the mobile market, gradually adding new features and support as those features become widely available in handsets.

A collection of optional features for Java ME is called a JSR, or Java Specification Request. You will encounter some of the more popular JSRs later in this book. JSRs cover features like filesystem access, media playback, XML parsing, and more. RIM has been pretty good at adopting the most widespread and useful JSRs. You can find some of a BlackBerry's supported JSRs by visiting the device's Options menu, and then selecting About. You will likely see several options such as "Micro Edition File" and "Micro Edition Bluetooth."

Many handsets besides BlackBerry devices support Java ME. Due to different display sizes, supported JSRs, and other discrepancies, MIDlets rarely actually offer "Write once, run everywhere" functions. Still, you can port between two Java ME phones much more easily than between two different platforms.

MIDlet Behavior

When a user launches a MIDlet, the device will run it in a stripped-down version of the Java Virtual Machine. Unlike a regular Java SE application, which is entered through a static `main()` function and runs until its threads are terminated or it calls `System.exit()`, a MIDlet is a *managed* application. The managing platform will invoke the managed application's methods when it needs to respond to something, such as the app pausing or the user selecting a button. This architecture should look familiar to developers of Java servlets and other Java EE applications.

The simplest MIDlets need to reply to only three events: the application starting, pausing, or exiting. An application should handle necessary initialization when starting, release scarce resources when pausing, and perform any remaining cleanup when exiting.

MIDlet UI

MIDlet programming supports several choices for user interface programming. The simplest, but most limited, uses `Screen` objects. Each `Screen` instance corresponds to an application screen. A `Form` is a type of `Screen` that can contain multiple `Item` objects. Examples of items include text entry fields, labels, and images. Using screens allows you to very quickly build up an application UI with your desired functions. Unfortunately, the UI usually looks unattractive. Screens tend to look better on BlackBerry devices than on most other Java ME devices, but they still do not look nearly as nice as other UI frameworks.

When using a Screen, users will interact with your application through Command objects. Each Command defines a specific action the user can take. In an e-mail program, the commands might include choices to compose a new message, save the current message, run a spell checker, or exit the app. The application manager will notify your app when the user has selected a Command. In BlackBerry apps, available commands will display when the user presses the BlackBerry Menu key.

Instead of using Screen, you can choose to subclass Canvas. A Canvas allows you to completely control the appearance of your app, down to the pixel level. When your app needs to draw, it will receive a Graphics context. You can use this to directly draw images, text, rectangles, arcs, and even arbitrary blocks of pixels. This system offers maximum flexibility for creating great-looking apps. However, it is also considerably more complex.

A Canvas-based app can continue to use Command objects, but it also gains the ability to directly interact with the user. You will receive notifications when the user presses a key or interacts with the screen, both for non-touch BlackBerry devices and touch-based ones. With these capabilities, it becomes possible to write more advanced user interfaces. For example, you could add keyboard shortcuts to your e-mail program or flip between images when the user clicks them.

Finally, a GameCanvas offers a useful set of behaviors for developers who write games or other applications that demand a high degree of interactivity. Screen and Canvas apps are primarily reactive, waiting for notifications and deciding how to respond. GameCanvas allows you to directly query the key states and immediately start painting in response. This gives you maximum control over application speed and responsiveness. Additionally, a GameCanvas offers an offscreen Graphics context that you can progressively draw to before copying it directly to the screen.

A MIDlet Example

Follow these steps to write a simple MIDlet that will be your first BlackBerry app.

1. Start Eclipse and select a fresh workspace.

2. Click File ➤ New ➤ Project.

3. Expand BlackBerry and select BlackBerry Project. Click Next. Verify that the JRE matches your intended target, such as BlackBerry JRE 6.0.0. Name the project "HelloWorld". If you hate the idea of writing another Hello World application, call it something else. Click Finish.

4. Expand the HelloWorld project, and open BlackBerry_App_Descriptor.xml.

5. Fill out the Title, Version, and Vendor fields. You may enter any text you like. To avoid confusion, I like to keep my MIDlet title and project title consistent, so I enter HelloWorld here.

6. Select MIDlet from the Project Type drop-down, as shown in Figure 1–3.

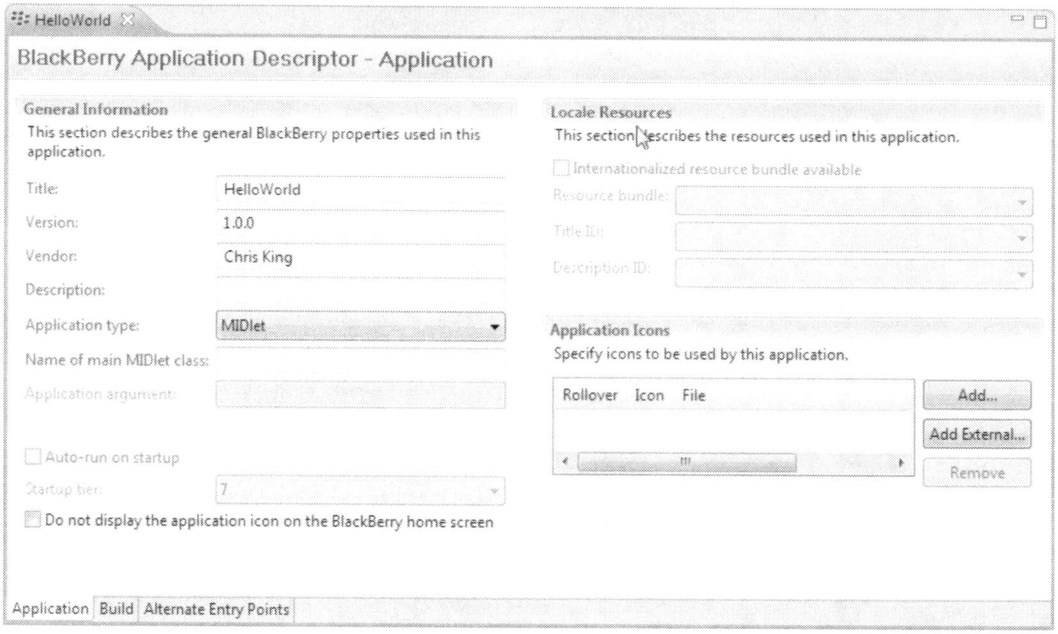

Figure 1–3. Making a MIDlet

7. If you like, click the top X to close this window.

8. Right-click the src folder in your Project Explorer, select New, and then select Class. (If you can't see your src folder, try expanding the project by pressing the + sign near the project name.)

9. Give this class a name. I chose HelloWorld. Also provide a package name. I will be using packages under com.apress.king throughout this book.

10. Set the superclass to javax.microedition.midlet.MIDlet.

11. Keep "Inherited abstract methods" checked.

12. Click Finish.

You now have an empty MIDlet. If you wanted, you could run it right now. There isn't much point, though, since it doesn't do anything yet.

Listing 1–1 shows how to implement a simple MIDlet. This app uses the screen-based approach to development. It displays a simple message on the screen and offers an option to quit the app. Because the app is so simple, there is nothing to do when the app is paused, and it always destroys itself in a straightforward manner. As you can see, you need only a little boilerplate code to get this running.

Listing 1–1. A Basic MIDlet

```java
package com.apress.king;

import javax.microedition.lcdui.*;
import javax.microedition.midlet.*;

public class HelloWorld extends MIDlet implements CommandListener
{
    protected void startApp() throws MIDletStateChangeException
    {
        Form form = new Form("Welcome!");
        StringItem text = new StringItem(null, "Hello, World!");
        form.insert(0, text);
        Command quitCommand = new Command("Quit", Command.EXIT, 0);
        form.addCommand(quitCommand);
        form.setCommandListener(this);
        Display.getDisplay(this).setCurrent(form);
    }

    public void commandAction(Command c, Displayable d)
    {
        if (c.getCommandType() == Command.EXIT)
        {
            try
            {
                destroyApp(true);
                notifyDestroyed();
            }
            catch (MIDletStateChangeException e)
            {
                e.printStackTrace();
            }
        }
    }

    protected void destroyApp(boolean arg0) throws MIDletStateChangeException
    {
        notifyDestroyed();
    }

    protected void pauseApp()
    {
        // This method intentionally left blank.
    }

}
```

Running a MIDlet

It's now time to run your first app on the simulator. To do this, select the Run menu in Eclipse, choose "Debug As," and finally choose "BlackBerry Simulator." Your default simulator will appear and begin booting.

NOTE: Later in this chapter, we will see how to start a simulator with networking enabled.

Happily, RIM's device simulators faithfully represent the actual devices. On most non-BlackBerry Java ME phones, simulators provide an overly idealized depiction of the runtime environment. Those simulators usually run fast and bug-free, while the actual mobile device suffers from slowness and defects. If you have thoroughly debugged your application on a RIM simulator, you can reasonably believe that it will run well on the actual device. (Of course, you will not know for sure until you actually try it. We'll cover that step at the end of this chapter.)

The downside to this accuracy, though, is that the simulator tends to be rather slow. It takes about as long to boot up as an actual device does. Be patient, and eventually you will see the home screen.

Now, locate the HelloWorld app. For OS 6 devices, click All to expand the main menu, and then scroll down and look for HelloWorld. On older devices, you can find the icon on your home screen or within a Downloads folder. Once you find your app, click the icon. It will launch, looking something like Figure 1–4. Note that the exact appearance will vary based on the simulator you are using.

Figure 1–4. A simple MIDlet running in the simulator

MIDlet Evaluation

You should pick the MIDlet form if you plan to write an application for both BlackBerry and Java ME devices. The consistent programming APIs will make the whole process much simpler, and you'll minimize the amount of rework.

However, you will give up the chance to take the fullest advantage of the BlackBerry user interface if you go this route. Even the best-looking MIDlets won't visually integrate cleanly with other applications on the phone, and discerning users will detect something different about them.

If you choose to write a MIDlet, I suggest using `Screen` classes for writing a demo or an app where you don't care about the UI. Use a `Canvas` for commercial applications, and a `GameCanvas` for games or other high-quality interactive apps.

The rest of this book contains a good amount of information that can be applied to MIDlets. To learn even more, particularly more details about the user interface options, consider reading *Beginning Java ME Platform,* by Ray Rischpater (Apress, 2008). Most of the content in that book also applies to writing MIDlets for BlackBerry devices. (Disclaimer: I am the technical reviewer of that book.)

CLDC Applications

MIDlets provide a good bridge of compatibility between Java ME and BlackBerry devices. On the other hand, RIM engineered BlackBerry CLDC from the ground up specifically for BlackBerry, and this framework provides the best integration with the native device behavior. Applications written with this platform tend to have a more polished feel familiar to BlackBerry users.

CLDC stands for Connected Limited Device Configuration. Somewhat confusingly, MIDlets are also technically CLDC applications. Java ME provides support for a wide range of applications; the most popular are the MIDlets, which are defined as part of MIDP, the Mobile Information Device Profile. RIM has taken the CLDC foundation and created its own custom user interface on top of it as a replacement for MIDlets. Within this book, I will use the terms "MIDlet" or "MIDP MIDlet" to refer to a MIDlet app, and the terms "CLDC" or "BlackBerry CLDC" to refer to a BlackBerry CLDC app.

> **NOTE:** The two types of apps can share almost all APIs, except for their UI classes. This means that BlackBerry CLDC applications should never import a class under the `javax.microedition.lcdui` or `javax.microedition.midlet` packages, and MIDlets should never import a class under the `net.rim.device.api.ui` package hierarchy. On the other hand, BlackBerry CLDC applications can freely use non-UI Java ME classes under the `javax.microedition` package, and MIDlets running on BlackBerry can use RIM classes under the `net.rim` package.

CLDC Behavior

BlackBerry CLDC apps function like a hybrid between Java SE and MIDlets. They do have a static main() function that starts the application and will run until completion. Your main class should extend UiApplication. UiApplication is the heart of a CLDC app; it provides the following crucial capabilities:

- An event dispatcher that manages all user input and updates the user interface

- A screen stack that maintains application state

- Standard controls for menu actions and other commonly used elements

Once your app starts the event dispatcher, it will behave similarly to a MIDlet: it will receive notifications when important events occur and respond appropriately.

CLDC UI

Screen objects form the building blocks for CLDC applications. CLDC screens are located in the net.rim.device.api.ui package, and, despite the similar name, they are completely different from the MIDlet screens located in the javax.microedition.lcdui package; you cannot use the classes interchangeably. A Screen typically contains one or more displayable items, and also performs specialized logic related to those items. If you were writing a calendar app, you might use one screen to show the entire calendar view, another screen for creating new appointments, and a third screen to view previously entered appointments. Each screen would offer different options depending on its purpose.

An app is composed of screens, and each screen is composed of fields. A CLDC Field is roughly analogous to a MIDlet Item. RIM offers a rich set of standard fields for things like displaying images and text, and even more advanced fields for displaying things like maps. One specialized type of Field is the Manager. A Manager controls the appearance and behavior of its own children fields. One Manager may lay out its children horizontally, another vertically, and another as a grid. By using managers, you can create elaborate and attractive user interfaces.

You can also subclass Field, Manager, or any other class to add your own desired functions and appearance. For example, you might override DateField in your calendar app to create dates that fit in with the visual style of your app, and you might add custom functions to immediately display appointments when the user selects a date.

In the most extreme cases, you may choose to override the paint() method for a Screen or a Field. This will allow you unlimited control over the look of your app. However, the existing Field implementations look quite good, and most allow ways that you can easily customize them. You can create attractive apps by sticking to the default toolkit.

A CLDC Example

Now that you've created a MIDlet, making a CLDC app will go more quickly. Create a new BlackBerry project called HelloUniverse. Follow the instructions in the previous section, "A MIDlet Example," but this time keep the Project Type as the default of "BlackBerry Application." Create a new class called HelloUniverse that extends net.rim.device.api.ui.UiApplication.

Listing 1–2 shows a simple CLDC app that performs the same basic function as the previous MIDlet application. For this example, we will configure a basic MainScreen with some non-interactive elements. Future examples in this book will show how to create more interactive CLDC applications.

Listing 1–2. A Basic BlackBerry CLDC Application

```
package com.apress.king;

import net.rim.device.api.ui.UiApplication;
import net.rim.device.api.ui.component.LabelField;
import net.rim.device.api.ui.container.MainScreen;

public class HelloUniverse extends UiApplication
{

    public void start()
    {
        MainScreen main = new MainScreen();
        LabelField label = new LabelField("Hello, Universe");
        main.add(label);
        UiApplication app = UiApplication.getUiApplication();
        app.pushScreen(main);
        app.enterEventDispatcher();
    }

    public static void main(String[] args)
    {
        (new HelloUniverse()).start();
    }
}
```

You'll note that this requires even less code than we needed in the MIDlet. When you build a CLDC app, you get a lot of useful capabilities for free, including automatic state management that allows a user to navigate back through your app and exit. You can override these behaviors if you want, such as managing your own history, but the default works correctly in most cases.

Run your app using the same steps as described in the previous section, "Running a MIDlet." If you had closed the simulator earlier, Eclipse will re-launch it; if the simulator is still running, your application will deploy to it.

Even though the code is different, you build, load, and launch BlackBerry CLDC applications the same way you do MIDlets, and they will go in the same location. Figure 1–5 shows the running CLDC application.

Figure 1–5. A BlackBerry CLDC application running in the simulator

NOTE: You'll observe that HelloWorld is still installed. Although you can debug only one project at a time, any changes you make to the BlackBerry simulator will persist across multiple launches or debug sessions. If you'd like to return to a clean slate, you can do so by clicking the Eclipse Project menu, clicking the BlackBerry sub-menu, and then selecting Clean Simulator.... There are multiple options for removing applications, the internal file system, the SD card, or resetting security settings. Note that you cannot clean a running simulator; if an option is grayed out, close your simulator and try again.

CLDC Evaluation

Use the BlackBerry CLDC UI if you are writing an app on your own BlackBerry for fun, if you know that your app will need to run only on BlackBerry devices, or if you want to achieve the highest level of visual integration with the BlackBerry platform. RIM has done a good job at providing attractive, flexible, extensible visual elements. It takes little effort to create a nice-looking app, and you can customize the look as much as you like.

For these reasons, I will use CLDC applications in my examples for the remainder of the book. Most of the topics also apply to MIDlet applications, and I will provide occasional directions on how to adapt to MIDlets.

To keep the focus on the advanced topics of this book, I tend to use simple Screen classes that are informative but not flashy. If you'd like to learn more about designing user interfaces for BlackBerry CLDC apps, please consult *Beginning BlackBerry 6 Development*, by Anthony Rizk (Apress, 2011).

Libraries

The last major type of application is a *library*. "Application" is a misnomer here, since a library is, by definition, headless. A library can provide functions to other applications and can perform tasks, but it cannot be directly launched by a user and does not provide any user interface. It resembles a Java JAR or a Windows DLL.

Library Functions

You'll rarely ever distribute a library by itself. Instead, you typically will bundle a library with one or more applications. You gain several benefits by doing this. It allows you to encapsulate functions and separate them from the application. If you have multiple apps that need to decode videos, then rather than writing video decoding functions and copying them to both apps, you could just place those functions within a library. When you fix bugs or add new video formats to decode, you need to update only the library and not each application.

Libraries can also perform simple tasks that don't require user interaction. You might use a library that scans for temporary files left behind by your main app and cleans them up, or that tells the device to start your application when the user receives a particular e-mail.

A Library Example

Create a new Eclipse workspace and start a third project, this one called GoodbyeWorld. Follow the instructions in the previous section in this chapter titled "A MIDlet Example," but this time select the Application Type "Library" and check the option for "Auto-run on startup." Leave the Startup Tier at 7 so this library runs after the system libraries have all finished initializing. Create a new class, GoodbyeWorld, with the default superclass of java.lang.Object.

This particular library will call some privileged API methods, so we will notify the build environment that our app has the proper access. Select Window in the Eclipse top menu, and then choose Preferences. Expand BlackBerry Java Plug-in in the left pane, select Warnings, and verify that all the options are checked. You should have RIM BlackBerry Apps API, RIM Crypto API, and RIM Runtime API selected. If you happen to know that you cannot access one or more of these—for example, if you have not yet acquired signing keys—leave those options unchecked. The compiler will generate a warning if your code attempts to call these restricted methods. You can still call them on the simulator, but they will fail on the device.

Listing 1–3 shows this library's implementation. You'll notice a special entrance function called libMain(). Not every library needs one, but if you selected "Auto-run on startup," then the system will run this method if it is available. In this example, we check to see if the HelloUniverse application is installed. If so, we wait for the device to finish booting up, and then launch it.

Listing 1–3. A Basic Library

```
package com.apress.king;

import net.rim.device.api.system.*;

public class GoodbyeWorld
{

    public static void libMain(String[] args)
    {
        System.out.println("GoodbyeWorld launching");
        int handle = CodeModuleManager.getModuleHandle("HelloUniverse");
        ApplicationDescriptor[] descriptors = CodeModuleManager
                .getApplicationDescriptors(handle);
        if (descriptors.length > 0)
        {
            ApplicationDescriptor descriptor = descriptors[0];
            try
            {
                ApplicationManager manager = ApplicationManager
                        .getApplicationManager();
                manager.waitForStartup();
                manager.runApplication(descriptor);
            }
            catch (ApplicationManagerException e)
            {
                System.out.println("I couldn't launch it!");
                e.printStackTrace();
            }
        }
        else
        {
            System.out.println("HelloUniverse is not installed.");
        }
        System.out.println("Goodbye, world!");
    }
}
```

Exit the simulator if it is open, and then start debugging to launch it again. You will see the same screen display as in Figure 1–5, but this time, you don't need to manually launch the app. Also, if you look in the Console view for the BlackBerry Simulator Output Console in Eclipse, you will see the message GoodbyeWorld launching included within the app startup messages.

Library Evaluation

Libraries offer nearly endless possibilities. They can enhance your other applications by providing useful utilities or running common tasks. They are especially useful when you have a portfolio of apps and want to share existing technology between them.

That said, most applications don't use libraries, and most don't need them. Think carefully about what your library is supposed to accomplish, whether it's actually useful, and whether a library is the best place to put those functions. It might be fun to automatically start up an application, but many users would likely be annoyed by that behavior.

Use your best judgment, and you may find situations where libraries are the best solution to a problem. The examples in this book do not use libraries often, but most of the code that does not have a UI component can run within a library. For example, you cannot play video or show pictures within a library, but you can use cryptography and access personal information.

Connecting to Files and Networks

Java ME added a new framework to the Java language. The Generic Connection Framework, or GCF, provides a generic mechanism for accessing many different kinds of resources that exist outside your app. You will likely use the GCF in all but the most trivial applications, regardless of whether you build a MIDlet or a BlackBerry CLDC app. In the remainder of this chapter, we will look at how to use the GCF to access local files and remote network locations.

A GCF Overview

The Connector class provides an entry into the GCF. Connector is a *factory* class—one that is responsible for creating other objects. When you call Connector.open(), you provide a connection string describing the resource you want to access. Connection strings look like URLs, but can describe a wide variety of connection types. Examples include http://apress.com, sms://+14155550100 and file:///SDCard/BlackBerry/Music/.

If the device supports the requested connection type, it will return an object that implements the appropriate subclass of Connection. Figure 1–6 shows the relationship between Connector and Connection, along with a few representative Connection types. If the device does not support a particular type of connection, Connector will throw a ConnectionNotFoundException. You may encounter an IOException in a variety of situations—for example, if networking is disabled when your app requests a network connection.

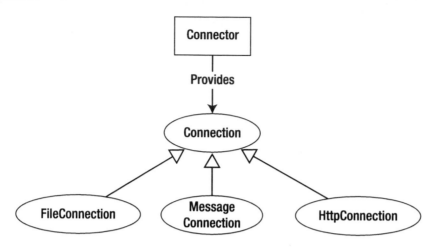

Figure 1–6. BlackBerry GCF connections

Because connections represent scarce resources, your app should gracefully deal with situations in which they are not available. Depending on the type of resource and the error, you might prompt the user to try again later. Also, because they are scarce, you should take care to clean up Connection objects by calling their close() method once you have finished with them. This will return underlying resources, such as file handles or Internet sockets, to the BlackBerry operating system. The following sample code shows how to open a particular type of connection and clean it up once done.

```java
String connectString = "http://www.apress.com";
HttpConnection connection = null;
try
{
    connection = (HttpConnection)Connector.open(connectString);
    // Read from the connection here.
}
catch (ConnectionNotFoundException cnfe)
{
    System.err.println("Couldn't find connection for " + connectString);
}
catch (IOException ioe)
{
    System.err.println("IO exception for " + connectString + ":" + ioe);
}
finally
{
    if (connection != null)
    {
        try
        {
            connection.close();
        }
        catch (IOException ioe) {}
    }
}
```

File Access

Java ME originally did not support file connections, but added them in JSR 75, which all modern BlackBerry devices offer. File connections allow you to read and write files within the BlackBerry device's built-in storage or an SD (Secure Digital) card. This capability allows you to offer extra storage in your app, produce useful files for the user, or communicate with other apps on the phone.

Paths

RIM devices offer two filesystem roots. One, located at /store/home/user, corresponds to the device's internal memory. This has limited size and should be used for small files only. However, it is also fast, responsive, and reliably available.

The other root, /SDCard, corresponds to the device's Secure Digital card. This removable memory card often stores large media files. SD cards also offer ways to encrypt files and protect them with Digital Rights Management (DRM). SD cards for BlackBerry devices can be quite large—several gigabytes in size—and users will rarely mind if you use them to store files for your app. However, you have no guarantee that any given user will have an SD card inserted in his or her device, and you should handle situations where it is unavailable.

You indicate a file URL by attaching the file:// prefix. An example of a full path to a local file is file:///SDCard/BlackBerry/Music/song.mp3. Note that there are three slashes after file:, not two.

Access

You can open each connection in one of three modes:

- Connector.READ indicates that your app will only read data from this resource.

- Connector.WRITE indicates that your app will only write data to this resource.

- Connector.READ_WRITE allows your app to both read from and write to this resource.

By default, connections will open with READ_WRITE access. You generally want this mode, particularly since bugs in some early versions of BlackBerry device software cause read operations to fail if a connection is opened with only READ access.

Even when you request these access levels, users still may choose to override your selection. If they do so, you can show an error message to the user asking him or her to make changes that will allow your app to function properly. Chapter 9 will discuss in more detail how to do this.

Streams

A `Connection` object by itself represents a resource. In order to interact with a file, you will need to open an appropriate stream by calling one of the following methods:

- `openInputStream()` returns a raw byte stream for reading.

- `openOutputStream()` returns a raw byte stream for writing.

- `openDataInputStream()` allows your app to read basic Java types, such as `int` and `String`, from the stream.

- `openDataOutputStream()` allows your app to write basic Java types to the stream.

> **NOTE:** BlackBerry does not support many standard Java I/O classes, such as `BufferedInputStream`.

Although you have successfully obtained a `FileConnection` object, opening the stream may still fail. The device generally does not check security until you attempt to access the file. The file itself also might not exist yet, or another app might hold a lock on it. Be prepared to handle `SecurityException`, `IllegalModeException`, and `IOException`.

Once you have an appropriate stream, you can read or write to it as you would in a standard Java application. Operations on streams are synchronous and blocking. This means that when you call a stream method like `read()` or `write()`, the method will not return until the operation is complete or an error occurs. If you read or write a large file, this may take a long time. Because of this, you should perform stream I/O operations in a separate thread.

The following code shows an example of opening a stream from an already opened file connection. As with connections, streams hold scarce resources that you should clean up when no longer needed.

```
DataInputStream dis = null;
try
{
   dis = connection.openDataInputStream();
   String bestPlayer = dis.readUTF();
   int highScore = dis.readInt();
   System.out.println(bestPlayer + " scored " + highScore + " points.");
}
catch (IOException ioe)
{
    System.err.println(ioe);
    ioe.printStackTrace();
}
finally
{
    if (dis != null)
    {
        try
        {
```

```
        dis.close();
    }
    catch (IOException ioe) { }
    }
}
```

When you write to a stream, the operating system may buffer the output. If your app writes individual bytes to a file, it would be highly inefficient to access the filesystem at each byte. All pending bytes will be written out when you call the close() method, or when the program calls flush() on the stream, as demonstrated in the following code snippet.

```
DataOutputStream dos = connection.openDataOutputStream();
dos.writeUTF("Sally Jones");
dos.writeInt(100);
dos.flush();
dos.writeUTF("Joe Smith");
dos.writeInt(98);
dos.close();
```

Other Operations

Although streams are the most important resources provided by a FileConnection, the interface offers several other useful methods, including the following:

- exists() checks to see whether the file or directory exists on the filesystem.

- create() creates a new, empty file at this location.

- mkdir() creates a directory at this location.

- delete() destroys this file or directory.

- list() returns all the files and subdirectories in this directory.

- fileSize() reports how many bytes a file occupies on the filesystem.

> **NOTE:** Always include the trailing / character when specifying a directory path, such as file:///SDCard/BlackBerry/Music/. If you don't, the BlackBerry operating system cannot determine whether you are referring to a file or to a directory of that name.

The following code snippet checks to see whether a file exists. If it doesn't, it will create it. The create() method does not automatically create directories, so this code first checks to see that the containing directory exists.

```
String directoryPath = "file:///SDCard/BlackBerry/Music/";
FileConnection connection = (FileConnection)Connector.open(directoryPath);
if (!connection.exists())
{
    connection.mkdir();
}
connection.close();
```

```
String filePath = "file:///SDCard/BlackBerry/Music/song.mp3";
connection = (FileConnection)Connector.open(filePath);
if (!connection.exists())
{
    connection.create();
}
connection.close();
```

Networking

Almost every interesting mobile app includes some sort of networking. It might share messages with other users, back up data on a remote server, or download new game levels. The GCF provides access to a variety of network types, and RIM's custom extensions to the GCF allow you to write networking code that takes advantage of BlackBerry device features. Recently, RIM has also provided ways to bypass complex network negotiations and more readily find an appropriate network path, as we'll see in the "Simpler Networking" section ahead.

Types of Connections

On BlackBerry devices, the Connector.open() factory method understands a variety of *protocols*. Table 1–1 lists some of the most useful.

Table 1–1. Network Connection Types

Protocol Name	Returned Interface Type	Comments	Example	Required Permission
http	HttpConnection		http://eff.org	javax.microedition. io.Connector.http
https	HttpsConnection	Secure version of http	https://www.amazon.com	javax.microedition. io.Connector.https
socket	StreamConnection	Raw TCP socket	socket://mysite.com:1066	javax.microedition. io.Connector.socket
udp	DatagramConnection	UDP socket	udp://streamingsite.com: 1812	javax.microedition. io.Connector. datagram

The platform also supports more esoteric connections, including to USB ports and raw SSL. This book will use HTTP for examples as this is one of the most common and feature-rich protocols.

HTTP Requests

RIM has defined a set of custom optional parameters that you can include when requesting a network connection. These control features outside the standard Java ME interfaces or that apply only to BlackBerry connections. Table 1–2 shows the optional parameters that you can apply to an HTTP connection.

Table 1–2. Optional Parameters for HTTP Connections on BlackBerry

Parameter Name	Meaning	Valid Values
ConnectionTimeout	Number of milliseconds to wait before timing out an MDS connection	Integer
deviceside	Whether to connect via direct TCP or a proxy connection	true or false
interface	Non-cellular connection to use	wifi
WapGatewayAPN	The Access Point name to use as a gateway	Domain name
WapGatewayIP	The gateway to use for a WAP connection	IP address
WayGatewayPort	The port to use for a WAP connection	Integer
WapSourceIP	Local IP address	IP address
WapSourcePort	Local port for this connection	Integer
WapEnableWTLS	Whether to force a secure WAP connection	true or false
TunnelAuthUsername	User name for APN	String
TunnelAuthPassword	Password for APN	String

You append optional parameters to the end of your connection string and separate them with semicolons. To open a direct TCP connection over Wi-Fi to the CIA's web site, you would use the connection string `http://www.cia.com;deviceside=true;interface=wifi`.

CAUTION: If you specify a Wi-Fi connection and no Wi-Fi is available, the connection will throw an exception instead of failing back to a regular cellular connection.

When calling `Connector.open()` for a network connection, you may choose to specify whether the connection should time out. By default, a connection will wait until the other server replies or an error occurs; however, sometimes no response will come, either because the server does not respond or a network connection has quietly dropped. It's a good practice to request the timeout notification so you can display an error to the user. Not every connection type supports timeouts; TCP connections will have a default timeout of two minutes, and timeouts on a BES (BlackBerry Enterprise Server) can be overridden with a ;ConnectionTimeout URL parameter, while direct TCP connections and WAP connections do not allow configuring timeout. An example of requesting a connection with a timeout follows. The final true parameter indicates that we want to receive an exception if the connection does not successfully open in a timely manner.

```
HttpConnection conn = (HttpConnection) Connector.open(
        "http://www.cia.gov;deviceside=true", Connector.READ, true);
```

Once you have an HttpConnection, you can choose to set the request method (GET, POST, or HEAD) by calling setRequestMethod(), and specify any custom headers (such as the User-Agent or accepts) by calling setRequestProperty(). Once the connection is set up and you are ready to send or receive data, open the corresponding stream type and begin using it. All the same rules that applied to FileConnection objects also apply here: run within a separate thread, be prepared for errors, and clean up after yourself when done.

Simpler Networking

Since OS 5.0, BlackBerry devices have supported the ConnectionFactory, a streamlined way to negotiate and open network interfaces. The raw method of opening connections just described offers developers a great degree of fine control, but only a small fraction of developers will actually care whether their request travels over Wi-Fi, the BES, or WAP. In most cases, you just want to access a URL and get a response. Even worse, developers used to need to manually query the current status of the device and follow a complicated set of choices to decide which transport to use.

With ConnectionFactory, you can just request the URL you want. It will return a ConnectionDescriptor, an intermediate object that holds your connection and lets you inspect the details of the connection. After you retrieve the actual Connection object, you can open an InputStream and use it exactly as you would a Connection returned from Connector.open(), as shown here.

```
ConnectionFactory factory = new ConnectionFactory();
String url = "http://www.apress.com";
ConnectionDescriptor descriptor = factory.getConnection(url);
HttpConnection connection = null;
DataInputStream input = null;
try
{
    connection = (HttpConnection)descriptor.getConnection();
    input = connection.openDataInputStream();
    String text = input.readUTF();
    System.out.println("Read: " + text);
}
```

By default, ConnectionFactory will use the first available transport it finds. Apps will often prefer to use particular transport if available; for example, you might want to use Wi-Fi because of its faster speed, but you would still rather make a slower connection than no connection at all. You can specify your preferred transport types by constructing an array of types defined in TransportInfo, as shown in the following snippet.

```
ConnectionFactory factory = new ConnectionFactory();
int[] transport = new int[]{TransportInfo.TRANSPORT_TCP_WIFI};
factory.setPreferredTransportTypes(transport);
```

The foregoing example uses an HTTP connection, but ConnectionFactory supports all major transport types, including HTTPS, SSL, UDP, and raw socket connections. The factory has enough intelligence to try connections only over transports that work for the requested connection type; for example, it won't attempt to negotiate a UDP connection over WAP.

Note that only RIM devices support ConnectionFactory and the related classes in the net.rim.device.api.io.transport package. If you use these APIs, your code will not run on other Java ME devices. However, because they ultimately produce a Connection object, you should be able to re-use the majority of your code other than the initial setup.

App: Media Grabber

You now know enough essentials to create a functional BlackBerry app. Throughout this book, we will build a media-sharing application through examples at the end of every chapter. By the time we finish, the app will let you record and play back media, encrypt it, send it to friends, and plug in to the browser. This first chapter will concentrate on building up the framework of the app so you can launch it, access the network, and see messages. It will give you practice with running and debugging apps, and in the process, we'll also use some of the features covered in this chapter.

Writing the App

Follow the instructions from earlier in this chapter to start a new Eclipse workspace and create a new BlackBerry CLDC application called MediaGrabber. Within that project, create a class called MediaGrabber that extends UiApplication. We'll write a static main() function that starts running the app, a simple UI to display, and a custom thread that uses the GCF to download a file and compare it to the local filesystem. Listing 1–4 shows the complete class.

Listing 1–4. An App That Grabs and Stores Data from the Internet

```
package com.apress.king;

import java.io.IOException;
import java.io.InputStream;
import java.io.OutputStream;
import java.util.Date;

import javax.microedition.io.Connector;
import javax.microedition.io.HttpConnection;
import javax.microedition.io.file.FileConnection;

import net.rim.device.api.io.transport.ConnectionFactory;
import net.rim.device.api.ui.UiApplication;
import net.rim.device.api.ui.component.LabelField;
```

```
import net.rim.device.api.ui.container.MainScreen;
import net.rim.device.api.util.Arrays;

public class MediaGrabber extends UiApplication
{

    public static void main(String[] args)
    {
        MediaGrabber app = new MediaGrabber();
        app.begin();
    }

    public void begin()
    {
        MainScreen s = new MainScreen();
        LabelField label = new LabelField("Kilroy Was Here");
        s.add(label);
        pushScreen(s);
        (new WebChecker()).start();
        enterEventDispatcher();
    }

    private class WebChecker extends Thread
    {
        public void run()
        {
            HttpConnection http = null;
            FileConnection file = null;
            InputStream is = null;
            OutputStream os = null;
            ConnectionFactory factory = new ConnectionFactory();
            try
            {
                http = (HttpConnection) factory.getConnection(
                        "http://www.google.com").getConnection();
                is = http.openInputStream();
                // Read the first 4 kilobytes.
                byte[] networkBuffer = new byte[4096];
                is.read(networkBuffer);
                is.close();
                http.close();
                file = (FileConnection) Connector
                        .open("file:///store/home/user/last.html");
                if (file.exists())
                {
                    System.out.println("We last checked Google on "
                            + new Date(file.lastModified()));
                    byte[] fileBuffer = new byte[4096];
                    is = file.openInputStream();
                    is.read(fileBuffer);
                    is.close();
                    if (Arrays.equals(networkBuffer, fileBuffer))
                    {
                        System.out.println("Google hasn't changed.");
                    }
                    else
                    {
                        System.out.println("Google's doing something new.");
```

```
                }
                file.delete();
            }
            else
            {
                System.out.println("Looks like the first time we've run!");
            }
            file.create();
            os = file.openOutputStream();
            os.write(networkBuffer);
        }
        catch (IOException ioe)
        {
            System.err.println("An I/O error occurred: " + ioe);
        }
        catch (Exception e)
        {
            System.err.println("An unexpected error occurred: " + e);
        }
        finally
        {
            try
            {
                if (os != null)
                    os.close();
                if (file != null)
                    file.close();
                if (is != null)
                    is.close();
                if (http != null)
                    http.close();
            }
            catch (Exception e)
            {
                // Ignore
            }
        }
    }
  }
}
```

Debugging on the Simulator

Because this app requires network support, we need to enable connections within the simulator.

1. You can do this in an already running simulator by opening Manage Connections from the main menu.

2. Check the option for Wi-Fi if it is not already selected.

3. Next, select Set Up Wi-Fi Network.

4. Choose the Default WLAN Network. This causes the simulator to view your personal computer's connection as its own Wi-Fi connection.

5. To verify the connection, return to the main menu, select the browser, and open a web page.

Certain device simulators do not offer an option for Wi-Fi, and older simulators may not direct traffic over that connection properly. In these cases, you must take an extra step before launching the simulator.

1. Click Run, and then click Debug Configurations.

2. Click the BlackBerry Simulator entry, and click the new launch configuration icon in the upper left. A new configuration will display. Name it what you like, such as "MediaGrabber BlackBerry".

3. Select the projects you wish to deploy.

4. Click the Simulator tab, and select the device you want to use. Mark the check box by the message that starts with "Launch Mobile Data System," as shown in Figure 1–7.

5. Finally, click the Common tab, and check both options under "Display in favorites menu." Click Debug.

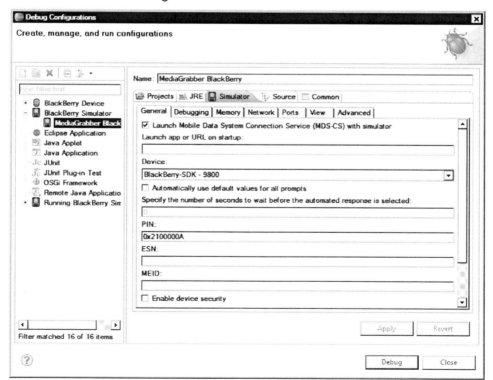

Figure 1–7. Configuring Eclipse to launch the MDS

> **CAUTION:** Only one copy of the BlackBerry simulator can run at a time. When changing the configuration to add MDS, close any previously running simulators.

The simulator window will launch again, but this time you will also see a black-and-white terminal window display with a lot of rapidly scrolling text, as shown in Figure 1–8. This is the Mobile Data System terminal. As mentioned before, the BlackBerry Simulator is very accurate to real device behavior, and this accuracy extends to the way BlackBerry devices access the Internet. The simulator cannot directly access the Internet connection on your development computer; instead, it connects to the MDS, which simulates a real wireless connection, and behind the scenes uses your computer's Internet connection to provide data.

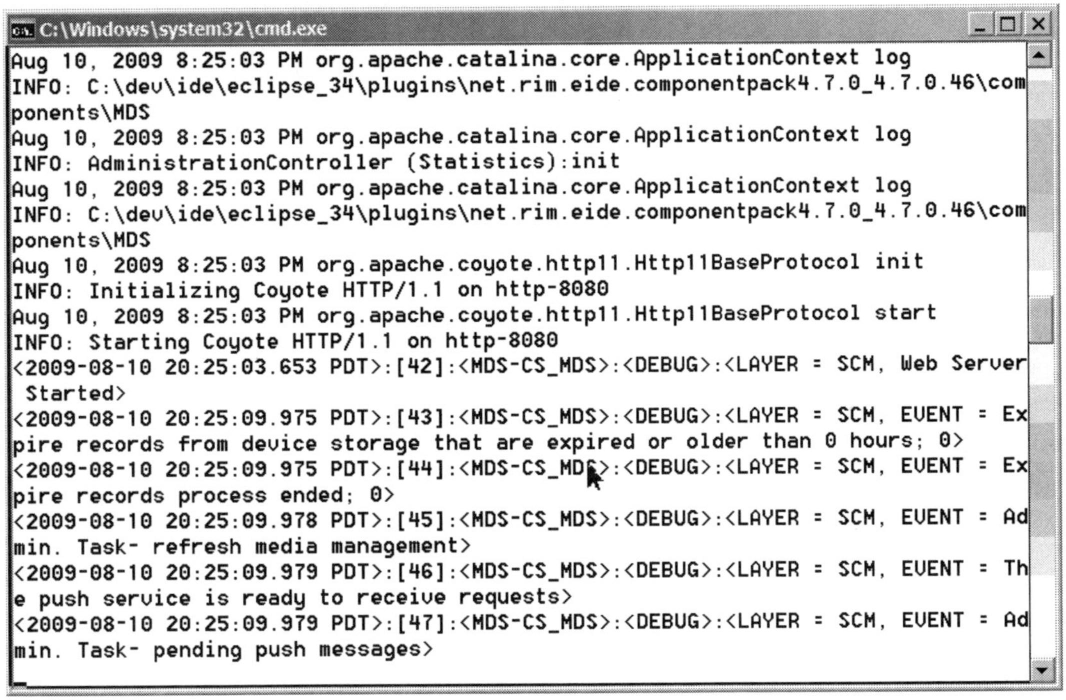

```
C:\Windows\system32\cmd.exe                                          _ □ ×
Aug 10, 2009 8:25:03 PM org.apache.catalina.core.ApplicationContext log
INFO: C:\dev\ide\eclipse_34\plugins\net.rim.eide.componentpack4.7.0_4.7.0.46\com
ponents\MDS
Aug 10, 2009 8:25:03 PM org.apache.catalina.core.ApplicationContext log
INFO: AdministrationController (Statistics):init
Aug 10, 2009 8:25:03 PM org.apache.catalina.core.ApplicationContext log
INFO: C:\dev\ide\eclipse_34\plugins\net.rim.eide.componentpack4.7.0_4.7.0.46\com
ponents\MDS
Aug 10, 2009 8:25:03 PM org.apache.coyote.http11.Http11BaseProtocol init
INFO: Initializing Coyote HTTP/1.1 on http-8080
Aug 10, 2009 8:25:03 PM org.apache.coyote.http11.Http11BaseProtocol start
INFO: Starting Coyote HTTP/1.1 on http-8080
<2009-08-10 20:25:03.653 PDT>:[42]:<MDS-CS_MDS>:<DEBUG>:<LAYER = SCM, Web Server
 Started>
<2009-08-10 20:25:09.975 PDT>:[43]:<MDS-CS_MDS>:<DEBUG>:<LAYER = SCM, EVENT = Ex
pire records from device storage that are expired or older than 0 hours; 0>
<2009-08-10 20:25:09.975 PDT>:[44]:<MDS-CS_MDS>:<DEBUG>:<LAYER = SCM, EVENT = Ex
pire records process ended; 0>
<2009-08-10 20:25:09.978 PDT>:[45]:<MDS-CS_MDS>:<DEBUG>:<LAYER = SCM, EVENT = Ad
min. Task- refresh media management>
<2009-08-10 20:25:09.979 PDT>:[46]:<MDS-CS_MDS>:<DEBUG>:<LAYER = SCM, EVENT = Th
e push service is ready to receive requests>
<2009-08-10 20:25:09.979 PDT>:[47]:<MDS-CS_MDS>:<DEBUG>:<LAYER = SCM, EVENT = Ad
min. Task- pending push messages>
```

Figure 1–8. The MDS status terminal

To test that the network works properly, click the Browser icon within the BlackBerry simulator and enter the URL of your favorite web page. You should see it load in this window, similarly to how it would look on an actual device.

Now you are ready to debug your app. Double-click the side of the Java editing window on line 46, at the line that starts with `http = (HttpConnection)`. A blue breakpoint marker should appear here, as shown in Figure 1–9. Launch your application. The simulator will freeze, and you may get a prompt in Eclipse asking if you'd like to open the Debug perspective. Answer Yes here, and check "Remember my decision."

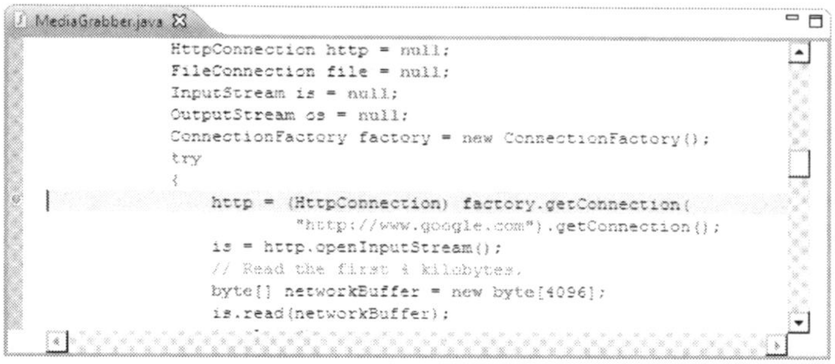

Figure 1–9. Setting a debug breakpoint in Eclipse

You are now in the Eclipse debug view. Even if you have never used Eclipse before, you should recognize its capabilities as similar to other IDEs you may have used, such as NetBeans or Visual Studio. You can inspect the values of local variables, add watches to expressions, and control execution of the code. You can press F5 to step into a method, F6 to step over the next line, and F7 to step out of a method. Press F8 to continue running until the next breakpoint.

You might encounter a ControlledAccessException. Through debugging, you can trace this down to the call to file.exists(). This exception indicates that you need additional permissions to successfully work with the file. We will examine permissions in more depth in Chapter 9. For now, if you encounter this problem, navigate to the applications menu. On BlackBerry 6 devices, you can find this in Options ➤ Device ➤ Application Management. Press the Menu key, and then choose Edit Default Permissions. Change all the permissions to Allow, press the Menu key again, and select Apply Defaults to All. When you re-run MediaGrabber, you should now succeed in the file operations.

Spend a few moments experimenting. You'll see that you can observe all the data that comes down from the network connection. If a problem occurs, you can view the thrown exception and determine how to solve it. Launch the app again, noting the different path it takes the second time. Once you feel comfortable in the debugger view, you can move on to the actual device.

Debugging on the BlackBerry Device

1. To debug on the BlackBerry, you first must load the application. The simplest way to do this is via the following steps: Stop any already running debug sessions.

2. Attach your device to the computer, and install any necessary drivers.

3. Right-click the project, select Debug As, and then select BlackBerry Device.

4. Enter the signing password you created from the section "The Keys to Development," and click OK.

5. Observe the device connecting to your computer and attaching the debugger.

6. If Eclipse warns about missing .debug files, click "Don't ask this again."

Once your app loads, navigate to it and launch the app. When prompted, grant it Trusted Application Status. It may ask you for permission to access www.google.com; we'll see how to avoid that request in a little while.

The device will freeze when it hits the breakpoint, and you can step through the code as you did with the simulator. For the most part, the debugger behaves the same in both places: you can view variables, control progress through the application, and so on. You may notice that sometimes execution will pause within a RIM class; you can view the entire call stack but not the specific executing code. This typically happens when RIM code throws an exception, sometimes due to an action within your code. You can usually step back out of this function or press F8 to continue running and observe what happens; sometimes the OS handles such exceptions internally before they reach you.

You also may see that sometimes debugger progress stops altogether. This happens when the device needs input from the user. This happens most often when a security prompt displays in response to an operation in your program. Answering Yes or No to this prompt will determine whether an exception is thrown in your app.

If you cannot debug your app on the device, or if you cannot view variable values, please carefully review the foregoing steps. In particular, make sure you have installed the simulator that corresponds to the device you are debugging on and double-check the device software version numbers and model numbers.

Finally, sometimes the debugger just detaches while your program is debugging, which can be annoying. Make sure your USB cable is firmly connected; if the problem persists, it may help to carefully set your breakpoints and avoid inspecting certain variables, since certain combinations can result in disconnection.

Working with Devices

On-target debugging is a powerful tool. There is no substitute for running your code on an actual phone and being able to see exactly what is happening. However, running on the phone is more complex than running on the simulator, and you should keep a few points in mind.

First, make sure that your particular phone is in a good state for running the app. Devices acquired secondhand through eBay or elsewhere can come with configurations that may block certain operations or fail to make connections. Chapter 9 will specifically address the issue of security policies on ex-corporate phones. If your device was originally created for another carrier, you may need to fill out the APN (Access Point Name) information for the current carrier; this is usually accessed via Settings ➤ Options ➤ Advanced ➤ TCP or Options ➤ Device ➤ Advanced System Settings ➤ TCP IP. You can find the proper APN settings on your carrier's web site or in an Internet search.

If you write your app for one particular device or for a known configuration, such as devices for a particular company's BES, you just need to set it up to work with those device settings. However, if you want to run on a variety of device types and carriers, you'll need to more carefully think about how to support those differences. You can create a single binary that attempts to detect a user's configuration and uses appropriate settings for them; or, you can create separate versions of the app for each configuration and let users choose which one to install. Chapter 10 addresses this choice in more detail.

Eclipse makes it convenient to deploy your app, but it can get a little tedious if you frequently make changes to test on the device. To learn about alternate ways of deploying your app, consult *Beginning BlackBerry 6 Development*, by Anthony Rizk (Apress, 2011).

BlackBerry devices can take a very long time to reboot after installing an app. To minimize the need to reboot, exit your app before deleting it or installing an updated version.

Sign Me Up

Hopefully you have received your BlackBerry code signing keys by now. If not, you can skip this part and continue with the later chapters in this book. Return here once you have installed the keys and are ready to start signing.

In Eclipse, click Project ➤ BlackBerry ➤ Sign with Signature Tool.... If you have previously signed within this session, such as when debugging on the device, Eclipse will remember and automatically supply your password; otherwise, it will prompt you to enter it again, as shown in Figure 1–10. The Signature Tool window will display, and then the tool will contact the RIM signing servers and apply the signatures. Depending on the size of your application and the code you call, you may see many more items. You will see some extra SignerID entries that you cannot receive signatures for; this is normal, as these are for advanced cryptography or internal RIM use. Also, you may not see some SignerID entries for keys you do possess. Again, don't be concerned; you won't need all keys, especially for simple apps.

Usually, the tool will automatically request signatures and close after success. To modify the signature collection process, run it again to receive a No Signatures Required prompt, which will leave the window open. If you are behind a proxy, click Properties and then fill in your proxy information. Click OK, and then click Close to dismiss the window.

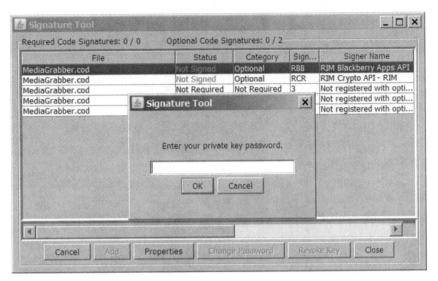

Figure 1–10. Requesting a signature

CAUTION: Whenever you sign an application, you must request a signature from the RIM signing servers. These servers notoriously suffer from occasional outages of varying lengths that can strike at any time. If you have a deadline for your project, do yourself a favor and plan to finish ahead of time so you aren't stuck if the signing servers happen to drop offline right before you need to ship.

Signed applications gain certain privileges, among them less frequent prompting of users. More importantly, though, only signed applications have permission to access certain protected RIM APIs. Much of the content in this book requires signing to run.

Signing doesn't add as much overhead as some other OEMs' solutions require. Still, signing can feel tedious when you frequently make changes to test on the device. Try to do as much work on the simulator as you can. If you are in a professional environment, consider some of the techniques discussed in Chapter 11. Ideally, though, you should be able to happily develop 95% of your app on the desktop, maybe 5% testing on the device, and then just apply a final set of signatures before distributing it.

WANT MORE?

MediaGrabber doesn't actually grab any media yet—we'll start doing that in the next chapter. However, this is a good opportunity to play around with the basic app now and get a feel for how development works on the BlackBerry. Try the following suggestions.

- Spruce up the MainScreen and text. Use a layout Manager to position the text in the center of the screen. Style the LabelField to make it more attractive.

- Try checking multiple web pages in addition to Google. Save each to a separate file. Make sure you clean up your connections after each one. Tip: Create a helper method that can handle any URL.

- Try running the app on different devices from different carriers. Do you need to make any changes for them, such as different network parameters?

Spend as much time as you like on these or other improvements. Once you feel comfortable with making and testing changes, you are ready to move on.

Excelsior

You have crossed the first threshold for writing advanced BlackBerry apps. Although the treatment in this chapter has been brief, you have learned the essentials for writing useful BlackBerry apps. You now have a functioning environment that allows you to write, test, and deploy your application on the simulator and on BlackBerry devices. You have learned the differences between MIDlets, BlackBerry CLDC applications, and library modules, and when to use each. You have built simple user interfaces. Most importantly, you know how to send and receive data over the wireless network, how to save and read files, and the essential structure of the Generic Connection Framework.

With these tools at your disposal, you can write a variety of useful apps. The remainder of this book will take that core knowledge to the next level by introducing you to the advanced tools and techniques of BlackBerry development. We'll start by examining the advanced features for media capture.

Chapter 2

Media Capture

For years, manufacturers have sold phones with promises of increased convenience. They say you shouldn't carry a phone, a camera, and a tape recorder—instead, buy one device that combines all those functions. This once-exotic bundling now feels standard, and today, even inexpensive phones generally can record media.

BlackBerry phones have embraced this trend as they have evolved from a business-centric tool to a general-purpose device, and most new BlackBerry devices contain a camera and microphone. While people appreciate the convenience factor, they typically won't get a camera that's as good as a stand-alone camera. A camera on a phone, though, becomes another tool for software developers. An analog camera just takes pictures, but a camera phone can do much more: display and manipulate those pictures, share them with your friends, detect the brightness of your surroundings, try to recognize faces, and more. This chapter introduces the media APIs that allow you to consume the information coming from your device and start doing interesting things with it.

BlackBerry vs. Java ME APIs

Because RIM's Java ME platform includes the standard set of multimedia APIs (MMAPI), developers already comfortable with Java ME development can immediately use these familiar interfaces in their programs. The Java ME concept of media revolves around a media `Player` object that plays and records media.

In addition to these standard APIs, BlackBerry has also added its own set of functions that allow access to abilities unavailable to most Java phones, such as e-mail and cell tower info. Throughout this book, you will notice that such packages start with "net.rim". In contrast, Java packages start with "java" or "javax". Generally, the RIM APIs will offer more compelling features, but at the price of greater difficulty when porting to other platforms.

The Java ME Standard: A MediaPlayer Connection

Historically, Java's development seesawed between two extremes. The initial release of Java included an enormous set of libraries with a bewildering array of packages, classes, and methods. Each individual component had a very well-defined role, but that meant learning many new components. With Java ME, the pendulum swung the other way with the introduction of the Generic Connection Framework (GCF). Now you had a single component, like a Connector, that was responsible for a wide variety of tasks such as accessing the network or writing a file. The MMAPI resembles the GCF because it provides only a few classes to learn, but a great deal of nuance in their use.

The MMAPI broadly defines media to include all audio operations and all visual operations except for the display of still images. In the same way that you access Connection subtypes by making requests to the Connector class, you access Player instances by making requests to the Manager class. Unlike the GCF, though, Player has no subclasses; instead, each Player can support an arbitrary number of Control objects. Each Control allows you to manipulate some aspect of the recording/playback operation. For example, playing back a video may provide access to a VideoControl, FramePositioningControl, and VolumeControl, while playing back an audio file will offer only the VolumeControl. Figure 2–1 illustrates two possible configurations of Player objects. This sort of separation allows RIM and other manufacturers to add additional functionality based on new features, and not the specific media type.

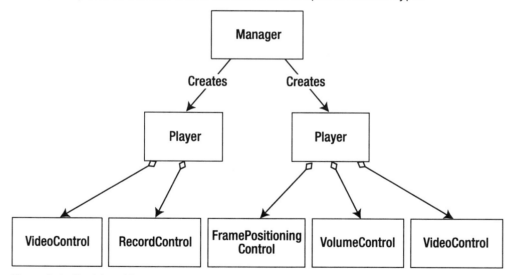

Figure 2–1. *Obtaining different Players from a Manager*

> **NOTE:** You can find Manager and other media classes under the javax.microedition.media package hierarchy.

The MMAPI has many components and may feel a little overwhelming at first. You may want to revisit earlier parts of this chapter as you become more comfortable with its structure and behavior. Don't worry—we'll take it slowly, and by the end of the chapter you'll be able to integrate media capture into your own apps.

Push Me/Pull You

The MMAPI distinguishes between two general tasks involved in any media operation. First comes the data delivery protocol. You can think of this like the TCP/IP stack that you use to download a file over the network. TCP/IP doesn't care whether you're downloading a movie, audio, or text; it's concerned only with how to get the data to you. The MMAPI uses the interface DataSource to represent the data delivery protocol. A DataSource might represent a network connection, a file connection, or even a randomized source of data. In the case of media recording, the DataSource will be the piece of hardware used to provide that media. After the data arrives, the framework handles that data content. Content handling involves looking at the raw bytes that have arrived and then performing some task with them. The MMAPI's Player class is a content handler. Depending on what type of content you've asked for, it might decode an audio stream and direct it to the phone's speakers. When recording media, the Player will generally translate the raw input data into a usable format for you to consume.

Interestingly, the same two objects have totally opposite roles when recording or playing. In a recording scenario, the DataSource deals with phone hardware and the Player writes to a representation; in a playback scenario, the DataSource reads a representation and the Player writes to phone hardware. This flexibility can make the MMAPI difficult to understand, but it also accounts for its power. By not tying themselves to the scenarios they could imagine, the MMAPI's authors have created a system that can evolve to accomplish tasks that were not possible at the time the standard was written.

> **NOTE:** The one aspect of the MMAPI that does not follow this DataSource/Player design stands out badly. At the time of its creation, the majority of phones did not support compressed audio formats, and programs relied on simple tone-based audio playback. Rather than creating a DataSource for those notes and a Player to output them, the MMAPI authors created a method **Manager.playTone()** that would generate a single note. The widespread adoption of compressed audio has rendered this method largely useless, and its presence in the API feels like an anachronism.

The Life of a Player

Player instances follow a standard life cycle. Handheld devices have less memory, slower processors, and usually slower network connections than desktop computers, so the MMAPI strives to keep as light a footprint as possible. It acquires resources only when necessary. You can queue up multiple media operations without worrying too much about memory usage, because the MMAPI will automatically provide them appropriate access as needed and not pre-allocate resources ahead of time.

Each step through the life cycle means you have taken more resources and moved closer to actually performing the media operation. The Player generally advances forward, but in certain cases it can return to an earlier state, as shown in Figure 2–2. The following list shows details on each state:

- *UNREALIZED*: This indicates that you have requested the media operation, nothing more. In a sense, it "isn't real" yet.

- *REALIZED*: Once a Player enters the REALIZED state, it knows what it has to do in order to complete the operation. Depending on the request type, it may need to communicate with the filesystem, check capabilities, or perform other initial setup. A realized Player should generally be "ready," but not holding on to any scarce resources. For example, if you are going to take a picture, the Player will not be holding an exclusive lock on the camera hardware in this state.

- *PREFETCHED*: This state must be entered before the operation starts; but for recording tasks, it will likely not do anything. In playback operations, this is generally where data will download and buffers will fill.

- *STARTED*: A Player that has started continues to operate. When recording, you have exclusive control of the recording hardware while in this state. When playing back, the media is playing during this time.

- *CLOSED*: Once you have finished with a Player, it enters this state. A closed Player has released nearly all of its resources and cannot be restarted; you must create a new Player if you wish to repeat the operation.

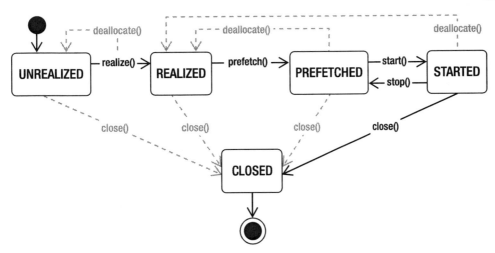

Figure 2–2. *The life cycle of a* Player *object*

Anytime you have a Player object, you can call close() to shut it down. This will release all of its resources and make it unavailable for further operations. Alternately, you can call the deallocate() method. This will return it to the REALIZED state unless it hasn't yet been realized, in which case it will keep the Player in the UNREALIZED state. Use deallocate() when you need to give up resources but intend to continue using this Player. For example, if your application contains both an audio and a video recorder, you could create two Player objects. Both can't use the microphone at the same time, so you could record using the audio Player, and then call deallocate() on it. You could repeat the process using the video Player, and then switch back to audio again, thus sharing the microphone between them. This would be more efficient than tearing down and recreating the Players from scratch each time you record.

The five states certainly offer a lot of options for managing your Player objects. Fortunately, you don't need to explicitly deal with them unless your app requires it, such as the foregoing example for sharing a microphone. A Player knows enough to automatically move through the required states so, for example, if you instruct an UNREALIZED Player to start playing, it will automatically handle any realization and prefetching necessary.

Media operations can block execution, so you may want to create, configure, and start your Player on a separate thread from the main UI thread. While most methods on Player synchronously block until their operation completes, start() simply begins the recording or playing operation, which will operate in the background while your calling thread continues execution. You will often want this thread to exit or wait until the Player's operation completes; do not assume that the Player is done after it returns control to you.

Listen to Me

The five states give a big picture of your media's actions, but sometimes you'll want more granularity than that. For example, you may want to know exactly when it first starts capturing data, or if another application is interfering with your operations.

RIM supports these use cases by offering a standard listener interface. By implementing PlayerListener, your application can register with a Player instance, as shown in Figure 2–3. PlayerListener defines a single method, playerUpdate(), which will be invoked whenever something interesting happens.

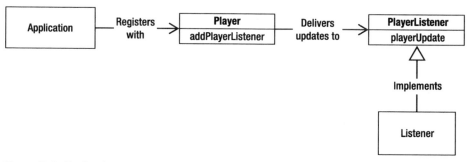

Figure 2–3. *Registering a* Listener *with a* Player

The framework tags updates as Strings, and optionally provides additional information in an accompanying Object. This flexible design allows manufacturers to define their own event types without requiring changes to the interface. The MMAPI defines a broad set of standard event names and makes them available as public fields in the PlayerListener interface. You will need to add references to any RIM-specific event types in your own code. Table 2–1 shows the Player events that can be generated during media capture.

Table 2-1. *Player Events During Recording*

String	Definition	Meaning	EventData Type	EventData Value
deviceAvailable	DEVICE_AVAILABLE	A previously unavailable device, such as a microphone, is now free.	N/A	N/A
deviceUnavailable	DEVICE_UNAVAILABLE	An exclusive device, such as a microphone, has been taken by a more important application, such as for an incoming call.	N/A	N/A
recordError	RECORD_ERROR	An error occurred while recording. Call setRecordLocation or setRecordStream on the RecordControl to try again.	String	Detailed error message
recordStarted	RECORD_STARTED	Recording has begun.	Long	Time
recordStopped	RECORD_STOPPED	Recording has stopped.	Long	Time
net.rim.device.internal .media.recordCommitted	N/A	Recording commit completed	N/A	N/A

Listing 2–1 implements a basic listener class that provides updates about the current status of a recording operation. However, a similar class could perform additional tasks as well, such as automatically restarting capture if an error occurs.

Listing 2–1. *A Status Update* PlayerListener

```
import javax.microedition.media.*;
import net.rim.device.api.ui.component.LabelField;

public class RecordingListener implements PlayerListener
{
    private LabelField status;

    public RecordingListener(LabelField status)
```

```
        {
            this.status = status;
        }

        public void playerUpdate(Player source, String event, Object data)
        {
            if (event.equals(PlayerListener.RECORD_STARTED))
            {
                status.setText("Recording started...");
            }
            else if (event.equals(PlayerListener.RECORD_STOPPED))
            {
                status.setText("Recording stopped...");
            }
            else if (event.equals(PlayerListener.RECORD_ERROR))
            {
                status.setText("Uh-oh!  Error:" + data);
            }
            else if (event.equals("net.rim.device.internal.media.recordCommitted"))
            {
                status.setText("Recorded data saved.");
            }
            else
            {
                status.setText(event + ":" + data);
            }
        }
    }
}
```

Attach the PlayerListener to the Player, and you will start receiving updates automatically.

```
player.addPlayerListener(new RecordingListener(status));
```

You don't need to add a PlayerListener for every Player. Most advanced applications will want to receive these sorts of notifications so they can update the user and take other actions, but for simple operations like playing background music, you'll be fine sticking with the basic Player API.

Have Content, Will Travel

Once the Player finishes and your capture completes, what's next? Depending on the type of capture you're doing, you'll have access to different Control objects, each with its own mechanism for accessing the correct data. If you took a snapshot, you could call a synchronous method on VideoControl that would return you the bytes for that shot. If you captured audio, you could obtain a RecordControl object and provide it with a file name or output stream that would store the data.

Generally speaking, once you have finished your recording, you should retrieve the data and then close the Player as soon as possible. This will make your application and the rest of the phone more responsive, freeing up memory and resources for other tasks.

What Else Is There?

So far, everything described is part of the standard MMAPI. This solution will work for most developers, and fortunately, RIM has implemented most of its media capabilities within this interface. In some situations, though, you may prefer to use the native RIM applications to perform capture instead of doing it all yourself. This can provide advantages. Users have already run the RIM applications before, so they will feel more familiar than a custom version you create. Additionally, the built-in apps may contain more features than you will implement in your own; you might not want to implement camera controls, for example. However, invoking RIM apps generally requires complicated interactions with the OS to display the app and then retrieve the captured files. The package net.rim.blackberry.api.invoke contains a class, Invoke, which can launch a variety of native applications. For example, to start the camera, you would simply call Invoke with the proper parameters.

```
Invoke.invokeApplication(Invoke.APP_TYPE_CAMERA, null);
```

The second parameter provides an optional set of arguments for the application. To launch in video record mode, use the appropriate parameter in CameraArguments.

```
Invoke.invokeApplication(Invoke.APP_TYPE_CAMERA, new
    CameraArguments(CameraArguments.ARG_VIDEO_RECORDER));
```

At this point, your application will enter the background, and you cannot interact with the user. However, your application can monitor the filesystem for newly created files, and then use them as if they were created by your application. You'll see an example of this later in the chapter.

Creating a MediaPlayer

As noted earlier, any media operation requires both a DataSource and a Player. In practice, the Manager class can provide an appropriate DataSource for most request types, so you may request a Player by simply passing in the proper String for the type of capture you want to make.

This raises a very important question: What happens if Player creation fails? On a BlackBerry device that has a built-in camera, such as a Torch, it should work; but on a device without a camera, like an 8800, it will obviously fail. If you are developing for your own personal device, this isn't a problem—you know its capabilities. However, if you hope to run on many different devices, you will need to handle situations where the device doesn't support an operation.

Chapter 10 provides much more detail on strategies to solve this problem. Fortunately, though, a clean way exists to determine at runtime whether the user's device supports an operation. The MMAPI defines a standard set of system properties, including the media-related properties shown in Table 2–2. By calling System.getProperty() with a given property name, you can determine what the device supports. Based on this, you can show an appropriate message to the user or disable an option entirely instead of waiting for it to fail.

Table 2–2. *MMAPI System Properties*

Key	Description	Returns
supports.audio.capture	Whether audio capture is supported	"true" or "false"
supports.video.capture	Whether video capture is supported	"true" or "false"
supports.recording	Whether recording is supported	"true" or "false"
audio.encodings	Supported audio capture formats	Space-delimited set of audio formats (e.g., "audio/pcm audio/amr"). null if not supported.
video.encodings	Supported video capture formats	Space-delimited set of video formats (e.g., "video/3gpp video/mp4"). null if not supported.
video.snapshot.encodings	Supported video snapshot formats for the getSnapshot method	Space-delimited set of image formats (e.g., "image/jpeg image/bmp image/png"). The first format is the default. null if not supported.

Once you have checked that this device supports your desired operation, simply issue the request to the Manager.

```
if (System.getProperty("supports.video.capture").equals("true"))
{
    Player player = Manager.createPlayer("capture://video");
}
```

> **CAUTION:** In order to keep the listings as focused and useful as possible, the short code snippets that you'll see like this will show only the most pertinent parts of an operation. They omit standard boilerplate that actual apps must include (like catching exceptions) or should include (like checking return values for validity). The longer listings at the end of each chapter show fully functioning programs, and these do include all required exception handling. That being said, it is very important to think about those exceptions. They aren't there just to inconvenience you, but to warn about very likely possibilities. Even if you have verified that your device supports an operation, there is a host of reasons that it might fail. For example, some other application might have an exclusive lock on the resource, or you may have insufficient permissions. You should be prepared to catch a MediaException and IOException from nearly every MMAPI method call, and take a sensible action in response.

Controlling Output

Your Player will contain at least one Control—a RecordControl—which determines what will happen with your recorded audio or video data. Obtain the RecordControl by asking the Player for it.

```
RecordControl recorder = (RecordControl)player.getControl("RecordControl");
```

The RecordControl contains a variety of useful functions. For our purposes, the most interesting are the options for determining where to direct output. The more generic option is setRecordStream(), which takes an OutputStream. Theoretically, you could use this to send the captured data to an HTTP server, an encryption layer, or some other fancy stream. In practice, you will use this method when you're interested in getting the raw bytes of the audio. This capture would require outputting to a proper stream.

```
ByteArrayOutputStream out = new ByteArrayOutputStream();
recorder.setRecordStream(out);
// Record here
byte[] rawData = out.toByteArray();
```

The method setRecordLocation(), which takes a URL, provides a very convenient alternative to an OutputStream. This choice will write output directly to the specified location, freeing you from any responsibility for handling the actual recorded data.

```
recorder.setRecordLocation("file:///SDCard/BlackBerry/Music/recording.amr");
```

RecordControl offers several other useful operations. You will almost always use the following options:

startRecord() indicates that capture can begin. If necessary, it will wait until the associated Player has entered the STARTED state.

stopRecord() pauses capture. You can call startRecord() later to resume capture.

commit() will cease capture and deliver the recorded data as earlier directed by setRecordStream() or setRecordLocation(). A commit occurs asynchronously: the data may not actually be saved until some time after the method returns. Your program should not attempt to access the output, whether a stream or a file, until after the "net.rim.device.internal.media.recordCommitted" event has been delivered to a PlayerListener.

For certain apps, the following choices may be useful, as well:

reset() will erase the current recorded contents. If you call reset(), none of the data up to this point will be written out.

setRecordSizeLimit() will set a cap, in bytes, on the amount of data to record. You might use this method if, for example, you let the user record video onto limited internal memory, or if you otherwise wish to cap the size of the output. The platform will automatically call commit() after reaching the specified limit.

getContentType() reports the format of the recorded media, such as "audio/amr" or "video/3gp". In practice, you will probably already know this, but it can be informative if you use the default unspecified format.

TIP: You cannot control the format of the output. Your format is set to what you specify when creating the Player; you cannot, for example, capture in AMR and output in MP3. If you want such a conversion, you will need to do so yourself by capturing in one format, examining the bytes, and writing out in the other format.

Recording Audio

By now you should have a general idea of how the recording process works. You will request a Player, configure it for your desired capture, start it to begin recording, and then stop it once the recording is complete. At that point, you can retrieve the recorded audio data.

Audio Formats

Before you start, though, you should ask yourself whether you care what format that data will be in. RIM offers several choices for audio encoding. Table 2–3 describes your choices. Note that each choice has a required minimum device software version and will not work on versions below this.

Table 2–3. *Audio Capture Formats*

URL	Recorded Format	Available with Version
capture://audio	AMR	4.2
capture://audio?encoding=amr	AMR	4.2
capture://audio?encoding=audio/amr	AMR	4.2
capture://audio?encoding=pcm	PCM	4.2
capture://audio?encoding=audio/basic	PCM	4.2
capture://audio?encoding=gsm	GSM	4.6
capture://audio?encoding=x-gsm	GSM	4.6
capture://audio?encoding=qcelp	QCELP	4.7

NOTE: BlackBerry devices currently support AMR narrow band, not the higher-quality AMR wide band. PCM recording is mono, 8 kHz, 16-bit.

Compared to the options available for playback, this isn't as rich a set of choices; for example, you cannot record in MP3 format. However, depending on your application needs, you might prefer certain formats. Some are more widely compatible, some compress better, and others offer more fidelity. AMR is a very highly compressed format that is optimized for speech, so it would be perfect for applications like a voice memo recorder. On the other hand, PCM is more appropriate for general non-voice audio capture, and it produces files that are more likely to be compatible with other programs.

You can determine at runtime what formats are supported by calling `System.getProperty("audio.encodings")`. Do this if you prefer to record in a particular format, but can fall back on another format if you can't use your first choice. This is especially important because even if a device has the appropriate software version number, it will not necessarily support every capture mode. For example, CDMA devices (such as phones on the Sprint or Verizon networks in the United States) may not support PCM regardless of their version.

Capture

At the time you request the `Player`, you ask for a particular format. However, you still need to decide where the data will end up. You can use a `RecordControl` for this purpose. `RecordControl.setRecordStream()` offers a generic way to output to any desired stream type, such as a byte array or a network connection. For convenience, `RecordControl.setRecordLocation()` will allow you to write out to a particular file.

The following pseudocode example shows the simplest way to record a 5-second audio clip.

```
Player player = Manager.createPlayer("capture://audio?encoding=amr");
RecordControl recorder = (RecordControl)player.getControl("RecordControl");
recorder.setRecordLocation("file:///SDCard/BlackBerry/Music/recording.amr");
recorder.startRecord();
player.start();
Thread.sleep(5000);
recorder.commit();
player.close();
```

NOTE: This example assumes that the device has a BlackBerry-formatted SD card inserted. In an actual application, you would want to verify that it is available. If you'd prefer to save to internal memory, you could write to a path under `file:///store/home/user`. For the best portability, use `FileSystemRegistry.listRoots()` to obtain a list of all currently mounted filesystems.

Considering everything that takes place, it's rather impressive that this takes only about eight lines of code to write. Real-world applications will be longer, but you can quickly and easily implement the essential steps.

Using the Camera

Image capture requires a bit more complexity than audio capture. The MMAPI does not actually provide an interface for grabbing data directly from the camera. Instead, it allows you to capture a screenshot from the device screen. This means you'll need to display the camera viewfinder on the device screen, and then do your capture from that.

> **TIP:** BlackBerry devices with OS 5.0 and higher support JSR 234, Advanced Multimedia Supplements (AMMS). AMMS builds on top of the MMAPI to provide much finer control over recording operations, including zoom, flash, focus, image and audio effects, and more. See the classes in `javax.microedition.amms.control` and subpackages for details.

Image Formats

As with audio capture, you have several choices when it comes to image capture. Unlike with audio, you do not need to make your choice at the time you create the `Player`. Instead, once you have access to a `VideoControl`, you can pass your requested format to `VideoControl.getSnapShot()`. Some supported image types follow:

```
"rgb565"

"encoding=jpeg&width=1600&height=1200&quality=superfine"

"encoding=jpeg&width=1600&height=1200&quality=fine"

"encoding=jpeg&width=1600&height=1200&quality=normal"

"encoding=jpeg&width=1024&height=768&quality=superfine"

"encoding=jpeg&width=1024&height=768&quality=fine"

"encoding=jpeg&width=1024&height=768&quality=normal"

"encoding=jpeg&width=640&height=480&quality=superfine"

"encoding=jpeg&width=640&height=480&quality=fine"

"encoding=jpeg&width=640&height=480&quality=normal"
```

You can easily understand most options in this list: the device supports JPEG images for capture, and you have a choice of several different resolutions and three levels of quality. What about that "rgb565" outlier? This choice retrieves raw pixel data instead of a compressed JPEG format. In RGB565, every 2 bytes refer to a single pixel. Within those 16 bytes, the top 5 bits represent the red value, the next 6 bits represent the green, and the final 5 bits represent the blue. You'll want to avoid this format unless you plan on manually manipulating the pixels in memory. Also, confirm that your target device does actually support capture in this format.

Even though RIM offered MMAPI support starting with device software version 4.2, it initially did not implement all aspects of the JSR. The JSR does allow manufacturers to support only parts, but the omission may confuse developers, since the API defines the getSnapShot() method even when the device does not support it. As with audio, you should check to make sure that the particular device you are running on supports image capture and that it provides the format you need.

Taking a Picture

When taking a picture, you must display the viewfinder within your app screen, as shown in Figure 2–4.

Figure 2–4. *A picture-taking app*

Capturing an image still requires obtaining a Player, but as the following pseudocode shows, the rest of the process differs from audio capture.

```
Player player = Manager.createPlayer("capture://video?encoding=video/3gpp");
player.start();
VideoControl control = (VideoControl)player.getControl("VideoControl");
Field cameraView = (Field)control.initDisplayMode↵
    (VideoControl.USE_GUI_PRIMITIVE, "net.rim.device.api.ui.Field");
screen.add(cameraView);
Thread.sleep(1000);
byte[] snapShot = control.getSnapshot↵
    ("encoding=jpeg&width=640&height=480&quality=normal");
player.close();
```

Several things are worth noting here.

- initDisplayMode() can take one of two arguments. USE_GUI_PRIMITIVE returns a UI element that you can place into your screen. When building a RIM CLDC application, pass "net.rim.device.api.ui.Field" as the second parameter to retrieve a Field. When building a MIDP MIDlet, pass "javax.microedition.lcdui.Item" to retrieve an Item that you can insert into your Form.

- If building a MIDlet, you also have the option of calling initDisplayMode() with the parameters USE_DIRECT_VIDEO and "javax.microedition.lcdui.Canvas" or "javax.microedition.lcdui.game.GameCanvas". This will return a special Canvas that you can set with Display.setCurrent(), offering a full-screen viewfinder.

- In all cases, the viewfinder must actually display on the screen prior to calling getSnapShot().

- Unlike audio recording, once we obtain a VideoControl, nothing remains to do with the Player. You can continue to take as many snapshots as you want until you close the Player. If you attempt to take pictures too quickly, however, getSnapShot() may return null. The camera requires time to clear out its buffer and prepare for the next shot.

Video Capture

BlackBerry devices support video capture starting with device software version 5.0. As you might expect, video capture combines features of audio capture and image capture. Like audio capture, you record throughout a duration instead of at a particular point in time. Like image capture, you must place a viewfinder on the screen. As with both, you should query system properties for "supports.video.capture" and "video.encodings" to determine whether the device supports recording and what formats you can use for capture.

```
Player player = Manager.createPlayer("capture://video?encoding=video/3gpp");
player.start();
VideoControl control = (VideoControl)player.getControl("VideoControl");
RecordControl recorder = (RecordControl)player.getControl("RecordControl");
Field cameraView = (Field)control.initDisplayMode↵
    (VideoControl.USE_GUI_PRIMITIVE, "net.rim.device.api.ui.Field");
screen.add(cameraView);
recorder.setRecordLocation("file:///SDCard/BlackBerry/videos/recording.3gp");
recorder.startRecord();
Thread.sleep(5000);
recorder.stopRecord();
recorder.commit();
player.close();
```

Video recording offers the same options as audio recording for controlling where your output data goes. It offers the same options as image capture for initializing the display mode and placing the viewfinder on the display.

Invoking the RIM Alternative

As discussed earlier, sometimes you may want to launch a native RIM application to handle media capture instead of using the MMAPI. Sometimes you will have no other choice, such as if you need to take a picture on a device without software version 4.6 or take a video on a device without version 5.0. Even if your device supports your desired operation, you may prefer the interface of the native application to what you can create on your own.

You can very easily start recording in this way: it takes only a single line to start. On the other hand, getting data back out requires more work. Because Invoke does not offer a mechanism for passing capture information back to the invoker, you will need to observe the filesystem. Once you see a valid file appear, you can assume that the capture application created it, and then perform whatever processing you want on the file.

The listener must implement the FileSystemJournalListener interface. It will receive notifications whenever the filesystem changes. Listing 2–2 shows a basic listener that will notify via system output when a video has been saved. At the same point, it also could prompt the application to do something with that file.

Listing 2–2. *A Class That Listens for Recorded Video Files*

```
public class VideoFileListener implements FileSystemJournalListener
{
    private long lastChangeNumber = 0;
    public void fileJournalChanged()
    {
        long nextChangeNumber = FileSystemJournal.getNextUSN();
        for (long change = nextChangeNumber - 1; change >= lastChangeNumber
            && change < nextChangeNumber; --change)
        {
            FileSystemJournalEntry entry = FileSystemJournal.getEntry(change);
            if (entry == null)
            {
                break;
            }

            if (entry.getEvent() == FileSystemJournalEntry.FILE_ADDED)
            {
                String path = entry.getPath();
                if (path != null && path.indexOf(".3gp") != -1)
                {
                    System.out.println("Video saved in " + path);
                    break;
                }
            }
        }
        lastChangeNumber = nextChangeNumber;
    }
}
```

Then, just register your listener before invoking the camcorder app. It will launch after a brief delay, as shown in Figure 2–5.

```
VideoFileListener listener = new VideoFileListener();
Application.getApplication().addFileSystemJournalListener(listener);
Invoke.invokeApplication(Invoke.APP_TYPE_CAMERA, new ↵
    CameraArguments(CameraArguments.ARG_VIDEO_RECORDER));
```

> **NOTE:** If you want to run this code on an actual device, you will need to sign your COD to provide access to the RIM APIs. Read more about this process in Chapter 9, which discusses the RIM security model.

Figure 2–5. *An image captured by the native camera app*

Several items in Listing 2–2 bear closer examination.

- RIM uses a journaled filesystem, which gives file operation a unique number. For performance reasons, you should search backward from the most recent operation to the oldest, as shown earlier in Listing 2–2. Otherwise, it may take a very long time to find the event you're looking for.

- fileJournalChanged() will be invoked every time a file is added, deleted, or modified. It's very possible that it will be called for a file other than our video. Keeping track of lastChangeNumber ensures that even when it is called multiple times, each entry is checked only once.

- Likewise, because this can be called for any file, we should verify that the correct type of file was added before accepting it. Here we just print it out; in a real application, you would likely pass the file name back to the main application for more processing.

- Don't forget to unregister your listener once you have the data or detect that the user has canceled and returned to your application. Do this with Application.removeFileSystemJournalListener().

- APP_TYPE_CAMERA has been available since software version 4.2 to capture still images. ARG_VIDEO_RECORDER was added in version 4.6 to record videos.

Most developers will likely view the Invoke system as a stop-gap measure. It's good to have available for phones that do not support your desired capture mode in a given software version, but it provides less control and will generally provide a poorer user experience. Fortunately, as devices increasingly migrate to more advanced software versions, the need for this alternative will fade away.

App: Media Grabber

Let's start .Connector;

import javax.microedition.io.work on our media-sharing application. The end of each chapter will tie together the various topics and examples given so far and provide a complete, functioning application. This first entry creates a stand-alone app that, depending on your device capabilities, allows you to record audio, still images, and/or video and save them to a specified location. Listing 2–3 presents the heart of the program: a Screen that will capture media. It supports all types of capture.

Listing 2–3. *A Media Capture Screen Class*

```
package com.apress.king.mediagrabber;

import java.io.*;

import javax.microedition.iofile.FileConnection;
import javax.microedition.media.*;
import javax.microedition.media.control.*

import net.rim.device.api.ui.Field;
import net.rim.device.api.ui.MenuItem;
import net.rim.device.api.ui.component.*;
import net.rim.device.api.ui.container.MainScreen;
public class RecordingScreen extends MainScreen implements PlayerListener
{
    public static final int RECORD_AUDIO = 1;
    public static final int RECORD_PICTURE = 2;
    public static final int RECORD_VIDEO = 3;
```

We'll use a simple state machine to keep track of the current operation and guide recording progress. The other instance variables will handle the actual media operations and the visual interface.

```
public static final int STATE_WAITING = 1;
    public static final int STATE_READY = 2;
    public static final int STATE_RECORDING = 3;

    private volatile int state = STATE_WAITING;

    private int type;
    private String location;

    private Player player;
    private RecordControl recorder;
    private VideoControl video;
    private Field cameraView;

    private LabelField status;

    private ByteArrayOutputStream dataOut;
```

Each MenuItem will display in the BlackBerry menu. To keep these class definitions compact, we call helper methods to perform each actual task. If you use the OS 6 version of the SDK, you'll notice a deprecation warning for the MenuItem constructor calls. This is because in a real commercial application, you should use internationalized text instead of hard-coded string literals like we show here. However, hard-coded strings make the examples easier to read, so we will continue using this constructor while building MediaGrabber. In Chapter 10, you will see how to use localized resources and avoid this warning.

```
    private MenuItem goItem = new MenuItem("Go", 0, 0)
    {
        public void run()
        {
            go();
        }
    };
    private MenuItem stopItem = new MenuItem("Stop", 0, 0)
    {
        public void run()
        {
            stop();
        }
    };
    private MenuItem doneItem = new MenuItem("Return", 0, 0)
    {
        public void run()
        {
            close();
        }
    };

    public RecordingScreen(int type, String location)
    {
```

```
        this.type = type;
        this.location = location;
        status = new LabelField("Waiting");
        add(status);
        dataOut = new ByteArrayOutputStream();
        initMedia();
    }
```

We initialize the media objects when first constructing the screen. As a result, the media operations execute on the main thread and not a separate thread. Some `Player` methods, such as starting and stopping, execute asynchronously, so you can safely call them from any thread without delay. Other operations, like the `realize()` and `prefetch()` that implicitly occur when you first call `start()`, block until they complete. This may seem dangerous to astute readers, as we should call blocking operations from a separate thread. Fortunately, BlackBerry devices do not delay long when starting capture, so you can safely fudge the rules here. This is handy, because you need to start your `VideoControl` before you can obtain the `Field`, and you must add your `Field` to the screen from the main UI thread. In other words, doing these tasks synchronously greatly simplifies the code. You'll see examples of handling media on separate threads in Chapter 3. We will grab the first available video capture format when building a video recorder. In a commercial application, you might present all the available choices to the user, or perform some analysis to find the best option, such as searching for the highest or lowest resolution available.

```
    public void initMedia() {
        try
        {
            switch (type)
            {
            case RECORD_AUDIO:
                player = Manager.createPlayer("capture://audio");
                player.start();
                break;
            case RECORD_PICTURE:
                player = Manager.createPlayer("capture://video");
                player.start();
                video = (VideoControl) player.getControl("VideoControl");
                cameraView = (Field) video.initDisplayMode(
                        VideoControl.USE_GUI_PRIMITIVE,
                        "net.rim.device.api.ui.Field");
                add(cameraView);
                break;
            case RECORD_VIDEO:
                String capture = "capture://video";
                String format = System.getProperty("video.encodings");
                if (format != null && format.length() > 0)
                {
                    int encodingSpace = format.indexOf(' ');
                    if (encodingSpace != -1)
                    {
                        format = format.substring(0, encodingSpace);
                    }
                    capture += "?" + format;
                }
                player = Manager.createPlayer(capture);
```

```
                player.start();
                video = (VideoControl) player.getControl("VideoControl");
                cameraView = (Field) video.initDisplayMode(
                        VideoControl.USE_GUI_PRIMITIVE,
                        "net.rim.device.api.ui.Field");
                add(cameraView);
                break;
        }
        player.addPlayerListener(this);
        state = STATE_READY;
        status.setText("Ready");
    }
    catch (MediaException me)
    {
        status.setText(me.getMessage());
    }
    catch (IOException ioe)
    {
        status.setText(ioe.getMessage());
    }
}
```

We add the appropriate MenuItem objects to the menu based on the current state of the application. For example, "Go" will display only when we enter the READY state.

```
public void makeMenu(Menu menu, int instance)
{
    if (instance == Menu.INSTANCE_DEFAULT)
    {
        if (state == STATE_READY)
        {
            menu.add(goItem);
        }
        else if (state == STATE_RECORDING)
        {
            menu.add(stopItem);
        }
        menu.add(doneItem);
    }
    super.makeMenu(menu, instance);
}
```

Our actual media operations require just a few simple method calls. Because image capture differs so much from audio/video capture, it uses a separate helper method.

```
private void go()
{
    if (type == RECORD_PICTURE)
    {
        takeSnapShot();
    }
    else
    {
        recorder = (RecordControl)player.getControl("RecordControl");
        if (recorder != null)
        {
            recorder.setRecordStream(dataOut);
            recorder.startRecord();
```

```
                        state = STATE_RECORDING;
                        status.setText("Recording");
                    }
                }
            }

            private void takeSnapShot()
            {
                try
                {
                    byte[] imageData = video.getSnapshot↵
                        ("encoding=jpeg&width=640&height=480&quality=normal");
                    if (imageData != null)
                    {
                        writeToFile(imageData, location + "/image.jpg");
                        status.setText("Image taken");
                    }
                    else
                    {
                        status.setText("Please try again later.");
                    }
                }
                catch (IOException ioe)
                {
                    status.setText(ioe.getMessage());
                }
                catch (MediaException me)
                {
                    status.setText(me.getMessage());
                }
            }
```

This helper method moves data from an in-memory buffer to a persistent store. You'll notice that we open the FileConnection with READ_WRITE access, even though we require only WRITE permission. We do this because of a bug in older versions of BlackBerry device software that caused writes to fail unless you requested READ_WRITE. This has not been a problem since around the time of OS version 4.5, but it doesn't hurt to ask for the extra access. Also, note that we close the file OutputStream before the FileConnection. Certain versions of BlackBerry device software do not respond well if you close the FileConnection first, which can leave you unable to reopen the file later.

```
            private void writeToFile(byte[] data, String fileName) throws IOException
            {
                FileConnection file = null;
                OutputStream output = null;
                try
                {
                    file = (FileConnection)Connector.open(fileName, Connector.READ_WRITE);
                    if (file.exists())
                    {
                        file.delete();
                    }
                    file.create();
                    output = file.openOutputStream();
                    output.write(data);
```

```
        }
        finally
        {
            if (output != null) { output.close(); }
            if (file != null) { file.close(); }
        }
    }

    private void stop()
    {
        try
        {
            if (type == RECORD_AUDIO || type == RECORD_VIDEO)
            {
                recorder.commit();
                if (type == RECORD_AUDIO)
                {
                    writeToFile(dataOut.toByteArray(), location + "/audio.amr");
                }
                else
                {
                    writeToFile(dataOut.toByteArray(), location + "/video.3gp");
                }
                status.setText("Data saved");
                state = STATE_READY;
            }
        }
        catch (IOException ioe)
        {
            status.setText(ioe.getMessage());
        }
    }

    public void playerUpdate(Player arg0, String arg1, Object arg2) {
        System.out.println("playerUpdate: " + arg1);
    }


}
```

Listing 2–4 presents the RecordingChoiceScreen. The user will see this screen first; it offers minimal text as well as menu options for supported forms of media capture.

Listing 2–4. *Examining Device Capabilities and Presenting Options*

```
package com.apress.king.mediagrabber;

import net.rim.device.api.ui.*;
import net.rim.device.api.ui.component.*;
import net.rim.device.api.ui.container.MainScreen;

public class RecordingChoicesScreen extends MainScreen
{
    private BasicEditField location = new BasicEditField↩
        ("Save location:", "file:///SDCard/BlackBerry", 100, ↩
        Field.FIELD_VCENTER | BasicEditField.FILTER_FILENAME);
    private MenuItem audioItem = new MenuItem("Record Sound", 0, 0)
    {
```

```
        public void run()
        {
            launchRecorder(RecordingScreen.RECORD_AUDIO);
        }
    };
    private MenuItem pictureItem = new MenuItem("Take a Picture", 0, 0)
    {
        public void run()
        {
            launchRecorder(RecordingScreen.RECORD_PICTURE);
        }
    };
    private MenuItem videoItem = new MenuItem("Record Video", 0, 0)
    {
        public void run()
        {
            launchRecorder(RecordingScreen.RECORD_VIDEO);
        }
    };

    public RecordingChoicesScreen()
    {
        setTitle("MediaGrabber");
        add(new LabelField("Please enter a save location, then select↵
            a recording choice from the menu."));
        add(location);
    }

    public void close()
    {
        location.setDirty(false);
        super.close();
    }

    public void makeMenu(Menu menu, int instance)
    {
        if (instance == Menu.INSTANCE_DEFAULT)
        {
            String property = System.getProperty("supports.audio.capture");
            if (property != null && property.equals("true"))
            {
                menu.add(audioItem);
            }
            property = System.getProperty("video.snapshot.encodings");
            if (property != null && property.length() > 0)
            {
                menu.add(pictureItem);
            }
            property = System.getProperty("supports.video.capture");
            if (property != null && property.equals("true"))
            {
                menu.add(videoItem);
            }
        }

        super.makeMenu(menu, instance);
    }
```

```
        private void launchRecorder(int type)
        {
            String directory = location.getText();
            RecordingScreen screen = new RecordingScreen(type, directory);
            UiApplication.getUiApplication().pushScreen(screen);
        }

        public boolean onSavePrompt()
        {
            return true;
        }
    }
```

In this class, we override onSavePrompt() to suppress a user-visible warning about editing the location field. Since we don't actually save this field, we can safely skip the warning.

Finally, Listing 2–5 shows the application's entry point, which creates and starts our RecordingChoicesScreen.

Listing 2–5. *MediaGrabber Application*

```
package com.apress.king.mediagrabber;

import net.rim.device.api.ui.UiApplication;

public class MediaGrabber extends UiApplication
{
    public static void main(String[] args)
    {
        new MediaGrabber().enterEventDispatcher();
    }

    private MediaGrabber()
    {
        pushScreen(new RecordingChoicesScreen());
    }
}
```

Go ahead and try running the application, ideally both in the simulator and on the device. After you successfully run the app, you can find the newly created files by entering the native Media application, pressing Menu, and selecting Explore. Navigate to the directory you selected.

You may notice a few problems at first in the simulator. First of all, because the simulator doesn't have a real camera, you must provide the camera image. You can do this by opening the native Camera application, or by selecting the Camera Image... option from the simulator menu. Figure 2–6 shows this option in a simulator.

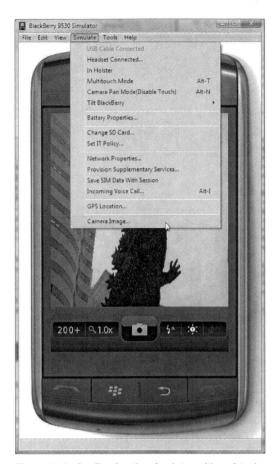

Figure 2–6. *Configuring the simulator with a virtual camera image*

Second, you'll need to insert a virtual SD card for the simulator, which you can do by configuring the simulator. I prefer the option of using a directory on the host PC filesystem, which allows me to easily view files as they are created, modified, and destroyed. In Eclipse, you can find this option in the run configuration, as shown in Figure 2–7.

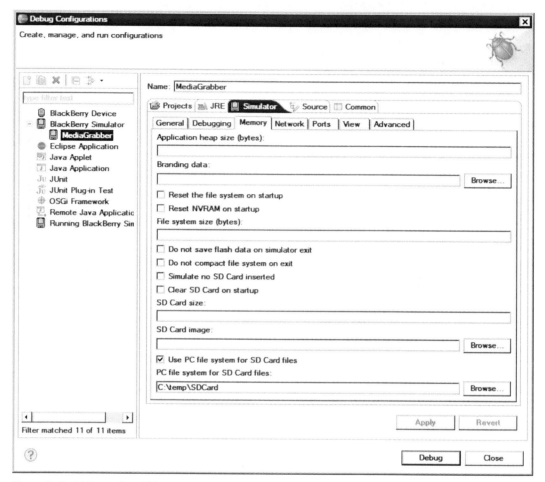

Figure 2–7. *Adding a virtual SD card to the simulator*

You will probably encounter security prompts when you run the application on the device. We cover these prompts in depth in Chapter 9. For now, simply provide all permissions whenever the device asks for them.

How do you debug when things go wrong? Most developers have their favorite techniques. Remember, you can view any information that is printed to the System.out log. When the application runs on the device, never underestimate the usefulness of attaching it to your IDE for an interactive debugging session!

WANT MORE?

If you would like to further enhance the behavior of this app, here are some tasks you can try for extra credit. These go above and beyond the improvements made in later chapters.

- Instead of using hard-coded media formats, parse the supported types provided by `System.getProperty()` and provide the user with a list of options.

- Let the user choose the file name. Check to make sure he or she picks a valid location.

- Suggest alternatives locations to save the file, such as internal storage.

Touches like this will make an app particularly intuitive and useful.

Excelsior

Congratulations! You have taken a giant step forward in mastering BlackBerry programming. As you have seen, RIM offers powerful media capture APIs that provide control over the hardware capabilities of recent devices. You must consider your target market and decide what devices to support, and then check for available media capture options on that target. You can use the MMAPI to embed media capture functions into your own application, giving you a high level of control over the user experience. Alternately, you can use RIM's Invoke API to pass off control to a native application, and then observe the results on your own.

Media capture can be a compelling application by itself; it's no coincidence that new RIM phones come pre-loaded with a camera app. The most exciting apps, though, obtain media and then do interesting things with it. In Chapter 3, we'll start looking at ways to display the media you have captured.

Chapter **3**

Media Playback

Modern mobile phones offer the chance to deliver high-quality media experiences. People have founded entire companies to provide personal television delivery, radio station rebroadcast, or similar repackaging of media. In many other applications, you can use media to enhance the features of your app. You might add background music to your game, a tutorial video to a productivity app, or a slideshow mode to a real estate app.

You must rely on your own judgment to decide whether media fits into your app, and, if so, to select the appropriate content. Once the time comes to actually present the media, BlackBerry devices offer a set of APIs for locating and playing that content. As with media capture, you can choose between standard MMAPI interfaces that embed playback within your app, and RIM interfaces to use a native app.

Finding Content

Because BlackBerry devices offer solid hardware features and live on the network, you have a plethora of choices for finding and delivering media files to play. This section discusses the various options and the trade-offs each offers.

Local Filesystem

You can use the `FileConnection` API to discover and load content. BlackBerry devices offer both internal memory and external SD card storage. The former responds quickly and reliably, but has limited size. You can use this to store app data, but you will annoy your users if you fill it up with large media files. The SD card offers a large amount of storage, but the user won't necessarily have a card inserted at any time.

How to Use

You should first use the `FileSystemRegistry` to verify the availability of the file system you want to use. You can then use the `FileConnection` API to look up content, recursing into subdirectories if necessary. Alternately, if you know the absolute path of the media file you're looking for, you can directly test for its existence.

Once you have verified the presence of your media file, you can directly create a `Player` for it by passing the file's URL to `Manager.createPlayer()`. If you prefer, you can also open the file contents as an `InputStream` and pass that stream to `Manager.createPlayer()`. In the latter case, you should also provide the media's MIME type, such as "audio/mpeg." If you omit the MIME type, `Manager` will attempt to detect it based on the initial contents of the `InputStream`, which may or may not succeed. In practice, developers generally use URLs to play media, unless they need to extract the media data from a more complex stream, such as applying custom decryption.

When to Use

A local filesystem offers several advantages:

- *Speed*: Your media can load and start playing more quickly than it could when loaded over the network, even on a fast location.

- *Reliability*: Particularly when using internal device memory, you can feel relatively sure that you can access the media, assuming the user hasn't manually deleted it.

Balance the advantages against the drawbacks.

- *Capacity*: The device's internal memory store has limited space, and the user may not want you to take up space on the SD card.

- *Authority*: Users may choose to grant or deny your app permission to read files at all, and you will be stuck if they deny it.

An Example

The following code snippet demonstrates how to search for the first available MP3 file.

```
public String getFirstMP3Path() throws IOException
{
    Enumeration roots = FileSystemRegistry.listRoots();
    while (roots.hasMoreElements())
    {
        String root = (String) roots.nextElement();
        String match = getFirstMP3Path(root);
        if (match != null)
        {
            return match;
        }
    }
    return null;
}

public String getFirstMP3Path(String directoryPath) throws IOException
{
    FileConnection directory = (FileConnection) Connector
            .open(directoryPath);
    Enumeration children = directory.list();
    while (children.hasMoreElements())
```

```
    {
        String path = (String) children.nextElement();
        if (path.indexOf(".mp3") != -1)
        {
            return directoryPath + path;
        }
        else if (path.indexOf("/") != -1)
        {
            String match = getFirstMP3Path(directoryPath + path);
            if (match != null)
            {
                return match;
            }
        }
    }
    return null;
}
```

Network Download

The MMAPI can automatically retrieve and play remote media resources. Therefore, you might want to place media files on an HTTP server and request them when necessary. You won't need to handle the actual network connection and download yourself, although you should still handle errors if the file cannot be accessed.

How to Use

Pass the media file location to the Manager using a URL that begins with http:// or https://. If you know at the time you create your application where the file will exist, you can simply hard-code the string. However, if you create a networked application, consider having the server pass the URL down to the client. This gives you greater flexibility if you later decide that you need to place the files on another server, change their format, or make other modifications.

When to Use

Of course, network download offers both advantages and disadvantages. The pros include:

- *Flexibility*: You can update the media file contents without requiring the user to download a new version of the file. For example, you could offer new music for a game.

- *Size*: Because you load off the network, you don't need to place any additional files in your app or in permanent memory. This keeps your users happy.

The cons are:

- *Reliability*: You must deal with network failures. Depending on your app, you may offer an offline mode if the app cannot reach the file; otherwise, it will not run correctly without a connection.

- *Speed*: The file may take quite some time to download, especially for large files or slow connections.

- *Memory*: Because the file isn't streaming, the entire contents must be buffered in RAM. Large video files will likely cause you to run out of memory.

An Example

Simply pass a URL to `Manager.createPlayer()`. The URL should contain the complete path to the network resource, such as "`http://example.com/files/sample.mp3`".

Network Stream

The MMAPI offers an impressive ability to handle streaming protocols. Streams allow the device to play the media while it downloads, without requiring you to acquire the entire file first. Not every manufacturer supports this, but RIM handsets do, starting with device software version 4.3. Streaming involves a lot of complexity—the player needs to judge how much content to buffer, decide when to start playing, and react properly when the network connection speeds up, slows down, or drops out. Fortunately, the MMAPI hides these details from you, and you can simply pass the proper URL and let the `Player` work its magic.

How to Use

Pass the media file location to the `Manager` using a URL that begins with `rtsp://`. The Real Time Streaming Protocol is the standard for streaming media over the Internet. As with media download, you can hard-code the string or obtain it from another resource. Make sure that the RTSP server you connect with has the right configuration for serving up mobile content. A stream designed for a desktop web browser will likely have far too much data for a mobile device, and trying to access it directly will result in choppiness or other problems.

> **NOTE:** If you'd like to experiment with creating your own RTSP server, you can check out LIVE555 Media Server at `www.live555.com/mediaServer/`.

When to Use

Keep the following tradeoffs in mind. The pros are:

- *Speed*: Compared with a regular network download, streams allow you to start playing content much more quickly.

- *Flexibility*: As with network downloads, you have control over a stream's content and can update it without modifying installed apps.

- *Live media*: Unlike regular audio files, which must be of a fixed length, streams can run indefinitely. This allows support for radio stations, live commentary, or other on-the-fly audio delivery.

The cons are:

- *Reliability*: While streams have some ability to recover from temporary network problems, they will not help if the user cannot reach the network.

- *Speed*: While faster than a network download, streaming proceeds more slowly than a locally served file.

- *Quality*: RTSP allows for lossy data transmission—if it does not receive certain packets, the player simply won't play them. If the device has a bad connection, the resulting media will seem choppy or worse.

An Example

Create the Player as just shown, but use the rtsp scheme, as in "rtsp://myserver.com/streams/live.m4a".

Manual Buffering

What should you do if you want to stream on an older version of BlackBerry device software, or implement a custom streaming protocol? You can write your own streaming client implementation. This requires an investment in time and effort, but it allows you to have streaming capabilities even when the device doesn't support it.

How to Use

In the previous chapter, we discussed how DataSource objects handle the data delivery protocol. When you use a URL that starts with http://, file:///, or rtsp://, the Manager automatically creates an appropriate DataSource for that type of protocol. However, you can implement your own version of DataSource and SourceStream to provide whatever functionality you want, including support for streaming. Define this DataSource, and then pass it to Manager.createPlayer(). The Manager will then obtain the necessary data from the DataSource's provided streams, as shown in Figure 3–1.

Note that you will now be responsible for all the complexity of streaming. You will likely need to experiment and tune your DataSource's behavior to get the best results on different devices.

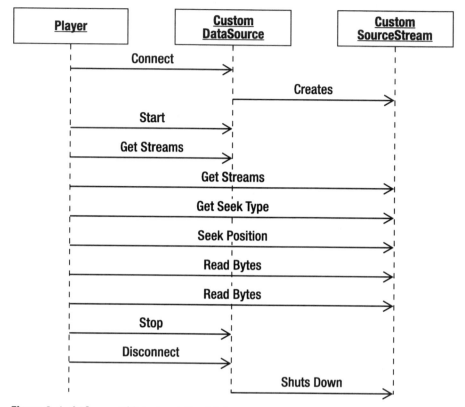

Figure 3–1. *A* Player *with a user-defined data source*

When to Use

Of course, manual buffering includes its own tradeoffs. Consider these pros:

- *Compatibility*: Your DataSource can run on any BlackBerry device that supports media playback and network connections.

- *Control*: You will gain a far greater level of control over media playback, beyond what is provided by the standard MMAPI behavior. For example, you could automatically shut off playback when the user's time expires.

Balance that against these cons:

- *Complexity*: Creating a DataSource is fairly tricky, and it requires tuning to get the best performance.

- *Coordination*: If using a custom protocol, you will need to make sure that the server is set up to provide data in the format you expect.

An Example

This skeleton class shows a DataSource implementation that could create a streaming Player.

```
public class StreamingDataSource extends DataSource
{
    public StreamingDataSource(String locator)
    {
        super(locator);
    }

    public void connect() throws IOException
    {
        // Connect to the locator and create the stream(s).
    }

    public void disconnect()
    {
        // Close the stream(s).
    }

    public String getContentType()
    {
        // Return content type of underlying stream.
        return null;
    }

    public SourceStream[] getStreams()
    {
        // Return stream(s) created in connect()
        return null;
    }

    public void start() throws IOException
    {
        // Start acquiring content with the stream(s).
    }

    public void stop() throws IOException
    {
        // Stop acquiring content.
    }

    public Control getControl(String controlType)
    {
        // Can return null unless adding custom controls.
        return null;
    }

    public Control[] getControls()
    {
```

```
            // Can return null unless adding custom controls.
            return null;
        }
    }
```

The associated SourceStream will do most of the actual work. A skeleton example
follows. An implementing class will generally re-use one or more existing InputStream
objects, adding any extra necessary logic.

```java
public class StreamingSourceStream implements SourceStream
{

    public ContentDescriptor getContentDescriptor()
    {
        // Returns descriptor for content being retrieved.
        return null;
    }

    public long getContentLength()
    {
        // Returns total amount of data to read.
        return 0;
    }

    public int getSeekType()
    {
        // Return one of NOT_SEEKABLE, RANDOM_SEEKABLE, or SEEKABLE_TO_START.
        return 0;
    }

    public int getTransferSize()
    {
        // Return size of a logical chunk to read.
        // Useful to influence the size of requested reads.
        return 0;
    }

    public int read(byte[] dataOut, int offset, int length) throws IOException
    {
        // Retrieve actual data. Can block until sufficient data available.
        return 0;
    }

    public long seek(long position) throws IOException
    {
        // Advance stream to desired position, if supported.
        return 0;
    }
    public long tell()
    {
        // Return current position within the stream.
        return 0;
    }

    public Control getControl(String controlType)
    {
        // Can return null unless adding custom controls.
```

```
        return null;
    }

    public Control[] getControls()
    {
        // Can return null unless adding custom controls.
        return null;
    }
}
```

COD Resource

Developers usually deliver media by packaging it with the application. When users install your COD file, they will receive all the bundled media files along with it. Because the entire COD loads into memory when the application starts, you can confidently access the media.

How to Use

Simply include the media file in your BlackBerry project. In Eclipse, right-click the `src` folder, choose Import, General, File System, Next, Browse, and then navigate to and add your resource. It will appear in the `src` folder, as shown in Figure 3–2, and will automatically build into the COD. Note that you can include any type of file as a resource. In your application, get an `InputStream` for that resource, and then pass that stream to `Manager.createPlayer()`. If you know the MIME type, include it here; otherwise, pass `null`. The `Manager` will create an appropriate `Player` for the file.

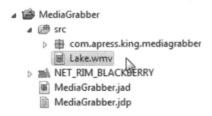

Figure 3–2. *Adding a resource to the COD*

When to Use

This simple approach offers the following pros:

- *Speed*: Because the device already loaded the COD into RAM, this is the absolute fastest way to access any media.

- *Reliability*: You can always access the media, no matter what the user does.

Remember these cons:

- *Size*: Every byte of media directly increases the size of your app. Users may not want to even install it if the app seems very large.

■   *Inflexible*: You cannot change the media without creating a new version of the app.

An Example

Retrieve the stream and create the player as shown here.

```
InputStream is = getClass().getResourceAsStream("/Lake.wmv");
Player player = Manager.createPlayer(is, "video/wmv");
```

Other

Do you have another source of media that doesn't fit into the foregoing choices? Not to worry! Manager accepts an InputStream, and an InputStream can wrap anything you want. Your underlying data may come from a big byte array, an algorithm, or multiple sources spliced together. When you want to hand off arbitrary bytes to the Player, create an InputStream.

How to Use

Java ME defines some useful standard implementations of InputStream. One of the most popular is ByteArrayInputStream, which wraps a block of bytes. You can also create your own subclass of InputStream. This class defines many methods to override, but most importantly you must provide an implementation of read() that returns the next bytes.

When to Use

The pros and cons of this approach depend on how the underlying data is obtained—whether in memory, from a file, over the network, etc. It will generally perform similarly to one of the foregoing methods. If writing your own InputStream, expect more time required to implement and debug it.

An Example

A fairly common use case is to store media contents in memory, and then wrap it with a valid InputStream.

```
byte[] mediaData;
// Fill in the contents.
InputStream input = new ByteArrayInputStream(mediaData);
```

Playing Audio

After you have identified and prepared the content you want to play, you can bring it into your app. Once again, the MMAPI hides many of the details from you, but the following section will show you what happens behind the scenes. You'll learn how to choose appropriate formats and encodings and see how to handle problems with playback.

The Player Returns

Playback involves the same classes we saw for capture: Manager, Player, and multiple Controls. You may want to review Figure 2-2 from the previous chapter to observe the states that a Player moves through.

Let's take a look at the particular states a Player might encounter when playing a particular type of media, such as a streaming audio file:

- UNREALIZED: In this state, the Player has been created, so it knows that it supports the transport protocol (in this case, RTSP).

- REALIZED: The Player has communicated with the server, verified that the stream exists, and determined that it supports the stream's media type.

- PREFETCHED: The Player has downloaded the initial contents of the stream as an audio buffer. It also has verified that it can direct audio to the output hardware, acquiring an exclusive lock if necessary.

- STARTED: The Player is actively streaming. The Player will usually produce audio during this time, although if it needs to rebuffer, it will remain in the STARTED state while fetching more data.

- CLOSED: The Player has finished streaming and released all network and hardware resources.

You can explicitly move a Player through each state by calling realize(), prefetch(), and start(). You can also just call start() to automatically move it through all the states. However, remember the underlying operations and what they involve. If you call start() on a video stream from your main UI thread, and the Player is still in the UNREALIZED state, then your app will appear to freeze during the seconds (or minutes!) that it takes to buffer the video. On the other hand, if you call prefetch() in another thread, calling start() will return almost immediately.

The previous chapter discussed the importance of exclusive locks and how you can use deallocate() to surrender those locks. You can still use deallocate() when playing media, but exclusive locks tend not to be as severe of an issue. Only one application can access the microphone or camera at a given time, but more than one application may be able to play sound. However, you may still want to use deallocate() to manage memory. Imagine you write a video app with 12 channels, each with its own Player. If the user switches between channels, the nonplaying streams will still hold expensive buffers. However, if you call deallocate() on each when it goes away, the 11 nonplaying channels will have minimal overhead.

Listening In

As it runs, the Player will deliver information about its current status to all registered PlayerListener objects. You will almost always want to register at least one PlayerListener with each Player. At an absolute minimum, this will provide you with useful debugging information about what is happening. In most cases, you will want to take some action based on certain important events. For example, you may show a Loading screen when a stream buffers, or exit the current screen once a song finishes playing. Figure 3–3 shows the potential sequence of one media play execution.

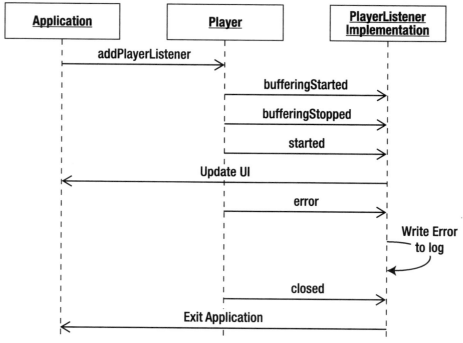

Figure 3–3. *A PlayerListener responding to Player events*

The MMAPI spec defines many events, and RIM can send custom events, as well. Whenever your PlayerListener is called, it will receive a String with the event name, and an Object containing more information about the event. Table 3–1 shows the most common events.

Table 3–1. *PlayerListener Events*

String	Definition	Meaning	EventData type	EventData value
bufferingStarted	BUFFERING_STARTED	Player enters buffering mode.	Long	Media time when buffering starts
bufferingStopped	BUFFERING_STOPPED	Player exits buffering mode.	Long	Media time when buffering stops
closed	CLOSED	Player closed; end of events.	N/A	null
deviceAvailable	DEVICE_AVAILABLE	An exclusive device is now available to this Player in the REALIZED state.	String	Name of device
deviceUnavailable	DEVICE_UNAVAILABLE	This Player has lost access to an exclusive device and placed back in the REALIZED state. The next event must be DEVICE_AVAILABLE or ERROR.	String	Name of device
durationUpdated	DURATION_UPDATED	The duration for this Player has changed. This generally occurs when the duration cannot be known at start but becomes available later.	Long	Duration of the media
endOfMedia	END_OF_MEDIA	The Player has reached the end of the media.	Long	Media time for the end of media
error	ERROR	The Player encountered an error.	String	Detailed error message (see ahead)
sizeChanged	SIZE_CHANGED	A playing video's size has changed; for example, the screen may have changed orientation.	VideoControl	Object with new video dimensions
started	STARTED	Player has begun to play.	Long	Media time when player started
stopped	STOPPED	Player has received a stop() call and returned to the PREFETCHED state.	Long	Media time when player stopped

String	Definition	Meaning	EventData type	EventData value
stoppedAtTime	STOPPED_AT_TIME	Player has reached the time specified by a previous call to StopTimeControl.setStopTime and returned to the PREFETCHED state.	Long	Media time when player stopped
volumeChanged	VOLUME_CHANGED	Volume has changed; for example, user has pressed a volume key.	VolumeControl	Object with new volume level
com.rim.mediaLoaded	N/A	Player has loaded the media, e.g., the first playable section of an RTSP stream.	N/A	N/A
com.rim.playableStreams	N/A	Player has found playable streams.	Long	How many playable streams were found, or -1 if unknown
com.rim.seekableUpdate	N/A	Player now knows whether the stream supports seeking to an arbitrary location.	Boolean	true if you can seek within the stream, false otherwise
com.rim.timeUpdate	N/A	Media has advanced; called about once per second. Not included in OS software versions 5.0 and later due to its effect on performance.	Long	Current media time in microseconds
com.rim.loading	N/A	Media is loading.	N/A	N/A

NOTE: The MMAPI does not specify what units "media time" corresponds to. On BlackBerry devices, each unit of media time is one microsecond. Multiply by 1,000 to convert to milliseconds (useful when comparing to system time), and by 1,000,000 to convert to seconds (useful when showing elapsed play time).

No app will need to respond to all the foregoing events, but every app will likely care about at least a few of them. You should just look for the ones you care about and ignore the rest. Certain media operations might generate a slew of events—for example, you might receive a "com.rim.timeUpdate" every second while a stream plays. Because of this, you may want to avoid actions like logging every event that is passed, because doing so would slow down the operation of your app.

Pay particular attention to errors, and distinguish between transient errors and permanent errors. If media will not play because of a network hiccup or temporary loss of the output device, you may want to retry the operation to save your user the hassle. On the other hand, if the media itself is corrupt or incompatible, you cannot do anything to fix it. To facilitate more deterministic handling of errors, RIM has decided to use integer values as the ERROR extended message. Table 3–2 shows the currently defined codes and their meaning. Note that some correspond to particular RTSP errors.

Table 3–2. *RIM Media Error Codes*

Code	Meaning
1	Player is busy.
2	Bad parameter
3	Out of memory
4	Stream has exhausted available data.
5	Other error
6	Media file is corrupt.
7	Server is not responding.
8	Connection is unavailable.
9	Invalid URL
10	File is unseekable.
11	Streaming server is not responding.
12	Missing DRM rights. RTSP error 401.
13	Streaming server rejected streaming request; other 400-range RTSP error.
14	Streaming server error; other 500-range RTSP error.
15	Payment is required; RTSP error 402.
16	Streaming server forbids client connection; RTSP error 403.
17	Item to stream not found; RTSP error 404.
18	Client must authenticate with a proxy prior to streaming; RTSP error 407.
19	Request URI too large; RTSP error 414.
20	Insufficient bandwidth for streaming; RTSP error 453.
21	Session expired; RTSP error 454.
22	Unsupported UDP or TCP transport streaming; RTSP error 461.

As you can see, most of the errors relate to streaming content. This level of granularity helps greatly when configuring a streaming solution, as it lets you quickly identify whether the problem comes from the client or the server.

Listing 3–1 shows a simple PlayerListener. This PlayerListener updates a Screen with status information and closes it when playback finishes.

Listing 3–1. *A Custom Listener for Media Playback*

```java
import javax.microedition.media.*;
import net.rim.device.api.ui.Screen;
import net.rim.device.api.ui.component.LabelField;

public class WatchdogListener implements PlayerListener
{
    private LabelField status;
    private Screen screen;

    public WatchdogListener(LabelField status, Screen screen)
    {
        this.status = status;
        this.screen = screen;
    }

    public void playerUpdate(Player player, String event, Object data)
    {
        if (event.equals(PlayerListener.BUFFERING_STARTED))
        {
            status.setText("Buffering, please wait.");
        }
        else if (event.equals(PlayerListener.BUFFERING_STOPPED))
        {
            status.setText("Buffer complete.");
        }
        else if (event.equals(PlayerListener.STARTED))
        {
            status.setText("Playing.");
        }
        else if (event.equals(PlayerListener.STOPPED))
        {
            status.setText("Stopped.");
        }
        else if (event.equals(PlayerListener.ERROR))
        {
            status.setText("Encountered error: " + data);
        }
        else if (event.equals(PlayerListener.END_OF_MEDIA))
        {
            screen.close();
        }
        else
        {
            status.setText (event + ":" + data);
        }
    }
}
```

All About Codecs

Imagine you have an app that plays humorous comedy clips. You find a bit on the Web that you like, add it to the app, and…nothing happens! It played just fine on your desktop—what gives?

Welcome to the wonderful world of media codecs. The options available for playback can bewilder, and they seem to grow more complicated every year. Investing some time up front in understanding codecs and selecting the appropriate formats for your app can save hours of last-minute scrambling.

Containers and Content

A media file resembles a box. Depending on the file format, it will contain various types of things: perhaps the author's name, some metadata about the contents, maybe some DRM. It will also contain one or more smaller locked boxes, which hold the actual audio or video data.

We call that outer box a container. Containers have names like MP4 and AVI, which refer to the way they package media pieces together. The locked boxes are the actual components. These must be opened with the corresponding key—the codec. Codecs have names like MPEG4 or AAC+, and describe how the actual audio or video bytes should play. Figure 3–4 shows three of the many possible configurations of codecs and containers.

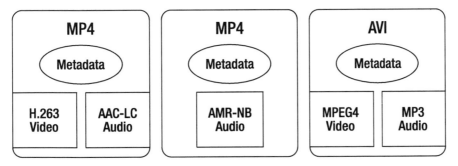

Figure 3–4. *Containers and codecs*

People sometimes get confused because containers and codecs have generally had a 1–1 correspondence historically. An MP3 file always uses the MPEG1 audio encoding, so all MP3 files are more or less compatible. However, an M4A file may use H.263, H.264, or MPEG4 encoding, so you cannot simply ask for an M4A file—you also need to know what codec it uses. You may have experienced this problem occasionally when using your desktop computer; mobile devices encounter this problem far more frequently.

The moral of the story is if you produce your own content, select a compatible format and use it for everything. If you acquire content from others, verify that you support each given piece of content.

Codec Support

Once the device identifies what encoding a piece of content uses, it must decide how to handle playback. Codecs are implemented in one of two ways: in software or in hardware. A software codec analyzes the byte stream, translates it from the compressed format into the device's native format, and then passes the translated bytes to the output device. This can consume a lot of time, and on a limited device like a mobile phone, the CPU may not translate fast enough to play at an acceptable rate. A hardware codec is embedded into the graphic or audio chip, and can directly translate the encoded data into sound or video. This faster process frees up the CPU for other tasks, but also costs more, and therefore it is often missing from cheaper devices.

Software codecs are limited by processor speed. Hardware codecs are limited by hardware design. Therefore codecs are among the few items in the world of BlackBerry development that are controlled by phone hardware, not just the version of BlackBerry device software installed. Fortunately, RIM has documented their codec support well. Please see the appendix for a list of currently supported codecs on a range of popular BlackBerry models.

You can also attempt to determine at runtime what types of content a given device supports. This lets you future-proof your app, so if a newer device or software version becomes available, the same version of your app will automatically know that it can handle a better codec. Use the method `Manager.getSupportedContentType(null)` to obtain an array of all valid MIME types on this device. You can even pass in a particular protocol to be used for filtering, so `Manager.getSupportedContentType("rtsp")` will return only the types that the device can stream, while `Manager.getSupportedContentType("file")` will return all types that can be played from a local file.

Where Does the Sound Go?

The default audio behavior of BlackBerry devices will usually satisfy you. Sound will play from the device when you want and automatically move to the headphones when you plug them in.

However, in certain circumstances you might want to exercise more control over where audio goes. If your app delivers voice messages, you might prefer the sound to be sent through the earpiece for privacy, rather than through the speakerphone, where anyone can hear. Figure 3–5 shows some of the more common audio outputs for a BlackBerry.

Figure 3–5. *Audio connections on a device*

A `Player` with an audio component will offer an `AudioPathControl`. You may use this to see where audio is currently being directed, and send it somewhere else if appropriate. The following options are supported.

- `AUDIO_PATH_BLUETOOTH`: Bluetooth Synchronous Connection Oriented (SCO) link, such as a car kit

- `AUDIO_PATH_BLUETOOTH_A2DP`: Paired A2DP-compatible device, like a stereo Bluetooth headset

- `AUDIO_PATH_HANDSET`: The earpiece

- `AUDIO_PATH_HANDSFREE`: The speakerphone

- `AUDIO_PATH_HEADSET`: Hands-free headset

- `AUDIO_PATH_HEADSET_HANDSFREE`: The speakerphone and the hands-free headset

> **NOTE:** `AudioPathControl` is available starting with software version 4.2.
> `AUDIO_PATH_BLUETOOTH_A2DP` was added in version 4.3.

The following code demonstrates how to force audio to be played through the speakerphone.

```
Player player = Manager.createPlayer("file:///SDCard/BlackBerry/Music/Walrus.mp3");
player.prefetch();
AudioPathControl control = (AudioPathControl)player.getControl("AudioPathControl");
if (control.getAudioPath() != AudioPathControl.AUDIO_PATH_HANDSFREE)
{
    control.setAudioPath(AudioPathControl.AUDIO_PATH_HANDSFREE);
}
```

Starting with software version 6.0, you can query a particular path's availability; this will let you know that the route is available. You can also reset audio to the default path, which frees you from keeping track of the previous setting if you wish to return to it later. The following snippet continues the previous example, connecting to a stereo Bluetooth headset if it's available, and later returning to the original setting.

```
if (control.canSwitchToPath(AudioPathControl.AUDIO_PATH_BLUETOOTH_A2DP))
{
    control.setAudioPath(AudioPathControl.AUDIO_PATH_BLUETOOTH_A2DP);
}
// After playback finishes...
control.resetAudioPath();
```

Mixing Music

Sometimes you might like to play more than one audio file at once. Perhaps you are playing background music for a boxing game, and you also want to play an audio clip of someone landing a punch. How does this work? Well, it depends on the device. The MMAPI defines a system property called "supports.mixing". If this is true, the device must support playing at least two audio sources at the same time. If it is false, then only one can play at a time. In this case, the second attempt to play will either fail or interrupt the first player.

Currently, most GSM devices support mixing up to two audio sources. Most CDMA devices do not support any mixing. For the best compatibility, you should check for the system property.

What should you do if the device does not support mixing? You have limited options. If you want to mix two pieces of music, you can try combining them into a single file for playback. If you want to combine music and effects, you will generally need to stop the first Player before starting the second, and then restart the first once the second is done. Depending on the application, this may sound annoying, and you might prefer to disable either music or effects entirely.

This example demonstrates deciding whether to start a second Player based on the capabilities of the device. All users will hear the song, but only mixing devices will play the claps.

```
Player music = Manager.createPlayer("file:///SDCard/BlackBerry/Music/ObLaDi.mp3");
Player sound = Manager.createPlayer("file:///SDCard/BlackBerry/Music/clap.amr");
music.realize();
sound.realize();
music.start();
if (System.getProperty("supports.mixing").equals("true"))
{
```

```
    for (int i = 0; i < 5; ++i)
    {
        sound.start();
        Thread.sleep(1000);
        sound.stop();
    }
}
```

Bringing It Together

You've found your media and you know its format. Now you can create a Player, set it up, and start it going.

With audio, you can create a Player through any of the three createPlayer methods offered by Manager.

- One takes a URL, such as "http://myserver.com/files/clip.mp3".

- Another takes an InputStream and a type, such as myByteStream and "audio/mpeg".

- The last takes a custom DataSource (described earlier in the section titled "Manual Buffering").

You can simply call start() to get it going, or queue it up for later playback. You will likely want to handle media operations in a separate thread for the best performance. You also might want to control other aspects of playback. By calling Player.getControl(), you can obtain a VolumeControl and a StopTimeControl. The VolumeControl allows you to set the volume level (at a value between 0 and 100) and mute/unmute the audio, while StopTimeControl offers a way to specify when the Player should stop. You could combine the two to play a softer five-second preview of a full audio clip. The code that follows demonstrates how to play audio.

```
InputStream is = getClass().getResourceAsStream("/crowdNoise.mp3");
Player player = Manager.createPlayer(is, "audio/mpeg");
player.realize();
StopTimeControl time = (StopTimeControl)player.getControl("StopTimeControl");
VolumeControl volume = (VolumeControl)player.getControl("VolumeControl");
if (time != null)
{
    time.setStopTime(5000000); // Microseconds
}
if (volume != null)
{
    volume.setLevel(50);
}
player.start();
```

> **TIP:** Not all platforms support StopTimeControl. As usual, you should check for a non-null value returned from getControl. If not available, you can work around this by creating a separate Timer and manually stopping playback once it expires.

Other Audio Options: MIDI and Tones

The MMAPI defines several options for playing programmatically generated audio. This approach was much more popular when devices were highly limited. As support for playing standard audio formats has improved, these alternatives have fallen out of favor because of their complexity and nonportability. However, they still may be appropriate when porting legacy software, creating sound effects for games or when working on specialized apps such as a virtual piano.

If you look through RIM's documentation, you will notice that it includes references to MIDIControl. This specialized Control offers methods to program MIDI channels and send MIDI events to be played. Theoretically, this would offer a standardized way to play generated music. However, as with much of the MMAPI, it does not require vendors to implement it, and RIM has chosen not to do so. Attempts to create a MIDIControl will result in an "unsupported media type" exception. Note that you can still play existing MIDI files as just shown, just not create low-level MIDI events.

However, RIM does support a similar alternate mechanism, the ToneControl. Unlike other audio playback, you do not need a file or input stream to gain access to this player and control. Instead, Manager offers a custom string, TONE_DEVICE_LOCATOR (with the value "device://tone"), which you can use to retrieve a compatible Player.

Once you have a ToneControl, you can program a monotonic tone sequence. Bytes define the tempo, note pitch, note duration, and volume, and they control progress through the song. The following snippet shows how to play the opening of Beethoven's Fifth Symphony using a ToneControl.

```
byte tempo = 30; // 120 bpm
byte eight = 8;  // eighth-note
byte whole = 64; // whole note
byte C4 = ToneControl.C4; // Middle C
byte eFlat = (byte)(C4 + 3);
byte gMajor = (byte)(C4 + 7);
byte[] beethoven = {
    ToneControl.VERSION, 1,
    ToneControl.TEMPO, tempo,
    gMajor, eight, gMajor, eight, gMajor, eight, eFlat, whole //  Buh-buh-buh BUH!
};
Player player = Manager.createPlayer(Manager.TONE_DEVICE_LOCATOR);
player.realize();
ToneControl control = (ToneControl)player.getControl("ToneControl");
control.setSequence(beethoven);
player.start();
```

If this looks like something you might want to use, see the complete documentation in the ToneControl class. In practice, ToneControl has too many limitations for most developers. It can play only a single note at a time and is cumbersome to program. Unless you need the ability to play arbitrary notes at runtime, look elsewhere.

If you do want to play arbitrary notes, consider using Manager.playTone(). Unlike other methods in Manager, this will directly play sound without going through a Player. You can specify a pitch, length, and volume. As with the ToneControl, it is far too cumbersome to try to play elaborate music with this interface, but it can be useful in certain circumstances, such as if you want the device to make a loud noise when it encounters an error condition.

Playing Video

Video playback resembles audio playback, with the extra wrinkle that you need to display the video somewhere. We will follow a process similar to the camera viewfinder we created in the last chapter. You will create the Player, obtain a VideoControl, place it somewhere on the Screen, and then start it playing. Unlike video capture, starting playback takes longer, especially if you are playing a video delivered over the network. The code that follows shows a simple case of playing a video for about five seconds and then stopping, such as for a preview.

```
Player player = Manager.createPlayer("file:///SDCard/BlackBerry/Video/clip.3gp ");
player.realize();
VideoControl control = (VideoControl)player.getControl("VideoControl");
Field cameraView = (Field)control.initDisplayMode
    (VideoControl.USE_GUI_PRIMITIVE, "net.rim.device.api.ui.Field");
screen.add(cameraView);
player.start();
Thread.sleep(5000);
player.close();
```

The VideoControl offers the following useful options for positioning your playback window:

- getDisplayWidth and getDisplayHeight return the current dimensions of space occupied by the video playback window, in pixels.

- getSourceWidth and getSourceHeight return the dimensions of the actual video file, in pixels.

- getDisplayX and getDisplayY return the coordinates of the upper-left corner of the playing video, relative to the containing GUI object.

- setDisplayLocation allows you to position the video if the display mode is USE_DIRECT_VIDEO.

- setVisible controls whether the video is displayed.

- setDisplaySize will adjust the size of the video image. This may scale the video to fit the requested dimensions, or may just clip the video. You'll need to experiment with your particular videos and devices to determine which happens.

- setDisplayFullScreen attempts to make the video fill the entire screen.

Displaying Images

While audio and video may impress users, far more apps rely on images. Images range from simple bitmaps to animated GIF and Scalable Vector Graphics (SVG) files. While you probably already know the simplest ways to display images, more advanced techniques may prove useful in certain cases.

Static Image Display in BlackBerry CLDC Applications

The first or second BlackBerry program you wrote when first learning the platform most likely included an image. The `Bitmap` class underlies most image creation and drawing. Note that bitmap refers to any rastered image format, including JPEG and PNG in addition to BMP files. You have a wide variety of options available for creating images.

- Reference a resource in the COD file:
  `Bitmap.getBitmapResource("clip.png");`

- Create a blank image that you can later draw into: `new Bitmap(300, 300);`

- Obtain a built-in system bitmap:
  `Bitmap.getBitmapResource(Bitmap.HOURGLASS);`

- Create from raw image data: `Bitmap.createBitmapFromBytes(rawData, 0, -1, 1);` or `Bitmap.createBitmapFromPNG(rawData, 0, -1);`

After you have a `Bitmap` object, you can adjust the raw pixels if necessary by calling `getARGB()` and `setARGB()`. In most cases, though, you can then proceed to display the image by creating a `BitmapField` and then add it to the screen as you would any other `Field`.

```
screen.add(new BitmapField(bitmap));
```

As an alternative to the `Bitmap` class, you can use the `EncodedImage` class to obtain a drawable image. `EncodedImage` has separate subclasses for each of the supported image types and methods that provide more detail about each than a standard `Bitmap` describes. For example, a `PNGEncodedImage` offers information about the alpha bit depth for a particular image. However, unlike `Bitmaps`, `EncodedImages` are not mutable: you cannot alter the images once created. As with `Bitmap`, you can create an `EncodedImage` in multiple ways.

- Reference a resource in the COD file:
  `EncodedImage.getEncodedImageResource("clip.png");`

- Create from bytes: `EncodedImage.createEncodedImage(rawData, 0, -1);`

You can create a `BitmapField` for an `EncodedImage` in order to display it on the screen.

```
BitmapField imageField = new BitmapField();
imageField.setImage(encodedImage);
```

As with other `Field` objects, you can adjust the size and layout to fit your particular `Screen`.

SVG Image Playback

BlackBerry devices with software version 4.6 or later include support for JSR 226, a standard approach for control and display of SVG animations. If you'd like to learn more about SVG, you can view the official specification online at www.w3.org/Graphics/SVG/. Apress publishes a good book on the topic called *SVG Programming: The Graphical Web,* by Kurt Cagle (2002). BlackBerry SVG images must conform to the W3C SVG Tiny 1.1 profile.

SVG animations rely on classes in the javax.microedition.m2g package. If you will only play existing animations, and not create or manipulate them, you will generally need to use only two classes: SVGImage and SVGAnimator. SVGImage contains the data, while SVGAnimator understands how to parse and present it. The following example shows how to create and start an animation.

```
InputStream svgSource = getClass().getResourceAsStream("sample.svg");
SVGImage image = (SVGImage)ScalableImage.createImage(svgSource, null);
SVGAnimator animator = SVGAnimator.createAnimator(image, "net.rim.device.api.ui.Field");
Field field = (Field)animator.getTargetComponent();
screen.add(field);
animator.play();
```

You may notice some similarities between this code and what we did for video capture and playback. In both cases, we needed to specify the full class name for the component that will display the content. "net.rim.device.api.ui.Field" indicates that you wish to display the SVG animation in a CLDC application. To display animations in a MIDlet, ask for a "javax.microedition.lcdui.Item" instead.

As usual, you can manipulate the Field to control how the content will display within your application. SVGAnimator uses a simplified version of the Player life cycle with only three states: playing, stopped, and paused. Figure 3–6 shows how the methods play(), pause(), and stop() affect playback.

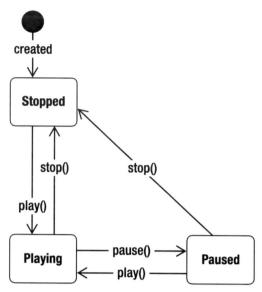

Figure 3–6. *SVG animation states*

If you would like to capture user action on the SVG image and take some action in response, register an SVGEventListener with the SVGAnimator by calling setSVGEventListener(). The platform will notify your listener when the user presses a key or touches the screen, or the visibility of the animation changes.

Getting Plazmic

Long before SVG support became available on its devices, RIM provided a semi-custom 2D vector graphics package of its own. Plazmic, a subsidiary of RIM, offers a content creation tool that allows Flash-like authoring, but the generated content compiles down into a compact binary format much terser than standard SVG. Because of its smaller size, Plazmic usually loads faster over the network. For several years, Plazmic was the only choice for adding rich media content to BlackBerry devices. The introduction of APIs discussed in this chapter changes that situation, but because of the compact size and large quantity of existing content out there, you may wish to add Plazmic content to your own app.

Authoring Plazmic is beyond the scope of this book, but you should understand how to create and deliver it. An artist creates content using the proprietary Plazmic Content Developer Kit (CDK). The kit offers support for importing some elements of SVG and Flash format animations, which may allow for quicker porting of content. The artist's design compiles into a binary PME (Plazmic Media Engine) file. This contains the information necessary to describe the animation contents and behavior. Many animations will also include raster graphics or music. Together with the PME, these will be bundled into a PMB, or Plazmic Media Bundle, as shown in Figure 3–7.

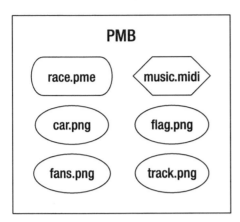

Figure 3–7. *A possible PMB configuration*

On the client side, Plazmic often displays in the browser. It also can theme BlackBerry devices and make visual changes to native apps. If you'd like to include Plazmic content in your own app, RIM has offered APIs since device software version 3.7—ancient by RIM standards. You need to use only a few classes, all in packages `net.rim.plazmic.mediaengine` and `net.rim.plazmic.mediaengine.io`.

> **CAUTION:** Although Plazmic support exists as far back as 3.7, there are many different versions of the CDK, and not all content will display in all versions. Even if your target phone supports Plazmic playback, check to ensure that you can create content that will display in it.

Unlike SVG, Plazmic includes logic for handling the download of content. If you load a PMB over the network, you will receive regular updates about the status of that operation. You can use this information if you wish to show a loading message, progress bar, or other feedback to the user while waiting. You can also bundle Plazmic content directly into your COD, which creates the standard trade-offs between fast delivery and updateability.

> **TIP:** Due to a limitation in the RIM JDE, you cannot directly include Plazmic PMB files in your COD. Instead, ask for the PME file and all media files separately, and then add them to your project. If image files are not in PNG format, configure your project to prevent them from being automatically converted to PNG.

Plazmic internally represents content in SVG, so it's no surprise that Plazmic playback resembles that of SVG. Plazmic offers three states: UNREALIZED, REALIZED, and STARTED. You move between the states by invoking methods on a MediaPlayer object, as shown in Figure 3–8. An UNREALIZED MediaPlayer is "blank," with no content assigned to it. A REALIZED player has obtained its content, which can be a time-consuming operation: even once the content file has been loaded, all media resources within that file must be initialized and prepared. A STARTED player is actively playing its content.

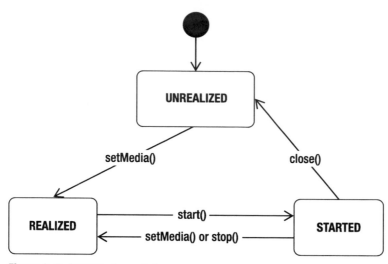

Figure 3–8. *Plazmic player states*

Plazmic has a single listener interface, MediaListener, which is used by both MediaManager and MediaPlayer. MediaListener defines a single method, mediaEvent(), which delivers messages about content download or playback status. Table 3–3 shows the possible results.

Table 3–3. *Plazmic Media Events*

Event	Data Type	Data Contents
MEDIA_REQUESTED	String	URI of requested content
MEDIA_IO	LoadingStatus	Current status of the loading operation
MEDIA_LOADING_FAILED	String	URI of requested content
MEDIA_REALIZED	Object	Opaque media data
MEDIA_COMPLETE	Object	Opaque media data

Unfortunately, Plazmic doesn't offer many opportunities for interactive content. Unlike the SVG APIs, it has no mechanism for determining when the user has clicked within the animation, so you can't use Plazmic to create simple games. On the other hand, MediaPlayer does include these standard mechanisms for controlling playback:

start() starts playback.

setMediaTime() will instruct a realized player to begin at the specified millisecond time.

getMediaTime() returns the current elapsed media time in milliseconds.

stop() pauses playback.

close() stops playback and releases the Plazmic resources.

NOTE: Unlike an MMAPI `Player`, you can re-use a `MediaPlayer` after calling `close()`.

You have several options when retrieving content to play. You can simply call `createMedia()`, providing the location of the Plazmic content, which may indicate a file or a network location. This method blocks until it fully retrieves the content and returns an `Object`, which you can then provide to the `MediaPlayer`. Alternatively, you can add a `MediaListener` and call `createMediaLater()`, which will return immediately. Sometime later the platform will invoke your listener with a `MEDIA_REALIZED` event and the media object. Finally, in rare circumstances you may want to define your own `Connector` and provide it via `MediaManager.setConnector()`. This allows you to define custom behavior for retrieving Plazmic content, such as removing encryption.

In its simplest form, creating and starting Plazmic content takes only a few lines of code.

```
MediaManager manager = new MediaManager();
MediaPlayer player = new MediaPlayer();
Object content = manager.createMedia("http://myserver.com/racing.pmb");
player.setMedia(content);
Object ui = player.getUI();
screen.add((Field)ui);
```

Because Plazmic associates so strongly with native RIM behavior, you cannot embed it into a MIDlet. Consider using Plazmic if you want a compact animation that will run on many RIM devices; avoid it if you want to use a more widely supported format or create interactive content.

GIF Animation

Animated GIFs are probably the most widespread form of animation on the Web, and people often turn to them first when creating simple animations. Unfortunately, animated GIFs on BlackBerry devices require special handling. If you include the GIF as a resource in your COD, the program compiler won't have a good way of telling whether a given GIF file will animate. Because PNG files require less decoding on the device than GIF files, by default the compiler will translate all non-PNG images (including GIF and JPEG) into PNG format. Therefore you will lose all animation information.

To avoid this problem, you can either rename the file extension to something else (like .gxx), or instruct your build environment to leave all images alone. If you use the Eclipse plug-in, open the BlackBerry App Descriptor, select Build, and then verify that the "Convert image files to png" box is unchecked, as shown in Figure 3–9. Note that you should use this last approach only if your program uses just PNG files and animated GIF images; otherwise, you will miss out on the valuable optimizations for display decoding. Also note that the PNG problem is moot if you load a GIF file over the network or from a file outside your COD.

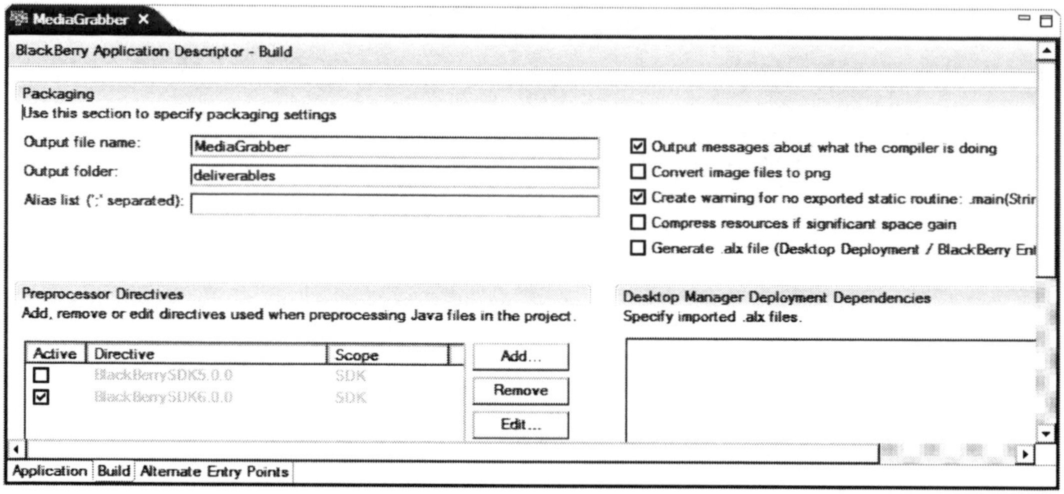

Figure 3–9. *Eclipse settings to retain all GIF files*

Once you actually have a GIF image, you face another problem. By default, a `BitmapField` will display only the first frame of the image. Fortunately, RIM created `BitmapField` as an extensible class, so you can override it to add animation support. Load the image as a `GIFEncodedImage`, and then use the methods exposed by that class to determine how many frames and animation loops the image includes. Create a separate thread that walks through the frames, sleeps for an appropriate time at each frame, and then invalidates the `BitmapField`. The custom BitmapField's `paint()` method should retrieve the current frame position and then draw it to the `Graphics` context. You can find examples of this process on RIM's developer web site.

MIDP Images

While this book focuses on RIM CLDC UI, some programmers may use the MIDP user interface for display, so we will briefly touch on how those apps handle images.

If you use a `Form`, you can directly append an `Image` to your `Form`, or create an `ImageItem` and then add that.

```
Image image = Image.createImage(getClass().loadResourceAsStream("clip.png"));
pmyForm.append(image);
```

However, most MIDlets will probably use a Canvas or GameCanvas to handle their UI. In these cases, you can draw directly to your graphics context when directed to do so.

```
public class MyCanvas extends Canvas()
{
    public void paint(Graphics g)
    {
        g.drawImage(image, 50, 50, TOP_LEFT);
    }
}
```

> **TIP:** The standard MIDlet API does not provide any support for animated images. If you try to draw an animated GIF, only the first frame will display. You can create simple animations yourself by using a timer to repeatedly call `repaint()` on the canvas and draw the next frame with each invocation.

Invoking Native Apps

On occasion, you may need or want to let a built-in application handle media playback instead of doing it yourself. Perhaps your app will run on an older version of device software that does not support the desired APIs; perhaps you prefer the interface of the native app; or perhaps you just want to simplify the code in your own app. Whatever the reason, RIM has made it relatively simple to communicate your desire to the built-in applications.

Playing Video Through the Browser

BlackBerry devices have supported video playback for a while, but support in the SDK is relatively recent. If you want to play a video but can't or don't want to do so in your own app, you can pass the location of the video file to the device browser. Note that this works even if the video file is present on the local filesystem.

The following sample code shows how to launch media through the browser on RIM software versions 4.0 and later.

```
BrowserSession browserSession = Browser.getDefaultSession();
browserSession.displayPage("http://myserver.com/video/awards.3gp");
```

This invokes the default browser, which works for most uses. In some cases, though, you might need to launch a particular browser in order to access the content. For example, the hosting server might deliver content only over WAP, or it may be reachable only through a BES. If this is the case, you will need to search for the corresponding `ServiceBook` entry and get a `BrowserSession` for that type. You can see examples of finding other browsers in Chapter 7.

> **NOTE:** This method does not allow you to play a video that was bundled within your COD. To play this type of video, first save it out to a temporary file and then invoke the browser.

Using CHAPI to Play Audio

CHAPI, the Content Handler API, finally provides a good generic way of allowing different apps on the same phone to communicate with one another. Certain apps can register as content handlers for particular MIME types or URL schemes. When other apps make a request to handle that type of content, the device AMS (Application

Management System) will invoke the registered app and allow it to service the request. When complete, the results will pass to the requesting app. Figure 3–10 illustrates the basic sequence that takes place when requesting content handling through CHAPI.

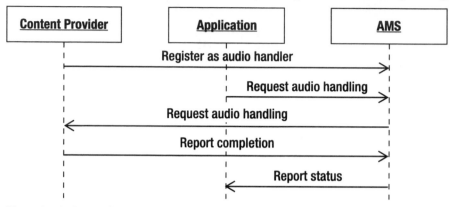

Figure 3–10. *Requesting audio playback through CHAPI*

NOTE: If you have programmed for the Android platform, this may sound familiar. A BlackBerry CHAPI request closely resembles an Android Intent.

RIM has embraced the CHAPI system for several forms of inter-app communication. Because the native media application already registers as a CHAPI handler, you only need to make a request to handle the type of audio, as shown in the code that follows.

```
Invocation request = new Invocation("file:///SDCard/BlackBerry/temp/train.mp3");
Registry registry = Registry.getRegistry
    ("net.rim.device.api.content.BlackBerryContentHandler");
registry.invoke(request);
```

You'll learn more about CHAPI in Chapter 8, including how to register your own apps to handle special types of content.

App: Media Reviewer

Chapter 2's exercise created an app that could capture media. There's a problem, though: how do you know if you captured something good? It would be much more useful if you could play back what you captured to make sure that your thumb wasn't over the camera and you can't hear the neighbors in the background.

To get started, copy over your current version of MediaGrabber into a new project. We will build on the previous version of the app, adding a media reviewer screen that plays back captured audio and video content. Listing 3–2 uses a separate class to handle display; this will allow us to support playing back arbitrary content in the future.

Listing 3–2. *A Content Reviewing Screen*

```
package com.apress.king.mediagrabber;

import java.io.InputStream;

import javax.microedition.media.*;
import javax.microedition.media.control.VideoControl;

import net.rim.device.api.ui.Field;
import net.rim.device.api.ui.MenuItem;
import net.rim.device.api.ui.UiApplication;
import net.rim.device.api.ui.component.*;
import net.rim.device.api.ui.container.MainScreen;

public class PlayingScreen extends MainScreen implements PlayerListener
{
```

The PlayingScreen uses a state machine similar to what we created in the last chapter for the RecordingScreen. Both screens display many of the same components, although we will use them very differently.

```
    public static final int STATE_WAITING = 1;
    public static final int STATE_LOADING = 2;
    public static final int STATE_LOADED = 3;

    private int state = STATE_WAITING;

    private UiApplication app;
    private LabelField status;

    private InputStream source;
    private String type;
    private String location;

    private Player player;
    private StatusUpdater updater;

    private MenuItem startItem = new MenuItem("Start", 0, 0)
    {
        public void run()
        {
            start();
        }
    };

    private MenuItem playItem = new MenuItem("Resume", 0, 0)
    {
        public void run()
        {
            try
            {
                player.start();
            }
            catch (MediaException e)
            {
                status.setText("Couldn't resume: " + e);
            }
        }
```

```
    };

    private MenuItem pauseItem = new MenuItem("Pause", 0, 0)
    {
        public void run()
        {
            try
            {
                player.stop();
            }
            catch (MediaException e)
            {
                status.setText("Couldn't pause: " + e);
            }
        }
    };

    private MenuItem rewindItem = new MenuItem("Rewind", 0, 0)
    {
        public void run()
        {
            try
            {
                player.setMediaTime(0);
            }
            catch (MediaException e)
            {
                status.setText("Couldn't rewind: " + e);
            }
        }
    };
```

Superficially, this appears similar to the earlier RecordingScreen; both make heavy use of a Player object to get work done. However, PlayingScreen is much more general-purpose. It will accept any type of media, either a file or an arbitrary stream. There's no guarantee it will play, but it will try. While we will use this class to play back captured local content from a file location, it can also play back networked content or other remote files accessed through an InputStream. We will define multiple constructors for these different uses.

```
    public PlayingScreen(String location, String message)
    {
        this(message);
        this.location = location;
    }
    public PlayingScreen(InputStream in, String type, String message)
    {
        this(message);
        this.source = in;
        this.type = type;
    }

    private PlayingScreen(String message)
    {
        add(new LabelField(message));
        status = new LabelField("Waiting.");
```

```
        add(status);
        app = UiApplication.getUiApplication();
        updater = new StatusUpdater();
    }
```

We override the onClose method to call close() on the Player. This is an important step, as Player objects are not automatically unloaded when they can no longer be referenced. If you keep multiple Player instances hanging around, they may hold on to scarce resources, making it impossible to play additional media until the garbage collector unloads them some time later.

```
    public boolean onClose()
    {
        if (player != null)
        {
            player.close();
        }
        return super.onClose();
    }

    public void makeMenu(Menu menu, int instance)
    {
        if (instance == Menu.INSTANCE_DEFAULT)
        {
            if (state == STATE_WAITING)
            {
                menu.add(startItem);
            }
            else if (state == STATE_LOADED)
            {
                if (player.getState() == Player.STARTED)
                {
                    menu.add(pauseItem);
                }
                else
                {
                    menu.add(playItem);
                }
                menu.add(rewindItem);
            }
        }
        super.makeMenu(menu, instance);
    }
```

This class finally introduces extra threads. We could cheat when recording and avoid them because capture starts so quickly, but there's no way a user would accept waiting a minute for an audio file to download over the network. When the user requests the media to start playing, we defer the work of actually initializing the Player to a separate Thread. Doing this allows the UI thread to retake control and provide updates while this thread retrieves or loads the media. In turn, when we need to update the UI, we synchronize on the global UI event lock, which ensures that our update does not clash with other actions.

```
    private void start()
    {
        state = STATE_LOADING;
```

```
              status.setText("Loading");
              if (player == null)
              {
                  (new Thread()
                  {
                      public void run()
                      {
                          try
                          {
                              if (location != null)
                              {
                                  player = Manager.createPlayer(location);
                              }
                              else
                              {
                                  player = Manager.createPlayer(source, type);
                              }
                              player.addPlayerListener(PlayingScreen.this);
                              player.realize();
                              state = STATE_LOADED;
                              VideoControl vc = (VideoControl)player.getControl↵
                                  ("VideoControl");
                              if (vc != null)
                              {
                                  Field video = (Field) vc.initDisplayMode(↵
                                          VideoControl.USE_GUI_PRIMITIVE, ↵
                                          "net.rim.device.api.ui.Field");
                                  synchronized (Application.getEventLock())
                                  {
                                      add(video);
                                  }
                              }
                              player.start();
                          }
                          catch (Exception e)
                          {
                              status.setText("Error: " + e);
                          }
                      }
                  }).start();
              }
          }
```

As usual, adding a thread complicates the picture. We want to provide updates to the UI about the status of the media, but if we attempt to modify the Screen from outside the main UI thread, something else may also attempt to modify it at the same time, resulting in corruption. To operate safely, we can either explicitly claim the event lock, as just shown, or take advantage of UiApplication.invokeLater(), which makes code run on the UI thread. Using the event lock tends to require less code, while invokeLater can make the application more responsive since your UI updates proceed independently of your worker thread. We re-use a single object, updater, for all of the status updates in order to avoid creating tons of garbage objects.

```
    public void playerUpdate(Player player, String event, Object eventData)
    {
        if (event.equals(PlayerListener.END_OF_MEDIA))
```

```
    {
        app.invokeLater(new Runnable()
        {
            public void run()
            {
                close();
            }
        });
    }
    else
    {
        updater.setMessage(event);
        app.invokeLater(updater);
    }
}

private class StatusUpdater implements Runnable
{
    private String message;
    public void setMessage(String message)
    {
        this.message = message;
    }
    public void run()
    {
        status.setText(message);
    }
}
}
```

Now that we have a playback screen available, we can modify the RecordingScreen. Listing 3–3 shows the modifications made to this file. Unchanged portions have been replaced with comments; refer to the previous chapter for the original contents, or download the listing from the Apress web site.

Listing 3–3. *A Recording Screen That Automatically Presents Recorded Content*

```
package com.apress.king.mediagrabber;

// Imports go here.

public class RecordingScreen extends MainScreen implements PlayerListener
{
    // Instance variables here.

    // Constructor and initial methods here.
```

PlayingScreen doesn't make much sense for the camera, since we don't need a Player to show a static image. In the case of the camera, then, we directly create a new Screen and put the Bitmap on it. This will nicely resize the screen to show the entire image, as shown in Figure 3–11.

```
    private void takeSnapShot()
    {
        try
        {
            byte[] imageData = video⏎
```

```
                    .getSnapshot("encoding=jpeg&width=640&height=480&quality=normal");
            if (imageData != null)
            {
                writeToFile(imageData, location + "/image.jpg");
                status.setText("Image taken");
                Bitmap taken = Bitmap.createBitmapFromBytes(imageData, 0, ↵
                        imageData.length, 1);
                Screen reviewer = new MainScreen();
                BitmapField bitmap = new BitmapField(taken);
                reviewer.add(bitmap);
                UiApplication.getUiApplication().pushScreen(reviewer);
            }
            else
            {
                status.setText("Please try again later.");
            }
        }
        catch (IOException ioe)
        {
            status.setText(ioe.getMessage());
        }
        catch (MediaException me)
        {
            status.setText(me.getMessage());
        }
    }

    // File output goes here.
```

stop() largely remains the same, except that we automatically start playing back captured data after persisting it.

```
    private void stop()
    {
        try
        {
            if (type == RECORD_AUDIO || type == RECORD_VIDEO)
            {
                recorder.commit();
                if (type == RECORD_AUDIO)
                {
                    String file = location + "/audio.amr";
                    writeToFile(dataOut.toByteArray(), file);
                    play(file, "Recorded Audio");
                }
                else
                {
                    String file = location + "/video.3gp";
                    writeToFile(dataOut.toByteArray(), file);
                    play(file, "Recorded Video");
                }
                status.setText("Data saved");
                state = STATE_READY;
            }
        }
        catch (IOException ioe)
        {
```

```
            status.setText(ioe.getMessage());
        }
    }
```

The `play()` method creates and displays a `PlayingScreen` for the recorded media.

```
    private void play(String location, String message)
    {
        Screen playback = new PlayingScreen(location, message);
        UiApplication.getUiApplication().pushScreen(playback);
    }
}
```

Figure 3–11. *MediaGrabber displaying a captured image in full-screen mode*

To show off the power of the new `PlayingScreen`, provide a way to directly enter it without going through `RecordingScreen`. Listing 3–4 shows how you can convert `RecordingChoicesScreen` from the previous chapter into `ChoicesScreen`. `ChoicesScreen` keeps the existing options for starting a record operation, but it also adds the ability to enter a file location or web URL and then select "Play Media" to launch it directly. Note that this will play only MMAPI-compatible media, so it will work for most audio and video, but not SVG, Plazmic, or other unsupported media types.

Listing 3–4. *A Screen to Start Recording or Playing a Particular File*

```java
package com.apress.king.mediagrabber;

import net.rim.device.api.ui.Field;
import net.rim.device.api.ui.MenuItem;
import net.rim.device.api.ui.UiApplication;
import net.rim.device.api.ui.component.BasicEditField;
import net.rim.device.api.ui.component.LabelField;
import net.rim.device.api.ui.component.Menu;
import net.rim.device.api.ui.container.MainScreen;

public class ChoicesScreen extends MainScreen
{
    private BasicEditField location = new BasicEditField("Location:", ↵
            "file:///SDCard/BlackBerry", 100, Field.FIELD_VCENTER↵
                    | BasicEditField.FILTER_URL);
    private MenuItem audioItem = new MenuItem("Record Sound", 0, 0)
    {
        public void run()
        {
            launchRecorder(RecordingScreen.RECORD_AUDIO);
        }
    };
    private MenuItem pictureItem = new MenuItem("Take a Picture", 0, 0)
    {
        public void run()
        {
            launchRecorder(RecordingScreen.RECORD_PICTURE);
        }
    };
    private MenuItem videoItem = new MenuItem("Record Video", 0, 0)
    {
        public void run()
        {
            launchRecorder(RecordingScreen.RECORD_VIDEO);
        }
    };
    private MenuItem launchVideoItem = new MenuItem("Play Media", 0, 0)
    {
        public void run()
        {
            launchPlayer();
        }
    };

    public ChoicesScreen()
    {
        setTitle("MediaGrabber");
        add(new LabelField(↵
                "Please enter a location, then select a choice from the menu."));
        add(location);
    }

    public void close()
    {
        location.setDirty(false);
        super.close();
```

```
    }

    public void makeMenu(Menu menu, int instance)
    {
        if (instance == Menu.INSTANCE_DEFAULT)
        {
            String property = System.getProperty("supports.audio.capture");
            if (property != null && property.equals("true"))
            {
                menu.add(audioItem);
            }
            property = System.getProperty("video.snapshot.encodings");
            if (property != null && property.length() > 0)
            {
                menu.add(pictureItem);
            }
            property = System.getProperty("supports.video.capture");
            if (property != null && property.equals("true"))
            {
                menu.add(videoItem);
            }
            menu.add(launchVideoItem);
        }

        super.makeMenu(menu, instance);
    }

    private void launchRecorder(int type)
    {
        String directory = location.getText();
        RecordingScreen screen = new RecordingScreen(type, directory);
        UiApplication.getUiApplication().pushScreen(screen);
    }

    private void launchPlayer()
    {
        String url = location.getText();
        PlayingScreen screen = new PlayingScreen(url, "Playing " + url);
        UiApplication.getUiApplication().pushScreen(screen);
    }

    public boolean onSavePrompt()
    {
        return true;
    }
}
```

Updating MediaGrabber.java is trivial: simply rename RecordingChoicesScreen to
ChoicesScreen. At this point, you can build and run the latest incarnation of
MediaGrabber. Give it a whirl! You'll want to run this on an actual device to get the best
impact; the canned images and audio in the simulator leave a lot to be desired. Try
recording whatever media your device supports, and also enter the URL for an external
media file.

Consider enhancing the app even more by adding these features:

- Save the most recently entered locations to allow quicker access.
- Allow the user to choose an audio device to play back sound.
- Write a new Screen that can play SVG or Plazmic content.

It doesn't make sense to go overboard with this app—after all, BlackBerry devices have a good Media application built in. However, these sorts of enhancements help a great deal when determining whether to add certain types of content into your own apps.

Excelsior

Phew! You covered a lot of ground in this chapter. As you can see, you have an incredibly wide range of options for adding compelling media content to your BlackBerry application. Fortunately, nobody expects your app to use all of them. Depending on your needs, you will likely choose just one or two types of content, a couple of formats, and one or two methods of delivery. You might choose the MMAPI Player interface for maximum compatibility and control, or Plazmic for a high level of integration with BlackBerry, or some other solution that takes advantage of your existing resources and interest. After you have made your decision, you can safely ignore the other media options—at least until you create your next app.

This chapter covered many ways of delivering content to the phone, including in your COD, on the filesystem, or over the Internet. However, an entire set of technologies that exist only for mobile phones offers unparalleled ways to exchange information with other people. The next chapter will dive into the sea of wireless messaging and show you how to create an app that's unlike what you can create on the desktop.

Chapter 4

Wireless Messaging

Nearly every application written today—whether on the server, desktop, or mobile—includes some form of networking component. If you've been programming for any length of time, you probably are familiar with TCP/IP, HTTP, and other standards of network communication already. When it comes to mobile phones, though, the available technologies quickly multiply. You can tap into the unique systems available to wireless devices and achieve features that are impossible to obtain on other platforms.

This chapter introduces several BlackBerry messaging options, looking at techniques unique to wireless, such as SMS and MMS messaging, as well as existing technologies that work slightly differently in this environment, such as e-mail. You will learn how to evaluate the different options when each technology makes sense to integrate into your application, and see how to access them from your Java app.

The various techniques share a common characteristic: all are very personal. Remember, whenever you send someone a wireless message, it will likely end up in his or her pocket. When you need that personal touch, wireless messaging provides the solution.

The Messaging Quiver

BlackBerry devices offer even more messaging options than most other mobile platforms. In addition to the ubiquitous wireless standard of SMS, and the slightly less ubiquitous standard of MMS, they offer a unique form of e-mail integration as well as a custom form of messaging available only between BlackBerry devices. This section provides a brief, high-altitude look at the available choices for wireless messaging.

SMS

Short Message Service, more often called SMS or simply text messaging, is the granddaddy of wireless messaging protocols. It was developed as a lightweight way to provide non-voice communication between mobile devices while not adding extra overhead to carrier networks.

Whenever you receive a call, the mobile tower pushes a packet of data to your phone, notifying it of the incoming call. This packet can be repurposed into a messaging packet, which means that its transmission is essentially free for the carrier. (This does not stop them from charging you for it, of course.) When your phone receives this packet, it extracts the content from it and, in most cases, displays the message on the screen or stores it in the inbox.

When you send a text, the phone packages it into a single packet and sends it to the tower. The tower passes it on to a Message Switching Center (MSC), a kind of junction point for nodes in the carrier's wireless network. The MSC ordinarily routes voice calls, but when it recognizes this as a text message, it will forward that message on to the Short Message Service Center (SMSC). The SMSC will examine the message to determine where it should go. If the recipient belongs to another wireless network, the SMSC will look up what carrier that number belongs to and then pass the message on to that network's SMSC. If the message specifies an e-mail recipient, the SMSC will send the message over the Internet.

Once the SMSC has a message intended for a recipient on its network, it will attempt to find that phone, using the same techniques as it would when placing an incoming call. If the recipient is available, the network will send the message. Otherwise, the SMSC will store the message and wait for the subscriber to become available. Depending on the requested configuration of the message, it may be stored for a period of time before it becomes invalid and is removed from the server.

Figure 4–1 shows two users, Patrick and Andrew, sending text messages to Kathryn. Patrick sends his from a mobile phone. In SMS jargon, this is a Mobile Originated (MO) message. When Kathryn receives it, it is a Mobile Terminated (MT) message. Andrew isn't using a mobile phone, but instead connects through an approved web portal to send his message. Most networks support integration points like this. If you plan to offer a service that will generate a large number of SMS messages, you will need permission from the wireless carriers to inject these messages into their network. Most often, developers will work with message aggregators who have standing deals with the major carriers and can provide you with this sort of access.

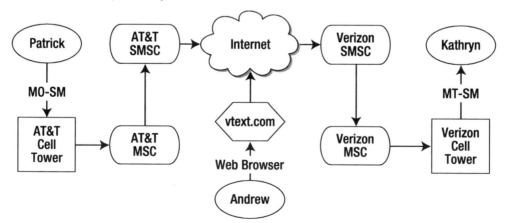

Figure 4–1. *Sending SMS messages to a mobile device*

So what, precisely, is an SMS? The exact representation can vary depending on the carrier, technology, and message configuration. As shown in Figure 4–2, all SMS messages contain a section of SMS headers and a 140-octet payload. The headers control things like the recipient address, delivery confirmation settings, validity intervals, and so on; third-party developers usually cannot access any of these fields other than the recipient. The payload, however, is standardized to facilitate compatibility between carriers. An octet is a collection of 8 bits—most people would call this a "byte." Using the word "octet" emphasizes that we can arrange these bits in nonstandard configurations. Phones often encode SMS messages using US-ASCII or GSM 7-bit character schemes, which allow 160 characters to fit within the 140 octets. If sending binary data, you can include up to 140 bytes. If senders use Eastern or Arabic languages, they can compose messages in 16-bit Unicode, allowing 70 characters. Sometimes, extra routing information or metadata that is not part of the SMS headers must be added to the SMS payload. For example, if the device is sending to an e-mail address, that address must be included in the payload, reducing the available number of characters.

Figure 4–2. *SMS message structure*

Different wireless carriers in the same country generally interoperate quite well. As long as your users remain primarily within a single region, you can feel fairly confident in sending messages to any wireless number. However, you should note that SMS does not include any delivery guarantees. The SMSC will make an effort to send the message, but it may fail for any of many technical reasons. If you ask for and receive a delivery confirmation, you will know that it arrived. Because of the lack of a strong service guarantee, you should use SMS in ways that supplement your app's functions and not make it a required component.

You should consider using SMS when you need to send a signal or provide an extremely short piece of data. Theoretically, you could send or receive multiple SMS messages and build them up into a larger binary message. Carrier support for such bundled messages is much less reliable, though, and if you try to implement such a system yourself, you multiply the risks of a lost message and incomplete data.

Pros

- Very quick transmission time
- Sent and received over carrier networks, so it remains available even without Internet service
- Strong interoperability between carriers

Cons

- Most carriers charge users for each message sent or received, or provide a limited number of free messages.

- Not available over Wi-Fi

- Extremely limited payload size

> **NOTE:** You may occasionally hear references to EMS, the Extended Message Service. EMS extends SMS by concatenating multiple SMS packets together into a single larger message. The EMS standard allows sending longer messages, and especially small binary data files such as sounds and images. Many handsets support the technology, but it has never really taken off in popularity. Given the increasing usage of standard Internet technologies such as e-mail, it seems unlikely that this situation will change in the future.

MMS

SMS has proven extremely popular, but, over time, its architecture has not allowed it to adapt to more data-intensive applications. Binary data delivery in SMS has always seemed a bit of a kludge, and ever-increasing data usage has eliminated it as a feasible delivery channel for large files. The rise of camera phones caused a corresponding increase in the desire to share photos with others, and the Multimedia Messaging Service (MMS) provided this kind of data transfer.

MMS came from the mobile world, but it was born in the Internet age. While SMS uses existing carrier technologies to deliver messages, MMS operates along an Internet backbone. Phones send and receive messages over an IP connection, meaning that MMS requires a data connection. On the other hand, carriers control the MMS service, and they do not allow just anyone access to their servers. Mobile subscribers with a data plan can send and receive messages almost without restriction; as with SMS, carriers require outsiders to be vetted before allowing them to send messages into the network.

The MMS system centers on the Multimedia Messaging Service Center, or MMSC. Each carrier has one of these centers, which routes all MMS messages to and from their subscribers. The WAP standard for MMS defines a set of standard interfaces, summarized here, that an MMSC must provide.

MM1: Connection to mobile devices over the carrier's network

MM3: Connection to other servers for this carrier, most importantly an SMTP e-mail gateway

MM4: Connection to other MMSCs for message routing

MM7: Connection to Value Added Service Provider (VASP) offered by third parties

Figure 4–3 illustrates three ways to create and send an MMS message to a mobile handset.

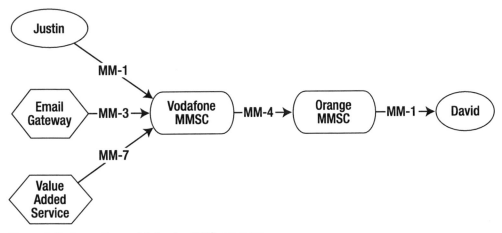

Figure 4–3. *Generating and delivering MMS messages*

You can generally send a few messages to MMS by sending to an e-mail address; these vary by carrier, and typically take a form like 4155551234@carrier.example.com. However, for large-scale message distribution, you will need to get an agreement with the carriers or go through a message aggregator. When this happens, you become a Value Added Service Provider. You can use MMS messages to communicate directly with your users, or to carry multimedia data to an application on their phone.

SMS messages are tightly constrained by existing carrier infrastructure and have to conform to size and format limits. In contrast, MMS messages were designed to be flexible and expandable. A Protocol Data Unit, or PDU, transmits a single MMS message. The PDU contains a set of message headers that include data such as the recipients, the size of the message, delivery confirmation requests, and other factors. After the headers come one or more attachments. Each carrier can mandate what media formats a phone must accept, and OEMs can choose to add additional formats, so you should check with your target carrier to see if they support your desired media on your targeted devices. However, all major MMSCs include transcoders, specialized services that translate attachments into compatible formats. For example, if you attempt to send a 640×480–resolution BMP to a device that supports only JPEG format up to 320×240, the MMSC will automatically convert the message attachment before it reaches the recipient. Most MMSCs can even split up a video file into a slideshow of still images. This can be very handy for ordinary use, but you should keep it in mind when sending messages: you cannot assume that the file you send will exactly match the file the phone receives. Again, support varies, but nearly all picture phones support JPEG and PNG images and MIDI and AMR audio, and nearly all video phones support 3GP video.

An MMS message also can include a Synchronized Multimedia Integration Language (SMIL) attachment. This special type of attachment describes how the other components within the message should display. The SMIL defines a series of slides, each of which will display for a specified length of time, and it can include some combination of text, image, and video. You can construct fairly elaborate messages with synchronized sound for an impressive impact. Figure 4–4 shows one possible configuration of such an MMS message. In practice, however, MMS messages rarely do anything more than send captured images or videos from the phone. The SMIL is almost never of any use when using MMS outside the phone's built-in messaging application, and you can safely omit it without any repercussions.

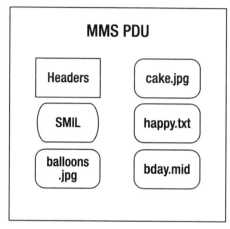

Figure 4–4. *A user-created MMS message*

MMS provides some useful applications, but has never really taken off in popularity the way SMS has. A variety of factors have played into this. Carriers do not interoperate as well for MMS as for SMS; some carriers eschew support altogether or offer different solutions. MMS is usually available only for camera phones with data plans, which includes most BlackBerry devices but not a lot of ordinary low-level phones. A user must also explicitly sign up for MMS messaging, which may or may not come with SMS messaging, and which has the same sorts of costs associated with it. Finally, the increasing availability of e-mail clients on smartphones and high-level feature phones has made it easier than ever to attach and send media off the device, which provides an alternative to the reason for MMS's existence.

From an application developer's viewpoint, MMS can offer a compelling choice when you want to send or receive multimedia content from a compatible phone, and you know the users' service plans include MMS. If you plan to run on a wide variety of devices across multiple countries and regions, though, consider another solution. As with SMS, you should view MMS as a channel to enhance the value of your app rather than a requirement for the app to function properly.

Pros

- Native support for sending and receiving multimedia content

- Based on an open standard that allows communication with non-BlackBerry devices

- Supports large message payloads

- Can generate attractive messages when sent directly to other users

Cons

- Most users must pay for each message sent or received, or have a limited number of free messages.

- Lower level of interoperability between carriers

- Requires connection to the carrier network; cannot send over Wi-Fi.

- Many users have devices that do not support MMS or do not include MMS in their subscription plans.

- Transcoder can modify message contents without your knowledge.

E-mail

BlackBerry devices famously work well with e-mail. Since their introduction, people have praised the combination of keyboard and network connection that, for better and worse, always makes it feasible to stay connected via e-mail.

Most BlackBerry devices have access to the public Internet, and depending on the device's configuration, most users can also add personal e-mail accounts to the device. This requires configuring the mail client for the device, a process similar to configuring a desktop e-mail program such as Outlook.

In most situations, outgoing e-mail messages travel through an SMTP server. When the user composes and sends mail from a private account, the BlackBerry infrastructure routes the message and sends it to the configured SMTP server. After entering the SMTP server, the message behaves exactly the same as if you sent it from your desktop computer. Unlike SMS or MMS, carriers do not control the routing; as long as you can reach the Internet, over the mobile network or through a Wi-Fi access point, you can send e-mail. Figure 4–5 shows how a BlackBerry device can access e-mail services over the network.

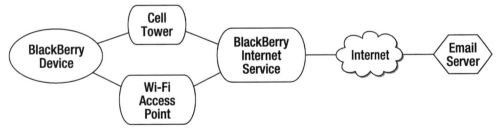

Figure 4–5. *A BlackBerry client sending an SMTP message*

Similarly, devices are often configured to retrieve e-mail from POP3 or IMAP servers. The BlackBerry Internet Service will check for new messages periodically or when prompted by the user, and it can automatically download new messages that it finds. Such incoming messages will arrive in the user's inbox. Depending on the device software version and user configuration, all e-mail may be dumped into a single inbox, or each account may have its own separate inbox.

When a device is sending or receiving messages this way, synchronization inconsistencies may appear. For example, if you send a message from your BlackBerry device, you probably cannot view it on your Outlook client later. Certain web-based e-mail providers, such as Gmail, do a better job at providing a unified view of all messaging activity on a given account. In all cases, though, the details will depend on how a given user has set up his or her particular accounts.

Almost everyone has at least one e-mail address, and most users will allow you to contact them. In the mobile world, smartphones almost always support e-mail, but feature phones and low-end consumer phones often lack it. Many BlackBerry users will have access to e-mail, but do not make this assumption for mobile users in general.

E-mail makes it convenient to exchange data, and allows sharing information via attachments. In some cases, you can attach arbitrary blocks of binary data to a message and pass it straight through to an application. However, given the constant threat of e-mail viruses, e-mail providers increasingly block attachments that they do not recognize, both on incoming and outgoing mail. These filters vary in quality. Sometimes you can simply rename to a well-known extension type such as .bmp, but most modern filters will scan the actual content of attachments and reject those that are unknown or not approved.

> **NOTE:** The native Messaging application can automatically resize attachments if they exceed the maximum size. Your own application does not automatically get this capability. Depending on your own app purpose, you can experiment with splitting an attachment into multiple parts, performing custom resizing, or setting limits on attachment sizes.

People can almost always send and receive e-mail for free, but may need to pay for the data usage and time on the network. Be sure to warn users if you will be transmitting large messages. Otherwise, you will be blamed when their next monthly service bill arrives. Additionally, individual e-mail providers' policies vary widely on the details of maximum message size, attachment size, and total traffic allowed.

Consider using e-mail when you need a message-based way to transmit data to and from the device, are primarily targeting BlackBerry and other smartphone platforms, and do not mind the possibility that your application's data will end up in the user's inbox. In most cases, you should probably first consider using a traditional HTTP server connection. That architecture is more traditional, reliable, and controllable. E-mail may provide a better solution if you want to develop a peer-to-peer application without a central server infrastructure, or if you intend to generate human-readable e-mails.

Pros

- Available over Wi-Fi and mobile networks

- Stored delivery: messages will arrive even if the recipient is not currently connected to the network.

- Can send and receive large messages

- Good support for text and binary attachments

- Excellent interoperability with all other e-mail addresses and nearly all other e-mail clients

Cons

- No guarantee any individual user will have a private e-mail account on his or her BlackBerry device

- Inconsistent policies on allowable attachments, message sizes, and so on

- Very visible to the user

- Not supported on many non-smartphone platforms

Push E-mail

Internet-based e-mail has grown more common on mobile phones, thanks to the increasing proliferation of well-designed smartphones. However, BlackBerry continues to hold the edge in e-mail thanks to its BlackBerry Enterprise Server (BES) and BlackBerry Internet Service (BIS). BES, used by corporate customers around the world, allows people immediate access to their business e-mail accounts, both within and outside the office. BES continues to evolve, and its details can seem fuzzy, but you can think of it as being a little like a Virtual Private Network (VPN). When users connect through their BES, they gain access to their company's secure infrastructure, including the e-mail accounts.

BES users are almost always corporate users. Their employer likely gave them the phone, and may subsidize their service bills as well. In exchange, they play by the company's rules. Keep this profile in mind when developing apps that depend on a BES e-mail account. However, individual users can gain access to a personal BES through subscription. This generally involves a monthly subscription fee in exchange for receiving the benefits of a BES. Similarly, RIM provides BIS, sort of a large public BES that consumers can use. BIS offers push functions similar to a BES, so instead of having instant access to work e-mail, users get instant access to consumer accounts like Gmail and Yahoo Mail.

A BES has several interesting features. First, it synchronizes enterprise e-mail. Unlike regular POP3 e-mail accounts, which may have messages scattered across multiple desktop and mobile devices, a BES e-mail account resides in a single canonical location, and all clients accessing it share a unified view into its contents. Changes made at any terminal will propagate to all of them, so deleting or reading a message on your phone means you won't need to deal with it again at work the next day.

The second, and most striking, feature of BES and BES e-mail is that they offer true push e-mail service. Unlike other mail programs that require you to press a button to check for mail, or that check for mail on an interval, your device will notify you the instant a new message becomes available. In this respect, push e-mail more closely resembles SMS than traditional e-mail. This also helps account for BlackBerry devices' infamous addictive properties. When people instantly receive notification of new messages, they tend to respond more quickly.

Figure 4–6 depicts a simplified view of the BES environment. As shown in this figure, a BES involves a level of integration between the company network, the wireless carrier network, and RIM's own custom infrastructure. All these pieces work together to provide a high degree of reliability and access. Recent versions of the BES environment support providing access to BES e-mail over Wi-Fi even if the device cannot reach the wireless carrier network.

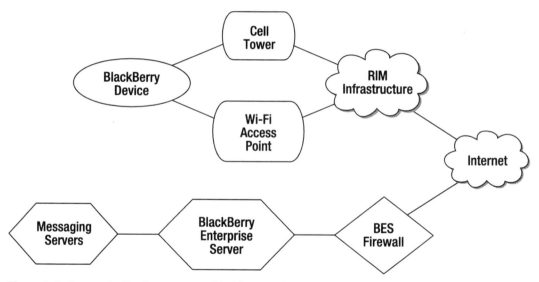

Figure 4–6. *Communicating from a remote BlackBerry device to a corporate e-mail account*

While the delivery mechanism for a BES looks more interesting than that of a regular e-mail account, the actual message contents themselves are identical. You can still create fairly large, long messages, and add attachments. However, BES administrators can strictly administer their users' accounts. This may involve actions such as blocking certain types of attachments or allowing communication only to certain other e-mail addresses. In all cases, you should avoid hijacking a user's BES e-mail account for a private application. At best you increase load on their servers; at worst, you may gain access to confidential information. On the other hand, if you write an app for one or more businesses, a BES can offer a great data transport mechanism: all of your users will have access to it, and you know the e-mail policies in advance. Just be sure to clear your plans with the appropriate administrator before getting too far, or they may cut you off.

Pros

- Push e-mail offers near-instant delivery, provided the device is available.

- Stored delivery: messages will arrive even if the recipient is not currently connected to the network.

- It can send and receive large messages.

- Good support for text and binary attachments

- Available over Wi-Fi and mobile networks

- Consistent environment for corporate users

Cons

- Not available to most private users

- Not available if porting to devices other than BlackBerry

- May involve restrictive security settings

- May be inappropriate to mix application messages with business e-mails

BlackBerry PIN Messaging

The previous section described how RIM's custom infrastructure—separate from, but integrated with, the wireless carrier network and private business network—provides push e-mail and other useful features to BES users. That infrastructure can also provide a truly unique form of messaging apart from e-mail.

Any given mobile device will have several numbers associated with it. These include the Mobile Device Number (MDN), which you dial to ring the device, the Mobile Equipment Identifier (MEID) or International Mobile Equipment Identity (IMEI), which uniquely identifies the physical phone, and possibly others as well. In addition to these numbers, every BlackBerry device has a BlackBerry Personal Identification Number (PIN). This number allows RIM's infrastructure to recognize every device that connects with it, even after reselling or changing wireless carriers.

Any BlackBerry connected to the Internet and the RIM infrastructure can be located, so if you know another user's PIN, you can directly message them through the network, as shown in Figure 4–7. Note that you can make contact even if you do not know the other user's e-mail address or phone number. PIN messages travel over the data channel, through the network, and are available even if the user cannot access the wireless network or is using the voice channel.

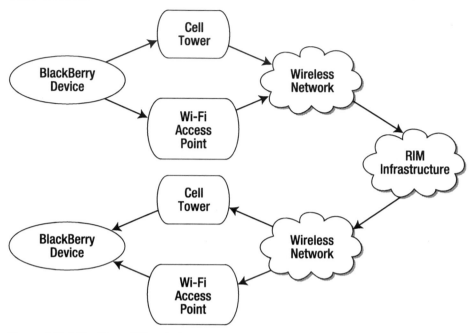

Figure 4–7. *A BlackBerry PIN-routed message*

Recent BlackBerry devices take advantage of this capability to offer a form of instant messenger, similar to AOL Instant Messenger or Skype. Once you receive a PIN message, you can immediately reply to the recipient. If you have saved the sender in your contacts, you can see the full name and not just the PIN.

PIN messages offer several interesting aspects. First of all, they are truly peer-to-peer. You cannot generate them outside a BlackBerry device, and they do not depend on any other server to store and forward. They also have an extremely high level of integration with BlackBerry devices. You cannot assume that every BlackBerry device uses a BES, and you cannot assume that every user has a text messaging plan, but by definition every device has a PIN.

> **NOTE:** In certain cases, such as a device being reported stolen, the PIN may be unavailable for messaging.

PIN messages have size limits. They are quite generous for text, but large sections of binary data may require more. Devices with software versions 4.2 or later currently can send messages with a subject of up to 255 Unicode characters and a body of up to 30,835 Unicode characters. On software version 4.1, the limit was still 255 characters for the subject, and only 16,385 for the body. These same limits apply to the text portion of a sent or received e-mail.

If you plan on targeting only BlackBerry devices and have access to your users' PIN numbers, this form of messaging may provide an appropriate platform. It can certainly make for a compelling technology demo.

Pros

- Instant push notification

- Available to virtually all BlackBerry devices

- No extra cost per message, other than for data used

Cons

- Restricted to BlackBerry devices only

- Must obtain the PIN number

- Not appropriate for large binary messages

Sending Text Messages

BlackBerry devices support JSR 205, the Wireless Messaging API (WMA) 2.0. This standard Java framework allows application developers to create applications that run on a variety of platforms and carriers, leveraging well-known techniques to easily integrate wireless messaging into their apps.

WMA expands upon the GCF, the Generic Connection Framework, which provides the basis for nearly all forms of resource access on Java ME devices. As with other GCF interfaces, you obtain a MessageConnection by issuing a request to the general `Connector.open()` method. When sending SMS messaging, use the protocol `sms://`. The contents after the protocol part should show the address to receive the messages. One possible address would be "sms://+14155550100". In this case, we are sending a message to a number in America (+1), in the city of San Francisco (415), with a seven-digit phone number (5550100). As when sending SMS messages using the phone's built-in messaging application, the phone will not know at the time you create the message whether the recipient can receive texts or even exists.

> **NOTE:** You can find SMS and MMS classes in the `javax.wireless.messaging` package. Many classes have generic names like `Message` that match the names of classes in other RIM packages. Therefore, you may need to selectively import the classes you reference, or else use fully qualified class names within your code. From the context of code examples, it should generally be clear what classes to import, but I will point out the package names in cases where it may seem ambiguous.

Creating Texts

Once you have obtained a MessageConnection, you can create the specific type of message that you intend to send by calling MessageConnection.newMessage(). You must provide the type of message to be sent, which can be one of MessageConnection.TEXT_MESSAGE, MessageConnection.BINARY_MESSAGE, or MessageConnection.MULTIPART_MESSAGE. You may also specify an address, although this is superfluous since messages will be sent to the address provided to Connector.open(). Figure 4–8 shows the interface hierarchy for objects returned from newMessage().

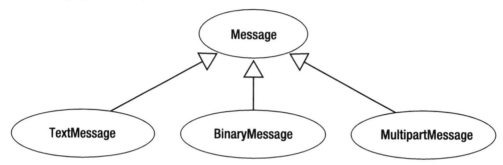

Figure 4–8. *Available message types on BlackBerry devices*

Both TextMessage and BinaryMessage objects will send over SMS. As discussed in the previous section, an SMS message payload has a fixed size, but you can encode it in different ways. A TextMessage can set its body with the setPayloadText() method, which allows up to 160 ASCII characters in a single message. The following code shows how to create and send a basic text message from your program.

```
MessageConnection smsConnection = (MessageConnection)Connector.open
    ("sms://+14155550100");
TextMessage bottle = (TextMessage)smsConnection.newMessage
    (MessageConnection.TEXT_MESSAGE);
bottle.setPayloadText("Sending out an SMS");
smsConnection.send(bottle);
```

> **NOTE:** send() is a blocking synchronous method, so this method will not return until after the message has finished transmission or an error occurs. As such, you will always want to send your messages from a separate thread. We'll see an example of this at the end of the chapter.

Sending Data

WMA provides a powerful tool for application developers by allowing you to specify a destination port number for your message. Regular messages like the one just shown will arrive in the recipient's built-in inbox, but messages sent to a particular port will be delivered to applications that listen on that port. This allows you to easily use messages to deliver data to and from applications. Note, though, that there are some complications to this process. First, under the hood, port numbers are included in the payload of the sent SMS message, and thus take away from the available space. Second, wireless carriers have only inconsistently implemented SMS ports. Most GSM (Global System for Mobile) carriers make ports available, but support in CDMA (Code Division Multiple Access) is rarer. Even when CDMA phones do support text message ports, they may use custom and incompatible methods for embedding the port number. This makes interoperability between carriers extremely difficult, particularly if you do not know what carrier a recipient uses.

WMA 2.0 helps circumvent the problem of port numbers occupying extra space by mandating that OEMs support message division and reassembly. Since an SMS has only 140 octets available, the messaging platform must split the single message into multiple SMS messages, each containing extra data describing reassembly, if an application attempts to send a message containing more than 140 octets. On the receiving end, phones must detect such split messages and reassemble them into a single message before delivering them to listening applications. WMA mandates that implementations support splitting an SMS into up to three messages, although they may choose to support more. This ability is useful, but you should carefully consider your audience. If you know that all users will have BlackBerry devices or similar phones that support WMA 2.0, you can rely on this behavior; however, if you send messages to other phones that do not implement message reassembly, the received messages will appear garbled.

The combination of binary message support and the ability to direct messages to particular applications can make text messages an attractive data delivery vehicle. Consider, for example, writing a play-by-SMS chess game. Both players would have a copy of the app on their phones showing the board. Whenever a player makes a move, the game sends the details of that move to the opponent's phone number. When that phone receives the move, it notifies the user and updates the local view of the board. This game takes advantage of the store-and-forward design of existing SMS infrastructure, so if one player turns off his or her phone, the message will wait until the phone becomes available. The following code demonstrates how to construct and send such a binary SMS message.

```
MessageConnection smsConnection = (MessageConnection)Connector.open↵
    ("sms://+14155550100:5000");
BinaryMessage chessMove = (BinaryMessage)smsConnection.newMessage↵
    (MessageConnection.BINARY_MESSAGE);
// Advance the king forward one space.
byte[] move = new byte[]{1, 3, 4, 'k', 3, 5};
chessMove.setPayloadData(move);
smsConnection.send(chessMove);
```

When Things Go Wrong

The previous code examples omit exception handling for clarity. However, real applications must recognize and respond to errors. Wireless messaging is fraught with connectivity issues, and other problems can arise, as well. You should be prepared to deal with the following exceptions:

- IOException can be thrown in a variety of situations, including when the network is unreachable or the message is rejected by the carrier.

- A SecurityException occurs if the application has not secured the necessary permissions, such as if it is unsigned or has not received PERMISSION_INTERNET.

- ConnectionNotFoundException is thrown if the protocol type is not known.

- An InterruptedIOException means that the message could not complete sending or receiving. This happens if a timeout occurs or another thread shuts the MessageConnection during transmission.

- IllegalArgumentException generally indicates a programming bug and means that the parameter is invalid.

Whenever exceptions occur, try to recover and continue gracefully. You will generally want to notify the user with a message such as "Unable to connect. Please confirm that your device has service and try again." If you let the user directly set the phone number or message payload, then suggest that he or she checks those, as well.

In all cases, clean up your connections in all exit situations. This is a good programming practice in general, and is especially important on limited-resource mobile devices. If you fail to clean up a MessageConnection, future attempts to send messages may fail. You can usually accomplish this best through use of a finally block, as shown here.

```
public void sendMessage() throws IOException
{
    MessageConnection conn = null;
    try
    {
        conn = (MessageConnection)Connector.open("sms://+14155550100");
        // Use the connection to create and send a message.
    }
    finally
    {
        if (conn != null)
        {
            conn.close();
        }
    }
}
```

The finally block ensures that regardless of whether an exception occurs, the connection is cleaned up.

CAUTION: I usually omit robust exception handling from the small samples of code within a chapter. The resulting code is usually easier to read, but certainly not appropriate for production-quality applications. Keep this in mind as you work through a chapter.

SMSC Lookup

WMA defines a system property for the SMSC. As discussed in the first section, the SMSC is the piece of equipment that handles the actual delivery of SMS messages. You can retrieve the SMSC by retrieving the `wireless.messaging.sms.smsc` system property as follows.

```
String smscAddress = System.getProperty("wireless.messaging.sms.smsc");
```

The SMSC is generally provided as a phone number on the carrier network, such as +15555550100. You won't access this number directly, but it lets you determine what SMS provider a given user has. Once you learn the SMSC addresses for carriers in your desired regions, you can use this information to make decisions about any special handling that a given carrier may require.

Sending SMS on CDMA

Speaking of special handling, when using wireless messages, you will eventually encounter differences between GSM and CDMA carriers. WMA was specifically designed to be carrier-agnostic, and on most other platforms you can happily re-use code for both GSM and CDMA. On several BlackBerry devices, though, SMS messages will fail to send from CDMA devices. This known issue affects the 7130, 7250, 8703e, 8830, Curve 8330, and Pearl 8130 phones. It appears to have been fixed for more recent CDMA models, including the Storm 9530 and beyond.

NOTE: Code Division Multiple Access (CDMA) and the Global System for Mobile (GSM) are the two most widely used wireless technologies. They use fundamentally different methods for wireless communication, so a GSM phone cannot be used on a CDMA carrier or vice versa. For the vast majority of applications, it makes absolutely no difference which type of phone you are running on. However, RIM and other OEMs must use different CPUs and architectures for the different types of devices, so in certain edge cases such as this, discrepancies will crop up. These can be frustrating, but the issues are generally fairly well documented. To determine what type of network your phone uses, call `RadioInfo.getNetworkType()`.

Fortunately, RIM has a workaround available for affected phones. Instead of using the WMA `MessageConnection` and Message interfaces, send a UDP packet via a `DatagramConnection`. This does make a certain amount of sense—SMS messages do appear somewhat similar to UDP in structure and purpose. You should still use the existing SMS protocol when addressing the recipient of the message. A short example follows.

```
if (RadioInfo.getNetworkType() == RadioInfo.NETWORK_CDMA)
{
    DatagramConnection backDoor = (DatagramConnection)Connector.open↵
        ("sms://+14155550100");
    byte[] data = "You cannot stop me".getBytes();
    Datagram dg = backDoor.newDatagram(backDoor.getMaximumLength());
    dg.setData(data, 0, data.length);
    backDoor.send(dg);
    backDoor.close();
}
```

Note that there is no distinction here between a regular text message and a binary message; you simply send bytes in both cases. Other BlackBerry devices will detect and interpret these messages correctly, but other phones may interpret them as binary data and not display regular text. In addition, note that this method generally does not work for GSM devices. If you plan to run on both types of networks and intend to use SMS messaging, you will need to create separate versions for each network or detect the current network and use one technique or the other.

Sending Multimedia Messages

SMS is a good choice for compact messages—either bits of human-readable text or small custom binary messages. When considering how to move large pieces of multimedia data on and off the device, think about MMS as an option. You can build MMS messages using the same WMA framework used by SMS messages, but they offer much more capacity and more flexibility in message construction.

> **CAUTION:** There were several bugs with RIM's initial implementation of MMS in device software version 4.6. These problems have been fixed starting with device software version 5.0, but to be safe, be sure to test on actual devices early in your development cycle. Also, because carrier MMSCs do not accept traffic from outside their wireless network, you will not be able to test MMS messages from the BlackBerry Simulator.

Talk to the World

You can address MMS messages to mobile phone numbers, but also to short codes, e-mail addresses, even IP addresses. This offers a great deal of flexibility when designing your application architecture. Instead of a peer-to-peer app design, you might choose to send data over MMS to an e-mail address and have a server component that receives those messages and acts on them. Therefore, while the general form of constructing a MessageConnection resembles that for SMS messages, you have more options available.

```
MessageConnection mms = (MessageConnection)Connector.open↵
        ("mms://+14155550100");
MessageConnection mms = (MessageConnection)Connector.open↵
        ("mms://sally@email.com");
MessageConnection mms = (MessageConnection)Connector.open↵
        ("mms://127.66.0.255");
```

Because MMS messages more closely align with the Internet world than the telephonic world, you also have the option of directing messages directly to an application ID. Similar to the port in an SMS message, this allows you to send a message directly to an application that has registered to handle those messages. To avoid conflicts, you should use a unique namespace when selecting an application ID. If you do not specify an application ID, the message will be delivered to the phone's default message client.

```
MessageConnection mms = (MessageConnection)Connector.open↵
        ("mms://+114155550100:com.apress.king.mms");
```

Constructing Parts

An MMS message can contain one or more pieces of content. Each piece is represented as a separate `MessagePart`. A `MessagePart` contains data, such as the actual sound, image, or text. You can set binary data directly on the `MessagePart`, or assign an `InputStream` to make it read in the data. In addition to the data, you can set the following pieces of metadata on the `MessagePart`:

- A MIME type describes the format of the data, such as "`image/jpeg`" or "`audio/amr`."

- The Content ID uniquely identifies this message part.

- The Content Location provides a file name.

The following code demonstrates how to create `MessageParts`. For convenience, this sets the text data directly from bytes and image data through an InputStream, but both could be set in either way.

```
String captionContent = "It's a boy!";
String captionContentId = "text_boy";
String captionContentLocation = "/boy.txt";
MessagePart textMessagePart = new MessagePart(captionContent.getBytes(), 0, ↵
    captionContent.length(), "text/plain", captionContentId, ↵
    captionContentLocation, null);
InputStream imageContent;
String imageContentId = "img_boy";
String imageContentLocation = "/photo.png";
imageContent = getClass().getResourceAsStream(imageContentLocation);
MessagePart imageMessagePart = new MessagePart(imageContent, "image/png",↵
    imageContentId, imageContentLocation, null);
```

If sending to another MMS-capable phone, you might consider adding a SMIL as well. This special type of `MessagePart` controls the display of other attachments in the message. It allows you to divide a message into multiple slides, specify how long each should display, group together audio, image, and text elements, and set up repeating loops. A full discussion of SMIL is beyond the scope of this book; for more details, you can view the specification defined by the W3C, available online at www.w3.org/TR/REC-smil/. An example of creating a simple SMIL follows.

```
String smilContent =
    "<smil>" +
        "<body>" +
            "<par dur='15000ms'>" +
                "<img src='photo.png'/>" +
                "<text src='boy.txt' />" +
            "</seq>" +
        "</body>" +
    "</smil>";
String smilContentId = "start";
String smilContentLocation = "/first.sml";
MessagePart smilMessagePart = new MessagePart(smilContent.getBytes(), 0, ↵
        smilContent.length(), "application/smil", smilContentId, ↵
        smilContentLocation, null);
```

You will almost always omit the SMIL if your MMS message transmits data to an application or a server, as you generally won't care about presentation.

Making the Message

Apart from the addition of attachments, MMS messages also add additional options to the message itself. We have already discussed the different addresses an MMS message can include, such as phone numbers and e-mail addresses. Unlike an SMS, which has only a single recipient, an MMS message can have multiple recipients. In addition, MMS messages support the e-mail–style address types of "to" (main recipients), "cc" (carbon copy, secondary recipients), and "bcc" (blind carbon copy). "bcc" recipients will receive the message, but their addresses will not appear in the message, so other recipients will not see those addresses. "bcc" may be a good choice if you want to send a single message to many recipients while protecting their privacy.

MMS messages offer several other fields that may be useful:

■ You can set the subject, which may be presented to the recipient before the recipient chooses to download the message.

■ The start content ID refers to the SMIL attachment, if one exists, and directs the MMS transport to place it appropriately in the final message.

■ The message header X-Mms-Delivery-Time specifies when the message may be delivered to the recipient. It may arrive later than this, but not earlier, so you can use this header when sending holiday greetings or similar timed messages in advance. Set the value to the desired time, in milliseconds since the Unix epoch. All clients can set this parameter, and most MMSCs will honor it.

- You can set the message header X-Mms-Priority to one of "high," "normal," or "low." This does not affect message delivery, but it may result in different presentation to the recipient.

The most important aspect of an MMS message, though, is the assembly of its attachment parts into the final message. You may add attachments in any order. As noted earlier, you can set the start content ID to indicate the SMIL if it is present; the SMIL information will control how to present the other parts.

You can construct large MMS messages, but carriers will generally set message limits on individual phones within their networks, based on factors such as network speed. You can usually send at least a few hundred kilobytes in a single MMS, and possibly as much as a megabyte or more for phones with high-quality cameras. In addition to the carrier limits when sending a message, you may run into limits when simply composing your message. If an attachment causes the message to exceed the size limit, or run out of memory, the operation will fail with a `SizeExceededException`.

The following code demonstrates how to create an MMS message, configure it, and attach the previously created media files.

```
MessageConnection mms = (MessageConnection)Connector.open↵
    ("mms://+14155550100");
MultipartMessage birthMessage = (MultipartMessage)mms.newMessage↵
    (MessageConnection.MULTIPART_MESSAGE);
birthMessage.addAddress("to", "+14155550101");
birthMessage.addAddress("to", "aunt.dotty@server.com");
birthMessage.addAddress("bcc", "my_email@work.com");
birthMessage.setSubject("The moment you've been waiting for...");
birthMessage.setStartContentId("start");
birthMessage.addMessagePart(textMessagePart);
birthMessage.addMessagePart(imageMessagePart);
birthMessage.addMessagePart(smilMessagePart);
```

Get Out of Here

Configuring an MMS requires a fair amount of work, but after the preparation, you send it using the exact same technique as an SMS. Again, the method will block until the message finishes sending or an error occurs. Keep in mind that long messages take even longer to send than short messages, and handle message sending in a separate thread.

```
mms.send(birthMessage);
```

Plugging into E-mail

If SMS dominates messaging on wireless devices, e-mail certainly dominates messaging in the rest of the world. Everybody has an e-mail address, and people increasingly send and receive e-mails while on the go. BlackBerry devices have always had a strong level of integration with e-mail, and you can take advantage of this affinity when moving data off the handset. Turn toward e-mail when you want to move a relatively large amount of data off the device in a standard format.

Taking Account

E-mail is so popular on BlackBerry devices that a given device may have many accounts registered. These may range from highly encrypted push e-mail accounts delivered over a BES to a basic free Gmail or Hotmail account. To support specialized network behaviors, RIM uses the concept of a service book to describe the configuration of each given account.

Service books are a unique property of BlackBerry devices that you will not find on other mobile operating systems. They perform several functions, but most importantly each book directs how an account connects to BlackBerry infrastructure, uses the mobile radio, handles encryption, and directs traffic. Even a basic user's device will contain multiple service books—perhaps one for handling WAP traffic through the carrier's wireless network, another for unencrypted Wi-Fi browsing, two for e-mail accounts, and several more for essential device functions. Figure 4–9 depicts a possible service book configuration.

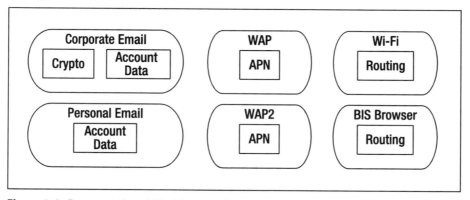

Figure 4–9. *Representation of BlackBerry service books*

> **NOTE:** Most documentation uses the term *service book* to describe these types of accounts. However, the RIM API uses the term *service record* to describe each individual account, and service book to describe the sum collection of all device accounts. I will use the term service book in this section due to its more common usage.

Any given device will contain many service books; only a few matter when sending e-mail, as we will see next. Once you have retrieved the appropriate service book, you can create an e-mail session for that account. The session associates your e-mail activity with the proper account and ensures that "Sent From" and other information appears correctly in outgoing messages. You can easily retrieve a session for the default e-mail account, as shown here.

```
Session defaultSession = Session.getDefaultInstance();
```

> **CAUTION:** While rare, some users will not have any e-mail account configured on their phones, in which case attempts to retrieve the default session will return null. Additionally, service book information may not be available immediately if the device has recently powered on, in which case you can try again later and retrieve the account.

You may want to send from another e-mail account. For example, a business BlackBerry device probably has a corporate e-mail address configured as the default, which should not send messages from a game. You can query the device for all e-mail service books. Each service book has a content ID describing the general function of the book. E-mail accounts use the content ID called CMIME (Compressed Multipurpose Internet Mail Extension). Once you have access to the accounts, you can select an appropriate one for your application to use—or, better, present your user with the choice of which to use. The following code shows how to scan through the available accounts on a device.

```
ServiceBook book = ServiceBook.getSB();
ServiceRecord[] records = book.findRecordsByCid("CMIME");
if (records != null)
{
    for (int i = 0; i < records.length; ++i)
    {
        ServiceRecord record = records[i];
        String name = record.getName();
        int type = record.getType();
        String description = record.getDescription();
        // Check to see whether to use this account. If so...
        ServiceConfiguration config = new ServiceConfiguration(record);
        Session emailSession = Session.getInstance(config);
    }
}
```

If you already know the account you wish to use, you can retrieve it via ServiceBook.getRecordById(), ServiceBook.getRecordByCidAndUserId(), or a similar method.

Creating the Message

Once you obtain an e-mail session for the account you wish to use, you can construct and configure the message. The BlackBerry API exposes a message store that holds all messages, both incoming and outgoing. The store, in turn, contains multiple folders. You cannot create a stand-alone message; instead, you must create a message within an existing folder. Create outgoing messages within the sent folder, as shown next.

```
Store msgs = Session.getDefaultInstance().getStore();
Folder[] sentFolders = msgs.list(Folder.SENT);
Folder sentfolder = sentFolders[0];
Message msg = new Message(sentfolder);
```

> **NOTE:** You can locate the BlackBerry mail classes in the `net.rim.blackberry.api.mail` package.

Observe that the `list()` method returns an array of folders. This allows greater flexibility with different mailbox configurations, but most users never have more than one `sent` folder. You can safely use the first returned `sent` folder.

Once you have constructed a `Message`, you can invoke appropriate methods on it to configure the message. These include all the options you would expect in a standard e-mail client, including choosing recipients, setting priority, and picking a subject. Be prepared to handle an `AddressException` if the recipient address is malformed. You also have access to fields that most other clients cannot access, such as configuring the date a message reports being sent, or requesting a read acknowledgment via a flag. The following code shows how you can programmatically write a message to a famous BlackBerry user.

```
Address to[] = new Address[1];
to[0] = new Address("obama@whitehouse.gov", "Barack Obama");
msg.addRecipients(Message.RecipientType.TO, to);
msg.setPriority(Message.Priority.HIGH);
msg.setSubject("Mission complete");
msg.setContent("The job is done. Awaiting further instructions.");
```

After composing your message, you can send it using the `Transport`. A `Transport` handles the sending and receiving activities of a given e-mail session. This operation may fail with a `MessagingException`, which can occur if the message could not be sent due to being rejected or encountering other problems.

```
Transport.send(msg);
```

Adding Attachments

You have now constructed a basic message, but what if you want to add attachments? Most of the message construction will still happen in the same way, but instead of setting the content directly as just shown, you will need to build a multipart message. Much like multipart MMS messages, with e-mail you can combine a series of `BodyPart` objects into a `Multipart` container. Each `BodyPart` consists of a chunk of binary data and a content type. For convenience, RIM offers several Part classes to use:

- `TextBodyPart` provides a simple way to set the text in a message that also contains attachments. You can set the content with a String, and it automatically has type text/plain.

- `SupportedAttachmentPart` defines a more generic kind of Part that can contain any type of content. You set the binary data and content type. You should also declare the file name used by the binary data.

> **CAUTION:** You will see several more Part subclasses in the Java API. Some of these classes work only for incoming messages, so you cannot use them when constructing an outgoing e-mail.

The following example shows how to construct and add attachments to a message. You can configure the rest of the message in the same way as in the previous example.

```
Multipart multipart = new Multipart();
TextBodyPart text = new TextBodyPart(multipart, "The job is done.");
SupportedAttachmentPart image = new SupportedAttachmentPart(multipart,
                "image/jpeg", "plans.jpg", imageData);
byte[] secretKey = new byte[]{17, 33, 0, 127};
SupportedAttachmentPart key = new SupportedAttachmentPart
    (multipart, "application/octet-stream", "key.dat", secretKey);
multipart.addBodyPart(text);
multipart.addBodyPart(image);
multipart.addBodyPart(key);
msg.setContent(multipart);
```

Testing Sending

If you try to run an app that sends e-mail from your device, the message will send properly (assuming you have properly configured your e-mail account and you have appropriate permissions). However, if you attempt to send from the device simulator on your desktop, the message will not send. What's going on?

You cannot configure an e-mail account on the desktop device simulator, because the simulator connects through a simulated MDS connection that does not actually connect to the real BlackBerry infrastructure. When you try to send a message from the default messaging client, it will appear to send properly, but will not actually generate a message.

To work around this issue, RIM has developed a separate stand-alone application. Much like the MDS, which simulates a BlackBerry network connection, the Email Server Simulator (ESS) simulates a BlackBerry-supported e-mail connection. The ESS provides a bridge between the MDS and outside e-mail, allowing you to test sending and receiving e-mail messages. If you plan on spending much time working with e-mail in your app, I highly recommend configuring the ESS early on. It will save you a great deal of time and allow you to complete most of your development on the desktop.

> **CAUTION:** The ESS is a local server, and you may need to modify your development machine to allow it to run properly. If you run into problems while setting it up, try disabling your firewall, turning off other local servers such as Apache, and running the ESS as an administrator.

You cannot directly access the Email Server Simulator through the BlackBerry Eclipse plug-in, but you can locate it under your Eclipse plugins folder. The full path should be something like `C:\eclipse\plugins\net.rim.ejde.componentpack6.0.0_6.0.0.29\components\ESS`. Run the `load.bat` file to launch the ESS. You can also install

ESS as part of the standard RIM JDE, which you can find on the BlackBerry web site. Once you have installed the JDE, you can find the Email Server Simulator in your Start menu under the `Research In Motion` folder, as shown in Figure 4–10. Both methods of installing and launching ESS work equally well. Running from the command line does give the advantage of displaying debug output from the ESS, which can help when tracking down issues.

Figure 4–10. *Locating the Email Server Simulator*

The Email Server Simulator offers two different modes. The Connected mode will connect to a third-party e-mail account. If the ESS is using connected mode, outgoing messages from the BlackBerry simulator will create actual e-mail messages from the configured account. Unfortunately, Connected mode doesn't work for several versions of the MDS/ESS combination. Even when it does work, it is extremely limited: it can send only through nonauthenticated, nonencrypted SMTP connections. There are very few of those left today, due to spammers and other abusers.

Instead, you should use the Standalone mode. Instead of sending to an external e-mail account, this mode causes the ESS to behave like a simple POP3/SMTP e-mail server. It will store outgoing messages, and you can connect a third-party desktop e-mail application, such as Outlook Express, to retrieve and send messages. Figure 4–11 shows one possible configuration of Standalone mode. You can pick any port numbers you want, which can help you avoid conflicts with ports in use on your machine. After you have set up the simulator, click "Launch" to start running. You won't see any log information about the ESS's actions.

Figure 4–11. *Configured Email Server Simulator*

Now, download a stand-alone e-mail client or open an existing one. Create a new account, and set both the POP3 and SMTP server addresses to "localhost." This directs the e-mail client to access your local machine instead of an external mail server. Consult your e-mail client's documentation to learn how to add an account. Figure 4–12 depicts adding an account using Windows Live Mail.

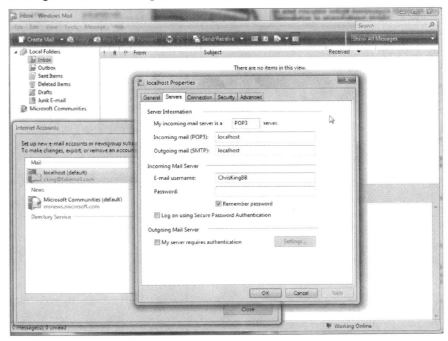

Figure 4–12. *Adding a dummy localhost e-mail account*

Be sure to set the port numbers that you configured in the Email Server Simulator window on the new account. You can usually find this under the advanced options, as shown in Figure 4–13. Without the correct port numbers, the client will not connect with the ESS.

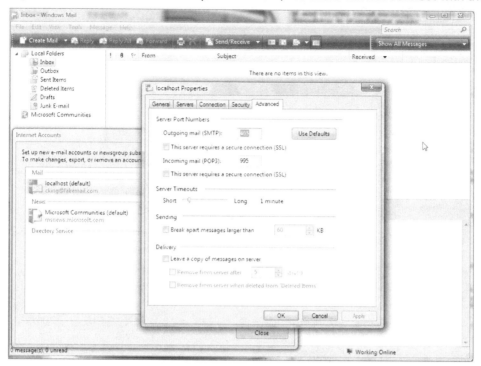

Figure 4–13. *Configuring matching port numbers on the e-mail account*

Before testing with your app, try to send a test message from the default BlackBerry message application. It doesn't matter what address you use, as all outgoing messages will go to the ESS. However, note that you will need to check the option Launch Mobile Data System Connection Service in your debug simulator configuration. This is required because ESS operates in a push e-mail system such as a BES, which works only with the simulated MDS environment, not with simulated Wi-Fi connections outside the BES. Compose the message like you would on an actual device, as shown in Figure 4–14.

Figure 4–14. *Creating a test e-mail message*

After you send, the message should shortly appear in your desktop e-mail client. Figure 4–15 shows a properly received message. Check your spam folder if you do not see it right away.

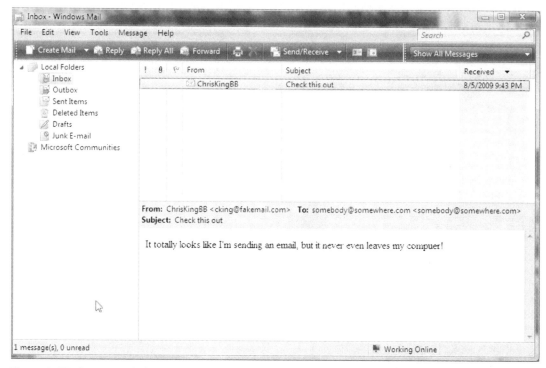

Figure 4–15. *A message delivered from the ESS to a desktop e-mail client*

After configuring your ESS, you can test sending messages from your app when running in the simulator. These will appear in the desktop client, where you can confirm that they contain the settings and attachments you expect to see.

> **CAUTION:** If the ESS stops running, outgoing e-mail messages will not send. This can prevent other networking operations, such as HTTP connections, from working properly. If you experience problems with e-mail, try shutting down your simulator, MDS, and ESS, and then bring the ESS back up, and then the simulator with the MDS option enabled.

Unfortunately, the simulator configuration puts a low limit on attachment sizes, meaning that you'll get an "Attachment too big" error when adding all but the smallest files. Also, the ESS does not handle attachments well and will not deliver them to your mail client. As a result, you should plan to test on an actual device if you send e-mails with attachments.

Receiving Text Messages

The earlier part of this chapter dealt with sending messages. Now we will look at how to receive messages. Not every app will need both kinds of functions. You may just send messages to share information about what your app is doing, or just receive messages in order to activate functions within your app. Some peer-to-peer apps will do both. The classes used to receive messages are usually the same as those used to send them, but we will use them in different ways.

Getting the Message

Suppose that you want to notify your already running app about incoming messages. To do this, you will open a special kind of MessageConnection that functions as a server instead of a client. In other words, you declare an intention to handle messages that others send to you.

The format of a server connection string resembles that of a client string, but you omit the phone number portion, and instead include only the port number. An example follows.

```
MessageConnection receiver = (MessageConnection)Connector.open("sms://:4000");
```

> **TIP:** On most BlackBerry devices, a connection string of "sms://:0" indicates that this app wants to receive ALL incoming SMS messages. Do not abuse this, as it will prevent messages from being delivered to other apps.

> **TIP:** As described earlier in this chapter, if you wish to send SMS messages to your app from a server, you will need to make an agreement with the wireless carriers or go through an SMS aggregator. SMS aggregators generally send regular SMS messages and not port-directed messages. To indicate that a message should be delivered to a particular GSM port, use the TP-User-Data/User-Data-Header header when sending your server request to generate the outgoing SMS message.

Once you have a MessageConnection, you can receive in one of two ways. The method MessageConnection.receive() blocks until a message arrives. If you write a separate message-handling thread, you may choose to just call receive() within a loop to handle all incoming messages. Alternately, you may choose to register a listener with the connection. By implementing the MessageListener class and calling setMessageListener(), your main thread can continue running normally. The platform will invoke your MessageListener class whenever a message becomes available. Note that the invocation may run on your app's main thread, so you should still spawn a separate thread in this situation. A simple anonymous MessageListener may look like the following:

```
receiver.setMessageListener(new javax.wireless.messaging.MessageListener()
{
    public void notifyIncomingMessage(MessageConnection connection)
    {
```

```
            Message incoming = connection.receive();
            // Handle the message here.
        }
    });
```

Notice that we have declared the `notifyIncomingMessage` method to process the message. Again, a real application should receive the message on a separate thread.

Waking Up

So far, this all works well as long as our app runs. But what if it hasn't started yet? If we expect to receive messages on port 4000, and the phone receives a message for that port while the app isn't running, the phone simply discards the message. The user will not see it, and the app will not be notified.

For BlackBerry CLDC applications, you can handle this by having your application automatically start on boot-up. It can then use the foregoing approaches to open a `MessageConnection` and either register as a listener or create a thread that calls `receive()`. Once a message arrives, you can process it, calling `UiApplication.requestForeground()` to bring up your UI if so desired.

MIDlets, however, cannot automatically start on boot-up. If you write a MIDlet, you must register with the push registry. The push registry, a component of the device AMS, starts up apps when certain circumstances occur. In our particular case, we want to register to handle incoming messages.

The push registry can take one of two forms: dynamic or static. We can dynamically register through application code. Imagine that someone is playing a mobile version of chess. They will start the game and start playing. The game notifies the push registry that it wants to handle incoming messages to port 6060. During a particularly long wait, the player exits the app in order to listen to some music. When the other player finally moves, his or her device sends your player a message to port 6060. The AMS notices the port number and automatically starts your chess game app back up again. At this point, you can retrieve the incoming message and show the latest move.

When registering with the push registry, you provide these three pieces of data:

- The connection URL describes the protocol and address of incoming connections; this is equivalent to the string that will be passed to `Connector.open()`.

- The MIDlet class name is the fully qualified MIDlet class to start after receiving the message.

- The allowed sender indicates that the app should start only if the connection came from this source.

To register for all incoming SMS messages to a particular port, use something like this:

```
PushRegistry.registerConnection↵
    ("sms://:4000", "com.apress.king.chess.ChessGame", "*");
```

If you want to receive only from one specific sender, specify it in the last parameter.

```
PushRegistry.registerConnection("sms://:4000", "com.apress.king.chess.ChessGame",
    "+14155550133");
```

This method will throw a `ClassNotFoundException` if it cannot find the class, and an `IOException` if it encounters some other problem, such as another application already reserving the same port. You can call this method from a different class than the one to register.

Dynamic registration has several advantages, such as letting you decide on the fly what port you want to use, perhaps based on what's available and what a server wants to use. It also makes it tougher for hackers to exploit a known port number and send your app data it doesn't expect. On the other hand, you cannot dynamically register an app until after it starts. That works fine for a chess game, but it means your app will no longer be registered after the user reboots his or her phone, until the user remembers to start the app on his or her own.

To get around this issue, consider using static registration. You declare a static registration in your application JAD or `MANIFEST.MF` file, which registers with the AMS at installation time. From then on, the phone will always invoke your app whenever it receives a matching message, even if it has never run before. As the following example shows, you provide the same information in static registration that you would use in dynamic registration, just as a standard name-value pair.

```
MIDlet-Push-1: sms://:4000, com.apress.king.chess.ChessGame, *
```

If your app registers for multiple types of incoming messages, or for other types of push notification, just keep incrementing the number after `MIDlet-Push` to `MIDlet-Push-2`, `MIDlet-Push-3`, and so on.

> **CAUTION:** Using static registration carries its own pitfalls. The phone guarantees that your app will start when an appropriate message arrives, so it will install your app only if the user has not already installed another app that registers for the same port number. To be as safe as possible, pick a random port number that is high in the available range, and stay away from well-known port numbers.

We've Got Incoming

The push registry doesn't use any special interfaces when launching your MIDlet for an incoming message: it uses the same `startApp()` method as when the user manually launches the app. To determine whether the AMD launched your app, you should query the pending connections from the `PushRegistry`. If your app has registered for multiple push types, there may be more than one push pending. Search to find the proper one. Once you have located it, you can open the `MessageConnection` and proceed as usual. The code that follows shows an example of retrieving the message that launched this MIDlet.

```
String[] pendingConnections = PushRegistry.listConnections(true);
if (pendingConnections != null && pendingConnections.length > 0)
{
    for (int i=0; i<pendingConnections.length; i++)
    {
        String url = pendingConnections[i];
        if (url.startsWith("sms"))
        {
            MessageConnection messageConnection =↵
                (MessageConnection)Connector.open(url);
            Message incoming =  messageConnection.receive();
        }
    }
}
```

CAUTION: RIM devices generally require a full phone reboot when you install an application with static push registry. This is because the static push registry is initialized when the phone boots up. This will slightly inconvenience your users, but can frustrate developers and testers who may load an app hundreds of times. Consider omitting the push registry entry on debug builds.

What Is It?

You now have a Message. Remember, though, that there are two types of SMS messages: TextMessage and BinaryMessage. If you know which kind of message to expect, you can cast directly to the form you want. Otherwise, test for the specific type in order to determine how to access its parts.

TIP: BlackBerry CDMA phones may receive incoming plain text messages as type BinaryMessage. To reconstruct the original text, just create a String from the byte payload.

You use the TextMessage and BinaryMessage classes for both creating and receiving messages, and you can retrieve the same type of information from both. In certain cases, the meaning of a method or piece of data changes. For example, the address in an outgoing message refers to the recipient address, whereas the address of an incoming message refers to the sender address. The following code shows how to retrieve information from a retrieved SMS message.

```
String sender = incoming.getAddress();
if (incoming instanceof TextMessage)
{
    TextMessage text = (TextMessage)incoming;
    String body = text.getPayloadText();
}
else if (incoming instanceof BinaryMessage)
{
    BinaryMessage binary = (BinaryMessage)incoming;
    byte[] payload = binary.getPayloadData();
}
```

Testing SMS

You can easily test sending SMS from the simulator. However, RIM does not currently support a good way to test receiving SMS. If you can, try to complete your testing on an actual device. If your app heavily relies on receiving SMS and you anticipate needing a great deal of testing, though, you might want to look at the smsdemo Java application released by RIM, which you can find on the BlackBerry developer web site; this utility echoes back SMS messages from a specialized client. Alternately, you can create a test harness within your app that bypasses the standard message receiving code, and instead directly hands a dummy payload to the rest of your app.

Receiving MMS Messages

Once you know how to receive SMS messages, you'll find receiving MMS to be very familiar. It uses the same MessageConnection interface to retrieve messages, just with the mms protocol instead of the sms one. As with sending, you can register a class name instead of a port number. You can use the push registry for MMS in the same way you would for SMS. To retrieve a message, simply receive it as shown here.

```
MessageConnection receiver = (MessageConnection)Connector.open
    ("mms://:com.apress.king.mms");
MultipartMessage mms = (MultipartMessage)receiver.receive();
```

> **CAUTION:** MMS messages can be quite large and take a long time to fully receive. Be sure to receive in a separate thread from your main app. Consider showing some sort of progress indicator to let your user know that the app is retrieving data.

Observe that the mms protocol will retrieve only MultipartMessage messages, so unlike with SMS, you do not need to test for the class type before casting.

Reading MMS

The incoming MMS message will have the same fields available that you could set for outgoing messages. Simply call the accessors to pull out whatever information you want, as shown here:

```
String sender = mms.getAddress();
String subject = mms.getSubject();
```

Of course, you wouldn't be using MMS if you just wanted the sender and the subject. To get at the attachment data for the message, retrieve the message parts. Each part will contain a content ID, a content location, a MIME type, and data. If you control the incoming messages to this app, you may know exactly what you will be receiving and can directly get the attachments you need; otherwise, you may want to scan all the attachments, and take appropriate behavior on each. The sample that follows shows how to look for JPEG image and text attachments.

```
MessagePart[] parts = mms.getMessageParts();
for (int i = 0; i < parts.length; ++i)
{
    MessagePart part = parts[i];
    String name = part.getContentID();
    String type = part.getMIMEType();
    String file = part.getContentLocation();
    if (type.equals("image/jpeg"))
    {
        InputStream is = part.getContentAsStream();
        // Could set this picture on the UI or save it.
    }
    else if (type.equals("text/plain"))
    {
        byte[] messageBytes = part.getContent();
        String text = new String(messageBytes);
        // Could display this text.
    }
}
```

Testing MMS

Unfortunately, you cannot test sending or receiving MMS messages within the simulator. MMS relies on a combination of SMS message delivery, a cooperative MMSC, and data delivery to send messages. The simulator cannot easily recreate this complicated environment.

Therefore, you should test on the actual device. Your phone will need to be able to send and receive MMS messages through the native Message application in order for it to send or receive MMS messages within your app. If it cannot, contact your wireless carrier or IT administrator to properly set up your wireless data plan and IT policy.

If your app uses MMS heavily, deploying to the device every time you make a change may be too labor-intensive. Consider writing a local test harness for the simulator instead. Test to see whether you are running on the simulator; if you are, you can omit the outgoing messages and invoke appropriate incoming methods. For example, you might programmatically construct a `MultipartMessage` and proceed as if it had been delivered from the `MessageConnection.receive()` method.

Reading E-mail

E-mail lets you easily move data off your BlackBerry app. It can also receive data, but you will need to deal with more complications. Because e-mail isn't exclusively a wireless technology, its policies and standards tend to be more complex. If you can clear those hurdles, though, e-mail usually provides the fattest message-oriented pipe at your disposal.

Listening

The previous two sections discussed how your app could directly receive incoming SMS and MMS messages. These capabilities allow an app to use wireless messaging as a pure data channel, meaning the user will never see the actual messages. However, e-mail doesn't have this sort of exclusive relationship. Your app cannot intercept incoming e-mail—if it could, just imagine the potential for abusive programs to wreak havoc with business e-mail accounts.

What you can do is listen for messages. After a message arrives on the handset, the BlackBerry device will check to see if anyone has registered to be notified of changes in a particular folder. You can join this notification list by implementing the FolderListener interface. The following code shows the skeleton of a listener class.

```
public class ArrivingListener implements FolderListener
{
    public void messagesAdded(FolderEvent event)
    {
        if (event.getType() == FolderEvent.MESSAGE_ADDED)
        {
            // Handle arrived messages here.
        }
    }
    public void messagesRemoved(FolderEvent event)
    {
        // This method intentionally left blank.
    }
}
```

You must attach your FolderListener to a particular message store. The previous section on sending e-mail described how to find and retrieve an appropriate store. The next example sets a store on the user's default e-mail account.

```
Session session = Session.getDefaultInstance();
Store store = session.getStore();
ArrivingListener listener = new ArrivingListener();
store.addFolderListener(listener);
```

> **NOTE:** You may want to use a dedicated e-mail folder for your app. Because the user will see incoming e-mail messages, it will probably annoy them to have a large number of app-directed messages delivered to their inbox. Depending on the user and the type of e-mail account, you may need the cooperation of an IT administrator to set up folders correctly.

Reading Messages

Incoming e-mail messages contain all the same fields that you can provide to outgoing messages. Once you have obtained the message, you can read those fields in directly, as shown in this example:

```
net.rim.blackberry.api.mail.Message arrived = event.getMessage();
```

```
Address sender = arrived.getFrom();
String senderAddress = sender.getAddr();
String senderName = sender.getName();
String subject = arrived.getSubject();
int size = arrived.getSize();
byte priority = arrived.getPriority();
```

Note that the `Address` object contains multiple pieces of information about the sender. Depending on your app design, you may care about the sending e-mail address, the associated name, both, or neither. The priority will correspond to one of `Message.Priority.HIGH`, `Message.Priority.MEDIUM`, or `Message.Priority.LOW`.

For basic e-mail messages with just a text component, you can retrieve the body text directly as shown here.

```
String text = arrived.getBodyText();
```

This will return `null` if the message has no body text.

Reading Attachments

If the message contains attachments, they will be collected in a multipart message part. Once you retrieve the multipart, you can iterate through the constituent parts and pull out the individual attachments.

If you are building a general-purpose app that handles messages in a variety of formats, this will require a fair amount of introspection. Individual parts might contain MIME data, a downloaded attachment, plain text, and other pieces of content. You may need to scan all the attachments to find what you are interested in, as shown in the following example. On the other hand, if you know exactly what attachments to expect, you can retrieve them directly.

```
Object contents = arrived.getContent();
if (contents instanceof BodyPart)
{
    // Read body
}
else if (contents instanceof Multipart)
{
    Multipart attachments = (Multipart)contents;
    int num = attachments.getCount();
    for (int i = 0; i < num; ++i)
    {
        Part part = attachments.getBodyPart(i);
        if (part instanceof SupportedAttachmentPart)
        {
            SupportedAttachmentPart attachment = ↩
                (SupportedAttachmentPart)part;
            String type = attachment.getContentType();
            if (type.equals("image/png"))
            {
                InputStream image = attachment.getInputStream();
            }
        }
    }
```

```
    else if (part instanceof TextBodyPart)
    {
        TextBodyPart body = (TextBodyPart)part;
        String message = (String)body.getContent();
    }
    else if (part instanceof MimeBodyPart)
    {
        MimeBodyPart attachment = (MimeBodyPart)part;
        String type = attachment.getContentType();
        if (type.equals("image/png"))
        {
            InputStream image = attachment.getInputStream();
            // Could display or save the image here.
        }
    }
    }
    }
}
```

The device may initially download only the first portion of a large message. The user can view important information like the sender and subject, and possibly the first few lines of the message. The user can then decide whether to download the entire message. To detect whether a particular part has fully downloaded, call hasMore() on the part. If additional data remains, your app can request to download it by calling Transport.more(). Provide the BodyPart and true if you want to download the entire part, or false to download the next available chunk. The following snippet provides an example. Note that this method is not synchronous. If you want a notification when the body part has been retrieved, attach a MessageListener to the message prior to calling Transport.more().

```
if (attachment.hasMore())
{
    Transport.more(attachment, true);
}
```

> **CAUTION:** It bears repeating that you should use extreme care when listening for e-mail messages. Don't put yourself in a position where you could be accused of eavesdropping on confidential messages. Be sure to clearly state to the user how your app will access e-mail, and ask for the user's permission when doing so.

PIN Messaging

All of the messaging technologies described so far exist on multiple platforms. However, only BlackBerry devices can use PIN messaging. Each BlackBerry has a unique PIN, and only BlackBerry devices have PINs. If your app is exclusively aimed at BlackBerry users, PIN messaging offers an interesting way to exchange information.

Getting Pinned

A PIN number exclusively belongs to one particular device. You may want to learn the PIN even if not using PIN messaging, as it provides a way to uniquely identify each of your devices. You can access the PIN by retrieving it from the device info with the call DeviceInfo.getDeviceId().

If you know the PIN number for another BlackBerry, you can send it a message. RIM uses the same interfaces for constructing PIN messages as it does for constructing e-mails: you will retrieve a store to an e-mail session, construct a message within that store, and send it. Once the message hits the network, though, the RIM infrastructure will intercept and route it to the corresponding device.

You flag an outgoing message as a PIN message by adding a PIN recipient. PINAddress takes the same form as a regular Address, but you will populate it with the recipient's PIN number (represented as a String) and name. You can configure the rest of the message as you would a regular plain-text e-mail. You cannot add attachments to a PIN message.

The following code shows how to construct, configure, and send a PIN message.

```
Store store = Session.getDefaultInstance().getStore();
Folder[] folders = store.list(Folder.SENT);
Folder sentFolder = folders[0];
Message msg = new Message(sentFolder);
PINAddress recipients[] = new PINAddress[1];
recipients[0]= new PINAddress("10000000", "Chris King");
msg.addRecipients(Message.RecipientType.TO, recipients);
msg.setSubject("Poke");
msg.setContent("You've been pinned!");
Transport.send(msg);
```

Receiving PINs

Receiving a PIN also resembles the process for an e-mail. You add a listener to the user's e-mail folder, which will be notified when an incoming message arrives. The listener will receive all incoming notifications, for both e-mail and PIN messages, so if you care only about PIN messages, you should check the message type as shown in the example here. Use the standard e-mail access methods to pull out the PIN message contents you are interested in.

```
public class PINListener implements FolderListener
{
    public void messagesAdded(FolderEvent event)
    {
        Message message = event.getMessage();
        if (message.getMessageType() == Message.PIN_MESSAGE)
        {
            String pinSubject = message.getSubject();
            String pinContent = message.getBodyText();
        }
    }
    public void messagesRemoved(FolderEvent event) {
```

```
        // No action necessary.
    }
}
```

> **CAUTION:** The message type functions are broken on several versions of the device software. If the previous example doesn't work on your particular platform, print out the value returned by `getMessageType()` for an incoming PIN message, and then change the code to test for that integer instead of `PIN_MESSAGE`.

Unfortunately, the BlackBerry device simulator does not support PIN messaging. I recommend using the Email Server Simulator and e-mail messages for development on the simulator, and then switch to PIN messages when running on the actual device. Most of your app logic should be able to remain the same; you will just switch between sending to a `PINAddress` instead of an `Address`, or switch whether you test for a `PIN_MESSAGE` type.

App: Sending and Receiving Media Messages

So far, our MediaGrabber can record media, save it to the local filesystem, and play media back to us. That's cool, but isn't it a bit of a shame that we're the only ones who can enjoy it? Let's enhance the app and come up with a way to pass media off the device so we can share it with friends and family.

First, let's take care of a little housekeeping. In Chapter 3, we saw how time-consuming operations should run in a separate thread to keep the UI responsive. We also saw that we needed to use a separate class to handle updates to our Screen that originated from a new thread. We will have the same issue with sending media as we did with playing it, so rather than reimplementing that special class again, let's create a general-purpose stand-alone class that is capable of handling asynchronous UI updates.

Listing 4–1 shows the implementation of `StatusUpdater`. Feel free to use this in any of your own projects, as this is a fairly common task. You may also want to adapt it for other types of `Field` objects other than simple text labels.

Listing 4–1. *A General Class for Updating Label Elements Asynchronously*

```java
package com.apress.king.mediagrabber;

import net.rim.device.api.ui.UiApplication;
import net.rim.device.api.ui.component.LabelField;

public class StatusUpdater implements Runnable
{
    private LabelField status;
    private String message;
    private UiApplication app;

    public StatusUpdater(LabelField status)
    {
        this.status = status;
```

```
        app = UiApplication.getUiApplication();
    }

    public void sendDelayedMessage(String message)
    {
        this.message = message;
        app.invokeLater(this);
    }

    public void run()
    {
        status.setText(message);
    }

}
```

Next, let's look at the main task of sending an outgoing message. To keep things nice and organized, we'll create a new class, SendingScreen. This Screen will allow the user to enter an e-mail address. Once the user selects send, the screen will compose a new e-mail message to that user, attach the media data, and then send it out. Listing 4–2 provides all the details.

Listing 4–2. *Sending Media from the Device to an E-mail Address*

```
package com.apress.king.mediagrabber;

import net.rim.blackberry.api.mail.*;
import net.rim.device.api.ui.*;
import net.rim.device.api.ui.component.*;
import net.rim.device.api.ui.container.MainScreen;

public class SendingScreen extends MainScreen
{
    private static final int STATE_INPUT = 0;
    private static final int STATE_SENDING = 1;
    private static final int STATE_SENT = 2;

    private int state = STATE_INPUT;

    private String contentType;
    private String filename;
    private String message;
    private byte[] data;

    private BasicEditField receiver;
    private LabelField status;

    private StatusUpdater updater;

    private MenuItem sendItem = new MenuItem("Send", 0, 0)
    {
        public void run()
        {
            send();
        }
    };
```

```
public SendingScreen(String contentType, String filename, String message, ↵
                byte[] data)
{
    this.contentType = contentType;
    this.filename = filename;
    this.message = message;
    this.data = data;
    status = new LabelField("Please enter an email address.");
    receiver = new BasicEditField("Recipient:", "", 100, ↵
                    BasicEditField.FILTER_EMAIL | Field.USE_ALL_WIDTH);
    add(status);
    add(receiver);
    updater = new StatusUpdater(status);
}

public void makeMenu(Menu menu, int instance)
{
    if (instance == Menu.INSTANCE_DEFAULT)
    {
        if (state == STATE_INPUT)
        {
            menu.add(sendItem);
        }
    }
    super.makeMenu(menu, instance);
}

private Message createMessage(String recipient, String type, ↵
                String filename, String message) throws MessagingException
{
    Store defaultStore = Session.getDefaultInstance().getStore();
    Folder sentFolder = defaultStore.getFolder(Folder.SENT);
    Message outgoing = new Message(sentFolder);
    Address friend = new Address(recipient, "");
    outgoing.addRecipient(Message.RecipientType.TO, friend);
    outgoing.setSubject(message);
    Multipart multipart = new Multipart();
    SupportedAttachmentPart file = new SupportedAttachmentPart(multipart, ↵
                    type, filename, data);
    multipart.addBodyPart(file);
    TextBodyPart text = new TextBodyPart(multipart);
    text.setContent("Check this out!");
    multipart.addBodyPart(text);
    outgoing.setContent(multipart);
    return outgoing;
}

private void send()
{
    status.setText("Sending, please wait.");
    state = STATE_SENDING;
    receiver.setEditable(false);
    (new Thread(new MessageSender())).start();
}

private class MessageSender implements Runnable
{
```

```
        public void run()
        {
            String address = receiver.getText();
            try
            {
                Message outgoing = createMessage(address, contentType, ⏎
                            filename, message);
                Transport.send(outgoing);
                updater.sendDelayedMessage("Message sent");
                state = STATE_SENT;
            }
            catch (Exception e)
            {
                updater.sendDelayedMessage("Problem sending: "⏎
                                        + e.getMessage());
                e.printStackTrace();
            }
        }
    }

    public boolean onSavePrompt()
    {
        return true;
    }
}
```

The rest of the changes are minor. We must update the RecordingScreen to use the SendingScreen once media has been recorded. The code that follows shows a new method to initiate the send, along with an example of updating the previous code to use the new functions. Most of the class remains identical to the Chapter 3 version; you can download the complete updated RecordingScreen from the Apress web site.

```
private void send(String location, String contentType, String message, ⏎
            byte[] data)
{
    SendingScreen sending = new SendingScreen(contentType, location, ⏎
                message, data);
    UiApplication.getUiApplication().pushScreen(sending);
}
// Within the stop() method, use the following:
if (type == RECORD_AUDIO)
{
    String file = location + "/audio.amr";
    writeToFile(dataOut.toByteArray(), file);
    send("audio.amr", "audio/amr", "Here's some sound!", ⏎
                dataOut.toByteArray());
}
```

Finally, update PlayingScreen to use the new version of StatusUpdater we created. In the constructor, use the following code.

```
updater = new StatusUpdater(status);
```

In PlayerUpdate, substitute the following code for the old updater reference.

```
updater.sendDelayedMessage(event);
```

Recall from earlier in the chapter that the ESS does not handle attachments well; therefore, you should run this on an actual device. If you haven't already, test sending e-mail from the built-in Messaging application. Include an attachment to make sure you can send those files properly. Then launch and run MediaGrabber. Record as before, enter any email address you like, and select Send. The outgoing message should shortly arrive in your inbox.

WANT MORE?

As you've seen in this chapter, you have a bewildering range of technologies available for wireless messaging. The current version of MediaGrabber works fine, so long as the user has a compatible e-mail account, but you could expand it to provide even more features to your users.

- Attach a `MessageListener` to your outgoing e-mail. When the message status updates, check to see whether it sent successfully or if an error occurred. Report the final message status to the user. Be sure to remove the `MessageListener` when the `SendingScreen` dismisses.

- If your device and plan support it, try sending MMS messages instead of e-mail.

- Listen for incoming e-mail messages. If the message contains one of the strings our app uses (like "Here's some sound!"), notify the user that a friend has sent a MediaGrabber file.

You can decide whether to add these new capabilities to the existing `SendingScreen`, or create new classes to handle those expanded functions. You can also improve the presentation by allowing people to enter their own custom messages on outgoing media.

Excelsior

This chapter has shown the many wireless messaging choices that you can use when developing an app. Each option has its own unique profile and advantages, without any one-size-fits-all solution. Depending on your app's needs, you may prefer the ubiquity of SMS, the presentation options of MMS, the desktop integration and wide capacity of e-mail, or the unique BlackBerry aspect of PIN messaging. Each has its own quirks, and now that you know them, you can take full advantage of each to its fullest.

Many successful BlackBerry apps will stick with conventional networking technologies, such as HTTP or socket programming. Those are great choices if you want to re-use existing server components, run on any device with a data connection, or require more continuous communication. Wireless messaging, on the other hand, allows you to connect with existing platforms of message delivery with very little extra effort on your part. Decide early in your project which approach best fits your needs.

Your app is now capturing information on the device and sending it over the network. Wouldn't it be bad, though, if your boss ended up seeing the pictures you took at that wild party? Chapter 5 will examine ways to protect the data we send from the device, keeping it secure and making sure that the intended recipient has access.

Cryptography

Next to their e-mail capabilities, BlackBerry devices are probably most famous for their security. Corporations love them because data sent over a BlackBerry Enterprise Server is automatically encrypted, because they can remotely wipe stolen devices, and because of their integration with corporate security policies. With this strong legacy, many BlackBerry users naturally pay attention to the strength of security offered by applications.

Cryptography is a broad topic that can and does fill many books. This chapter focuses on some of the tools available to an application developer like you when writing for the BlackBerry platform. We will look at some of the most common goals when writing secure apps, and the various APIs you can use to accomplish those goals. Keep in mind that security is a serious, multi-faceted issue. You should view this chapter's contents as a useful starting point that will continue with further education, security audits, and real-world testing.

Is It Secret? Is It Safe?

Suppose that you write a business expense–tracking app. This app allows users to enter their receipts onto the BlackBerry, then uploads the data to a server or sends the user an e-mail. So far, so good. Now, imagine that while the app transmits that data, a hacker uses a packet sniffer to observe the message being sent. Now, someone else has access to personal financial information from your users, which he or she may use to steal their identities or crack bank accounts.

Of course, not every app will need to worry about this sort of thing. Who cares if a hacker eavesdrops on a weather-predicting app? Early on in development, you should consider and discuss the security profile of your app.

1. Does the app have access to sensitive data?

2. Does the app store such data? Transmit it?

3. What are the risks associated with loss or interception of that data?

4. What would it take to protect the data?

5. How hard will it be to protect the data? How long will it take? Will it inconvenience the user?

If, after a thorough analysis, you decide that the app needs to protect its data, you can proceed to a consideration of the best method to do so.

Data Encryption

When most people hear the word cryptography, they may first think of cipher encryption—that is, transforming a plain text, such as "hello," into seeming gibberish called a ciphertext, such as "ifmmp." Ciphers have existed for millennia, and modern ones have grown incredibly sophisticated.

All but the most trivial ciphers rely on use of a key. The key is a secret piece of data that is used to encrypt a message. For example, consider a cipher that adds the key value to the plain-text value. We might have a plain text of "hello" and a key of "world." We can convert those letters into numeric values, starting with 1 for "A" and 26 for "Z". Then, for each letter, we add the value of the plain text to the value of the key. If the total is greater than 26, we subtract 26 so we end up with a value between 1 and 26. Finally, we convert the number back to the numeric value. In this example, "h" has a value of 8 since H is the eighth letter in the English alphabet; "w" has a value of 23 since it is the twenty-third letter. 8 + 23 = 31. We subtract 26 to get a value of 5, which corresponds to the letter "e." Table 5–1 shows how to apply these steps to the entire words.

Table 5–1. *Applying a Simple Cipher*

Plain-Text Letter	Key Letter	Plain-Text Number	Key Number	Sum	Cipher Letter
h	w	8	23	5	e
e	o	5	15	20	t
l	r	12	18	4	d
l	l	12	12	24	x
o	d	15	4	19	n

Without any other context, the word "etdxn" doesn't seem to mean anything, and any would-be attackers are left frustrated. Even if they know how the cipher works, without the extra information supplied by the key, they cannot crack it.

What happens if someone figured out your key, though? When this happens, the cipher becomes useless, and attackers can decrypt any ciphertext that they come across later. It is imperative to keep your keys secret. Some modern systems generate keys on the fly based on secret processes, such as the time of day or the motion of a lava lamp. Apart from the keys, modern ciphers are, of course, far more complex than the example just shown, and often involve scrambling the order of letters in addition to performing various permutations on each byte of data.

You can choose between many types of ciphers for software applications. Most fall into one of two major categories. A block-based cipher encrypts data in specific chunk sizes. In our previous example, since our key is five letters long, we would want to process plain text in sets of five letters. If the incoming plain text has only 13 letters, then we can substitute random characters for the last 2 letters and discard them when we decode the message. Alternately, a stream-based cipher can process plain texts of arbitrary length. Neither type is inherently more secure than the other.

Data Decryption

If a server sends your app encrypted data, you will need to write code to decrypt that data so you can process it. Similarly, if you encrypt your user's data and store it on the local filesystem, you'll decrypt that data when you need to access it. Decryption reverses encryption, and transforms a ciphertext back into a plain text, as shown in Figure 5–1.

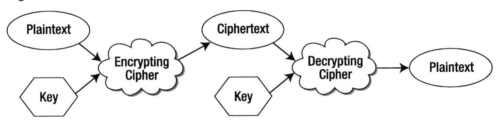

Figure 5–1. *Using a key to encrypt and decrypt a message*

We can easily decrypt the sample cipher from the previous section. For each cipher letter, convert to a number, then subtract the key's value. If this results in a negative value, count back from 26 to arrive at the plain text. Table 5–2 shows the decryption stage.

Table 5–2. *Reversing a Simple Cipher*

Ciphertext Letter	Key Letter	Ciphertext Number	Key Number	Sum	Plain-Text Letter
e	w	5	23	(26–18=)8	h
t	o	20	15	5	e
d	r	4	18	(26–14=)12	l
x	l	24	12	12	l
n	d	19	4	15	o

The most common ciphers rely on a shared secret, also known as a symmetric key, when performing decryption. This means that both the encoder and decoder must have access to the same key, which each uses to perform its operation. The past half-century has also witnessed the development of public key encryption, also known as an asymmetric key system. In this crypto system, the encryptor and the decryptor use two separate keys. This greatly helps applications like Internet commerce, where you want many strangers to send you encrypted data, but you do not want to allow any of those strangers to decrypt each other's messages. However, the private key for an asymmetric key system is still a critical secret that must be preserved.

Validation

You can use encryption and decryption when you want to protect an entire chunk of data so nobody else can read it. Sometimes, however, that provides more protection than you really need. Suppose your weather-predicting server sent messages to the BlackBerry telling it whether it will rain tomorrow. You don't really care if someone else intercepts that message; however, you still worry about another situation. What if a rival programmer starts sending messages to your users, claiming that tomorrow will bring a rain of frogs? Your users will get upset and delete the app.

In this situation, you actually want some way to determine the authenticity of a message. How can you know that this data came from your server and nobody else has tampered with it? You can best accomplish this goal by using a checksum, also known as a hash or a digest. A checksum is a formula that looks at all the data in your message, applies an algorithm over it, and then generates a hash representing that algorithm's result, as shown in Figure 5–2. Checksums run over the plain messages protect against inadvertent errors that may occur during transmission. To protect against intentional attacks, you can add a secret key to the end of the message, and then find the hash value generated by the combination of the message and the key. Using this method, you can pass the entire message through in unencrypted format, which allows for faster processing, and still protect against tampering. People sometimes refer to this process as a cryptographic signature, or more informally, signing. The signature proves authorship without the overhead and inconvenience of full encryption.

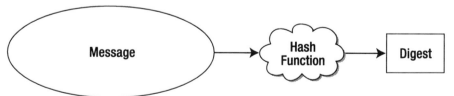

Figure 5–2. *A hash function generates a cryptographic digest for a message.*

When your app receives the message, it can add the same secret key and then run that same algorithm and compare the calculated result to the received hash. If the two match, you can reasonably trust the message's authenticity.

A trivial checksum might first convert every letter to a numeric value, as in our examples before, and then add the values together. It will then divide the sum by 26 and take the remainder (for a value between 0 and 25) plus 1 (for a value between 1 and 26). This final letter is then appended to the end of the string prior to submission.

Suppose we want to send the message "hello" and our secret key is "j". So, the message "helloj" is transformed to 8 + 5 + 12 + 12 + 15 + 10, which equals 62. Dividing by 26 yields a remainder of 10, so the hash value is 11, or "k". We transmit the value "hellok", keeping the secret key out of the message. If an attacker tries to send the message "aloha" to our app, but doesn't know the key, he may send "alohak". When the app receives this message, it will add the secret "j" to the text "aloha", and then transform "alohaj" to 1 + 12 + 15 + 8 + 1 + 10, which equals 47. We divide by 26, take the remainder of 21, add 1 to get 22, and end up with "v". However, we can see that the checksum value was "k". Therefore, we know this message is not authentic, and we discard it.

You may choose to combine a checksum and a cipher for a transmitted message. This is slower than just cryptographically signing, but helps ensure both that nobody else can read the message and that the message was not modified in transit. To do this, calculate a digest for your entire message, combine the two, and then run the entire result through a cipher before sending.

There are a variety of well-known checksum algorithms available. While on the Web, you have probably encountered MD5 hashes, which verify that a file has not been tampered with. Some potential weaknesses have been discovered in MD5, and today most new apps should use SHA or the more secure SHA-1. If you prefer, you can roll your own checksum algorithm. However, keep in mind that anything you come up with will likely not match the security of the more widely used technologies.

> **NOTE:** If you'd like to learn more about MD5, SHA-1, or any of the algorithms discussed in this chapter, Wikipedia provides good high-level discussions of each, along with links to academic papers discussing implementation and any vulnerabilities.

SATSA

Java ME introduced JSR 177, the Security and Trust Services API (also known as SATSA), to address some common security concerns. Like several other JSRs, SATSA ended up as a bit of a grab bag with several disparate elements thrown in together. It defines some standard Java classes to use for cryptography, ported over from the Java SE versions. It also defines interfaces for interacting with SIM cards and managing security certificates. Individual manufacturers can decide which components of SATSA they wish to implement and which they do not.

Thus, even though RIM has technically supported SATSA since device software version 4.2.1, they have adopted only the SIM card–related functions. They have also taken some, but not all, of the certificate-management classes. They did not adopt any of the cryptography. As such, you cannot use SATSA for encryption or decryption. This confuses some new RIM developers, so keep in mind that even devices that support SATSA do not include SATSA decryption.

As you will shortly see, you still have plenty of options available. RIM has offered its own security classes since long before it adopted SATSA, and it makes sense that RIM would not import the duplicate functionality of the SATSA crypto packages. The downside, of course, is that you cannot easily port Java ME applications written using SATSA crypto to run on BlackBerry.

Bouncy Castle

While SATSA offers useful encryption support, it implements only a subset of the many available cryptographic systems. Additionally, RIM and many other manufacturers have not added SATSA support to their devices. To make up for these deficiencies, an open source project called Bouncy Castle has gained a lot of attention and support. Bouncy Castle provides free access to a wide variety of crypto functions.

An Introduction

Most security algorithms are well documented in academic literature. However, the actual implementations of those algorithms tend to be written by for-profit companies who make money by licensing their use. Bouncy Castle started when two programmers grew tired of needing to reimplement standard security classes every time they switched projects. There is no great secret behind how each algorithm works—the real secret is the cryptographic key—but such ad-hoc rewrites are not only tedious and time-consuming, they also increase the risk of writing a flaw that may allow the code to be exploited. The programmers decided to start a new project that would allow them and other developers to re-use a stable, proven base of cryptographic classes.

Bouncy Castle contains a clean room implementation of major crypto classes, meaning that they were written based on documentation and not by looking at any pre-existing code. Therefore, no other company's patents or copyrights apply to Bouncy Castle. You can use this open source code under a version of the MIT X Consortium license, which is widely considered quite reasonable. The license is also quite short, so you should read it and understand it before using the code in your own project.

Adding Bouncy Castle to Your Project

Because Bouncy Castle is not part of the standard RIM environment, you must manually add the classes to your project. You can download the entire Bouncy Castle source from the web site at `www.bouncycastle.org`. Bouncy Castle exists for many different versions of Java; you will want to download the latest release of the lightweight J2ME implementation, a `.zip` file that contains the compiled classes, source code, tests, and documentation. When you see it, you may gulp, because it takes up several megabytes. Needless to say, this could have a significant impact on your binary size.

Fortunately, because you have access to the source, you can simply add the classes you need to your project and ignore the rest. Alternately, you can add everything at once, and later go back to trim it out. Pulling in all the code except for the tests and examples will increase the size of your program by about 600KB; it increases far less if you import only the classes you need.

To import the classes in Eclipse, right-click your project's source folder and select Import. Expand the General window, select File System, and then click Next. Browse to the location on your hard drive where you unzipped the Bouncy Castle .zip file, and select the src folder. You can check src to import everything, or expand it and select only the files you need. When done, click Finish.

> **NOTE:** If building outside of Eclipse, you might consider using Proguard, which both can both obfuscate and automatically remove unused code from your program.

When you import the source files, note that some of them are included in the java.* package tree. Java ME omits some common Java SE classes that Bouncy Castle requires to function properly, such as BigInteger. The download contains reimplementations of these classes. On some versions of the RIM software, you may need to rename the packages because the classloader does not approve of loading user-created code in the java namespace. You can easily rename by right-clicking a package in the Package Explorer, selecting Refactor and then Rename..., changing the name to something like xjava.io, and finally clicking OK. Eclipse will work its magic, searching for and automatically converting all references to the affected files. Repeat for any remaining packages.

Using Bouncy Castle in Encryption

Bouncy Castle offers a slew of functions too vast to completely cover here. This section focuses on the essentials for encoding or decoding messages. Consult the API documents to learn more details on how specific ciphers work.

The two most important types of classes in the package are ciphers and engines. A cipher describes a generic interface for how encryption or decryption operations behave. The root cipher classes include BufferedBlockCipher and StreamCipher. Each defines the core operations of a cipher: initializing with a key, processing blocks of bytes, and returning results. Subclasses of each can define custom behavior, such as how to pad extra bytes in a block cipher.

You can initialize any given cipher class with a variety of compatible engines. The engine takes care of the actual process of converting bytes into ciphertext, while the cipher takes care of passing around input and output. Engines implement one of two main interfaces. BlockCipher is used for a variety of symmetric key cipher engines, including AES. AsymmetricBlockCipher is used for asymmetric key cipher engines, including RSA. Each individual engine is usually initialized with a CipherParameters object, which provides the key or other data needed by the engine.

In many cases, your app will work within an existing crypto system. For example, you may already have a server that accepts data in Blowfish, in which case you can simply start using the BlowfishEngine class. If you are responsible for setting up a new crypto system, then read about each cipher to determine which ones best fit your needs. Most often you will need to decide between speed and protection. Of course, the strongest cipher won't help if you fail to keep your keys secure.

Once you have set up your cipher appropriately, you just need to feed it data. All ciphers work on arrays of bytes, so if your input comes from some other format, like a String or an InputStream, you will need to access the underlying bytes first. After encryption completes, you will have access to the encoded byte stream. The following code example demonstrates a sample encryption from a plain-text string into an encoded version. This sample uses the Twofish cipher, a very secure algorithm with pretty good performance. We initialize the cipher with a preshared secret string, and true to indicate that the cipher should perform encryption. Next, we encode the input bytes. Note that we need to call the doFinal() method for a block-based cipher like Twofish in order to fill out the remainder of the last block. At the end of the process, we have the raw bytes. Here we construct a string to display, but this step often doesn't make sense, since the encrypted ciphertext contains many nonprintable characters.

```
String plaintextString = "Five Tons of Flax";
byte[] plaintextBytes = plaintextString.getBytes();
String keyString = "illuminati";
byte[] keyBytes = keyString.getBytes();
KeyParameter key = new KeyParameter(keyBytes);

TwofishEngine twofish = new TwofishEngine();
BufferedBlockCipher cipher = new PaddedBufferedBlockCipher(twofish);
cipher.init(true, key);

byte[] cipherBytes = new byte[cipher.getOutputSize(plaintextBytes.length)];

int cipherLength = cipher.processBytes(plaintextBytes, 0, ↵
        plaintextBytes.length, cipherBytes, 0);
cipher.doFinal(cipherBytes, cipherLength);
String cipherString = new String(cipherBytes);
System.out.println("Encrypted cipher is [" + cipherString + "]");
```

> **TIP:** Notice that we allocate a byte buffer large enough to hold the entire ciphertext. This works fine for short messages like this one, but if we were encrypting a 10MB data file, we might not be able to allocate that much contiguous memory. Later in this chapter, you'll see an example of how to allocate a smaller buffer that can be re-used to progressively encrypt or decrypt a larger message.

You should prepare to catch a CryptoException, which will occur if any problems happen during the process. When you run the code, you should see the encrypted message.

> **CAUTION:** In an actual application, you should use a randomly generated binary key for maximum security. Using a dictionary word, or even a combination of printable characters, makes your key easier to guess.

Using Bouncy Castle in Decryption

The exact same classes can be used for decryption as for encryption. Typically, you only need to substitute false for true in your cipher's init() method. The overall process remains the same: after initialization, you feed the ciphertext bytes into the cipher, finalize if necessary, and then use the output decoded bytes. The following example continues the previous one, taking the encrypted cipherBytes and restoring them to their original state. Note that we can re-use the existing crypto classes here.

```
cipher.init(false, key);
byte[] decryptedBytes = new byte[cipher.getOutputSize(cipherBytes.length)];
int decryptedLength = cipher.processBytes(cipherBytes, 0, ↩
        cipherBytes.length, decryptedBytes, 0);
cipher.doFinal(decryptedBytes, decryptedLength);
String decryptedString = new String(decryptedBytes);
System.out.println("Decrypted message is [" + decryptedString + "]");
```

Using Bouncy Castle to Create Digests

You can find classes for the most popular message digest algorithms in Bouncy Castle, including SHA1Digest and MD5Digest. Unlike ciphers, you do not need to initialize digests, and you interact with only one class to make the digest. If you just wish to create a simple checksum to ensure that the message was not corrupted, you can feed bytes directly to the digest. To cryptographically sign the message as discussed earlier, you should add a secret key to the beginning or the end of your message, generate the digest, and then attach the digest to the message. Digests typically follow the message body. The following code generates an SHA-1 hash for a message/key combination.

```
String message = "Yond Cassius has a lean and hungry look";
String postfix = "caesar";
byte[] messageBytes = message.getBytes();
byte[] postfixBytes = postfix.getBytes();
SHA1Digest digest = new SHA1Digest();
digest.update(messageBytes, 0, messageBytes.length);
digest.update(postfixBytes, 0, postfixBytes.length);
byte[] hash = new byte[digest.getDigestSize()];
digest.doFinal(hash, 0);
```

As with ciphers, digests generate their output as raw byte data. This poses a problem if your app transmits plain text, such as XML or JSON, because it cannot transmit the nonprintable characters. Developers customarily solve this problem by encoding hash values in Base64. Base64 converts raw byte values to a 64-character alphabet of printable characters, including A–Z, a–z, 0–9, "+", and "/". This will slightly expand the number of characters to send, but ensures that they can be transmitted. Bouncy Castle includes a useful `Base64Encoder` class that converts between binary and Base64. Despite the name, the class supports both encoding and decoding. The next example uses this class to convert the previous hash into a regular `String`, and then attaches it to the message for transmission. Depending on your message format, you may place the final hash in an XML tag or similar element.

```
Base64Encoder base64 = new Base64Encoder();
ByteArrayOutputStream out = new ByteArrayOutputStream();
base64.encode(hash, 0, hash.length, out);
byte[] base64Bytes = out.toByteArray();
String hashString = new String(base64Bytes);
String transmitted = message + "\n" + hashString;
System.out.println("Transmitted message is [" + transmitted + "]");
```

Using Bouncy Castle to Verify Digests

As you would expect, verification of a digest is the reverse of creating one. Once you receive the complete message, separate the digest from the message body. If the message is cryptographically signed, attach the key to the body. Use the same digest algorithm to calculate a hash. If the received hash used Base64 encoding, either decode the received hash or encode your calculated one. Finally, confirm whether the two hashes match. If they do, you know that the message sender possessed the proper key. The next example shows how to verify the message generated by the previous example.

```
String received;
int separation = received.indexOf('\n');
String receivedHash = received.substring(separation + 1);
String message = received.substring(0, separation);
byte[] messageBytes = message.getBytes();
String postfix = "caesar";
byte[] postfixBytes = postfix.getBytes();
SHA1Digest digest = new SHA1Digest();
digest.update(messageBytes, 0, messageBytes.length);
digest.update(postfixBytes, 0, postfixBytes.length);
byte[] calculatedHash = new byte[digest.getDigestSize()];
digest.doFinal(calculatedHash, 0);
ByteArrayOutputStream output = new ByteArrayOutputStream();
Base64Encoder base64 = new Base64Encoder();
base64.decode(receivedHash, output);
byte[] receivedHashBytes = output.toByteArray();
if (Arrays.equals(calculatedHash, receivedHashBytes))
{
    System.out.println("Message is valid.");
}
else
{
    System.out.println("Et tu, Internet?");
}
```

Bouncy Castle Analysis

Bouncy Castle offers several advantages that make it worth serious consideration:

- You can easily port your code to Java ME devices.

- Because of its wide use, it has received a lot of scrutiny and is widely considered to be quite secure.

- It provides classes for most major cryptographic algorithms.

You should look elsewhere if any of the following issues concern you:

- You must follow the terms of the open source license.

- No commercial support is available.

- Using Bouncy Castle will increase your application size.

RIM Crypto Classes

BlackBerry devices use a host of security options as part of their ordinary operations, and many of those algorithms are available for you to use as a developer. Most of these algorithms are the same as those available in Bouncy Castle, but these have been implemented specifically for Research In Motion and are available exclusively for development on BlackBerry devices.

> **CAUTION:** Depending on your geographic location, agreement with RIM, and other factors, you may not have access to the RIM Crypto API code signing keys required for these classes. If this is the case, consider using Bouncy Castle or another crypto solution.

An Introduction

While the RIM crypto libraries do not contain quite as many algorithms as Bouncy Castle, they do offer a wide range. You can start using them immediately as you would any other RIM-specific classes. You can find the available items in the `net.rim.device.api.crypto` package. Encryption and decryption happen through a set of standard elements:

- A key, implementing the `Key` interface, initializes a cipher with the secret or public key. The major types are `PublicKey`, `PrivateKey`, and `SymmetricKey`. Each cipher has its own particular implementing key class.

- Stream-based ciphers are provided as subclasses of `StreamEncryptor` or `SteamDecryptor`. Note that, unlike Bouncy Castle, the RIM API uses separate classes to handle decryption than are used for encryption.

- Block-based ciphers implement `BlockEncryptorEngine` or `BlockDecryptorEngine`. Subinterfaces define the type of key used, such as `PublicKeyEncryptorEngine` and `SymmetricKeyEncryptorEngine`.

- Block-based ciphers can use implementations of the `BlockFormatterEngine` interface to provide padding to their crypto tasks.

> **TIP:** Make use of Eclipse's auto-complete feature by typing the start of a class name, then holding down Ctrl while pressing Space. A list of valid selections will display. As a bonus, Eclipse automatically adds the required import statements to your `java` class. For example, if you wish to use RC5 encryption, you can type RC5 and press auto-complete, and you will see `RC5Key`, `RC5EncryptorEngine`, and `RC5DecryptorEngine`.

The actual classes are very well named, with all relevant classes sharing a common prefix. RIM divides its classes into a set of libraries. For space considerations, only a limited subset may be available on a given device. RIM guarantees that all devices will, at a minimum, include classes for SHA-1 checksums. Devices may optionally also include classes for WTLS, Wireless Transport Layer Security. This will be delivered in the file `net_rim_crypto_1.cod`, and includes support for additional digest and encryption algorithms, as shown in Table 5–3.

Table 5–3. *Crypto Resources in* `net_rim_crypto_1`

Digests	Encryptions
SHA256	AES
SHA384	ARC4
SHA512	DES
MD5	TripleDES
	RC4
	RC5
	RSA PKCS v1.5

To see if your device includes crypto1, select Options from the main menu, click Advanced Options, and then click Applications. Press the menu key and select Modules. This will bring up the list of every COD file loaded on the device. Scroll down and see if `net_rim_crypto_1` is included. Most modern devices include this library, along with its companions `net_rim_crypto_2` and `net_rim_crypto_3`.

Devices will offer net_rim_crypto_2 only if they have the first one. This library adds support for SSL/TLS (Secure Sockets Layer/Transport Layer Security), which introduces support for RSA PKCS (Public Key Cryptography Standard) version 2.0.

Finally, a device may have net_rim_crypto_3 if it has the first two. It adds a somewhat random assortment of additional, less commonly used crypto resources, as shown in Table 5–4.

Table 5–4. *Crypto Resources in* net_rim_crypto_3

Digests	Encryptions
MD2	CAST-128(CAST5)
MD4	RC2
RIPEMD-128	Skipjack
RIPEMD-160	ECIES
	ElGamal
	RSA-PSS
	RSA ANSI X9.31

In practice, unless you know that your users will likely have severely limited devices, you can write your app assuming all these algorithms are available, and instruct users to acquire the libraries if they happen to not be installed.

Encryption with the RIM Crypto Classes

While the general process of encryption proceeds similarly regardless of whether you use Bouncy Castle or the RIM libraries, the actual details vary. You start by creating the secret key for the operation. Next, create either a stream encryptor or a block encryptor engine. If using a block cipher and your messages are not already padded, create a formatter engine. The RIM BlockEncryptor class plays a similar role to the Bouncy Castle Cipher classes: it manages the details of passing around the input plain text, running the engine appropriately, and generating the output ciphertext. Unlike Bouncy Castle, which outputs directly to a byte array, RIM will write the ciphertext into an OutputStream. This lets you direct the encoded message to a file or network connection if you wish, without managing the actual bytes. The code that follows shows how to encrypt a message using the RIM RC5 classes.

```
String messageString = "The falcon cannot hear the falconer.";
byte[] messageBytes = messageString.getBytes();
String keyString = "beast";
byte[] keyBytes = keyString.getBytes();
```

```
RC5Key key = new RC5Key(keyBytes);
RC5EncryptorEngine engine = new RC5EncryptorEngine(key);
PKCS5FormatterEngine padder = new PKCS5FormatterEngine(engine);
ByteArrayOutputStream output = new ByteArrayOutputStream();
BlockEncryptor encryptor = new BlockEncryptor(padder, output);
encryptor.write(messageBytes);
encryptor.close();
output.flush();
byte[] cipherBytes = output.toByteArray();
String cipherString = new String(cipherBytes);
System.out.println("Encoded message is [" + cipherString + "]");
```

You can adapt this example for any other type of block cipher. For stream encryption, you will provide the OutputStream directly to the StreamEncryptor subclass's constructor and omit the padder.

Several exceptions may occur during encryption and decryption operations. CryptoUnsupportedOperationException indicates that this particular algorithm is not supported. CryptoTokenException occurs when the operation requires a physical token, such as a smart card, that is not present or has a problem. Finally, a generic IOException may occur due to problems writing to the requested OutputStream.

Decryption with the RIM Crypto Classes

As mentioned before, the RIM libraries include separate classes to handle the decryption step. For example, the RC5DecryptorEngine is the counterpart of RC5EncryptorEngine, and a BlockUnformatterEngine matches a BlockFormatterEngine. The most significant difference between encryption and decryption is that decryption writes its output into a provided byte array, not an OutputStream. If you do not know in advance how large a message will be, you will need to progressively build up the decrypted message yourself. The following example illustrates how to do this, decrypting the ciphertext that we generated in the previous section. You'll notice the loop that repeatedly reads data in small chunks. This is a common pattern that is used in many I/O operations other than crypto.

```
byte[] cipherBytes;
String keyString = "beast";
byte[] keyBytes = keyString.getBytes();
RC5Key key = new RC5Key(keyBytes);
RC5DecryptorEngine engine = new RC5DecryptorEngine(key);
PKCS5UnformatterEngine unpadder = new PKCS5UnformatterEngine(engine);
ByteArrayInputStream input = new ByteArrayInputStream(cipherBytes);
BlockDecryptor decryptor = new BlockDecryptor(unpadder, input);
ByteArrayOutputStream decryptedStream = new ByteArrayOutputStream();
byte[] buffer = new byte[1024];
int bytesRead = 0;
do
{
    bytesRead = decryptor.read(buffer);
    if (bytesRead != -1)
    {
        decryptedStream.write(buffer, 0, bytesRead);
    }
```

```
} while (bytesRead != -1);
byte[] decryptedBytes = decryptedStream.toByteArray();
String decodedMessage = new String(decryptedBytes);
System.out.println("Original message was [" + decodedMessage + "]");
```

Using RIM Crypto with Digests

The RIM crypto packages include several popular hash algorithms, including multiple versions of SHA and MD. As when creating digests for Bouncy Castle, you may run a digest over an entire message and obtain a hash. For this section's examples, we'll create unsigned digests to simply verify message integrity, but you can apply the exact same principles as before to cryptographically sign your messages.

RIM does add some convenient classes to use in digest operations. Unlike Bouncy Castle digests, which focus mainly on byte arrays for operations, RIM digests can work with streams. You may choose to wrap several streams together to obtain a desired result. The following code example demonstrates how to use two useful utility streams, Base64OutputStream and DigestOutputStream, to automatically Base64 encode the digest value. Data flows from the input bytes, through the digest algorithm, out to the digest stream, then through Base64 encoding, and finally to the destination bytes.

```
String message = "Not all who wander are lost.";
byte[] messageBytes = message.getBytes();
MD5Digest digest = new MD5Digest();
ByteArrayOutputStream bytesOut = new ByteArrayOutputStream();
Base64OutputStream base64 = new Base64OutputStream(bytesOut);
DigestOutputStream digestOut = new DigestOutputStream(digest, base64);
digest.update(messageBytes);
digestOut.flush();
byte[] base64Checksum = bytesOut.toByteArray();
String base64String = new String(base64Checksum);
```

If you wish to verify the checksum for data you have received, follow the exact same code as before, comparing the calculated base64Checksum with the version you received. If they are identical, the message was not corrupted since it was sent. You may also use a cryptographic signing strategy if you wish to verify the authenticity of the sender.

RIM Crypto Analysis

Turn to the built-in RIM solution in the following situations:

- You want to minimize the size of your application.

- You cannot accept the conditions of an open source library.

- You expect to run only on BlackBerry devices.

- You control the BlackBerry devices that will be running your app.

Consider another solution if the following are high priorities for you:

- There is a chance that users have removed support for advanced crypto from their devices.

■   Certain crypto algorithms are not supported.

Using the Certicom Classes

Several classes in the `net.rim.device.api.crypto` package are not available for use in most applications. However, if you are developing commercial applications with needs such as secure electronic commerce, you may find them very useful.

An Introduction

You can safely write all RIM crypto classes into your code and even run with them in the simulator, but when you try to run your app on the device, you may face an error message like the following:

```
Uncaught exception: Missing RCC signature. Not allowed to access Certicom
functionality.
```

To access these classes, you must contact Certicom, a subsidiary of Research In Motion that owns the rights to these functions. You can do this by accessing its web site at `http://certicom.com/rim`, where you can contact a member of its sales team. Once you receive approval, you will receive additional code signing keys that permit access to these restricted APIs. Certicom classes will appeal most to "serious" applications with strong business aspects, particularly mobile commerce. Most applications can consider using other forms of encryption instead, including the RSA classes included in Bouncy Castle.

You can determine which classes require the use of a Certicom license by consulting the API javadocs. They include some interesting ones based on public key systems, including the Elliptic Curve Integrated Encryption Scheme (ECIES), the Digital Signature Algorithm (DSA), Diffie-Hellman (DH), Key Exchange Algorithm (KEA), and RSA.

Public key encryption tackles the difficult problem of how to establish secure communication with another party if you have not previously agreed upon a secret key to use. Our previous encryption example required both the sender and the receiver to use the same key, which is reasonable if we are writing the code for both parties, but would not work in situations where we expect to receive messages from other applications or senders. Public Key Infrastructure (PKI) is based upon some interesting modern mathematics that shows how you can create a system with multiple keys that allows for one-way encryption. In other words, everyone can know a public key that allows them to encrypt a message, but only one person knows the secret private key used to decrypt it. Public key encryption is most often thought of as encoding and decoding messages, but it also plays a useful role in determining another party's authenticity. If you receive a message from someone else, and can decrypt it using his or her public key, then you know that it was signed by the actual sender's private key. RSA, the most famous public key system, relies on modulus operations and the difficulty of finding very large prime numbers. If you're interested in learning more about the history and mathematics behind public key encryption, I highly recommend *The Code Book*, by Simon Singh (Anchor, 2000), the most intelligent and approachable book I've found yet on the topic of cryptography.

Encryption with Certicom Public Keys

RIM's asymmetric ciphers are based around the CryptoSystem interface. Each also includes a PublicKey, a PrivateKey, and several other classes relating to that crypto system's operation. The issue of key distribution is outside the scope of this chapter. If your app only needs to encrypt outgoing messages, it can be configured with the recipient's public key, but if the app needs to decrypt incoming messages, you must decide how best to give senders access to the client's public key. With that in mind, the following code demonstrates how you can use Certicom's implementation of RSA cryptography to encrypt a message. Here, we construct a random pair of public and private keys; in real applications, these would likely be generated from known key values. Because the underlying cipher is a block cipher, we wrap and pad it as before, and then run the input through the cipher to generate the encrypted message.

```
String message = "Purple monkey dishwasher";
byte[] messageBytes = message.getBytes();
RSACryptoSystem rsa = new RSACryptoSystem(1024);
RSAKeyPair keyPair = new RSAKeyPair(rsa);
RSAEncryptorEngine rsaEncryption = new RSAEncryptorEngine(↵
        keyPair.getRSAPublicKey());
PKCS5FormatterEngine padder = new PKCS5FormatterEngine(rsaEncryption);
ByteArrayOutputStream output = new ByteArrayOutputStream();
BlockEncryptor encryptor = new BlockEncryptor(padder, output);
encryptor.write(messageBytes);
encryptor.close();
output.flush();
byte[] ciphertextBytes = output.toByteArray();
```

Decryption with Certicom Public Keys

To decrypt this message, the receiver will use a private key part of the pair, and then run the received message through the decrypting system. The BlockDecryptor class operates on a byte array, so the following example builds up a total output array through repeated operations on a byte buffer.

```
RSADecryptorEngine rsaDecryption = new RSADecryptorEngine(↵
        keyPair.getRSAPrivateKey());
PKCS5UnformatterEngine unpadder = new PKCS5UnformatterEngine(rsaDecryption);
ByteArrayInputStream input = new ByteArrayInputStream(ciphertextBytes);
BlockDecryptor decryptor = new BlockDecryptor(unpadder, input);
byte[] buffer = new byte[1024];
ByteArrayOutputStream out = new ByteArrayOutputStream();
int bytesRead = 0;
do
{
    bytesRead = decryptor.read(buffer);
```

```
    if (bytesRead != -1)
    {
        out.write(buffer, 0, bytesRead);
    }
} while (bytesRead != -1);
byte[] decryptedBytes = out.toByteArray();
String decryptedMessage = new String(decryptedBytes);
System.out.println("Decrypted message is " + decryptedMessage);
```

As with the regular RIM crypto package, you will need to catch `CryptoException` and `IOException`. Even if your application has received Certicom signatures, there's still a small chance that the required crypto libraries will not be loaded on the device, in which case your app may choose to present an error message.

> **CAUTION:** Several class names in the RIM crypto package clash with those found in the standard Java libraries and other packages. For example, `RSAPrivateKey` is used both in `net.rim.device.api.crypto` and in `java.security.interfaces`. Double-check the package names of your imports.

If you wish to store keys for crypto operations, consider using the keystore classes located in the `net.device.api.crypto.keystore` package. You can choose from a variety of keystore types, including stores that persist only until the device is reset and stores that can be synced to the user's computer via the desktop manager. Also available under the crypto package are classes for certificate management, useful to help control and determine the authority that backs keys you receive.

Certicom Analysis

For the most part, use of Certicom requires the same choices considered for RIM Crypto. Specifically, you keep your code size small and avoid potential licensing issues, but are restricted to a particular set of ciphers and locked in to RIM's API. The extra detriment for Certicom is the additional cost involved in acquiring the keys. Balanced against this is the confidence many institutions and individuals have in dealing with a business as a provider of strong encryption.

Other Encryption Choices

So far, this chapter has examined how to implement cryptographic systems within your app. You have seen how this requires making appropriate choices about the specific crypto algorithm you will use, how to create and distribute keys, and other issues. However, you can get cryptographic security through existing systems. Consider the options covered in this section if you want more passive protection.

HTTPS Encryption

If your app communicates with a server that already supports HTTPS, you may be able to omit additional encryption in your messages. BlackBerry devices support HTTPS out of the box, and a connection between your app and an HTTPS server will be as secure as the connection between your web browser and an HTTPS web site. You can create an HTTPS connection by using the proper protocol string, as in the example that follows:

```
HttpsConnection https = (HttpsConnection) Connector↵
        .open("https://www.amazon.com");
```

HTTPS encryption uses public key encryption. When your app first issues a request to a server using the https:// protocol, the TLS/SSL will take over. A handshake begins between the client and the server. The client will notify the server what types of encryption it supports (DES, DSA, etc.) and provide a random string to the server. The server will respond with its own random string, along with a certificate and its public key. The client will inspect the certificate to see whether it is valid; if it is, it can trust that it is dealing with the actual server. The client then creates a random premaster secret that will be used as the basis for an encryption key, encrypts that premaster secret with the server's public key, and then transmits it to the server.

Even if an attacker intercepts this transmission, he will not be able to decrypt the premaster secret without the server's private key. The server can decrypt the premaster secret. Both the client and the server then use that premaster secret to generate a master secret, and finally create session keys from the master secret. The session key is a symmetric key that will be used to encrypt all future traffic between the client and the server during this session (that is, until it times out).

The initial handshake can be a little slow. Once the symmetric key is determined and encrypted traffic begins, transmission will be a little slower and take a little more space than it would in regular HTTP communication due to the overhead of encryption. The difference tends not to be very noticeable.

If your application uses lower-level socket programming instead of higher-level HTTP communication, you can use the ssl:// or tls:// protocols, which will generate an SSL or TLS session. These perform handshakes similarly to HTTPS, but subsequent traffic is carried over a low-level socket instead of higher-level HTTP. The following code demonstrates how to create each type of connection.

```
SecureConnection ssl = (SecureConnection) Connector↵
        .open("ssl://myserver.com:5555");
SecureConnection tls = (SecureConnection) Connector↵
        .open("tls://myserver.com:5556");
```

After the connection opens, you can use each SecureConnection as you would an ordinary SocketConnection. You can also call getSecurityInfo() to obtain additional details about the negotiated security, such as the server's certificate and the cipher being used for crypto.

> **NOTE:** After establishing a secure connection, encryption is applied in both directions, on both outgoing and incoming data.

MDS Encryption

All traffic between the BlackBerry device and the Mobile Data System is automatically encrypted. As a result, if you make sure that outgoing traffic goes to a server on your corporate BES environment and travels over the BES network, you will not need any extra encryption. However, traffic sent between the MDS and the ultimate destination server is not encrypted. You still may need to use encryption if the receiving server expects encrypted traffic, or if you are concerned about eavesdropping from other entities within the corporate network.

File Encryption

In addition to manual file encryption using Bouncy Castle or the RIM Crypto APIs, you may also choose to apply built-in support for file encryption. RIM offers a custom interface called `ExtendedFileConnection` that extends the standard `FileConnection` interface. You can cast any `FileConnection` to an `ExtendedFileConnection` to gain access to several additional encryption features.

- `enableDRMForwardLock()` will allow other applications on the device to read this file, but make it unreadable when transferred off the device. If the user copies the file to his or her computer, it will transfer in an encrypted format. This method works on both the /store and the /SDCard roots.

- `setControlledAccess()` controls access to this file so that only your application can read or write it. You must obtain a `CodeSigningKey` for your module and then set it on the `ExtendedFileConnection`. When the file is accessed in the future, the OS will verify that the request comes from the module that signed it. This method works on the SD card but not on the internal memory store.

In both cases, you must set any protection before you create the file. You can access standard file encryption as shown in the following example.

```
ExtendedFileConnection file = (ExtendedFileConnection)Connector.open
    ("file:///SDCard/BlackBerry/purchase.mp3");
file.enableDRMForwardLock();
file.create();
```

After creating the file, you can open streams to read and write data as you normally would. The operating system automatically applies and removes encryption, with no extra intervention needed.

App: Securing MediaGrabber

MediaGrabber provides a convenient way to record your thoughts, take pictures of your surroundings, and send such info off to a place where you can review it later. Occasionally, though, you might be a little nervous about what happens to your media once it leaves your phone. Perhaps your musings about pursuing another job will be overheard by a bored IT worker monitoring your business e-mail account. Or maybe you don't want your father or son to accidentally open pictures from your Vegas trip sent to your shared home computer. Let's add an extra layer of security by providing the ability to encrypt the media we send out.

Adding Encryption

We will use the DES encryption algorithm for this enhancement, using the version provided in the RIM crypto packages. DES has some shortcomings; modern computers can use brute force to crack it. I chose it here because the key size is nice and short. You may choose to use AES-128 or a similar block cipher for added security at the cost of greater complexity.

To add an extra layer of security, we will also use an initialization vector. The vector, known as IV, provides a bit of random information that combines with the key in the encryption. This helps protect the secrecy of the key. If you encrypt two messages with the same key, then attackers can more easily decrypt the messages; using a random IV is one of several ways to help avoid this problem. The IV protects the key but is not itself secret, so we will send it along with the message so the recipient can decrypt it.

The actual changes to add encryption are rather brief. We will add the following two new instance variables to the SendingScreen to manage the crypto operations.

```
private boolean encrypt;
private String iv;
```

We will update the constructor to accept encryption as an additional parameter. Then we can write a new method encryptData() that applies our secret DES key to binary data. I find it easiest to represent key values in hexadecimal strings. Each character in a hex string can represent 16 characters, and so it holds 4 bits of data. We can write simple utility functions that will translate hex string values to and from the byte arrays that the crypto classes prefer to work with.

Finally, we need to update the createMessage() method, which will check to see whether the caller requested encryption. If so, it will call our new method to encrypt the attachment data and include the initialization vector information in the plain text of the message. The rest of the send operation runs the same as before. Listing 5–1 shows the modified methods.

Listing 5–1. *Optionally Encrypting Attachments Prior to Sending*

```java
private byte[] bytesFromHexString(String input)
{
    int length = input.length();
    // Each hex character represents 4 bits, so 1
    // byte is 2 characters.
    byte[] bytes = new byte[length / 2];
    for (int i = 0; i < length; i += 2)
    {
        bytes[i / 2] = (byte) Integer.parseInt(input.substring(i, i + 2),
                16);
    }
    return bytes;
}

private String hexFromBytes(byte[] input)
{
    int length = input.length;
    StringBuffer builder = new StringBuffer(length * 2);
    for (int i = 0; i < length; ++i)
    {
        byte value = (byte) input[i];
        String hex = Integer.toHexString(value);
        if (hex.length() == 8)
        {
            // Integer.toHexString assumes "negative" 4-byte inputs yield an
            // 8-character string, so trim off all but the last 2
            // characters.
            hex = hex.substring(6);
        }
        builder.append(hex);
    }
    return builder.toString();
}

private byte[] encryptData(byte[] in) throws CryptoException, IOException
{
    ByteArrayOutputStream out = new ByteArrayOutputStream();
    String hexKey = "2BEAFABBABE4AFAD";
    byte[] binaryKey = bytesFromHexString(hexKey);
    DESKey key = new DESKey(binaryKey);
    DESEncryptorEngine encryptor = new DESEncryptorEngine(key);
    InitializationVector vector = new InitializationVector(8);
    byte[] ivValue = vector.getData();
    iv = hexFromBytes(ivValue);
    CFBEncryptor cfb = new CFBEncryptor(encryptor, vector, out, true);
    cfb.write(in);
    out.flush();
    return out.toByteArray();
}
private Message createMessage(String recipient, String type,
        String filename, String message) throws MessagingException,
        CryptoException, IOException
{
    if (encrypt)
        data = encryptData(data);
    Store defaultStore = Session.getDefaultInstance().getStore();
```

```
        Folder sentFolder = defaultStore.getFolder(Folder.SENT);
        Message outgoing = new Message(sentFolder);
        Address friend = new Address(recipient, "");
        outgoing.addRecipient(Message.RecipientType.TO, friend);
        outgoing.setSubject(message);
        Multipart multipart = new Multipart();
        SupportedAttachmentPart file = new SupportedAttachmentPart(multipart,
                type, filename, data);
        multipart.addBodyPart(file);
        TextBodyPart text = new TextBodyPart(multipart);
        if (encrypt)
        {
            text.setContent("The attached file is encrypted, the vector is "
                    + iv);
        }
        else
        {
            text.setContent("Check this out!");
        }
        multipart.addBodyPart(text);
        outgoing.setContent(multipart);
        return outgoing;
}
```

Better Choices

Our little app is getting quite feature-rich. Let's allow our users to easily decide what operation they want to take on each piece of media they record. We can easily do this by adding additional menu items in the recording screen: rather than automatically perform a particular operation once they acquire the media, we will allow them to make a selection from a menu. We will add two new states, STATE_RECORDED and STATE_RECORDED_IMAGE, to represent the condition where the user has finished media capture. We also will store information about the captured media. Based on these states, we present additional options in the menu. Best of all, the user can now perform multiple operations on the same media; for example, the user can first view it, and then send two encrypted copies. Listing 5–2 shows the modifications to our improved recording screen.

Listing 5–2. *A Better Recording Screen*

```
package com.apress.king.mediagrabber;
// Imports here

public class RecordingScreen extends MainScreen implements PlayerListener
{
    public static final int STATE_WAITING = 1;
    public static final int STATE_READY = 2;
    public static final int STATE_RECORDING = 3;
    public static final int STATE_RECORDED = 4;
    public static final int STATE_RECORDED_IMAGE = 5;

    // Additional member variables
    private String filename;
    private String contentType;
```

```
    private String message;
    private byte[] data;

    // New menu items
    private MenuItem playItem = new MenuItem("Play", 0, 0)
    {
        public void run()
        {
            play();
        }
    };
    private MenuItem showItem = new MenuItem("Show", 0, 0)
    {
        public void run()
        {
            showPicture();
        }
    };
    private MenuItem sendItem = new MenuItem("Send", 0, 0)
    {
        public void run()
        {
            send(false);
        }
    };
    private MenuItem sendEncryptedItem = new MenuItem("Send Encrypted", 0, 0)
    {
        public void run()
        {
            send(true);
        }
    };

    // New menu options
    public void makeMenu(Menu menu, int instance)
    {
        if (instance == Menu.INSTANCE_DEFAULT)
        {
            if (state == STATE_READY)
            {
                menu.add(goItem);
            }
            else if (state == STATE_RECORDING)
            {
                menu.add(stopItem);
            }
            else if (state == STATE_RECORDED)
            {
                menu.add(playItem);
                menu.add(sendItem);
                menu.add(sendEncryptedItem);
            }
            else if (state == STATE_RECORDED_IMAGE)
            {
                menu.add(showItem);
                menu.add(sendItem);
                menu.add(sendEncryptedItem);
```

```
                }
            menu.add(doneItem);
        }
        super.makeMenu(menu, instance);
    }

    // Modified capture
    private void takeSnapShot()
    {
        try
        {
            data = video
                    .getSnapshot("encoding=jpeg&width=640&height=480&quality=normal");
            if (data != null)
            {
                String file = location + "/image.jpg";
                writeToFile(data, file);
                status.setText("Image taken");
                filename = "image.jpg";
                contentType = "image/jpeg";
                message = "Here's a picture!";
                state = STATE_RECORDED_IMAGE;
            }
            else
            {
                status.setText("Please try again later.");
            }
        }
        catch (IOException ioe)
        {
            status.setText(ioe.getMessage());
        }
        catch (MediaException me)
        {
            status.setText(me.getMessage());
        }
    }

    private void stop()
    {
        try
        {
            if (type == RECORD_AUDIO || type == RECORD_VIDEO)
            {
                recorder.commit();
                data = dataOut.toByteArray();
                if (type == RECORD_AUDIO)
                {
                    String file = location + "/audio.amr";
                    writeToFile(data, file);
                    contentType = "audio/amr";
                    message = "Here's some sound!";
                    filename = "audio.amr";
                }
                else
                {
                    String file = location + "/video.3gp";
```

```
                    writeToFile(data, file);
                    contentType = "video/3gp";
                    message = "Here's a video!";
                    filename = "video.3gp";
                }
                status.setText("Data saved");
                state = STATE_RECORDED;
            }
        }
        catch (IOException ioe)
        {
            status.setText(ioe.getMessage());
        }
        finally
        {
            if (dataOut != null)
            {
                try
                {
                    dataOut.close();
                }
                catch (Exception e)
                {

                }
            }
            dataOut = new ByteArrayOutputStream();
        }
    }

    // New option implementations
    private void play()
    {
        Screen playback = new PlayingScreen(location + "/" + filename, message);
        UiApplication.getUiApplication().pushScreen(playback);
    }

    private void send(boolean encrypt)
    {
        SendingScreen sending = new SendingScreen(contentType, filename,
                message, data, encrypt);
        UiApplication.getUiApplication().pushScreen(sending);
    }

    private void showPicture()
    {
        Bitmap taken = Bitmap.createBitmapFromBytes(data, 0, data.length, 1);
        Screen reviewer = new MainScreen();
        BitmapField bitmap = new BitmapField(taken);
        reviewer.add(bitmap);
        UiApplication.getUiApplication().pushScreen(reviewer);
    }
}
```

Decryption

Run the app in the simulator first. You should be able to send both encrypted and decrypted versions. Now, load it on the phone and send yourself an encrypted message.

When you try to open the attached file, at best you'll get an error message. In the worst case, you may crash your player application. Looks like the encryption works—now, how to reverse it? Unless you already have a tool in place, I recommend using the popular openssl program. openssl is installed by default on modern Linux and OS X machines, and is also included as part of the Cygwin package for Windows, available at www.cygwin.com. openssl is mainly used for secure connections, but also contains a very useful and powerful set of tools for encryption and decryption.

Save your encrypted file to your local disk, and then navigate there in a command line. You can perform the decryption with a single step that should look like the following:

```
openssl enc -d -des-cfb8 -K 2BEAFABBABE4AFAD -iv 36bd3018c8116220 ↩
    -in audio.amr -out decrypted.amr
```

Let us break this apart and see what each option does:

- enc tells openssl to run in crypto mode.

- -d is used for decryption; use -e to encrypt instead.

- -des-cfb8 corresponds to the encryption we used, a DES key and a CFB encryptor with an 8-byte IV. You can type openssl enc --help to see a complete list of supported ciphers.

- -K provides the secret key.

- -iv is the random initialization vector. You should substitute the value received in the e-mail.

- -in and -out control input and output respectively. Substitute the actual file names here.

The operation should run without any errors. If it doesn't, please double-check your encryption code and the arguments to openssl. Now, open your attachment again. Huzzah! You can now safely view it. Congratulations on creating a secure application.

Paranoia

Or is it secure? At a minimum, you'll want to change the key value; otherwise, anyone reading this book will be able to easily crack your security. Even a new key may not suffice, though. Let's perform a quick audit of the app.

In the same directory as your .project and MediaGrabber.alx file, you will see a MediaGrabber.cod file. This contains the code that is actually loaded onto the BlackBerry device. Open this file with a hex editor. On Windows, I prefer XVI32, a freeware hex editor that you can find with a simple web search. You will see the program data, much of which is unreadable. Now, search in this file for our secret key, 2BEAFABBABE4AFAD or whatever you have substituted for it. Eep! There it is, plain as day.

This is a habitual problem in computer security. In order to perform crypto, the program must contain crypto keys. It must keep those keys secret. And yet, those keys must be distributed within, generated by, or sent to the app. How can you keep attackers from discovering these keys?

There are several strategies available. The more obfuscation you use, the more casual attackers you will deter. You can split up the key into multiple parts and then recombine the pieces. You can generate the key in memory—for example, by shifting every letter one position down the alphabet. You can encrypt a key with another key, although this leads to a chicken-and-egg problem. Ultimately, a sufficiently determined hacker with unlimited time and resources can theoretically decompile and reverse engineer your program to discover your keys. Depending on your app design, you may be able to use public key encryption where it does not matter if an attacker discovers the public key.

WANT MORE?

Cryptography is a fascinating area, and, if it interests you, you can easily spend hours, days, or years reading about different options and experimenting with them. You can pursue a few extra items in MediaGrabber to make it more secure for your users.

- Allow the user to enter his or her own key that will be used for encryption instead of using a hard-coded one. *Extra credit:* Generate a strong key based on text that the user enters (e.g., generate a value like 0x42FAAB783C10CE77 from the password tristero). *Super extra credit:* Securely store the user's key so the user doesn't need to type it in every time he or she sends an encrypted message.

- Add support for multiple ciphers to the app, such as AES, TripleDES, and RC5. Allow the user to select which encryption method to use when sending. Keep in mind that this also will require support for multiple key sizes.

- Experiment with using the Bouncy Castle library instead of the RIM crypto library. The encryption logic can remain largely the same while you modify your code to fit the Bouncy Castle API.

- Make your app as secure against hackers as you can. Conceal your key within the .cod file. Experiment with ways to generate key values that also allow the receiver to figure out the key.

Program security requires constant vigilance, so completing these exercises will help you develop the mindset of constant paranoia and inquisitiveness that will help you discover flaws before they can be exploited.

Excelsior

Choices abound in the world of security. The rich resources of the built-in RIM crypto libraries and the free offerings of Bouncy Castle make it very unlikely that you will ever find yourself lacking crypto options. The bigger challenge is to make sense of what's out there and pick what makes the most sense for your app. If your app is for personal use or you just want to discourage potential hackers, you won't need very strong cryptography. Applying even the simplest cipher will deter the vast majority of abusers, who will move on to easier targets. However, if you need to craft a system that manages people's money, personal information, or sensitive data, you must fulfill the mission of protecting that trust. Involve others, consult experts, and make sure others review and test your app.

Please keep in mind that the examples in this chapter included hard-coded keys for maximum readability, but you will rarely hard-code keys in true applications. Consider whether each user will need his or her own key, and if so, how to distribute them. Think about whether you can algorithmically generate a key, and if you can, how to ensure both parties stay in sync.

"Security through obscurity" persistently thwarts good design. Too many people convince themselves that, by not talking about how their app works, they are protecting against intrusion. You will know your app is secure if you can tell people every detail about how it works and still know that they will not be able to crack it.

Fortunately, simply by thinking about these issues, you already have a head start on many other developers. Not to mention, you have more than a head start on using advanced BlackBerry APIs—you have completed the race!

Part 1 of this book has provided you with the tools for creating feature-rich applications that exploit the best built-in capabilities of BlackBerry devices. Up until this point, our apps have been growing upward, gaining new functionality. Next, we will turn our focus inward and start exploring ways to more tightly integrate with other systems on the device.

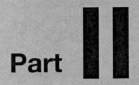

Device Integration

You now have the tools to make a useful and interesting mobile BlackBerry app. If you're lucky, lots of people will get it... and it will sit in the Downloads folder or at the bottom of their home screen. It may be great while people are using it, but even the best app becomes forgettable if people don't see it often.

This next section focuses on *integration*, the process of connecting your app with other powerful apps and features on the device. You will gain access to the user's personal address book, calendar, and more, so that you can access information and provide new updates. You will learn how to use the BlackBerry web browser in your app, and use your app in the BlackBerry web browser. Finally, you will learn how to elevate your app to the level of a first-class application, capable of providing services to other apps on the phone and displaying custom icons from the BlackBerry menus.

By the end of this part, your apps won't just have more features: they'll also be irresistible. Obtaining this level of polish and mutual cooperation with built-in device applications can turn your app from something you download into a part of your daily routine.

Chapter 6

Personal Information

If you work for a large company, your boss probably has a large Rolodex with all his business contacts' information in it. The boss may have a secretary who manages scheduling and appointment reminders. If you're like most programmers, you likely don't have either of those. What you do have is a computer in your pocket with the capability of storing all sorts of personal information: your friends' names, their phone numbers and email addresses, your plans for the weekend, a grocery list, and more. Our mobile phones have become intensely personal devices, one of the few things that we bring with us almost all day long. We trust the phone with a great deal of information, and, if users are willing to share that information, your apps can become far more useful, immediate, and personal.

This chapter looks at the various options offered by the BlackBerry API for integrating with the user's personal information. Their friends will be your friends, their calendar an open book, their notes a reminder to you. Of course, not every app will need to connect in these ways, but almost everything can benefit from a little personal touch.

Contacts

People buy phones to communicate. Specifically, they buy to communicate with other people through voice calls or messaging. The built-in address book app (sometimes labeled Contacts) is usually one of the first items a user will see when they turn on their BlackBerry, and even the most die-hard luddites take the time to enter their friends' information for easier calls. RIM exposes every piece of information about those contacts through the Personal Information Management (PIM) interface, which also forms the basis for other types of information. In this section you will learn how to use PIM in order to query and manipulate the user's contacts.

An Overview of PIM

The PIM API was first deployed as part of JSR 75, the same standard that brought us the FileConnection API. It has proven extremely successful, and now runs on the vast majority of Java ME phones as well as all BlackBerry devices with software version 4.0

or higher. This common basis makes it much easier to port applications between BlackBerry and other devices.

PIM and Lists

PIM took a different approach from FileConnection, eschewing the GCF in favor of a more specialized interface. Rather than allowing for arbitrary types of personal information stores, it defined a particular set of the most common. These stores include a user's address-book, calendar, and to-do list. Each type of store is presented as a list—conceptually, an ordered sequence of records, whether those records are contacts or appointments. Because PIM predefined the lists, RIM could not add specialized classes directly; however, because the lists are presented as interfaces, RIM derived from those interfaces to add their own specialized behavior. Figure 6–1 illustrates the current class hierarchy for list management on BlackBerry devices.

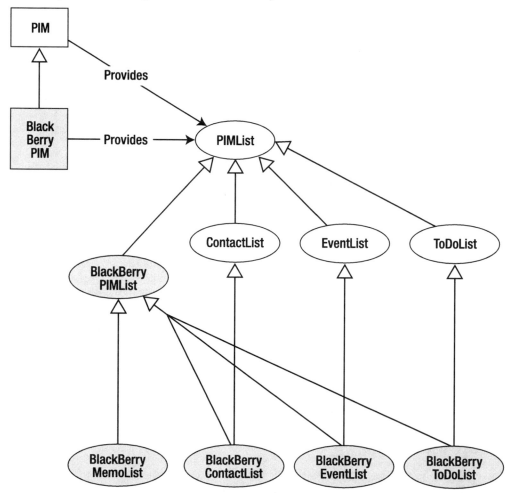

Figure 6–1. *PIM access to information lists*

The factory classes PIM and BlackBerryPIM provide access to the lists, as well as methods for serializing or deserializing individual list items. These two classes actually refer to the same singleton object, and you can safely cast them back and forth. BlackBerryPIM defines access to RIM-exclusive lists and capabilities. Each PIMList comes in both a standard and a BlackBerry-specific flavor. The BlackBerry versions of these classes offer additional useful features on top of those included in the original JSR specification. For example, a ContactList presents ways to look up contacts by searching for certain criteria, while a BlackBerryContactList adds the ability to search for contact groups, or to directly retrieve a contact by their unique ID. As with PIM and BlackBerryPIM, each PIMList and BlackBerryPIMList is a singleton object, so you can cast each into the other version.

> **TIP:** If you need the extra abilities offered by the BlackBerry version of a list, go ahead and use it. Otherwise, stick with the plain version to ease porting to other platforms.

RIM created a special type of list, BlackBerryMemoList, exclusively for BlackBerry devices. As you might expect, this provides access to the Memos application.

Any changes you make to personal information will appear in other PIM-related apps and vice versa. So, if you add a ToDo list item within your app, it will appear the next time the user opens their Tasks application.

You open a list by providing the enumerated type to the PIM singleton and casting to the appropriate type. The returned lists share many characteristics with I/O connections: you can open lists in read-only, write-only, or read-write modes, and you should close them when finished, as shown below. Keeping PIMList instances open may block others from accessing the associated data.

```
PIM pim = PIM.getInstance();
ContactList contacts = (ContactList)pim.openPIMList(
        PIM.CONTACT_LIST, PIM.READ_ONLY);
// Use the contacts here.
contacts.close();
```

> **NOTE:** You can find the PIM classes in the javax.microedition.pim package.

Almost every PIM-related operation can fail with a PIMException. The exact reason for the exception will vary from operation to operation; when opening a PIMList, it may fail if the requested list isn't available. A variety of methods can also throw SecurityException, usually because the user hasn't authorized the app to read or modify personal data.

Certain device configurations may support multiple lists of each type. One ContactList may expose contacts stored on a SIM card, while another ContactList represents the contacts on a Microsoft Exchange server. The PIM class provides methods to determine what list names are available and to grab those particular lists, as shown in the example below.

```
PIM pim = PIM.getInstance();
String[] listNames = pim.listPIMLists(PIM.EVENT_LIST);
for (int i = 0; i < listNames.length; ++i)
{
    EventList contacts = (EventList)pim.openPIMList(
            PIM.EVENT_LIST, PIM.READ_WRITE, listNames[i]);
    // Use the list
    contacts.close();
}
```

Starting with BlackBerry OS 6, you can create your own custom PIM lists by using `BlackBerryPIM.createPIMList()`. As of this writing you can only create new contact lists, but future versions may support creating custom calendars, tasks, and so on. Creating a custom list allows you to segregate one set of contacts from the user's other contacts; for example, a fleet management app might place all customers' contact information in a separate list separately from the user's personal or corporate contacts. You can delete a custom contact list by calling `BlackBerryPIM.removePIMList()`.

> **NOTE:** Custom contact lists only exist on the client, and do not sync like the regular contact lists.

The device maintains each list separately from other lists. You cannot combine all lists of one type into one master list.

Categories

Each type of PIMList can contain an arbitrary number of categories. Categories logically group together groups of items. In a ToDo list, you might have separate categories for Sales, Research, Projects, and Personal. Then, when adding a new ToDo item, you could choose to assign it to an appropriate category.

> **NOTE:** Preloaded BlackBerry applications sometimes refer to a category as a Filter.

Categories are entirely optional. `PIMList` includes a special type of category called `UNCATEGORIZED` that is associated with every item in the list that does not belong to any category. If you do choose to assign a category to an item, that category must already exist. You can determine this by querying the associated list as shown below.

`String[] categories = contacts.getCategories();`

Categories in PIM resemble tags more than folders. Each individual item might belong to zero, one, or many categories. If you need to pick up flowers for a co-worker's birthday party, you might file that in your ToDo list under both Projects and Personal. Later, when you filter by Projects, Personal, or all, you will see that reminder. Figure 6–2 shows a theoretical user's address book as organized by categories.

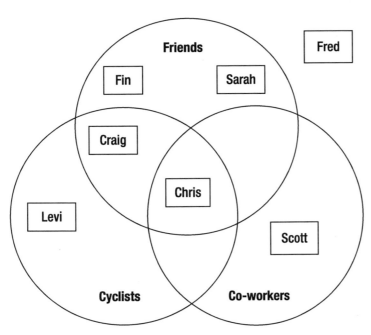

Figure 6–2. *Contacts shown by category*

Items

Up until now, all the classes in this chapter have offered organization and access. However, items are the heart of PIM. They provide the actual data that users care about: a person's name, the time of an appointment, and the priority of a task.

Each PIMList provides access to a set of PIMItem objects. Every item in a PIMList has the same class type: an EventList will only contain Event objects, a ContactList contains Contact objects, and so on. As with the PIMList class, each PIMItem subclass has an associated BlackBerry version as well. Figure 6–3 shows the complete hierarchy for Contact items; the same structure applies to all other types of items as well. Once again, you can always downcast from a PIMItem to its BlackBerry counterpart, such as from a Contact to a BlackBerryContact.

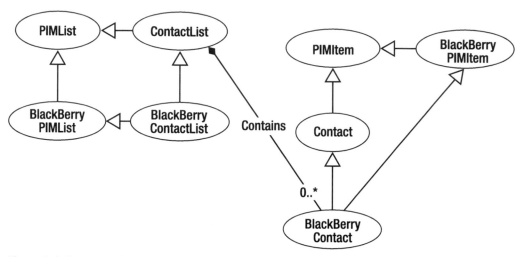

Figure 6–3. *Items contained in a ContactList*

Each list contains methods for creating and removing items, as discussed later in this chapter. You can also search lists to find and edit existing items.

To manage an item's categories, call addToCategory(), providing the name of the desired category. Conversely, call removeFromCategory() to detach a category from this item. The method maxCategories() indicates how many categories an item can belong to, with -1 indicating that there is no limit.

Fields

If you have completely filled out a contact's information in the address book, you have seen the wide variety of data types that are included. Some things, such as the name and phone number, are simply text. Others are collections of text items; for example, an address contains separate entries for the street, city, and so on. You can enter the birthday or anniversary through a special date control. All of these pieces of information are referred to as fields, and together they tell you everything there is to know about a particular item.

To support the many different kinds of information that items require, fields are fairly complex. They can theoretically support many data types, so each individual field must declare what particular type it provides. Examples include strings, arrays of strings, Date objects, and binary data. Each field may have zero or more values with that data type. For example, if you enter three email addresses for the same contact, one field will provide all three entries. Certain fields support attributes. An attribute provides more detailed information about the data it contains, such as distinguishing between a home and a work phone number. Finally, the field also has a human-readable label that describes what information it provides.

> **CAUTION:** Depending on your application's internationalization language needs, the human-readable label may not be in the language you wish to display.

Contacts usually have the most complex data structure, and are the only type of item that uses attributes. Use `PIMItem.ATTR_NONE` whenever you work with fields that do not support attributes.

At runtime, you can query a `PIMList` about the fields it supports. `getSupportedFields()` returns an array of integers, with each integer corresponding to an enumerated field value, such as `Event.START` or `ToDo.PRIORITY`. You can use this to determine whether to provide or display values for particular fields. BlackBerry offers consistent support for particular sets of fields, so you do not need to check for fields if your app will only run on BlackBerry devices. However, you should include these checks if you plan to run it on other devices as well. You can also look up the data type, label, maximum number of values, and attributes for a field, as shown in the following code.

```
int[] supportedFields = contacts.getSupportedFields();
for (int i = 0; i < supportedFields.length; ++i)
{
    int field = supportedFields[i];
    String label = contacts.getFieldLabel(field);
    int type = contacts.getFieldDataType(field);
    int[] attributes = contacts.getSupportedAttributes(field);
    for (int j = 0; j < attributes.length; ++j)
    {
        int attribute = attributes[j];
        String attrLabel = contacts.getAttributeLabel(attribute);
    }
}
```

Support for fields is consistent across all the items in a given list. You will never have one Contact that supports a birthday and another that doesn't. However, not every field will necessarily have a value. In some cases, a field may be mandatory, meaning it cannot be stored without having some value. When this happens, the system usually provides an initial default that your app can choose to overwrite.

Contacts

Contacts are probably the most complex item in the PIM database. They certainly have the greatest number of fields, and are the only items that support field attributes. Contacts also tend to be the most widely used piece of personal information. Access to contacts can greatly enhance the usefulness of your app, so you should understand their structure.

Hello, Stranger

A contact describes an entity with whom you can communicate. Contacts are most often people, but may also include companies, automated response lines, or other things. At a minimum, we will likely assign a name to each contact, whether it is "Bob" or "Apress" or "That one weird guy who's always in the coffee shop." Around that name, we attach a lot of associations and information.

In the world of PIM, we can quantify a lot of that information into data. People have phone numbers, so we enter that into the contact record. We further distinguish between a person's fax number, their work number, and their mobile number. Any individual contact may have multiple versions of the same type of data, and omit other types of data entirely. Figure 6–4 shows the set of fields included for a hypothetical item in the address book.

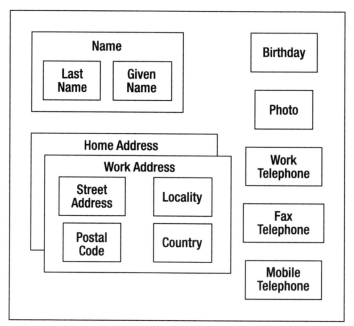

Figure 6–4. *Data fields provided by a contact*

This data is extremely malleable. People might change their address when they move, change their name when they marry, and change their photo when they grow a beard. The contact record remains the same, because it refers to the same entity, but the fields within it may change entirely.

Representing a Contact

Prior to the creation of the PIM API, a consortium of technology companies defined a standard format for contact data. They named this standard vCard, and you might have seen them attached to emails or included in web pages. A vCard stores information about a particular entity in a well-structured format that can be parsed by any application. The most widely used format is vCard 2.1, created in 1996, while the most advanced version is vCard 3.0. A sample vCard follows.

```
BEGIN:VCARD
VERSION:2.1
N:Maas;Oedipa
FN: Oedipa Maas
ORG:Inverarity Estate
TITLE:Executor
TEL;WORK;VOICE:(818) 555-0144
TEL;HOME;VOICE:(707) 555-0135
ADR;WORK:;;400 Inverarity Drive;San Narciso;CA; 91340;United States of America
LABEL;WORK;ENCODING=QUOTED-PRINTABLE: 400 Inverarity Drive =0D= San Narciso,↵
  CA 91340=0D=0AUnited States of America
ADR;HOME:;;303 Palm Avenue; Kinneret;CA; 95418;United States of America
LABEL;HOME;ENCODING=QUOTED-PRINTABLE: 303 Palm Avenue =0D= Kinneret, CA 95418↵
  =0D=0AUnited States of AmericaStates of America
EMAIL;PREF;INTERNET:oedipa@waste.example.net
END:VCARD
```

Although a vCard provides a useful standard for data interchange, the actual storage will hopefully not look anything like this. Each contact will most likely be broken apart and stored in a compact database. The vCard specification includes a large number of fields that mobile devices do not support, such as LOGO and AGENT fields. The standard also allows anyone to create additional fields by prefixing them with an X-. Some nonstandard fields that have gained widespread adoption include X-ANNIVERSARY and X-SKYPE-USERNAME. Some of these fields might be useful on a mobile phone, while others won't. The PIM Contact API was derived from vCard 3, and selected a subset of fields from the standard that seemed most useful. However, each individual manufacturer could decide which of those fields to implement. There is usually a 1–1 correlation between the fields exposed in the Java PIM API and what is shown by a device's native contacts app. If there is no Assistant entry in the address book, the API doesn't need to bother supporting Contact.ASSISTANT. This allows for far better efficiency in storing contact information in the device's native format.

A BlackBerry Contact

Fortunately, RIM has standardized the fields they make available. Besides selecting a subset of the standard PIM fields listed in the Contact class, they have added several additional fields as well in BlackBerryContact. Table 6–1 shows the available fields along with their supported attributes and the total allowed quantity.

Table 6–1. *Supported BlackBerryContact Fields*

Name	Field	Type	Attributes	Total Allowed
Address	Contact.ADDR	PIMItem.STRING_ ARRAY	Contact.ATTR_WORK Contact.ATTR_HOME	1
Anniversary	BlackBerryContact. ANNIVERSARY	PIMItem.DATE		1
Birthday	Contact.BIRTHDAY	PIMItem.DATE		1
Direct Connect ID	BlackBerryContact.DCID	PIMItem.STRING		1
Email	Contact.EMAIL	PIMItem.STRING		3
Notes	Contact.NOTE	PIMItem.STRING		1
Organization	Contact.ORG	PIMItem.STRING		1
Photo	Contact.PHOTO	PIMItem.BINARY		1
PIN	BlackBerryContact.PIN	PIMItem.STRING		1
Telephone	Contact.TEL	PIMItem.STRING	Contact.ATTR_FAX, BlackBerryContact.ATTR_ FAX2, Contact.ATTR_HOME, BlackBerryContact.ATTR_ HOME2, Contact.ATTR_ MOBILE, BlackBerryContact.ATTR_ MOBILE2, Contact.ATTR_ OTHER, Contact.ATTR_ PAGER, Contact.ATTR_ WORK, BlackBerryContact. ATTR_WORK2	8
Title	Contact.TITLE	PIMItem.STRING		1
Unique ID	Contact.UID	PIMItem.STRING		1
User 1	BlackBerryContact.USER1	PIMItem.STRING		1
User 2	BlackBerryContact.USER2	PIMItem.STRING		1
User 3	BlackBerryContact.USER3	PIMItem.STRING		1
User 4	BlackBerryContact.USER4	PIMItem.STRING		1

NOTE: The Direct Connect ID is only supported on Integrated Digital Enhanced Network (iDEN) devices. iDEN is most often used for push-to-talk mobile phones that behave similarly to walkie-talkies. `BlackBerryContact.PIN` must be a hex number represented as a string.

As Figure 6–5 shows, this list precisely corresponds to the native BlackBerry address book app. The user will see any changes you make to a contact within your app the next time she views her address book.

Figure 6–5. *A native BlackBerry contact*

Adding Contacts

Sometimes you might want your app to introduce the user to someone new. You might include contact information for technical support, or perhaps allow them to import friends from a social networking app into their address book. PIM provides two options for adding new items: creating a blank item from scratch, or importing an existing item from an outside source.

Creating Blank Contacts

Each `PIMList` subinterface includes a factory method for creating a new, blank item within that list. For a new contact you would use `ContactList.createContact()`, as shown here.

```
PIM pim = PIM.getInstance();
ContactList contacts = (ContactList) pim.openPIMList(PIM.CONTACT_LIST,
        PIM.READ_WRITE);
Contact contact = contacts.createContact();
```

When your blank contact is initialized, it actually comes with some preliminary default values. This is a minimal set on BlackBerry devices. Each contact must have a name, so by default this will be "Empty Contact." Additionally, the device will create four entries for telephone numbers, two for work and two for home; however, these do not have any values set by default.

If you create multiple contacts, each of them will have the name "Empty Contact." It is perfectly valid to have two separate contacts with the exact same name—otherwise, it wouldn't be possible to have two friends named "John Smith." If your app will create contacts, such as a tech-support contact for your product, it should check first to make sure that those contacts do not already exist in the address book in order to avoid duplicates. Later in the chapter, you'll see how to search for existing contacts.

Importing a Contact

The PIM class provides the method `fromSerialFormat()` for importing an item from a stream. The following code demonstrates how to do this from an array of UTF-8 bytes. You can just as easily load a vCard over the network, from a file, or through any other type of input stream source. However, keep in mind that `fromSerialFormat()` expects to receive plain characters; if the data has been received over an HTTP or email connection, you should remove any encoding prior to deserializing.

```
ByteArrayInputStream input = new ByteArrayInputStream(cardData);
PIM pim = PIM.getInstance();
PIMItem[] items = pim.fromSerialFormat(input, "UTF-8");
if (items.length > 0 && items[0] instanceof Contact)
{
    Contact imported = (Contact) items[0];
}
```

When importing a contact, the first byte in the input stream should be the "B" character of the `"BEGIN:VCARD"` or `"begin:vcard"` tag. (vCard tags are not case-sensitive.) The vCard must be in the 2.1 or 3.0 format. PIM will continue processing all characters until it reaches the `"end:vcard"` tag or an error occurs. As it reads in data, it will import any compatible tags (such as name, email, mobile, etc.) into the `Contact` object's data fields. If it comes across any incompatible tags (such as nickname, public key, or photo URL), it silently drops those fields. If the card does not include the mandatory name field, PIM will use "Empty Contact" as a default.

Even though this method returns an array of PIMItem objects, it will only read in a single Contact. The method returns an array because sometimes a single data entry can result in multiple PIMItem instances. For example, a calendar appointment can be represented as both a ToDo and an Event. If the stream contains multiple vCards, you must call fromSerialFormat() multiple times to import them all.

> **CAUTION:** Versions of BlackBerry device software prior to 4.6.1 have flawed implementations of fromSerialFormat() that may throw exceptions when you try to import vCards. In some cases, you can avoid this by restricting the set of fields in the vCard; test on your target devices if you plan on using this method.

Editing Contacts

After you have created, imported, or looked up an existing Contact, you can start making changes to it. This might involve adding new fields, editing existing fields, or removing fields. Keep in mind that you can only edit items from a list that was opened with WRITE_ONLY or READ_WRITE access.

Modifying Basic Fields

Most of the fields in the Contact class have only a single value associated with them. To edit them, provide a new value of the appropriate type, as previously shown in Table 6–1.

Editing Strings

You can directly add strings to a contact record, as shown here.

```
contact.addString(Contact.ORG, PIMItem.ATTR_NONE, "Engineering");
```

You can modify an existing string value by calling the setString() method with an appropriate index.

```
contact.setString(Contact.TITLE, 0, PIMItem.ATTR_NONE, "Senior Engineer");
```

How can you know which version to call? Most string fields can only accept a single entry. If you try to add a new entry when one already exists, a FieldFullException will be thrown. Conversely, if you try to set a field and no value is currently set, you'll get an IndexOutOfBoundsException. If you have just created a blank new contact, you can safely call addString() since no fields currently exist. Otherwise, you should check to see whether the field already has any values, and then set or update it appropriately as in the following example.

```
if (contact.countValues(Contact.NOTE) > 0)
{
    contact.setString(Contact.NOTE, 0, PIMItem.ATTR_NONE, "Next victim");
}
```

```
else
{
    contact.addString(Contact.NOTE, PIMItem.ATTR_NONE, "Next victim");
}
```

If you have previously added a string, and then later call setString() with an index of 0, it will overwrite the previously added value. This occurs even if the Field supports multiple entries.

Finally, for maximum portability, you can check to see whether the device supports a field before you attempt to access it. This will protect you if you ever run on devices that do not provide the given field.

```
if (contacts.isSupportedField(BlackBerryContact.USER1))
{
    contact.addString(BlackBerryContact.USER1, PIMItem.ATTR_NONE, "BB user");
}
```

Editing Dates

A date in a Contact item is a long 64-bit integer in Unix epoch time—that is, the number of milliseconds since midnight on January 1, 1970 GMT. If you wish to use the current time, you can call System.currentTimeMillis(). You can also calculate the time value yourself. However, I find it easiest to use the Calendar class, which provides useful methods for converting a calendar date and time into a suitable long value. The following example assigns an anniversary value to a contact.

```
Calendar calendar = Calendar.getInstance();
calendar.set(Calendar.YEAR, 2008);
calendar.set(Calendar.MONTH, Calendar.JULY);
calendar.set(Calendar.DATE, 21);
long time = calendar.getTime().getTime();
contact.addDate(BlackBerryContact.ANNIVERSARY, PIMItem.ATTR_NONE, time);
```

NOTE: The getTime().getTime() call is not a typo. The first method converts a Calendar into a Date, the second from a Date into a primitive time value. The BlackBerry version of java.util.Calendar omits some useful functions from the Java SE version, including getTimeInMillis() and overloaded set() functions that specify multiple fields at once.

Editing Binary

A BlackBerry contact supports a single type of binary field, the photo. You can use any image format supported by EncodedImage, including PNG, BMP, WBMP, GIF, JPEG, and TIFF. However, pay attention for some quirks. First, not all specific images will be supported. I've noticed that most PNG files can be added successfully, while others generate an "Image type is not supported" error. Second, you can either Base64 encode the binary data or provide it in raw byte format; however, you must give the length of the data as the number of bytes in the unencoded format. On recent devices, you may directly set image bytes for the photo as shown here.

```
EncodedImage image = EncodedImage.getEncodedImageResource("silhouette.png");
byte[] data = image.getData();
contact.addBinary(Contact.PHOTO, PIMItem.ATTR_NONE, data, 0, data.length);
```

On devices with older software versions, you may need to Base64 encode the data first. Fortunately, a convenient class provides a quick way to do this, as shown in the following code.

```
EncodedImage image = EncodedImage.getEncodedImageResource("silhouette.png");
byte[] data = image.getData();
byte[] encoded = Base64OutputStream.encode(data, 0, data.length, false, false);
contact.addBinary(Contact.PHOTO, PIMItem.ATTR_NONE, encoded, 0, data.length);
```

Of course, you can obtain the image bytes any way you like. This example shows how to use a resource in your application, but you can also download an image from the Internet or select something from the local filesystem.

Modifying Email Addresses

The basic fields shown in the previous section all support a single entry. An email address is a String, but any given user may have multiple addresses. BlackBerry devices support up to three addresses for any given contact. You may simply call addField() multiple times, as in the following example.

```
contact.addString(Contact.EMAIL, PIMItem.ATTR_NONE, "westley@example.com");
contact.addString(Contact.EMAIL, PIMItem.ATTR_NONE, "farmboy@example.com");
contact.addString(Contact.EMAIL, PIMItem.ATTR_NONE, "dread.pirate@example.com");
```

Should you ever need to add another address after reaching the maximum, you must remove one of the existing addresses first. You can remove any field, not just email addresses, by calling the removeValue() method. The example below will remove the second item; if run after the preceding code, the two remaining addresses will be westley@example.com at index 0 and dread.pirate@example.com at index 1.

```
contact.removeValue(Contact.EMAIL, 1);
```

New email addresses will always be added to the end of the list. You can call setString() with the appropriate index to modify an existing email address slot.

Modifying Names

Contact.NAME has the type PIMItem.STRING_ARRAY. Sometimes you would like to access individual components of a name; for example, you can easily sort "John Smith" by first name, but you'd like individual access to the "Smith" part in order to sort by the last name. PIM defines five potential elements that make up the name array. BlackBerry supports a subset of these, as shown in Table 6–2.

Table 6–2. *Elements in the Name Array*

Name	Meaning	Example	Supported?
Contact.NAME_FAMILY	Last name	House	Yes
Contact.NAME_GIVEN	First name	Gregory	Yes
Contact.NAME_OTHER	Middle name, nick name, etc.	Greg	No
Contact.NAME_PREFIX	Honorific or title placed before name	Dr.	Yes
Contact.NAME_SUFFIX	Honors, offices, or generational information	M.D.	No

You cannot directly set an individual name element; instead, you must add or remove the entire string array at once. You can build up and apply the array as shown in the following example.

```
int nameCount = contacts.stringArraySize(Contact.NAME);
String[] names = new String[nameCount];
names[Contact.NAME_PREFIX] = "Dr.";
names[Contact.NAME_GIVEN] = "Nick";
names[Contact.NAME_FAMILY] = "Riviera";
names[Contact.NAME_SUFFIX] = "M.D.";
contact.addStringArray(Contact.NAME, PIMItem.ATTR_NONE, names);
```

You can include as few name parts as you like, although, if you don't include a given nor a family name, BlackBerry will apply a default of "Empty" and "Contact" respectively. You can safely include unsupported name parts such as NAME_SUFFIX, which the platform will silently discard. If you'd prefer to check at runtime whether a name is supported, use the method isSupportedArrayElement().

```
if (contacts.isSupportedArrayElement(Contact.NAME, Contact.NAME_SUFFIX))
    names[Contact.NAME_SUFFIX] = "M.D.";
```

Modifying Phone Numbers

The phone number field is the first field we have examined that supports attributes. As described previously, an attribute provides more detailed information about the data it contains. When you add multiple email addresses, you can not distinguish whether one email address will be more appropriate than another to use. For phone numbers, however, you can attach an attribute to each number describing its purpose, as the following code demonstrates.

```
contact.addString(Contact.TEL, Contact.ATTR_HOME, "5555550100");
contact.addString(Contact.TEL, Contact.ATTR_WORK, "5555550103");
contact.addString(Contact.TEL, BlackBerryContact.ATTR_WORK2, "5555550104");
```

As long as you stick to the defined attributes and don't repeat yourself, everything will work as expected. However, BlackBerry follows some unusual rules in other cases. If you try to add an unsupported attribute (such as `Contact.AUTO`), or one that already has a value assigned to it, then, rather than discarding the value or throwing an error, the number will be assigned to the next available slot. Therefore, your code might add a mobile number to a contact, and have that number stored as a pager number. There is a limit of eight numbers per contact, and adding any more after that will result in a `FieldFullException`.

To avoid this problem, you can use the `countValues()` method to determine how many entries a field already stores, and then a `getAttributes()` call to retrieve the attributes. Attributes are bit flags, so you can use a bitwise AND operator to determine whether a given attribute is set, as shown in the next example. This code will scan through all the telephone numbers already set on a contact and, if it finds a mobile number, update it.

```
int telCount = contact.countValues(Contact.TEL);
for (int i = 0; i < telCount; ++i)
{
    int telAttrs = contact.getAttributes(Contact.TEL, i);
    if ((telAttrs & Contact.ATTR_MOBILE) != 0)
    {
        contact.setString(Contact.TEL, i, Contact.ATTR_MOBILE, "5555550109");
        break;
    }
}
```

Modifying Addresses

The address field is the most complex field in a `Contact`, as it combines both the array elements we saw in the name field and the attributes found in telephone numbers. Now that you have mastered both of these concepts, addresses should seem relatively straightforward. First you will build up an array of address elements, and then assign that array to a specific address attribute. Table 6–3 shows the address array elements.

Table 6–3. *Elements in the Address Array*

Name	Meaning	Example	Supported?
Contact.ADDR_COUNTRY	Country	Canada	Yes
Contact.ADDR_EXTRA	Any other information	Head office	Yes
Contact.ADDR_LOCALITY	City, town, rural area	Waterloo	Yes
Contact.ADDR_POBOX	Post office box	54321	No
Contact.ADDR_POSTALCODE	ZIP or other postal code	N2L 3W8	Yes
Contact.ADDR_REGION	Province, territory, or state	Ontario	Yes
Contact.ADDR_STREET	Street number and name	295 Philip Street	Yes

As with phone numbers, if you try to add an unsupported address or one that already has a value, it will be assigned to the next available slot. However, with just two supported attributes, this is less of a problem. You may reuse an existing array to add multiple addresses, as the next example shows.

```
int addrCount = contacts.stringArraySize(Contact.ADDR);
String[] address = new String[addrCount];
address[Contact.ADDR_STREET] = "1600 Pennsylvania Ave NW";
address[Contact.ADDR_LOCALITY] = "Washington";
address[Contact.ADDR_REGION] = "D.C.";
address[Contact.ADDR_POSTALCODE] = "20500-0004";
address[Contact.ADDR_COUNTRY] = "USA";
contact.addStringArray(Contact.ADDR, Contact.ATTR_HOME, address);
address[Contact.ADDR_STREET] = "One First Street N.E.";
address[Contact.ADDR_LOCALITY] = "Washington";
address[Contact.ADDR_REGION] = "D.C.";
address[Contact.ADDR_POSTALCODE] = "20543";
address[Contact.ADDR_COUNTRY] = "USA";
contact.addStringArray(Contact.ADDR, Contact.ATTR_WORK, address);
```

You may remove or update individual address entries as discussed previously.

Saving Contacts

All modifications to a contact happen entirely in memory. In order to persist those changes to the device's long-term storage, you must commit them by calling Contact.commit(). Even if no errors have occurred when you add and modify fields, the call to commit() may still throw an exception. For example, if you try to add an invalid image to a contact via the Contact.PHOTO field, the platform may not detect the problem until you try to save the contact.

After you call commit(), you can continue using this Contact object, but it will not save additional changes unless you call commit() again.

Besides a local save, you might want to exporting contact data so you can send it to a server or other application. You can do this yourself by iterating through a contact's fields and writing the information to a custom format, but it's much easier to use PIM's built-in vCard support, assuming the receiving party can read that format.

You can serialize a Contact by calling PIM.toSerialFormat(). You provide the Contact and the output stream. Additionally, you must specify a character encoding; the method assumes UTF-8 if this is null. Finally, you must specify the data format. BlackBerry devices offer two: VCARD/2.1 and VCARD/3.0. If you'd like to dynamically check the supported formats, you can call PIM.supportedSerialFormats(PIM.CONTACT_LIST). This returns an array of all supported formats. The following example shows how to export a contact to an in-memory array.

```
ByteArrayOutputStream out = new ByteArrayOutputStream();
String[] formats = pim.supportedSerialFormats(PIM.CONTACT_LIST);
pim.toSerialFormat(contact, out, "UTF-8", formats[0]);
byte[] vCardData = out.toByteArray();
```

Searching for Contacts

A few users might never get around to creating any contacts in their address book, while others might have hundreds or thousands. The number of contacts is limited only by the available memory on the device. How do you go about finding the contacts you want? You have a variety of tools at your disposal, including both standard PIM APIs and special searches that are only available for BlackBerry devices.

I Want It All

If you need the entire haystack and not just the needle, `ContactList.items()` is the method for you. This method returns an `Enumeration` filled with `Contact` items. Why would you want to use this? It would be handy if you wanted to present the user with a list of all available contacts to pick one, or for a spam app that sent emails to everyone you know.

> **CAUTION:** Remember that some users will have a *lot* of contacts. You should never write an app that does something like create a new `LabelField` for every contact they have; this will thrash the memory and won't run on certain power users' devices. You can safely call `items()`, just pay attention to when and how you allocate new objects based on what it returns. Similarly, don't do a linear search through the enumeration, since it will take a long time if there are many contacts.

`BlackBerryContactList` offers an extra method and two more fields that provide a little more refinement to the raw `items()` call. `BlackBerryContactList.SEARCH_CONTACTS` will return only `Contact` entries, while `BlackBerryContactList.SEARCH_GROUPS` will return only `BlackBerryContactGroup` objects. By default this API will return both. Most of the other lookup methods described later in this chapter also have alternate versions that accept these two search types. The following code will first process all of the contacts in a user's address book, and then operate on all the groups.

```
PIM pim = PIM.getInstance();
BlackBerryContactList contacts = (BlackBerryContactList) pim↵
        .openPIMList(PIM.CONTACT_LIST, PIM.READ_WRITE);
Enumeration items = contacts.items(BlackBerryContactList.SEARCH_CONTACTS);
while (items.hasMoreElements())
{
    BlackBerryContact contact = (BlackBerryContact) items.nextElement();
    // Process contact here.
}
items = contacts.items(BlackBerryContactList.SEARCH_GROUPS);
while (items.hasMoreElements())
{
    BlackBerryContactGroup group = (BlackBerryContactGroup) items.nextElement();
    // Process group here.
}
```

> **NOTE:** A `BlackBerryContactGroup` is a special type of address-book entry that represents an address list, such as an email distribution or a working group. Your application can read these but cannot modify or remove them. A `BlackBerryContactGroup` is not compatible with a `Contact`, so do not attempt to cast between the two.

BlackBerryContactList provides a useful method, `getSortOrder()`, that tells you how it will sort returned items. Depending on the device configuration, this can be `BlackBerryContactList.SORT_ORDER_FIRST_NAME`, `BlackBerryContactList.SORT_ORDER_LAST_NAME`, or `BlackBerryContactList.SORT_ORDER_COMPANY`. Unfortunately, you cannot modify the sort order yourself, but this can be helpful for displaying a message to the user or to determine whether you need to sort the results yourself.

Particular Retrieval

If you're fortunate enough to know the unique ID for a contact, you can look up your contact directly by calling `BlackBerryContactList.getByUID()`. This presumes that you have previously stored the UID in RMS or another suitable medium. Only developers will see the UID `String`; it is not visible when users view their address book. Each `Contact` has its own unique ID, but IDs may be reused if a contact is deleted, so you should check for validity after retrieving a Contact through this method.

If you happen to know the name of a contact, you can try to retrieve it by using the `itemsByName()` method. This comes in several versions, including one where you provide a simple search string, like "Jon," and another version where you provide a `Contact` object. If using the string, PIM will run a case-insensitive search of the list for a contact whose first name or last name starts with that string. So "Jon" will match "Jonathan Myers" and "Ben Jonson" but not "Longjon Silver." If you provide a `Contact`, it will search the family and given names, and will only return contacts if both names start with the provided strings.

Keep in mind that these methods can return multiple results. You might hope that searching for "Horatio Xavier" will only return one result, but someone might know two people of that name. A search for "A" will almost certainly return multiple results. The next example demonstrates how to search for a particular name, and then act on the first result.

```
Contact nameTemplate = contacts.createContact();
String[] name = new String[contacts.stringArraySize(Contact.NAME)];
name[Contact.NAME_GIVEN] = "Daniel";
name[Contact.NAME_FAMILY] = "Waterhouse";
nameTemplate.addStringArray(Contact.NAME, PIMItem.ATTR_NONE, name);
Enumeration matches = contacts.itemsByName(nameTemplate);
if (matches.hasMoreElements())
{
    Contact daniel = (Contact)matches.nextElement();
}
```

NOTE: Even though a new `Contact` is created here, `commit()` is never called, so it will not be saved to the address book.

Broader Searches

Another version of `items()` accepts a `String`. This behaves somewhat similarly to `itemsByName()`, except that it checks all fields in an item, and the matching string can occur anywhere within them. Searching for "stan" would match "Stanley," "Pakistan," and "instant@example.com". As with `itemsByName()`, this method returns an `Enumeration` of all matches. This method tends to run slowly, because it must search every character of every field, and of limited use, because rarely would you want all possible matches.

You might also choose to call `itemsByCategory()` to retrieve all contacts belonging to a particular category. As mentioned previously, some items might belong to multiple categories while others don't belong to any. You can pass the field `PIMList.UNCATEGORIZED` to this method to retrieve all items without any associated categories.

Once you have retrieved an `Enumeration` by either method, you can walk it and downcast to `Contact` objects as shown previously.

In OS 6.0, RIM added a custom API called `BlackBerryContactList.getContactsByPhoneNumber()`. This behaves similarly to calling `items()` with a `String`, but it adds support for flexible matching. For example, a contact may have the phone number 4155550001. `items()` would require you to pass this exact string, while `getContactsByPhoneNumber()` could also find the match if you passed 415-555-0001 or (415) 555-0001. Once again, you can walk the returned `Enumeration` to find the `Contact` you want.

Template Matching

You can perform the most powerful searches by using a `Contact` object as a template. This performs similarly to the specialized version of `itemsByName()` used previously, but this time it matches all fields. You can use this to narrow in on a particular `Contact`, such as the entry with a particular email address, or to find a set of related items, such as all your contacts who belong to a given organiz ation.

Template matching follows several well-defined rules.

- Two `STRING` fields match if the template item's string is contained anywhere within the item's string value. So, "key" would match "Turkey."

- If the template item uses the empty string "" for a field, all items with any value for that field match.

- For items with multiple values in a field, the position of the value does not matter. So, if your template has an email address of "bob@example.com", it will match "bob@example.com" whether it is in slot 0, 1, or 2.

- If PIMItem.ATTR_NONE is supplied, any matching item will be accepted regardless of attribute type.

- Otherwise, the attribute type in the item must match the attribute in the template.

- Any type other than a STRING must match exactly. Keep in mind that DATE fields may not share the exact same millisecond value, even if they fall on the same calendar date.

Your templates can be as broad or as focused as you need. The following example shows how to locate all of your contacts who belong to the Guild of Calamitous Intent and have a San Francisco area code.

```
Contact template = contacts.createContact();
template.addString(Contact.ORG, PIMItem.ATTR_NONE, "Guild of Calamitous Intent");
template.addString(Contact.TEL, Contact.ATTR_WORK, "415");
Enumeration henchmen = contacts.items(template);
```

Remote Lookup

Corporate BlackBerry users typically access a BES that attaches to a large enterprise database with access to extended contact information, such as a Microsoft Exchange server. Even though an individual user might only have 100 contacts saved on their SIM card, they might be able to access thousands more through the remote address server.

Developers can access this data through the BlackBerryContactList.lookup() method. You can choose between two versions: one takes a String, the other takes a Contact. These perform searches in the same way as ContactList.items(). However, because the phone cannot immediately access the data, the interface behaves differently. Instead of blocking until the search is complete, calling lookup() will start an asynchronous search through the network for contacts. You must pass in an instance of RemoteLookupListener. The provided object will receive a notification through its items() callback function once the search completes.

You can safely call lookup() even on non-BES devices; they will simply never receive the callback. Once the items arrive, you can access them as you would items returned through the other searches. Because the items reside on an external server, you cannot update them. However, you can import the items into your own local contact list by calling ContactList.importContact(). The following code demonstrates how to kick off a remote search for root email addresses, and then import the results into your address book.

```
final BlackBerryContactList localContacts = (BlackBerryContactList) pim
    .openPIMList(PIM.CONTACT_LIST, PIM.READ_WRITE);
Contact remoteSearch = contacts.createContact();
remoteSearch.addString(Contact.EMAIL, PIMItem.ATTR_NONE, "root@");
```

```
contacts.lookup(template, new RemoteLookupListener() {
    public void items(Enumeration results)
    {
        while (results.hasMoreElements())
        {
            Contact contact = (Contact)results.nextElement();
            Contact imported = localContacts.importContact(contact);
            try
            {
                imported.commit();
            }
            catch (PIMException pime) {}
        }
    }
});
```

Reading Contact Data

Once you have found a contact, you can access its information through the defined fields. If you know that certain fields have assigned values, such as if you have done a search for those fields, you can access them directly. Otherwise, you should use Contact.countValues() first to ensure that you have something there to read. For maximum portability, you can initially call ContactList.isSupportedField() to check that the field is safe to access.

The following code shows how to unpack certain information from a retrieved contact. We retrieve the contact's organization, create a readable version of their birthday, and then grab all email addresses. Finally, we look through all the addresses in the record and, if we find a work address, pull out some relevant fields from it.

```
String org = contact.getString(Contact.ORG, 0);
long birthdayTime = contact.getDate(Contact.BIRTHDAY, 0);
Calendar birthday = Calendar.getInstance();
birthday.setTime(new Date(birthdayTime));
int emailCount = contact.countValues(Contact.EMAIL);
for (int i = 0; i < emailCount; ++i)
{
    String email = contact.getString(Contact.EMAIL, i);
}
int addrCount = contact.countValues(Contact.ADDR);
for (int i = 0; i < addrCount; ++i)
{
    String[] address = contact.getStringArray(Contact.ADDR, i);
    int attribute = contact.getAttributes(Contact.ADDR, i);
    if ((attribute & contact.ATTR_WORK) != 0)
    {
        String street = address[Contact.ADDR_STREET];
        String city = address[Contact.ADDR_LOCALITY];
        String state = address[Contact.ADDR_REGION];
    }
}
```

This technique works well when you want to find specific fields. Sometimes you might want to show all of a contact's fields that have data, or look for a set of fields. Rather than call `countValues()` for every single field you care about, you can use the method `getFields()`, which tells you what fields have data. Fields return as an array of integers, which you can then use to directly access the data. The following debugging code looks at every field defined on a particular contact and writes the information to standard out.

```
int[] fields = contact.getFields();
for (int i = 0; i < fields.length; ++i)
{
    int field = fields[i];
    String fieldLabel = contacts.getFieldLabel(field);
    int dataType = contacts.getFieldDataType(field);
    if (dataType == PIMItem.STRING)
    {
        int dataCount = contact.countValues(field);
        for (int j = 0; j < dataCount; ++j)
        {
            String fieldValue = contact.getString(field, j);
            System.out.println(fieldLabel + ":" + j + ":" + fieldValue);
        }
    }
    else
    {
        System.out.println(fieldLabel);
    }
}
```

Deleting Contacts

PIM has the ability to delete contact entries. Obviously, you should use this with great caution. You will infuriate people if you eliminate their friends. However, it is entirely appropriate to remove a contact that your app created itself, or to perform a deletion at the request of your user. You can only delete a contact from a list that you opened with `WRITE_ONLY` or `READ_WRITE` permissions.

To perform a deletion, first locate a Contact using one of the techniques described above. Then you can call `ContactList.removeContact()`. As with other PIM operations, you should deal with `PIMException` and possibly `SecurityException` as well if the user refuses to allow you to delete the contact.

Invoking the Native Address Book

Developers commonly use PIM in their apps to allow the user to select one or more contacts from her address book and then extracting some information from those selections. On many platforms, developers need to write custom screens using the PIM APIs that read in all of the user's contacts and then present a list of options. Fortunately, RIM has a better solution: `BlackBerryContactList.choose()` allows your app to directly launch into a customized version of the built-in address book. As shown in Figure 6–6, this option displays a familiar UI that lets the user scroll to find a contact, or type to narrow down the available field.

Figure 6–6. *Choosing a contact from the native address book*

The choose() method will block until the user has finished with the address book. One of three outcomes may result.

- The user might have selected an existing entry that will be provided as the return value.

- The user might have created a new Contact, also provided as the return value.

- The user might have dismissed the address book without making any selection, in which case null is returned.

The choose() method is very useful, but you should keep a few caveats in mind.

- You cannot control the sort order that it uses to display the choices.

- You cannot filter the contacts. For example, if you wish to select an email address, it will also display contacts without email, and the user may choose one of them.

- You can not select multiple contacts. If you wish to pick more than one, you must call choose() multiple times, and handle cases where the user picks the same contact more than once.

- You can only select local contacts through this API, not contacts stored on a remote server.

- The address book shows both Contact and BlackBerryContactGroup items, and the user may select either. If you only want contacts, you should check to see that you are getting one.

The next example shows how to launch the native address book and check that the user selected a contact with an email address. In a full application, you can repeatedly invoke this code, displaying "Please select an email contact" until one is provided.

```
PIM pim = PIM.getInstance();
BlackBerryContactList contacts = (BlackBerryContactList) pim⏎
        .openPIMList(PIM.CONTACT_LIST, PIM.READ_WRITE);
PIMItem selected = contacts.choose();
if (selected != null)
{
    if (selected instanceof Contact)
    {
        Contact selectedContact = (Contact)selected;
        if (selectedContact.countValues(Contact.EMAIL) > 0)
        {
            // Process the selection here.
        }
    }
}
```

The BlackBerry Calendar

Some users go for years without ever opening the calendar app on their mobile phone. Others depend on it to drive their day. Your app can integrate with the calendar to provide your users with reminders, set up appointments, or perform other tasks to help schedule their time.

BlackBerry allows you to access calendar information through the EventList class. This class behaves similarly to the ContactList class, except that it provides Event items in place of Contact items. You can obtain an instance as shown below.

```
PIM pim = PIM.getInstance();
EventList events = (EventList)pim.openPIMList(PIM.EVENT_LIST, PIM.READ_WRITE);
```

For the most part, events behave like contacts. An event list contains multiple events, and each event supports a certain collection of fields, any one of which may have zero, one, or more items. The following sections focus on the unique aspects of events.

Calendar Syncing

Users with a full-featured desktop email client such as Microsoft Outlook can set up their BlackBerry Desktop Manager program to automatically sync between their desktop and mobile calendars. This means that, when a user accepts a meeting invitation on Outlook and then leaves the office, his BlackBerry can vibrate to remind him when the meeting time approaches. Keep in mind that events you create or manipulate on the phone might propagate to other devices. Conversely, even if the phone does not modify any events, the calendar may change the next time the device connects to the desktop.

A standard interchange format supports this kind of syncing. The original PIM Event implementation derived from vCalendar 1.0, also known as vCal. The Internet Mail Consortium, the same organization responsible for vCard, created this standardized format. The newer iCalendar standard, developed by the Internet Engineering Task Force, has since supplanted vCalendar. BlackBerry PIM supports import from and export to both formats. The following shows a simple iCalendar event.

```
BEGIN:VCALENDAR
VERSION:2.0
BEGIN:VEVENT
SUMMARY:Mom's Birthday Breakfast
DTSTART:20110610T060000Z
DTEND:20110610T070000Z
END:VEVENT
END:VCALENDAR
```

Different calendaring programs have long had trouble with importing and exporting each other's calendar events, although the situation has improved in recent years. Despite the existence of a standard, different programs have added their own quirks, and some deal with those quirks better than others. If your app will share calendar data with a server or another program, you should check to make sure both parties can share data successfully.

Repeat After Me

For the most part, Event objects are simpler than Contact. They do not use string arrays, attributes, or binary data. However, events do add one significant new characteristic: the idea of repetition. Imagine that you have a daily appointment to walk your dog at 7pm. You'd like to create an appointment so you don't forget this duty. If your calendar program created an event for every single day, that would produce 365 events in a single year—quite a lot of data, and far too much space to take up on a mobile device.

Repeating events offer a way for you to create a single event within your calendar, and then specify rules about how often it repeats. Repeating events can be defined very flexibly; you can specify repetition on calendar days (such as every June 10), weekdays (every Tuesday), or more complex constructions (the first and fourth Saturday of every month). You can even specify exceptions—for example, if you leave on vacation next week, you can hire a dog-walker and remove those pesky reminders during the time you'll be gone.

Figure 6–7 shows how a single repeating event can be virtually represented multiple times within an event list.

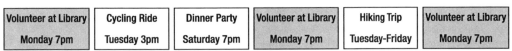

Figure 6–7. *A repeating calendar event*

PIM events support four fundamental types of repetition: RepeatRule.DAILY, RepeatRule.WEEKLY, RepeatRule.MONTHLY, and RepeatRule.YEARLY. You can set any of these alone on a RepeatRule to create a simple repetition. For example, to have an event repeat at the same time each week, you would define the FREQUENCY as shown below.

```
RepeatRule repeat = new RepeatRule();
repeat.setInt(RepeatRule.FREQUENCY, RepeatRule.WEEKLY);
```

You can control when an event stops repeating by also applying a COUNT or an END value. The former states that the event will recur a certain number of times at the provided frequency and then stop. The latter means that the event will keep recurring until a certain calendar time, at which point it will cease. You must provide COUNT as an int, while END needs a date. To make this event repeat for the next eight weeks, we would use the COUNT as shown below.

```
repeat.setInt(RepeatRule.COUNT, 8);
```

You can also specify multiple times at which an event will fire. To repeat an event on Monday, Wednesday, and Friday, you specify the DAY_IN_WEEK rule and provide a bitwise OR for those dates.

```
repeat.setInt(RepeatRule.DAY_IN_WEEK, RepeatRule.MONDAY | RepeatRule.WEDNESDAY↩
      | RepeatRule.FRIDAY);
```

Table 6–4 shows the available repetition modifiers. All the constants are defined in the RepeatRule class.

Table 6–4. *Repetition Modifiers*

Field	Values Allowed
DAY_IN_WEEK	SUNDAY, MONDAY, TUESDAY, WEDNESDAY, THURSDAY, FRIDAY, SATURDAY
DAY_IN_MONTH	1-31
DAY_IN_YEAR	1-365
WEEK_IN_MONTH	FIRST, SECOND, THIRD, FOURTH, FIFTH, LAST, SECONDLAST, THIRDLAST, FOURTHLAST, FIFTHLAST
MONTH_IN_YEAR	JANUARY, FEBRUARY, MARCH, APRIL, MAY, JUNE, JULY, AUGUST, SEPTEMBER, OCTOBER, NOVEMBER, DECEMBER

For certain frequencies, you can combine multiple modifiers to create a more fine-grained event time. If you want to celebrate American Thanksgiving, create a yearly event that occurs the fourth Thursday of every November.

```
repeat.setInt(RepeatRule.FREQUENCY, RepeatRule.YEARLY);
repeat.setInt(RepeatRule.MONTH_IN_YEAR, RepeatRule.NOVEMBER);
repeat.setInt(RepeatRule.WEEK_IN_MONTH, RepeatRule.FOURTH);
```

You can't use every modifier for every frequency; for instance, `DAY_IN_YEAR` doesn't make sense when applied to a `WEEKLY` recurrence. Frequencies can be controlled on a handset-by-handset basis depending on what the underlying calendar supports. To determine whether your device supports a certain modifier or set of modifiers, you can query `EventList.getSupportedRepeatRuleFields()`. If it accepts a combination of modifiers, the set will return as a bitwise AND. The next example checks to see how yearly recurring events are supported.

```
int[] supported = events.getSupportedRepeatRuleFields(RepeatRule.YEARLY);
for (int i = 0; i < supported.length; ++i)
{
    int rules = supported[i];
    if (rules == (RepeatRule.DAY_IN_MONTH & RepeatRule.MONTH_IN_YEAR))
        System.out.println("Can specify by month.");
    else if (rules == RepeatRule.DAY_IN_YEAR)
        System.out.println("Can specify by absolute date.");
}
```

Finally, you can specify exceptions to a repetition. You add one exception for each time that the event should not occur. Provide exceptions as `long` time values. If you decide to cancel next month's appointment but keep all future appointments, you could use the following code.

```
Calendar exceptionTime = Calendar.getInstance();
exceptionTime.set(Calendar.MONTH, 1);
repeat.addExceptDate(exceptionTime.getTime().getTime ());
```

You can check to see what exceptions have already been added by calling getExceptDates() and remove an existing exception by calling removeExceptDate(long date).

To query a previously created repeat rule, use the following methods.

- getFields() returns an array of all the fields that have been set.

- getInt(int field) retrieves a previously set field, such as the FREQUENCY or the DAY_IN_YEAR.

- getDate(RepeatRule.END) retrieves the specified end time.

- dates(long startdate, long subsetBeginning, long subsetEnding) allows you to provide a time window, and will return all of the repetitions that would occur within that window, excluding any exceptions.

Once you have a RepeatRule configured the way you want it, call Event.setRepeat(RepeatRule repeat). This will replace any previously configured repeat rule. You can query an event's current repetition by calling Event.getRepeat(); this will return null if the event only occurs once.

Eventful Data

As with contacts, you can access a variety of fields when editing or reading event data. Table 6–5 displays all the fields supported on BlackBerry. Most of these are very simple, with a single nonarray nonattribute value provided. LOCATION is a single string, which is easier than providing a structured address but also makes it more difficult to parse an event's location. The special ATTENDEES field can have multiple values, one for each attendee. Using the special convenience field ALLDAY will convert the event into an all-day event, running from midnight GMT of the start date through midnight GMT of the end date.

Table 6–5. *Supported BlackBerry Event Fields*

Field	Meaning	Type	Example
Event.SUMMARY	Title of this event	PIMItem.STRING	"Quarterly food strategy meeting"
Event.START	Date and time that this event begins	PIMItem.DATE	1207042400000
Event.END	Date and time that this event ends	PIMItem.DATE	1207042500000
BlackBerryEvent.ALLDAY	All day event	PIMItem.BOOLEAN	true
Event.ALARM	Time to display or sound a reminder, given in seconds before the time specified in START	PIMItem.INT	900 for an alarm 15 minutes before the event
BlackBerryEvent.FREE_BUSY	Status of the event	PIMItem.INT	BlackBerryEvent.FB_FREE, BlackBerryEvent.TENTATIVE, BlackBerryEvent.FB_BUSY, or BlackBerryEvent.OUT_OF_OFFICE
BlackBerryEvent.ATTENDEES	Email addresses of event attendees	PIMItem.STRING	bob@example.com
Event.LOCATION	Place where the event occurs	PIMItem.STRING	"Floor 13 Kitchen"
Event.CLASS	Visibility of this event	PIMItem.INT	Event.CLASS_PUBLIC, Event.CLASS_PRIVATE, Event.CLASS_CONFIDENTIAL
Event.NOTE	Additional information about this event	PIMItem.STRING	"Donuts will be served"
Event.UID	Unique identifier of this Event	PIMItem.STRING	"1234567890"

As with contact fields, the fields on an event correspond to what the BlackBerry Calendar app provides. The ALARM field matches the "Reminder" in an appointment. Both PRIVATE and CONFIDENTIAL classes will display as "Private."

The BlackBerry applies a few special rules for the standard event fields.

- Events have a minimum duration of one minute. If the END is less than one minute later than START, its duration will automatically be extended.

- Setting a NOTE to a value of "" will remove it from the event.

The Event and BlackBerryEvent interfaces both apply to the same objects; similarly, you can interchangeably cast EventList and BlackBerryEventList.

Using BlackBerry Calendar Events

Once you have gotten the hang of the Contact class, you can start working with Event objects. The specific data values you will work with vary, but the overall structure of building and accessing fields remains the same.

Creating and Editing Events

You can construct, import, and modify Event objects in the same way that you would Contact objects. The next example demonstrates how to create an Event from scratch. Here we assume that the app will run on a BlackBerry device, so we freely use BlackBerry-specific event fields and do not check for supported fields. This code will create a new five-hour-long event, set a reminder for 30 minutes before, include 3 attendees, and specify a location and a busy status before saving the event.

```
PIM pim = PIM.getInstance();
EventList events = (EventList) pim.openPIMList(PIM.EVENT_LIST, PIM.READ_WRITE);
Event event = events.createEvent();
event.addString(Event.SUMMARY, PIMItem.ATTR_NONE, "Radiohead Concert");
Calendar cal = Calendar.getInstance();
cal.set(Calendar.YEAR, 2001);
cal.set(Calendar.MONTH, Calendar.AUGUST);
cal.set(Calendar.DATE, 2);
cal.set(Calendar.HOUR_OF_DAY, 18);
event.addDate(Event.START, PIMItem.ATTR_NONE, cal.getTime().getTime());
cal.set(Calendar.HOUR_OF_DAY, 23);
event.addDate(Event.END, PIMItem.ATTR_NONE, cal.getTime().getTime());
event.addInt(Event.ALARM, PIMItem.ATTR_NONE, 1800);
event.addString(BlackBerryEvent.ATTENDEES, PIMItem.ATTR_NONE,↵
        "pat@example.com");
event.addString(BlackBerryEvent.ATTENDEES, PIMItem.ATTR_NONE,↵
        "chris@example.com");
event.addString(BlackBerryEvent.ATTENDEES, PIMItem.ATTR_NONE,↵
        "scott@example.com");
event.addString(BlackBerryEvent.LOCATION, PIMItem.ATTR_NONE, "Grant Park");
event.addInt(BlackBerryEvent.FREE_BUSY, PIMItem.ATTR_NONE,↵
        BlackBerryEvent.FB_OUT_OF_OFFICE);
event.commit();
```

Later, we might check to see if a repeat rule has already been set on the event. If not, we can say that this is a biennial event that will recur on the first Wednesday of every other August for the next decade.

```
if (event.getRepeat() == null)
{
    RepeatRule repeat = new RepeatRule();
    repeat.setInt(RepeatRule.FREQUENCY, RepeatRule.YEARLY);
    repeat.setDate(RepeatRule.MONTH_IN_YEAR, RepeatRule.AUGUST);
    repeat.setInt(RepeatRule.WEEK_IN_MONTH, RepeatRule.FIRST);
    repeat.setInt(RepeatRule.DAY_IN_WEEK, RepeatRule.WEDNESDAY);
    repeat.setInt(RepeatRule.INTERVAL, 2);
    repeat.setInt(RepeatRule.COUNT, 5);
    event.setRepeat(repeat);
}
```

And, as a reminder, you can check for existing fields before setting or adding them. You also can remove values from previously set fields. The following code does both.

```
if (event.countValues(Event.NOTE) == 0)
    event.addString(Event.NOTE, PIMItem.ATTR_NONE, "Bring a sweater");
else
    event.setString(Event.NOTE, 0, PIMItem.ATTR_NONE, "Bring a sweater");
event.removeValue(BlackBerryEvent.ATTENDEES, 1);
event.commit();
```

Searching and Reading Events

EventList offers the same set of items() methods as found in ContactList for retrieving all or a subset of items. You can also look up an event by its UID. The next example shows how you can use a template to discover all of a user's public busy events.

```
Event template = events.createEvent();
template.addInt(Event.CLASS, PIMItem.ATTR_NONE, Event.CLASS_PUBLIC);
template.addInt(BlackBerryEvent.FREE_BUSY, PIMItem.ATTR_NONE, BlackBerryEvent.FB_BUSY);
Enumeration matches = events.items();
```

EventList also defines a new items() method that searches for all events that occur within a given timeframe. You can specify whether to look for events beginning, ending, or occurring at any point during that time. You also can control whether all occurrences of a repeating event are returned or just the initial instance. The next example retrieves all events occurring in November, counts them, and writes their names to standard out. The events will return from oldest start date to newest start date; you can resort if you like.

```
Calendar calendar = Calendar.getInstance();
calendar.set(Calendar.YEAR, 2010);
calendar.set(Calendar.MONTH, Calendar.NOVEMBER);
calendar.set(Calendar.DAY_OF_MONTH, 1);
long startTime = calendar.getTime().getTime();
calendar.set(Calendar.DAY_OF_MONTH, 30);
long endTime = calendar.getTime().getTime();
int eventCount = 0;
Enumeration matches = events.items(EventList.OCCURRING, startTime, endTime, true);
while (matches.hasMoreElements())
```

```
{
    ++eventCount;
    Event match = (Event)matches.nextElement();
    if (match.countValues(Event.SUMMARY) > 0)
    {
        String summary = match.getString(Event.SUMMARY, 0);
        System.out.println(summary);
    }
}
```

Exporting and Deleting Events

You can write events out in a standard vCal or iCal format using PIM, as in the following example.

```
FileConnection saveCal = (FileConnection)Connector.open(↵
        "file:///store/home/user/app/schedule.ical");
OutputStream out = saveCal.openOutputStream();
PIM.getInstance().toSerialFormat(event, out, "UTF-8", "VCALENDAR/2.0");
```

This will write the iCal data to the specified file, where it can later be opened from this or another app, or copied to another device.

Once you have finished with an event, or wish to cancel one, you can delete it from the list by calling removeEvent, which takes an existing Event object as a parameter. Starting with OS 6, you can also provide an optional flag BlackBerryEvent.DO_NOT_NOTIFY_ATTENDEES, which will prevent the platform from telling other attendees of the cancellation.

Showing Calendars

While the EventList does not offer an equivalent of BlackBerryContactList.choose(), you do have some options for accessing nice built-in views of the calendar without needing a lot of extra work.

Invoking the Native Calendar

If you want to display a particular event or a period of time within the built-in Calendar app, you can do so using the Invoke class. You specify that you wish to open APP_TYPE_CALENDAR and then provide suitable CalendarArguments. You can choose one of the following time arguments.

- Provide a Calendar to open to a specific date and time.

- Open on a particular Event.

- If neither is specified, open to the default calendar.

You can also specify one of several view arguments.

- ARG_NEW brings up the "New Appointment" screen, where the user can create an event. If you provided an Event, it will set the initial fields accordingly.

- ARG_VIEW_AGENDA will open in the agenda view, with upcoming events stacked vertically on top of one another.

- ARG_VIEW_DAY brings up the daily view, divided by hours.

- ARG_VIEW_WEEK brings up the weekly view, with dates as rows and hours as columns.

- ARG_VIEW_MONTH displays a month grid.

- ARG_VIEW_DEFAULT displays the calendar in the current default format.

Unlike with choose(), the Invoke call does not return a value. You can check if the user has added or modified an event by adding a PIMListListener, as discussed later in this chapter.

Invoke lets you display event information to your user or show him a chunk of his schedule without writing your own user interface. The following example searches for a particular event and then shows the entire week in which it occurs, which can help show the context of an event.

```
PIM pim = PIM.getInstance();
EventList events = (EventList)pim.openPIMList(PIM.EVENT_LIST, PIM.READ_ONLY);
Enumeration matches = events.items("Hootenanny");
if (matches.hasMoreElements())
{
    Event event = (Event)matches.nextElement();
    CalendarArguments args = new CalendarArguments(↵
            CalendarArguments.ARG_VIEW_WEEK, event);
    Invoke.invokeApplication(Invoke.APP_TYPE_CALENDAR, args);
}
```

Although your app can create events directly, you might prefer to give your user a chance to review and approve the event before saving it to the address book herself. The next example does just that, setting up an event but presenting it in the native calendar instead of committing it.

```
Event proposed = events.createEvent();
Calendar time = Calendar.getInstance();
time.set(Calendar.YEAR, 2010);
time.set(Calendar.MONTH, Calendar.SEPTEMBER);
time.set(Calendar.DATE, 19);
proposed.addDate(Event.START, PIMItem.ATTR_NONE, time.getTime().getTime());
proposed.addString(Event.SUMMARY, PIMItem.ATTR_NONE, "Talk Like A Pirate Day");
proposed.addString(Event.NOTE, PIMItem.ATTR_NONE, "Arrrr...");
CalendarArguments view = new CalendarArguments(↵
        CalendarArguments.ARG_NEW, proposed);
Invoke.invokeApplication(Invoke.APP_TYPE_CALENDAR, view);
```

Picking a Date

You can use built-in UI components for date and time selection instead of creating them yourself. If building a BlackBerry CLDC app, use the DateField class in the net.rim.device.api.ui.component package. You can style this as you would any other Field, and can also specify one of DateField's special style constants to indicate whether to show the DATE, TIME, or both with DATE_TIME. You can optionally provide a DateFormat to give suggestions about how to display the date prompt; these may or may not be honored. You can construct the field and add it from within a Screen by using the following code.

```
Calendar initial = Calendar.getInstance();
initial.set(Calendar.MONTH, Calendar.JANUARY);
initial.set(Calendar.DATE, 1);
initial.set(Calendar.YEAR, 1980);
DateField birthday = new DateField(↩
        "Birthday", initial.getTime().getTime(),DateField.DATE);
add(birthday);
```

A representation of the currently selected time will display on the screen. When the user accesses the control, a special view that allows fairly easy modifications will be displayed, as shown in Figure 6–8.

Figure 6–8. *Activating a BlackBerry DateField control*

Assuming you save the `DateField` in an instance variable, you can query it later to discover what time the user has selected. If you'd like to immediately update your UI when a change occurs, you can call `setChangeListener()` to receive notifications of updates. The following code shows how you can read the selected Unix time into a more accessible `Calendar` object.

```
long selectedTime = birthday.getDate();
Calendar selected = Calendar.getInstance();
selected.setTime(new Date(selectedTime));
```

If you create a MIDP MIDlet, you have access to another class called `DateField`, this version in the `javax.microedition.lcdui` package. It has a more basic interface than the CLDC version, and does not support as much customization, but it is very simple to use: it is an Item that can be inserted into a `Form`. You provide the label and specify whether the user can select the date, the time, or both. Time has a granularity of one minute. You can set an initial default time to suggest via `setDate()` and read the final result via `getDate()`. The actual display of the MIDlet `DateField` exactly matches that of the CLDC `DateField`. You can set up a `DateField` with no initial time as follows.

```
Form form = new Form("Date Selection");
DateField wedding = new DateField("Wedding", DateField.DATE_TIME);
form.insert(0, wedding);
Display.getDisplay(this).setCurrent(form);
```

I Have A ToDo List?

The PIM concept of ToDo corresponds to the BlackBerry Tasks application. This app lets you track lists of things to be done. With access to the `ToDoList` interface, your app can chime in on what's important.

Each ToDo encapsulates a specific task. ToDo is based on the VTODO spec, a subset of the vCalendar specification. Calendar events and todo tasks have a close relationship, but they are not the same. An `Event` should have a time associated; ToDos may have due dates, but can also simply remind about outstanding tasks. The following example shows a simple VTODO.

```
BEGIN:VCALENDAR
VERSION:2.0
BEGIN:VTODO
DUE:20100401T235959
STATUS:NEEDS-ACTION
SUMMARY:Research practical jokes
END:VTODO
END:VCALENDAR
```

ToDo shares many of the same features as `Event`, as shown in Table 6–6. They are not interchangeable, so do not attempt to cast one to the other or use a field locator like `Event.SUMMARY` to read a ToDo summary.

Table 6-6. *ToDo Fields*

Field	Meaning	Type	Example	Supported
ToDo.SUMMARY	Title for this task	STRING	"Bring Goodies"	Yes
ToDo.NOTE	Complete details on this task	STRING	"Bring in enough cookies for 30 people"	Yes
ToDo.PRIORITY	Importance of this task	INT	0 for unspecified, 1 for highest, 9 for lowest	Yes
ToDo.CLASS	Visibility of this ToDo	INT	ToDo.CLASS_PUBLIC, ToDo.CLASS_PRIVATE, ToDo.CLASS_CONFIDENTIAL	No
BlackBerryToDo. STATUS	Current completion of this task	INT	BlackBerryToDo.STATUS_NOT_STARTED, BlackBerryToDo.STATUS_IN_PROGRESS, BlackBerryToDo.STATUS_DEFERRED, BlackBerryToDo.STATUS_WAITING, BlackBerryToDo.STATUS_COMPLETED	Yes
BlackBerryToDo. REMINDER	Day and time to sound or display a reminder alarm	DATE	1207042400000	Yes
ToDo.DUE	When this task should be done	DATE	1207050400000	Yes
ToDo.COMPLETED	Whether the task is finished	BOOLEAN	true	Yes
ToDo.COMPLETION_ DATE	When this task was finished	DATE	1207045400000	No
ToDo.REVISION	Last time this task was modified	DATE	1207032700000	No
ToDo.UID	Unique identifier	STRING	"5678901234"	Yes

NOTE: Although you can provide PRIORITY in a range from 0 to 9, BlackBerry devices only support 3 levels of task priority. 1-3 will be stored as 1 and displayed as "High," 7-9 will be stored as 9 and displayed as "Low," and everything else is stored as 5 and displayed as "Normal."

Other than the different fields, ToDo objects behave like Event objects. You access fields in the same way, and have access to the same kind of time-ranged search. You can use the extended BlackBerryToDo to access custom fields. The following sample demonstrates creating a new task for the user.

```
PIM pim = PIM.getInstance();
ToDoList todos = (ToDoList)pim.openPIMList(PIM.TODO_LIST, PIM.READ_WRITE);
```

```
ToDo todo = todos.createToDo();
todo.addString(ToDo.SUMMARY, PIMItem.ATTR_NONE, "Buy a new BlackBerry");
if (todos.isSupportedField(ToDo.CLASS))
{
    if (todo.countValues(ToDo.CLASS) == 0)
    {
        todo.addInt(ToDo.CLASS, PIMItem.ATTR_NONE, ToDo.CLASS_PUBLIC);
    }
}
todo.addInt(BlackBerryToDo.STATUS,↩
        PIMItem.ATTR_NONE, BlackBerryToDo.STATUS_IN_PROGRESS);
Calendar time = Calendar.getInstance();
time.set(Calendar.YEAR, 2010);
time.set(Calendar.MONTH, Calendar.NOVEMBER);
time.set(Calendar.DATE, 15);
time.set(Calendar.HOUR, 8);
todo.addDate(ToDo.DUE, PIMItem.ATTR_NONE, time.getTime().getTime());
time.set(Calendar.DATE, 8);
todo.addDate(↩
        BlackBerryToDo.REMINDER, PIMItem.ATTR_NONE, time.getTime().getTime());
todo.commit();
```

Take a Memo

The BlackBerryMemoList and its contained BlackBerryMemo objects are the easiest PIMItem classes to work with. These allow you to access the user's saved memos or add memos of your own. A BlackBerryMemo contains only three fields, all of which have the STRING data type.

▓   TITLE provides the name of the memo, which will be viewable from a list perspective.

▓   NOTE contains the memo's text.

▓   UID is the standard unique identifier.

You can create, edit, search, read, and delete memo objects just as you would other PIMItem objects. The next example shows a grocery list app that will look for a shopping list memo in the user's existing memos. If it finds one, it will add items to the list; otherwise, it will create a new memo. This shows how your app can integrate with other parts of the phone that the user can interact with even when your app is not running.

```
String ingredients = "Butter\nEggs\nChocolate Chips\nFlour";
PIM pim = PIM.getInstance();
BlackBerryMemoList memos = (BlackBerryMemoList)pim.openPIMList(↩
        BlackBerryPIM.MEMO_LIST, PIM.READ_WRITE);
BlackBerryMemo template = memos.createMemo();
template.addString(BlackBerryMemo.TITLE, PIMItem.ATTR_NONE, "Shopping List");
Enumeration matches = memos.items(template);
if (matches.hasMoreElements())
{
    BlackBerryMemo existing = (BlackBerryMemo)matches.nextElement();
    if (existing.countValues(BlackBerryMemo.NOTE) > 0)
    {
```

```
            String text = existing.getString(BlackBerryMemo.NOTE, 0);
            ingredients = text + "\n" + ingredients;
            existing.setString(↵
                    BlackBerryMemo.NOTE, 0, PIMItem.ATTR_NONE, ingredients);
        }
        else
        {
            existing.addString(BlackBerryMemo.NOTE, PIMItem.ATTR_NONE, ingredients);
        }
        existing.commit();
    }
    else
    {
        template.addString(BlackBerryMemo.NOTE, PIMItem.ATTR_NONE, ingredients);
        template.commit();
    }
```

You must set the TITLE before saving a note; if you fail to specify one, the method will throw a PIMException. This is different from required fields in other PIMItem objects, which provide a default value if you do not specify one.

Personal Changes

Every BlackBerryPIMList allows you to add and remove listeners. The listener will inform you when a change has come to the list: an item has been created, modified, or removed. You only need to respond to the events that interest you, and will continue to receive notifications until you remove the listener.

Listing 6–1 shows how to write a simple screen that instructs the user to delete a contact. By implementing the PIMListListener interface and adding itself as a listener, this screen will receive notifications whenever the contents of the list change. The class does not directly offer a UI for the deletion, but, if the user switches to the address book application and makes the deletion, this screen will be notified, and will update on-screen text using the same StatusUpdater we created for the MediaGrabber app. You can apply the same type of listener to any of the PIMList implementations.

Listing 6–1. Listening for Contact Deletion

```
import javax.microedition.pim.Contact;
import javax.microedition.pim.PIM;
import javax.microedition.pim.PIMItem;

import net.rim.blackberry.api.pdap.BlackBerryContactList;
import net.rim.blackberry.api.pdap.PIMListListener;
import net.rim.device.api.ui.UiApplication;
import net.rim.device.api.ui.component.LabelField;
import net.rim.device.api.ui.container.MainScreen;

public class RemoveContactListener extends MainScreen implements PIMListListener
{

    LabelField instructions;
    StatusUpdater status;
```

```
public RemoveContactListener()
{
    instructions = new LabelField();
    instructions.setText("It's time to vote someone off the island!");
    add(instructions);
    status = new StatusUpdater(instructions);
    try
    {
        BlackBerryContactList contacts = (BlackBerryContactList)PIM.↵
            getInstance().openPIMList(PIM.CONTACT_LIST, PIM.READ_ONLY);
        contacts.addListener(this);
        contacts.close();
    }
    catch (Exception e)
    {
        System.err.println(e);
        e.printStackTrace();
    }
}

public void itemAdded(PIMItem added)
{
    status.sendDelayedMessage("No!  You're supposed to get RID of people!");
}

public void itemRemoved(PIMItem removed)
{
    if (removed instanceof Contact)
    {
        if (removed.countValues(Contact.NAME) > 0)
        {
            String[] name = removed.getStringArray(Contact.NAME, 0);
            String message = "Goodbye, " + name[Contact.NAME_GIVEN] + "!";
            status.sendDelayedMessage(message);
        }
    }
}

public void itemUpdated(PIMItem oldContent, PIMItem newContent)
{
    status.sendDelayedMessage("Something changed, but they're still here.");
}
}
```

After you start the app and view the message, press the red end key on your BlackBerry to background the app. Open the address book and delete a contact. When you switch back to the app, you'll see the updated farewell message.

App: Selecting Recipients

BlackBerry devices have great keyboards, but entering a long email address can still feel cumbersome. If you know a lot of people, you probably cannot remember everyone's address. The rest of the world has had access to integrated contacts for a long while, so your users should as well.

The next iteration of MediaGrabber will allow you to select your recipient directly from the address book. For fun, after you send the message, use one of the extended BlackBerry user fields to keep track of how many messages you've sent. This could form the basis for later enhancements, like automatically suggesting the most frequently emailed contacts. All of your changes will occur within the SendingScreen class. Two new methods, selectRecipient() and updateContact(), do the bulk of the work. Listing 6–2 shows the sections of SendingScreen that have been modified to support your new features.

Listing 6–2. Integrating Media Sending with a User's Contacts

```java
package com.apress.king.mediagrabber;

// Newly imported packages.
import javax.microedition.pim.*;
import net.rim.blackberry.api.pdap.*;

public class SendingScreen extends MainScreen
{
    private MenuItem selectItem = new MenuItem("Select Recipient", 0, 0)
    {
        public void run()
        {
            selectRecipient();
        }
    };
    private void selectRecipient()
    {
        BlackBerryContactList contacts = null;
        try
        {
            PIM pim = PIM.getInstance();
            contacts = (BlackBerryContactList) pim.openPIMList(
                    PIM.CONTACT_LIST, PIM.READ_ONLY);
            PIMItem item = contacts.choose();
            if (item == null || !(item instanceof Contact))
                return;
            Contact contact = (Contact) item;
            if (contact.countValues(Contact.EMAIL) > 0)
            {
                String email = contact.getString(Contact.EMAIL, 0);
                receiver.setText(email);
            }
        }
        catch (Throwable t)
        {
            updater.sendDelayedMessage(t.getMessage());
        }
        finally
        {
            if (contacts != null)
            {
                try
                {
                    contacts.close();
                }
```

```
                    catch (PIMException pime)
                    {
                        // Empty
                    }
                }
            }
        }

        private void updateContact(String address)
        {
            BlackBerryContactList contacts = null;
            try
            {
                PIM pim = PIM.getInstance();
                contacts = (BlackBerryContactList) pim.openPIMList(
                        PIM.CONTACT_LIST, PIM.READ_WRITE);
                Contact template = contacts.createContact();
                template.addString(Contact.EMAIL, PIMItem.ATTR_NONE, address);
                Enumeration matches = contacts.items(template);
                while (matches.hasMoreElements())
                {
                    Contact match = (Contact) matches.nextElement();
                    if (match.countValues(BlackBerryContact.USER4) == 0)
                    {
                        // First time sending to them.
                        match.addString(BlackBerryContact.USER4, PIMItem.ATTR_NONE,
                                "1");
                    }
                    else
                    {
                        // Increment our counter.
                        String oldString = match.getString(BlackBerryContact.USER4,
                                0);
                        // If this isn't a number, will fall into the catch below.
                        int oldNumber = Integer.parseInt(oldString);
                        String newString = Integer.toString(oldNumber + 1);
                        match.setString(BlackBerryContact.USER4, 0,
                                PIMItem.ATTR_NONE, newString);
                    }
                    match.commit();
                }
            }
            catch (Throwable t)
            {
                updater.sendDelayedMessage(t.getMessage());
            }
            finally
            {
                if (contacts != null)
                {
                    try
                    {
                        contacts.close();
                    }
                    catch (PIMException pime)
                    {
                        // Empty
```

```
                }
              }
            }
          }

    private class MessageSender implements Runnable
    {
        public void run()
        {
            String address = receiver.getText();
            try
            {
                Message outgoing = createMessage(address, contentType,
                        filename, message);
                Transport.send(outgoing);
                updateContact(address);
                updater.sendDelayedMessage("Message sent");
                state = STATE_SENT;
            }
            catch (Exception e)
            {
                updater
                        .sendDelayedMessage("Problem sending: "
                                + e.getMessage());
                e.printStackTrace();
            }
        }
    }
}
```

WANT MORE?

PIM is one of the more entertaining areas of the BlackBerry API to play with, and you can enhance almost any application with a little extra integration. You might consider adding a few other features to MediaGrabber.

- Allow the user to select multiple recipients so they can send one file to many people at once.

- Show the recipients' names instead of their email addresses. Note that you will still need to store the addresses somewhere.

- Create a rolling ToDo that provides a random challenge for the user. For example, "Take 10 pictures in the next 5 days." Update their progress in the task, and provide a new one after they complete the challenge .

While you can easily go overboard with these kinds of features, you can also learn useful techniques. You can always remove features later if they seem cumbersome or aren't popular… and who knows, you may stumble across a really compelling feature.

Excelsior

You might know more about your users now than their own mothers do. With access to their daily schedule, circle of friends and business associates, and lists of what's important to them, your app has a great shot at making itself more useful and interesting. With this level of trust comes an enormous responsibility. Many users dislike sharing their private information, and you will quickly lose their trust if you start mining that data for your own purposes.

With that warning in mind, users are more amenable than ever before to sharing information about themselves so long as you reward them for doing so, whether in the form of entertainment, convenience, or achievements. Most successful apps that use PIM will fall into one of two categories. Either they fundamentally depend on personal information, or they use PIM to supplement their main purpose. If your app falls into the first category, you can use the information with confidence, so long as you disclose it; simply by installing your app, a user has indicated her interest in sharing data with you. In the latter case, in order for your app to be popular it should degrade gracefully in the absence of permission. If your app provides a carpooling service, and lets users upload their address books to find other carpoolers, it should continue to run even if the users don't feel comfortable sharing that data; people can still search and see who else wants to carpool. Once you have established a sufficient level of trust, most users will eventually choose to share their data for their own convenience. The key is to be forthright in what data you collect, how you will use that data, and what will happen if the data isn't shared.

In Chapter 7, you'll continue your tour through the powerful set of built-in applications by examining the browser. The few BlackBerry users who don't use the device's PIM features will almost certainly pop open a browser from time to time, and you will soon learn how to take advantage of it.

Chapter 7

Browser with Web Apps

BlackBerry devices have long offered the benefit of placing the Internet in your pocket. With strong data features, access to corporate intranets, a relatively large screen and high-quality keyboard, it's little surprise that the browser gets so much use. As we continue our tour through ways to integrate more deeply with BlackBerry devices, we will look at how to effectively tap the browser as a portal to rich content on the Web and construct lightweight web apps of your own.

Browser Types

Even though your BlackBerry might only display a single Browser icon, behind the scenes it supports several different browsing standards and technologies. Before you start coding, consider the various options available for mobile web sites.

WAP

When web browsing first came to mobile devices, it did not look anything like the desktop browsing experience. Devices had small screens, low resolution, and abysmal data transfer rates. If you visited a regular web page, loading it would take minutes and might be unreadable once complete.

Nonetheless, consumers have steadily demanded web access ever since mobile phones gained data capabilities. In order to support the extremely limited capabilities on a handheld, the Wireless Application Protocol (WAP) Forum developed a set of specifications in the late 1990s describing how to deliver mobile web content and how to display that content.

The first crack at the mobile Web was the development of the Wireless Markup Language (WML). It assumed that most phones could not display images, and made other assumptions about device capabilities in an effort to guide design and improve performance. WML used the metaphor of a deck of cards, with each WML document defining a single deck and each viewable screen a single card. See the following sample WML document.

```
<?xml version="1.0"?>
<!DOCTYPE wml PUBLIC "-//WAPFORUM//DTD WML 1.1//EN"
   "http://www.wapforum.org/DTD/wml_1.1.xml" >
<wml>
  <card id="index" title="Welcome">
    <p mode="wrap">Movie tickets on sale this weekend</p>
    <p>
      <b>Call Our Operators</b><br />
      <a href="wtai://wp/mc;14155550188">415-555-0188</a>
    </p>
  </card>
</wml>
```

> **NOTE:** You can find the entire specification for WML online at www.wapforum.org/what/
> technical/wml-30-apr-98.pdf. However, be aware that no mobile browser completely
> implements the spec. Look on the BlackBerry web site for the BlackBerry Browser Development
> Guide, which includes a complete list of supported WML tags.

Other than the oddness of the "card" element, this probably looks familiar if you've
worked with HTML before. The most interesting innovation of WML comes in that href
link. Instead of a standard web-style "http://" reference, it uses the protocol
"wtai://", Wireless Telephone Application Interface, which provides a powerful way for
mobile web content to gain access to phone hardware features: select a link in your
browser, and the phone automatically makes a call without your needing to remember
and dial the number yourself.

So how can you create WML? You can write and serve it up yourself as a document
with the MIME type text/vnd.wap.wml. More often, though, WML documents are
created by a WAP gateway. As Figure 7–1 illustrates, a WAP gateway handles traffic
from a mobile web browser, retrieves the requested content (which may be full HTML),
and then transcodes that content into WML. In other words, the WAP gateway rewrites
the document into a format appropriate for the browser. This may include stripping out
large images, removing styling information, flattening frames, and otherwise making the
content more accessible.

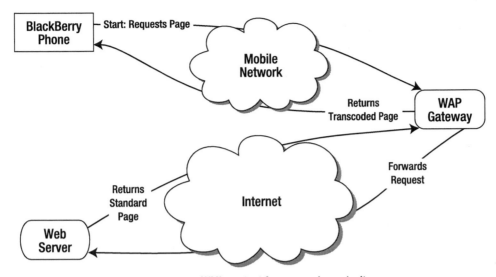

Figure 7–1. *A WAP gateway generates WML content from a regular web site*

WML is on the way out for multiple reasons. Modern mobile phones have far greater capabilities, larger and more detailed screens, access to faster wireless networks, and often unlimited data plans. Even lower-capability phones increasingly support WML's successor languages. Still, a large number of legacy WAP sites remain available, and these will continue to exist for a long time.

Figure 7–2 shows a sample mobile web page. You'll notice the numbered links; these would look unusual in a regular desktop web browser, but they allow very easy navigation for people using basic 12-key phone keyboards.

Figure 7–2. *Accessing a web site formatted for mobile content*

HTML and XHTML

The BlackBerry browser started adding support for full HTML with software version 4.0, and support has gradually improved with every new release. HTML is by far the most popular markup language on the Web, and you can use your BlackBerry to visit any site you would on your desktop computer. Still, the handheld HTML browsing experience on a mobile device is not as pleasant. While data speeds have gotten better, browsing can still feel painfully slow, especially if on a 2G connection. If pages are not specifically designed for mobile devices, they can be hard to navigate and view. The BlackBerry browser has historically had trouble rendering certain common HTML elements such as tables. Additionally, a lot of content that requires special Plug-ins simply will not display. As a result, while you can open just about any web page in your BlackBerry browser, only some of them will look good and operate well. If you choose to use HTML when deploying a mobile web site, you should view the pages with every version of the BlackBerry that you wish to support. If you have an existing page that looks good, you might not need to do any extra work. Figure 7–3 shows a full-featured HTML web page displaying within the BlackBerry browser.

Figure 7-3. *Full web content in a mobile browser*

The current best practice for deploying mobile web sites is to use XHTML mobile profile. This fully conforming document contains a specialized set of XHTML page elements, selected with a mobile browsing experience in mind. The most recent version is XHTML-MP2, and pages written in this language may load faster and render better than ordinary HTML. Best of all, XHTML-MP2 is very close in design to HTML, making it much easier to support both mobile and desktop views of the same type of content. Servers should provide XHTML-MP2 with a MIME type of `application/xhtml+xml` or `application/vnd.wap.xhtml+xml`. The following sample shows an XHTML-MP2 document.

```
<?xml version="1.0" encoding="UTF-8"?>
<!DOCTYPE html PUBLIC "-//WAPFORUM//DTD XHTML Mobile 1.2//EN"
  "http://www.openmobilealliance.org/tech/DTD/xhtml-mobile12.dtd">
<html xmlns="http://www.w3.org/1999/xhtml" xml:lang="en">
  <head>
    <title>Progressive Dinner</title>
  </head>
  <body>
    <p>Details on our <a href="http://example.net/may/">next dinner</a>.</p>
  </body>
</html>
```

NOTE: You can see a specification for XHTML-MP at http://www.openmobilealliance.org/ tech/affiliates/wap/wap-277-xhtmlmp-20011029-a.pdf. The document is short and mainly references other resources.

You will occasionally run across the term WAP2. Mobile carriers and developers have realized that today's phones have many more capabilities than those that motivated the original WAP system, and WAP2 removes many of the limitations present in WAP. When your phone uses a WAP2 connection, it still connects through a gateway, but in the case of WAP2 no special transcoding or transformation is done. The gateway may add some extra identifiers to your outgoing request that help identify the device or the mobile network, which can help your web server determine the appropriate content to provide.

BlackBerry devices do a good job at rendering this type of content. When dealing with full-featured pages like HTML or XHTML-MP, you should realize that the user has a great deal of control over the behavior of her browser. People may enable or disable Javascript, HTML tables, even images. Your application won't know how the user configured their browser, so if your app uses the browser and relies on certain features being enabled, it should provide instructions on how to configure the browser properly.

Embedding Content

HTML and XHTML documents support embedded content. You often see examples of this on the Web for special items such as Java applets or Flash video. BlackBerry devices have had supported embedding since device software version 4.0, and their support is considered complete as of version 4.6. You can embed a variety of content including midi files, Plazmic animations, and other HTML documents.

NOTE: If serving Plazmic content, your server must be configured to associate the .pme file extension with MIME type application/x-vnd.rim.pme and .pmb with application/x-vnd.rim.pme.b.

You can embed content by using the <object> tag, as in the following example. Use embedded objects when you want to present something within a larger context, or if you want to show something else if the browser cannot display the main content.

```
<OBJECT border=0 type="application/x-vnd.rim.pme" width="50" height="50"
data="spinner.pme">
```

HTML5

All browsers, desktop and mobile, will transition to HTML5. This new web standard modernizes the markup language to better match how people actually use the Web, and provides better performance, better functionality, and greater compatibility between vendors to support rich media features.

That said, HTML5 support continues to evolve. Some features may not make sense in a mobile browser, while others can be realized in multiple ways; for example, a date control can be presented using a keyboard or using a touch screen. RIM has partially supported HTML5 since OS 4.7, and continues to add support for more elements with additional releases of their software. Therefore, as with app development, before you start development with HTML5 you should first identify the oldest device that you need to support. Then investigate that device's capabilities, and restrict yourself to that feature set while building the mobile site. If it does not offer the features you want, you can investigate work-arounds using older HTML elements, or construct multiple versions of your web page and serve the appropriate version based on the User-Agent string provided by the mobile web browser.

> **NOTE:** BlackBerry devices running OS version 6.0 and beyond send a standardized User-Agent string that looks like `Mozilla/5.0 (BlackBerry; U; BlackBerry 9670; en-US) AppleWebKit/534.1+ (KHTML, like Gecko) Version/6.0.0.141 Mobile Safari/534.1+`. This format matches the User-Agent used by other mobile and desktop browsers, which makes it simpler for web servers to parse and serve appropriate data. Older devices use BlackBerry-specific User-Agent strings that look like `BlackBerry9530/5.0.0.93 Profile/MIDP-2.0 Configuration/CLDC-1.1 VendorID/179`.

Starting with BlackBerry OS 6.0, RIM has replaced their older browser rendering engine with a new version built on WebKit. WebKit started on the desktop, but has quickly become the standard for smartphone mobile browsers, and now BlackBerry joins the iPhone, Android, and Symbian devices with WebKit support. This means that most mobile websites should render quite similarly across all platforms, reducing the headaches that used to come with writing portable websites for a variety of mobile browsers. It also means that newly standardized features and bugfixes may arrive to the browser more quickly, as the open source WebKit project provides updates for compatible browsers. Best of all, WebKit supports HTML5, so you can start taking advantage of HTML5 on devices running OS version 6.0 and higher.

So, what benefits does HTML5 offer? You can find a complete list in the BlackBerry Browser HTML Reference guide, found on the BlackBerry developer documentation site. Some highlights that have been supported on BlackBerry devices include the following.

- Attractive input pickers for dates, colors, and more.
- Data lists that suggest available options.
- Video and audio elements.
- Timers for scheduling later events.
- Location information and notifications.
- Bitmapped canvas for dynamically creating images.

Widgets

For most of their history, the Browser has existed as a separate application from the main RIM OS. Starting with OS 5, and particularly with OS 6, the browser has grown more integrated with the main device. Widgets provide the clearest example of this. Widgets are small web programs that are stored and run on your device, exploiting HTML for their layout and display, while also integrating with device capabilities to provide more engaging and interactive features. Most smartphones support some form of widgets, although developers must generally rewrite a widget for each platform, particularly if it relies on device interaction. RIM has branded their widget platform as WebWorks.

Writing a widget typically follows a two-stage process.

1. First you or another designer will construct a skin for the widget, using HTML to create the interface.

2. Next, you use a special BlackBerry javascript widget API to add features to the widget. For example, when the user clicks a button, you might read data from a text file and then update a visible field. If necessary, you can write your own extensions to the javascript library that call into your own Java code.

Users can place widgets on their home screen, and interact with them without feeling like they're going through the browser at all. In this way, widgets can offer the best form of device integration: they are always visible and always available in a common location.

Other Browser Options

Third-party installable browsers have been popular on BlackBerry devices for years. They started making inroads when the official browser lagged behind in capabilities; a smaller portion of users install them now, but thanks to the increase in BlackBerry owners a growing number are turning to these alternative options. One of the most popular is Opera Mini, available at http://www.opera.com/mini/.

Unfortunately, you cannot integrate your app with third-party browser apps as you can with the native browser. You can't know for sure that all your users will have a particular browser, and, even if they do, they do not offer as rich a set of APIs for interaction as you can find with the built-in browser. Still, you should realize that other browsers exist, especially if you build a mobile web site and want to make sure all your visitors can view it properly.

Modern third-party browsers typically support HTML5, but do not offer access to the BlackBerry Javascript API. The device renders all widgets using the native browser's UI engine, so installing a new browser will not affect widget content.

BES administrators and users may be interested in BlackBerry push content. This is a very specialized application of the browser that allows corporations to send web content directly to their users' BlackBerry devices, where they can later view and use it. Pushing content requires some specialized server coding but no special support from the client. We will examine push content in more detail in Chapter 12.

Web, Widget, or App Development?

Since you've read this far into the book, you have probably already decided to write a "real" client app. Still, you should periodically take stock of the situation and see whether that is still the best way to deliver your app. You also might need to justify your decision to someone else, or provide advice on future projects. Therefore, consider the following tradeoffs before proceeding too far in BlackBerry development.

Lightweight Web

Browsers and browser-like applications are sometimes described as thin clients. Their only job is to send data, receive data, and format the results. They do not come with code describing how to play a game, read a patient's medical chart, or draw a map. They might seem to do all those things, but only because the content delivered to the client can do so.

Thin clients can have many advantages over their thicker counterparts.

- Easy Updates: Assuming you have access to the web server, you can easily make any changes you want. Whether you have one user or one million, everyone will see the change the next time their browser launches.

- Familiarity: People feel very comfortable using their browsers, and may trust a browser more than a random app they have installed.

- Cost: You don't need to pay RIM for signature keys.

- Security: The user won't see security prompts or other warnings when they visit your site.

- Consistency across Apps: Users appreciate how pressing Back will always take them back one page, pressing the BlackBerry Menu key will always bring up options for bookmarking and entering a URL, etc.

- Potentially Faster Startup Time: If your app contains a lot of content, it will take a while to load it all into memory. On the Web with a fast data connection, users can start using the app as soon as the first page loads.

You should keep some caveats in mind, especially if you are new to mobile web development.

- Browser Differences: If you develop a web site for the desktop, you'll probably be in good shape if it runs well in Firefox and Internet Explorer. If you're developing a general mobile web site, you need to be prepared to support dozens of different browsers, each with different versions and problems. Supporting all this can be a nightmare, especially if you use unusual features like location services or want a unique yet good-looking site.

- Lack of Control: The user drives the browser configuration, and many choose to speed things up by disabling images or otherwise lowering their feature set.

- Limited Capabilities: Basic web sites don't have access to many of a phone's capabilities, such as the microphone or the file system.

- Slow Connections: Some users still run on slower 2G data networks, and others may have a weak signal. Don't assume that everyone connects over a fat pipe. Make the pages as small as possible, and consider offering a link to an even more limited version for very slow connections.

- No Connections: If the phone goes into a tunnel, deep into an office building, or out in the woods, the user will be totally cut off from your web site. Consider when and how people will want to use your app to determine if this is acceptable. Note that users can choose to make certain bookmarked pages available in offline mode; this is a good solution if you just present text or use Javascript on a single page, but not if you use multiple pages or AJAX-style dynamic content loading.

Versatile Widgets

WebWorks widgets offer an attractive middle ground: they combine the flexibility and ease of web development with the feature set of full Java applications. Developers can often create a simple visual prototype widget within hours, rather than days, simply through HTML. They can then build on that prototype by writing the Javascript that will implement app features. Depending on the app's needs, they may also write their own custom Javascript extensions that call into native platform APIs to accomplish their tasks. Overall, widgets strive to make the easy things simple, and the hard things possible.Widgets will likely grow in popularity in the future, for the following resons.

- Ubiquity: Users can place widgets on their home screen, where they will always see and interact with it, increasing your exposure and usefulness.

- Right size: If you have a cool idea for a little app, a widget lets you simply present just what you want, without requiring the infrastructure of a full app.

- Extensible: With the ability to write custom Javascript extensions, you can support virtually any feature.

- No Network Required: Unlike regular web apps, a widget lives on your phone, and as long as it stores any necessary data locally, it can run under any network conditions

- Discovery: You package and distribute widgets as you would full-fledged BlackBerry apps, so you can take advantage of BlackBerry App World and other platforms for app distribution.

That said, widgets do not fit every situation. Keep the following points in mind when making your decision.

- Portability: Many smartphone platforms offer widget support, but often follow different standards. You may be able to re-use some of your HTML across different platforms, but will need to rewrite all Javascript and your custom libraries.

- Wrong size: If your app has many features or a complicated workflow, it probably needs a full-screen application so the user has sufficient space to see all relevant information at once. This includes most non-trivial games.

- Value perception: Unfortunately, users tend to associate widgets with lower functionality and lower value. Therefore, people may feel reluctant to pay for a widget when they would willingly pay for an app with equivalent features.

- Performance: For the majority of uses, widgets will perform well, but the web UI will limit your ability to drive some intensive operations like 3D rendering.

Heavy-duty Apps

Besides being a lot of fun to write, applications bring many improvements to the table. Often referred to as rich clients, apps arrive with knowledge about how to perform their tasks. An app actually understands how to play a game or read a medical chart, and doesn't need to support tasks it will never perform. Apps are specialized, and because of that they can deliver a much more satisfying experience to the user than a web app.

Rich clients offer quite a few improvements over the thinner web browser.

- Faster Performance: If your app is written well, it will run circles around a web site doing the same task.

- Full Capabilities: A signed app with the proper permissions can do practically anything at all on the phone.

- Offline Support: If your app doesn't contain networking components, it will be fully functional even if the phone's radio is turned off or the user doesn't subscribe to a data plan. Even if it does use networking, you have more options than on the browser: you can cache old data, offer a reduced-functionality mode, and so on. In contrast, a web app requires the user to be online.

- Monetization: You can use existing storefronts like BlackBerry App World to distribute and get paid for your app. With web apps, you'll need to manage billing and charges on your own.

Do consider the following caveats before starting to create a mobile app, especially if you have not previously developed for mobile platforms.

- Testing: Signing and loading your app takes much longer than simply hitting refresh, and can significantly slow down your development speed.

- Porting: A web page will at least render on most phones, even if it doesn't look good. A BlackBerry-compiled app won't even run on other phones like Android or iPhone.

- Distribution: You must work with a mobile storefront such as BlackBerry App World (and share your revenue) or be prepared to manage updates and sales yourself.

Launching the Browser

In many circumstances, you will want to offload some of your app's functions to a separate web browser. Perhaps you have a privacy policy that might be updated; rather than needing to release a new client every time it changes, you can instruct them to check it out and then direct the browser to a page with the updated policy. Or you might connect them to enhanced content, like leader boards or photo galleries, which you can quickly develop and deploy over the Web. Whatever the reason, opening the browser provides a useful portal into online content.

Starting the Browser

In Chapter 3, we saw how you can easily open the web browser, using only two lines of code.

```
BrowserSession browserSession = Browser.getDefaultSession();
browserSession.displayPage("http://www.sfgate.com");
```

However, this only tells one part of the story. While most users perceive a single "browser" application on their phone, most commercial BlackBerry devices actually contain multiple browsers. This is because of the different underlying radio technologies that each might use (such as cellular or Wi-Fi antennae), the different gateways to access (such as a BES gateway to corporate content or a WAP gateway to a carrier's subscriber page), and different rules configured on each account (the user may be charged for the mobile network but not for Wi-Fi).

In many cases, this need not concern you. If you are writing an app for your personal use, and know that the site is accessible from every gateway, then you can use the above code. However, if you need to open the browser content over a particular channel or wish to let the user decide, then you will have to dig a little deeper.

Service Options

You may remember service books from previous chapters. A service book describes a particular set of network configuration settings. As you'll see below, you can inspect the available service books, find the available connection types, and get the information necessary to open the correct browser.

Signed apps can freely examine service books, but the API doesn't document the books very well. Records contain a set of application data, which is a raw array of bytes that provide connection information. These bytes are in a format that allows the device to exchange information with the BlackBerry Desktop Manager over a serial or USB interface. The information is a sequence of tagged fields: each starts with a 2-byte size, followed by a 1-byte type indicator, followed by the actual data payload.

Fortunately, RIM has provided a couple of classes to help in extracting the necessary information from this opaque block. ConverterUtilities lets you scan through the types in the service book data to locate a particular type. ConverterUtilities in turn uses a DataBuffer, a general-purpose utility class that wraps a byte array and allows you to read and write basic types from that array, similar to the functions provided by DataInputStream and DataOutputStream.

Next comes the deep voodoo—the specific configuration type of the service book is stored in a record field with type 12. Once you retrieve that value, you must match it against the proper browser configuration, as shown in Table 7–1. You should also check to make sure that the record is active and valid; it does not make sense to launch a disabled browser.

Table 7–1. *Browser Configuration Types*

Number	Browser
0	WAP
1	BES
3	Wi-Fi
4	BIS
7	WAP2

Listing 7–1 shows a general-purpose class you can use to retrieve a desired type of browser session. You can call this repeatedly with different parameters in order to find your most preferred available browser. For convenience, the browser config types are provided as constants.

Listing 7–1. *A Convenient Wrapper Class for Retrieving a Specific Type of Browser*

```java
import java.io.EOFException;
import net.rim.blackberry.api.browser.*;
import net.rim.device.api.servicebook.*;
import net.rim.device.api.synchronization.ConverterUtilities;
import net.rim.device.api.util.DataBuffer;

public class BrowserLocator
{
    public static final int BROWSER_TYPE_WAP = 0;
    public static final int BROWSER_TYPE_BES = 1;
    public static final int BROWSER_TYPE_WIFI = 3;
    public static final int BROWSER_TYPE_BIS = 4;
    public static final int BROWSER_TYPE_WAP2 = 7;

    public static BrowserSession createBrowserSession(int browserType)
    {
        ServiceBook book = ServiceBook.getSB();
        ServiceRecord[] records = book.findRecordsByCid("BrowserConfig");
        int recordCount = records.length;
        for (int i = 0; i < recordCount; i++)
        {
            ServiceRecord record = records[i];
            if (record.isValid() && !record.isDisabled()
                    && getConfigurationType(record) == browserType)
            {
                return Browser.getSession(record.getUid());
            }
        }
        return null;
    }

    private static int getConfigurationType(ServiceRecord record)
    {
        try
        {
            byte[] appData = record.getApplicationData();
            if (appData != null)
            {
                DataBuffer buffer = new DataBuffer(appData, 0, appData.length,
                        true);
                // Skip past the first entry.
                buffer.readByte();
                // 12 is the magic field that holds the service
                // record's configuration type.
                if (ConverterUtilities.findType(buffer, 12))
                {
                    // Buffer is now pointing at the value.
                    return ConverterUtilities.readInt(buffer);
                }
            }
        }
```

```
            }
            catch (EOFException eofe)
            {
            }
            return -1;
        }
}
```

TIP: Just because a browser is available doesn't necessarily mean that it is usable; poor signal or other problems may prevent you from connecting. In the case of the Wi-Fi browser, you can at least check to see if the user has a valid access point by checking whether `WLANInfo.getWLANState()` returns `WLANInfo.WLAN_STATE_CONNECTED`. Otherwise, Wi-Fi may be on but disconnected.

After writing this class, you can retrieve an appropriate browser and display a page with very little code. The example below shows how to open a browser through a BES connection to view an online comic.

```
BrowserSession session = BrowserLocator.createBrowserSession(
        BrowserLocator.BROWSER_TYPE_BES);
if (session != null)
{
    session.displayPage("http://www.xkcd.com");
}
```

Launching with HTML

So far, we have focused on using the browser as a portal to dynamic, regularly updated external content. However, sometimes the browser can serve purely as a presentation tool. If your app can generate HTML, and runs on a device with software version 4.2 or later, it may use the browser to display its content. This may take less time to implement than developing a custom UI framework within your own app. This also provides a great option for applications that ordinarily do not contain any UI, such as libraries, but that occasionally want to show an error screen or other visual element.

To show your own HTML you use the same `BrowserSession.displayPage()` method that's used to show web sites, but, instead of prefixing with a protocol like `"http:"`, use the protocol `"data:"`. This instructs the browser that it should load the remaining content as its own page. Because there is no web server to provide the MIME type of the following content, you must supply it yourself with a string such as `"text/html"` or `"application/xhtml+xml"`.

NOTE: Because `BrowserSession.displayPage()` takes a regular String, it cannot handle binary data or other special characters. If your document will contain these, you should first Base64-encode the data using Base64OutputStream. Append `";base64"` to the end of your MIME type to indicate that the remaining content is Base64-encoded.

The next code sample demonstrates how to create a simple HTML document in memory and then display it using the default browser.

```
String content = "data:text/html,";
content += "<html>" +
    "<head><title>Party Alert</title></head>" +
    "<body>" +
        "<p>Only 243 days left until National Hangover Awareness Day!</p>" +
    "</body></html>";
Browser.getDefaultSession().displayPage(content);
```

This technique clearly has some limitations. You can't easily link to other local content, and handling images is also hard. Some users may be confused when they see the browser and not realize that it is connected to your app; you should clearly communicate where the content is coming from. Still, it is another handy tool to have in your toolbox, and offers the perfect solution to certain problems.

Embedding a Browser in Your App

After you've gone to the bother of writing an app and getting people to run it, it seems like a shame to send them packing when you want to display some Web content such as a high scores page hosted on your server. You are implicitly admitting that your app can't handle displaying that sort of content, and once they hit the browser you have no idea what they are doing. They may pop open their bookmarks and forget stop following your app flow.

You have an alternative: instead of going into a separate app, bring the browser into your own. You get to keep the user's attention within your app longer, and you get a great deal of insight into their actions: where they go, what they see, what they do. You can make the embedded browser as simple or as complex as you like.

An Overview

You can bring browser content into your app with a `BrowserField`. Like any `Field`, you can position it on the screen where you like, apply styling, and otherwise integrate it into your screen. `BrowserField` has many additional methods and associated classes that help you control the browsing experience. We will look at some of the most useful features supported. Developers can use these according to their needs, ranging from displaying simple static content to providing a fully functional embedded browser.

> **NOTE:** Somewhat confusingly, two classes named `BrowserField` exist. This section will use the classes in the package `net.rim.device.api.browser.field2`.

Supporting Players

BrowserField provides most functionality itself, but to fully tap into the browser, you can take advantage of several other classes. Some of the most useful are described below.

BrowserFieldConfig

This lets you specify additional properties associated with a browsing session, such as HTTP headers and cookie handling. You can create a BrowserFieldConfig and use it when creating your BrowserField, or you can retrieve the browser's current BrowserFieldConfig and modify its properties to affect future operations.

BrowserFieldListener

BrowserFieldListener provides you with reports about the progress of browser operations. By extending this class, you can receive notifications that you can use to display custom errors or progress indicators. You will also gain access to the DOM objects that are loaded through the browser, which may prove helpful if your app wants to take action based on the content loaded within the embedded browser.

An Example

To display an embedded browser you can simply create a BrowserField and insert it into your Screen. Listing 7–2 demonstrates this, sandwiching the browser content in between two text labels. We make it a little more interesting by implementing a custom BrowserFieldListener that observes browser activity, and reports it back to us through our status updater UI field.

Listing 7–2. *Embedding a Browser in a MainScreen*

```
import net.rim.device.api.browser.field.ContentReadEvent;
import net.rim.device.api.browser.field2.BrowserField;
import net.rim.device.api.browser.field2.BrowserFieldListener;
import net.rim.device.api.script.ScriptEngine;
import net.rim.device.api.ui.UiApplication;
import net.rim.device.api.ui.component.LabelField;
import net.rim.device.api.ui.container.MainScreen;

import org.w3c.dom.Document;

public class BrowserScreen extends MainScreen
{
    private LabelField status;
    private StatusUpdater updater;
    private String url;
    private BrowserField field;

    private BrowserFieldListener listener = new BrowserFieldListener()
    {
        public void documentAborted(BrowserField browserField, Document document)
        {
```

```
            updater.sendDelayedMessage("Aborted " + document.getDocumentURI());
        }

        public void documentCreated(BrowserField browserField,
                ScriptEngine scriptEngine, Document document)
        {
            updater.sendDelayedMessage("Created document "
                    + document.getDocumentURI() + " with engine "
                    + scriptEngine);
        }

        public void documentError(BrowserField browserField, Document document)
        {
            updater.sendDelayedMessage("Error in " + document.getDocumentURI());
        }

        public void documentLoaded(BrowserField browserField, Document document)
        {
            updater.sendDelayedMessage("Loaded " + document.getDocumentURI());
        }

        public void documentUnloading(BrowserField browserField,
                Document document)
        {
            updater
                    .sendDelayedMessage("Unloading "
                            + document.getDocumentURI());
        }

        public void downloadProgress(BrowserField browserField,
                ContentReadEvent event)
        {
            updater.sendDelayedMessage("Downloaded " + event.getItemsRead()
                    + " of " + event.getItemsToRead());
        }
    };

    public BrowserScreen()
    {
        status = new LabelField("Loading...");
        add(status);
        updater = new StatusUpdater(status);
        url = "http://www.bing.com";
        field = new BrowserField();
        add(new LabelField("Your search starts here."));
        add(field);
        field.addListener(listener);
        add(new LabelField("Don't forget to tip the service!"));
    }

    protected void onUiEngineAttached(boolean attached)
    {
        if (attached)
        {
            try
            {
```

```
            field.requestContent(url);
        }
        catch (Exception e)
        {
            updater.sendDelayedMessage("Failed to request URL " + url
                    + ": " + e.getMessage());
            e.printStackTrace();
        }
    }
}
}
```

If you create a simple app that pushes this screen and run the example, you will notice the Bing page load as shown in Figure 7–4 If you pay attention as it loads, you'll observe that the field automatically resizes to fit the amount of content inside. Many apps will prefer this behavior; if yours does not, you can wrap the field in another component and provide your own scrolling.

Figure 7–4. *A very simple browser field*

Play around with the browser for a while. It may impress you with its full feature set; with barely writing any code, you gained a complete browser with the ability to follow links, display images, and run javascript. You can easily add support for forward and backward history navigation if your app needs it, along with the other features described above.

> **NOTE:** You will need to have a phone running OS version 5.0 or later to take advantage of this version of `BrowserField`. Older phones can use the classes provided in the `net.rim.device.api.browser.field` package; these require considerably more code to integrate into your app.

Embedding Your App in a Browser

So far, we've looked at how to make your app call out to a browser, and how to pull the browser into your app. Both of these cases require the user to run your app in order to show web content. But wouldn't it be cool if you could control what the browser displayed whenever the user opened it?

MIME Type Providers

The BlackBerry browser identifies all pieces of content it finds on the Web by their content MIME types. Some of these it knows how to handle on its own, like `text/html`. For other pieces, like music, it must call out to other pieces of software in order to handle them. And, for some, it just doesn't know what to do with them.

This is where we come in. The BlackBerry browser has a pluggable architecture. Any piece of software can register itself as a provider for a particular type of content. When the browser finds something it doesn't recognize, it will query the providers to see if they want to take it. If they say yes, the browser will give them the content data and a space in which to render it.

> **NOTE:** The device does not allow you to hijack the browser by registering as a handler for built-in content types. You should check to make sure that your desired type is not already claimed on your target platforms. When you open that piece of content without a Plug-in, you should see a message such as "The item you selected cannot be displayed. Do you wish to save the item?"

Any given provider can register however many MIME types it wants. However, for simplicity, you usually will want to write a separate provider for each content type, unless multiple types have considerable overlap.

Writing a Plug-in

All browser Plug-ins must extend the `BrowserContentProvider` class. They must declare what MIME types they can accept by implementing two methods. `getSupportedMimeTypes()` indicates all the MIME types that this Plug-in can ever render, and controls whether the browser will consider it for a given piece of content.

getAccept() indicates what MIME types this Plug-in can render right now, given the current configuration of the browser. This may be a smaller returned set than getSupportedMimeTypes(); for example, if the Plug-in requires JavaScript support, it can decline to handle content if the user has disabled JavaScript.

The method getBrowserContent() contains the bulk of the Plug-in. This is the other side of the BrowserContent that we saw in the previous section: here, we create a BrowserContent of our own that handles the rendering of provided content. We have access to the requesting capabilities that we previously saw in RenderingApplication if we need them to complete the rendering task. BrowserContentBaseImpl is a useful base class that defines most of the necessary behaviors of a BrowserContent. You can configure or subclass this class as appropriate to show your content.

Browser content is fairly flexible: your Plug-in may be called to fill the entire screen if showing a single piece of content, or just a small region if embedded within a larger web page. The default behavior is usually acceptable, but you can exert more control over the visual behavior of the Plug-in by implementing the BrowserPageContext interface. The rendering process will invoke these methods to find out the rendering requirements. Most of these are currently unused; you should return the provided default values for future compatibility. If queried for DISPLAY_STYLE, you can return one or more of the style enumerations included in BrowserPageContext as a bit field.

Listing 7–3 shows how to create a custom browser Plug-in for viewing Java source files. To make it more interesting, you can compact the source files for easier viewing on a mobile phone. When you open a class file, you will see the fields and methods but not the definitions. You can handle two of the more common Java MIME types, text/x-java and text/x-java-source. When invoked to show one of these, open the input stream that contains the Java source, and then read it in byte-by-byte, determining whether to show or hide each part. To make the source more obvious, place the scrollbar on the left and fill the whole screen if it is available.

Listing 7–3. *A Browser Plug-in for Displaying Java Source Files in Compact Format*

```java
import java.io.*;

import javax.microedition.io.HttpConnection;

import net.rim.device.api.browser.field.*;
import net.rim.device.api.browser.plugin.*;
import net.rim.device.api.ui.component.RichTextField;

public class JavaViewer extends BrowserContentProvider implements
        BrowserPageContext
{
    String[] MIME_TYPES = new String[]
    { "text/x-java", "text/x-java-source" };

    public String[] getAccept(RenderingOptions context)
    {
        return MIME_TYPES;
    }

    public BrowserContent getBrowserContent(
```

```
                    BrowserContentProviderContext context) throws RenderingException
{
    if (context == null)
        throw new RenderingException("No context");
    BrowserContentBaseImpl browserContent = new BrowserContentBaseImpl(
            context.getHttpConnection().getURL(), null, context
                .getRenderingApplication(), context
                .getRenderingSession().getRenderingOptions(), context
                .getFlags());
    RichTextField contentField = new RichTextField();
    String fileName = "";
    try
    {
        HttpConnection conn = context.getHttpConnection();
        InputStream in = conn.openInputStream();
        fileName = conn.getFile();
        int numBytes = in.available();
        StringBuffer builder = new StringBuffer(numBytes);
        int depth = 0;
        int read = 0;
        do
        {
            read = in.read();
            if (read != -1)
            {
                if (read == '}')
                    --depth;
                if (depth < 2)
                    builder.append((char) read);
                if (read == '{')
                    ++depth;
            }
        } while (read != -1);
        String compressed = builder.toString();
        contentField.setText(compressed);
    }
    catch (IOException ioe)
    {
        throw new RenderingException("I/O Error: " + ioe.getMessage());
    }
    browserContent.setContent(contentField);
    browserContent.setTitle(fileName);
    browserContent.setBrowserPageContext(this);
    return browserContent;
}

public String[] getSupportedMimeTypes()
{
    return MIME_TYPES;
}

public boolean getPropertyWithBooleanValue(int id, boolean defaultValue)
{
    return defaultValue;
}

public int getPropertyWithIntValue(int id, int defaultValue)
```

```
{
    if (id == BrowserPageContext.DISPLAY_STYLE)
        return BrowserPageContext.STYLE_VERTICAL_SCROLL_ON_LEFT
                | BrowserPageContext.STYLE_SHOW_IN_FULL_SCREEN;
    return defaultValue;
}

public Object getPropertyWithObjectValue(int id, Object defaultValue)
{
    return defaultValue;
}
public String getPropertyWithStringValue(int id, String defaultValue)
{
    return defaultValue;
}

}
```

Registering the Plug-in

We still need to take one crucial step: registering the Plug-in with the browser. Use
BrowserContentProviderRegistry as shown in the following example in order to do the
registration.

```
BrowserContentProviderRegistry providerRegistry = BrowserContentProviderRegistry
        .getInstance();
if (providerRegistry != null)
{
    providerRegistry.register(new JavaViewer());
}
```

After this executes, any time you view a Java source file with the proper MIME type,
your Plug-in will automatically run and display the compressed source, as shown in
Figure 7–5. This is true even if your application is no longer running.

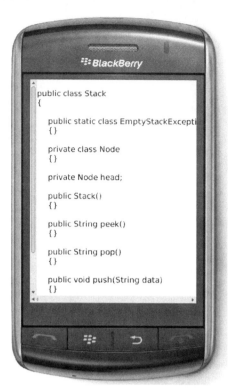

Figure 7–5. *A custom browser Plug-in displays a Java source file*

TIP: To test this, you will need to find a web server that attaches the correct MIME type to .java source files. Most online examples will serve these in `"text/plain"` for easier viewing. If you have access to a Linux box, you can easily install Apache 2, which has appropriate MIME defaults. Publish the Java file on your server, and then visit the file from a desktop web browser. If your server is properly configured, you will probably be prompted to download the file, which will be identified as having a Java file type.

If you are running a web server on your local machine, remember that you cannot use the IP address `"127.0.0.1"` or `"localhost"` within the BlackBerry simulator; these addresses are assumed to refer to the simulator itself, not your machine. Instead, use an appropriate network address like `"192.168.0.1"` or `"10.10.10.1"`. Also, make sure you are using a BlackBerry browser that can view pages within your local network. Within the Browser, try pressing the Menu key, then Options, then Browser Configuration. The Browser should be set to Wi-Fi, or a branded Wi-Fi name such as Hotspot Browser. Using the Internet Browser or other browser communicates with a gateway outside your local network, making those network IP addresses inaccessible.

Watch out for a significant catch: you can only register a Plug-in once. If you try to register it again, an exception will be thrown and you may see an error such as "A browser content provider for text/x-java MIME type has already been registered with the browser." BrowserContentProviderRegistry doesn't provide any methods to remove a loaded Plug-in, or to determine what Plug-ins are already registered, so you cannot make your registration conditional. How can you safely register the Plug-in within your app? You don't. In Chapter 1, you saw how to write a library that automatically runs on startup. You can stick the registration code in there and be confident that it will only execute once. As a bonus, the Plug-in will be ready to go from the moment the phone boots, even if the user never runs your app.

App: Friend Tracker

In Chapter 6, you saw how to piggyback on the existing contacts database in order to keep track of how many times you have shared media with each contact. It's an interesting piece of data, but currently users cannot view it without opening up the address book. Let's write a browser Plug-in that will display this information whenever the user views an appropriate piece of content in the Browser.

MIME Configuration

Before you start writing code, you'll need to decide how to deliver contact information that will integrate with your media-player app. Names starting with x- are available for use, and it makes sense to take advantage of existing VCard content, so define the new type text/x-vcard-media to hold this content. Because you invented this content type, it will not clash with any built-in types on the browser. If you have access to a web server, configure it to serve this MIME type. In Apache2, you can do this by adding the following to mime.conf, which instructs the web server to send .vcf2 files with the proper type and a content encoding of UTF-8. You will need to restart the web server after making any changes.

```
AddType text/x-vcard-media .vcf2
AddCharset UTF-8 .vcf2
```

Now you can create a sample vCard or two and upload them to the server. Many mail programs will allow you to export a contact's information in a .vcf or .vCard file. If you open it in a text editor, you should see something like the following. Change the file extension to .vcf2 and upload to your server.

```
BEGIN:VCARD
VERSION:2.1
N:Norton;Joshua
TITLE:Emperor
TEL;WORK;VOICE:(415) 555-0133
TEL;HOME;VOICE:(415) 555-0144
EMAIL;PREF;INTERNET:emperor.norton@sf.example.com
END:VCARD
```

If you access the .vcf2 file from within the BlackBerry browser, you will see an error message stating that the item cannot be displayed. The path is clear, and now you can write your Plug-in.

Creating the Plug-in Library

Open your existing MediaGrabber Eclipse workspace, or create a new one and import the current version of MediaGrabber. You won't modify the MediaGrabber code, but you will want to ensure that MediaGrabber and the Plug-in deploy together.

Create a new BlackBerry project. Name it "Friend Tracker," give it the Library type, and set it to run on startup.

The actual Plug-in looks similar to the compressed Java source viewer you wrote earlier in this chapter. Create a new Java source file called `FriendViewer` that extends the `BrowserContentProvider` class. Formatting for the friend tracker is not important, so you can omit the `BrowserPageContext` methods. You can make free use of the PIM interfaces you learned in Chapter 6 to import vCard data, search for matching contacts, and extract interesting fields. For simplicity's sake, display text describing the user's level of interaction with the provided contact; a more elaborate Plug-in might also include graphical elements like a check mark, highlighted text, and so on. Listing 7–4 contains the entire Plug-in.

Listing 7–4. *A Plug-in to Display a Web Contact's MediaGrabber Metadata*

```
package com.apress.king.mediagrabber;

import java.io.*;
import java.util.Enumeration;

import javax.microedition.io.HttpConnection;
import javax.microedition.pim.*;

import net.rim.blackberry.api.pdap.BlackBerryContact;
import net.rim.device.api.browser.field.*;
import net.rim.device.api.browser.plugin.*;
import net.rim.device.api.ui.component.RichTextField;
import net.rim.device.api.ui.container.VerticalFieldManager;

public class FriendViewer extends BrowserContentProvider
{
    String[] MIME_TYPE = new String[]
    { "text/x-vcard-media" };

    public String[] getAccept(RenderingOptions context)
    {
        return MIME_TYPE;
    }

    public BrowserContent getBrowserContent(
            BrowserContentProviderContext context) throws RenderingException
    {
        if (context == null)
            throw new RenderingException("No context");
```

```
BrowserContentBaseImpl browserContent = new BrowserContentBaseImpl(
        context.getHttpConnection().getURL(), null, context
                .getRenderingApplication(), context
                .getRenderingSession().getRenderingOptions(), context
                .getFlags());
VerticalFieldManager manager = new VerticalFieldManager();
RichTextField contentField = new RichTextField(
        RichTextField.USE_TEXT_WIDTH);
manager.add(contentField);
browserContent.setContent(manager);
String email = "";
try
{
    HttpConnection conn = context.getHttpConnection();
    InputStream in = conn.openInputStream();
    // Remove network encoding by reading in to a memory stream.
    byte[] bytes = new byte[in.available()];
    in.read(bytes);
    ByteArrayInputStream bais = new ByteArrayInputStream(bytes);
    PIM pim = PIM.getInstance();
    PIMItem[] items = pim.fromSerialFormat(bais, "UTF-8");
    if (items == null || items.length == 0)
    {
        contentField.setText("No contact found.");
    }
    else
    {
        Contact friend = (Contact) items[0];
        ContactList contacts = (ContactList) pim.openPIMList(
                PIM.CONTACT_LIST, PIM.READ_ONLY);
        // See if we know this person, based on their email address.
        if (friend.countValues(Contact.EMAIL) == 0)
        {
            contentField.setText("No email found.");
        }
        else
        {
            email = friend.getString(Contact.EMAIL, 0);
            Contact template = contacts.createContact();
            template.addString(Contact.EMAIL, PIMItem.ATTR_NONE, email);
            Enumeration matches = contacts.items(template);
            if (!matches.hasMoreElements())
            {
                contentField.setText(email
                        + " isn't in your address book.");
            }
            else
            {
                Contact match = (Contact) matches.nextElement();
                if (match.countValues(BlackBerryContact.USER4) == 0)
                {
                    contentField.setText("You haven't sent " + email
                            + " any media yet!");
                }
                else
                {
                    String sentString = match.getString(
```

```
                                   BlackBerryContact.USER4, 0);
                            contentField.setText("You have sent " + email + " "
                                   + sentString + " media files so far.");
                            }
                         }
                      }
                   }
                }
                catch (Exception e)
                {
                    throw new RenderingException("Error: " + e.getMessage());
                }
                browserContent.setTitle(email);
                return browserContent;
        }

        public String[] getSupportedMimeTypes()
        {
            return MIME_TYPE;
        }
}
```

Finally, we will write the Plug-in loader, shown in Listing 7–5. Because the FriendTracker project library runs on start-up, the phone will call this libMain method every time it boots. Claim the MIME type right away so the user can always view this kind of content.

Listing 7–5. *Plug-in Registration*

```
package com.apress.king.mediagrabber;

import net.rim.device.api.browser.plugin.BrowserContentProviderRegistry;

public class FriendTrackerLoader
{
    public static void libMain(String[] args)
    {
        BrowserContentProviderRegistry registry = BrowserContentProviderRegistry
                .getInstance();
        registry.register(new FriendViewer());
    }
}
```

Running the App

Run in the simulator first. You should be able to open the .vcf2 file you uploaded previously and view the appropriate text, as shown in Figure 7–6. If the browser still complains that it cannot display the file, double-check that the MIME types are correctly set on both the Plug-in and the web server, and that the Plug-in was loaded on the simulator. Depending on your simulator, you may need to exit and restart the simulator once to initiate the method. You should be able to set a breakpoint within the libMain() method and see it hit as the simulator starts.

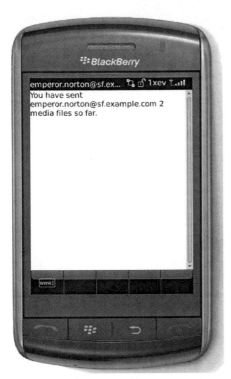

Figure 7–6. *Web content intercepted an interpreted with MediaGrabber data*

When loading the app on your BlackBerry device, sign and load both projects. (Since the MediaTracker project hasn't changed, if you have already loaded it on your device, you can just load the FriendTracker.) When you visit the .vcf2 file in the device browser, you should once again see an appropriate message.

This seems to work well so long as FriendTracker is installed, but, if a new user who did not have MediaGrabber visited that file, they would just see the unfriendly browser error message, with no instructions on how to solve the problem. Because of this, you should put custom content behind appropriate web page interfaces. You might write a simple HTML page with instructions such as "Click here to view Joshua Norton's public profile. If it doesn't load, you need to install FriendTracker: click here to get it today!" Alternately, you could embed the .vcf2 file within an iframe or other partitioned area. In these cases, the content will still render within the frame if the user has the Plug-in installed, and a blank space will appear if they do not. This allows you to attach appropriate messaging—"If you don't see the public profile, install FriendTracker here"—without requiring an extra click for the users who already have the proper content installed.

CAUTION: Unfortunately, the BlackBerry browser does not update its HTTP accept headers with Plug-in content MIME types. If it did, your web server could easily determine whether the Plug-in was installed and serve up appropriate content depending on whether it was present or not.

WANT MORE?

There's a lot that you can do in a web browser window. So far, the app presents a proof of concept that demonstrates how to hook in to other sources of data to render custom content. You can do a lot more with this idea, including the following.

- Display the vCard's name, address, and other PIM fields.

- Automatically import vCards for contacts not already in the user's address book.

- Use another extended BlackBerry user field to keep track of how many times a vCard has been viewed. Update the MediaGrabber app so every time you send media to a contact it displays how often you have viewed them in FriendTracker and how many pieces of media you have sent them.

- Create a widget that displays the top 3 most popular contacts in the address book, along with how many times you have sent them media.

Of course, you aren't constrained to using a vCard. Many apps will define their own custom data types; you might also want to experiment with options for exporting and viewing other friends' online media files.

Excelsior

The Web is still the killer app. This is as true for mobile devices today as it was for desktop computers a decade ago. More and more people turn to the Internet while on the go to discover information, connect with people, and entertain themselves. That's where the users are, and that's where you want to be too.

You have learned the relative merits of browser development, widget development, and app development, and seen that, while all have their uses, app development offers a lot of power. You don't need to choose one or the other, though. BlackBerry has a very flexible system that allows you to launch a browser from within your app, embed browser content within an app screen, or even allow your app to run when the user views certain web pages. You can also use your Java coding skills to write custom extensions for WebWorks widgets, marrying the power of app development with the speed and ease of web development. RIM's investment in HTML5 support significant improves the feature set available on the browser, making it feasible to create attractive user interfaces with standardized, portable markup. All of these techniques help bring your app closer to where users place their time and attention, making it even more accessible and irresistible.

We have seen many options for integrating with the device's major built-in applications. BlackBerry devices also offer frameworks that allow apps to define custom behaviors, making them more accessible to other developers and more attractive to users. Chapter 8 will examine ways to complete your integration with the device.

Chapter 8

Integrating with the BlackBerry OS

This chapter completes the tour of device integration by looking at various ways to tie into the device at a deeper level. These range from simple tasks, such as assigning attractive icons to your app, to more complex ones, such as providing a programming interface that other developers can use to invoke your app. When complete, you will have mastered most of the significant interfaces available for advanced BlackBerry development.

A Content Handling System

In Chapter 3, I briefly looked at the Content Handler API as a tool for launching media files in the native media player. However, the content handler system provides far more versatility and power than just a media player. This complex yet extremely useful set of interfaces allows the creation and use of almost any functionality imaginable.

The Content Handling Philosophy

Back when Java ME first started, mobile devices could barely handle running a single app at a time, let alone multiple apps. The early promoters championed the advantages of bringing the Java virtual machine sandbox to the mobile space: rogue apps could not infect users' phones with viruses, and buggy apps could not crash and prevent you from placing calls. Java ME aimed to enable simple, compact applications that could run with minimal resources in an isolated environment.

As the capabilities of mobile phones grow ever closer to those of desktop computers, this architecture has grown increasingly antiquated. Java ME phones now struggle against the richer multitasking operating systems found in other smart phones. One major shortcoming of the original Java ME design is the inability to launch one application from another application. Again, this made sense back in the 1990s when multitasking was beyond the physical capabilities of the device. Today, however, there are many situations where you might like to take advantage of existing app functionality. If a photo-viewing application already exists on the device, you could launch that app to show your photos rather than reimplementing the capability within a new app (and significantly increasing the app binary size, an unfortunate side effect).

Allowing the invocation of external apps can create complications, though. How do you know if the user has the other app installed? What do you do if they later delete the other app? How do you handle upgrades, where one version behaves slightly differently from the other? And how do you avoid a proliferation of incompatible APIs for every new app?

Enter JSR 211. The Content Handler API (CHAPI) seeks to resolve all these tensions by establishing a framework for communication between apps. CHAPI's philosophy encompasses the following desires:

- *Request/response framework*: Apps making requests should be able to ask for resources or for tasks and receive information when the request completes.

- *Loose coupling*: Apps should not need to know exactly which app services their request so long as it can fulfill the task.

- *Seamless transition*: The device should automatically pass control between requesting and servicing apps, bringing each to the foreground or background as needed. The user should never need to manually exit one app and start another in order to complete a request.

- *Enables discovery*: Apps should be able to learn which handlers are available to service desired requests and obtain basic information about them, such as their names.

- *Expandable:* New apps should be installable to provide additional capabilities, and apps should be able to initiate such installation. For example, a word processing app should be able to find and install a separate spell-checking app.

- *Supports delegation*: An app servicing a request should be able to enlist the assistance of other apps to complete its task.

RIM has embraced this platform, using it to allow communication with built-in BlackBerry applications and between third-party apps. It is available on all devices with software version 4.3 or higher.

The Content Handling Architecture

Think of content handling as a client-server application. The client wants to accomplish a task, such as purchasing extra credits for a game, or acquire a resource, such as searching for a file. The client expresses its desire with a class called Invocation, which combines the following elements:

- A verb, such as "edit," "open," or "print"

- A target, such as `"http://example.com/credits.do"` or `"file:///SDCard/BlackBerry/Music/NationalAnthem.mp3"`

- Optional extra parameters or data

> **NOTE:** The terms *client* and *server* strictly refer to the request/response system of communication. Unlike a typical client/server application, no network communication is involved. In this chapter, I use the terms *server* and *handler* interchangeably.

The client uses the `Registry` class to find any content handlers available to service the request and to actually issue the request. Once the `Registry` receives the `Invocation`, it checks to see what appropriate content handlers exist to handle it. The `Registry` then instructs the device AMS to deliver the `Invocation`. Because the client and the server are separate applications running in different processes, the AMS will first need to create a new Java process if the app is not already running, then serialize the `Invocation` and copy it into the server app's memory. Figure 8–1 illustrates how this system works at a high level; note that the client and the server do not directly interact with one another, nor do they technically share the same `Invocation` instance.

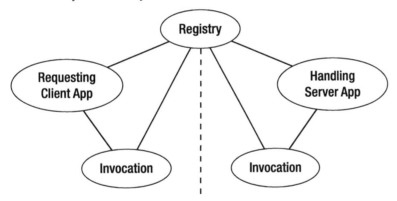

Figure 8–1. *A client/server view of CHAPI*

Server apps use the `Registry` to express their interest in handling certain types of content. Apps can register by content type, such as `"audio/mpeg"`, by extension, such as `".mp3"`, or both. In some circumstances, one app can specify which particular app should service the request. You will see examples covering all these invocations later in the chapter.

The life cycle of a request proceeds as follows:

1. The device AMS will start the server if it is not already running.

2. The server dequeues the `Invocation`.

3. If multiple invocations are pending, the server can handle them one at a time, or spawn multiple threads to process them simultaneously.

4. The server app receives its own copy of the `Invocation`, separate from the client's `Invocation`.

5. The server will examine the details of the request to determine what the requestor wants.

6. The server fulfills the request by taking an action, looking up data, or both.

7. It stores any return information that might be available, such as a file name or error code.

8. The server notifies the device about the success or failure of the operation.

9. The device AMS will copy the modified `Invocation` instance back across the address space boundary into the client application.

10. The client optionally receives a notification that the request was executed.

11. The client can retrieve any information that the server provided.

Figure 8–2 shows one potential flow between client and server CHAPI applications.

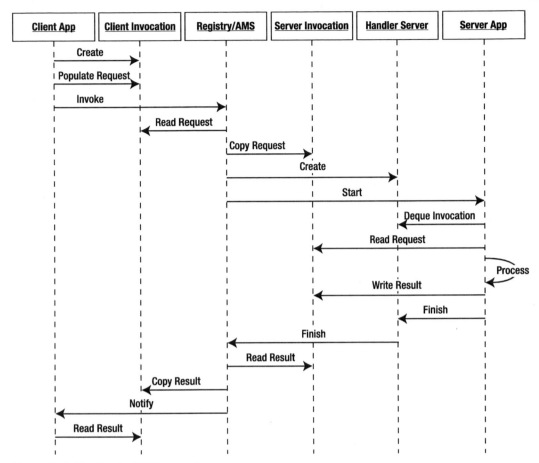

Figure 8–2. *The life of a CHAPI request*

The Major Players

Many classes are involved in smoothly fulfilling a content handling request. Some are only used by the client, others only by the server, and some by both. However, you should have at least a rough understanding of what each component does so you can anticipate what other apps might do.

Invocation

The Invocation embeds the data for a particular request. It holds information for locating an appropriate handler and will be serialized to communicate between the client and the server app.

Locating Hints

Because the device may have multiple content handlers, the Invocation can provide multiple levels of hints and information to help locate the best candidate.

Each content handler must have a unique ID. Java guarantees the uniqueness of these IDs: the BlackBerry will refuse to install or register a new application if it tries to claim a content handler ID already in use. Typically, developers name their IDs as they would fully qualified Java class names in order to distinguish between different authors; for example, if I wrote an image database, I might provide the content handler ID com.apress.king.imagestore. If you know the ID for a particular content handler you want to use, you can provide it to the Invocation. This takes priority over the other locating hints and instructs the AMS to use this particular provider.

Ideally, a client application shouldn't actually care what server component services the request. As with the "Software as a Service" model, components should be swappable after deployment without any client changes necessary. Therefore, the MIME content type determines most CHAPI handling. Any string is valid here; a component may register for a well-known content type, such as "text/html", or an invented one, such as "application/vnd.king.mediagrabber". The content type is the preferred method for finding providers if the handler ID is not provided, and all content handlers that have registered for that type will be considered.

In some cases, a client app may know that it needs to handle a particular piece of content, but not know the exact type of the content. For example, a browsing application may locate a link for http://example.com/card.vcf2. Absent any other information, the platform will select a content handler by searching for components that can handle the .vcf2 suffix. Alternately, after the client app sets the URL of a piece of content on the Invocation, it can call Invocation.findType(). This causes the platform to locate the provided content and try to determine its type; the web server may provide this if the content comes from an http:// link, or by the device if it is on the filesystem. After retrieving the type, this method automatically sets it on the Invocation, as if you had called Invocation.setType().

Actions

The various hints described so far are all nouns, describing the type, the target, or the desired handler. An Invocation can also specify a verb, the action to take. Content handlers can define actions using any string they want, such as "purchase". However, the ContentHandler class defines several standard actions, and when possible you should use these instead of inventing new action names. Table 8–1 lists the defined actions.

Table 8–1. *Content Handler Actions*

Action	Value	Definition
ACTION_EDIT	"edit"	Modify the content.
ACTION_EXECUTE	"execute"	Run the content.
ACTION_INSTALL	"install"	Install the content onto this device.
ACTION_NEW	"new"	Create new content.
ACTION_OPEN	"open"	Open the content.
ACTION_PRINT	"print"	Print the content.
ACTION_SAVE	"save"	Save the content.
ACTION_SELECT	"select"	Select from this content and return the value. This usually involves the user making an on-screen choice.
ACTION_SEND	"send"	Send the content off the device.
ACTION_STOP	"stop"	Cease processing a previously provided piece of content.

Content handlers must declare that they provide the requested action. If the Invocation includes an action, only handlers that have registered for that action will be invoked. If the action is null, the platform will only consider the hints and will ignore the action.

Parameters

Some content requests may only need a hint and an action to execute. If you provide a type of "audio/amr" and an action of "new", that may provide enough information to communicate that you want the user to record a new audio file. In other cases, you may need to provide additional information. If you provide a URL of "file:///SDCard/BlackBerry/game.dat" and a type of "edit", the handling application will probably need more data to edit the file properly.

Invocation supports two methods of providing extra data. First, you can use Invocation.setArgs() to provide a String array. This allows the handler to receive arbitrary parameters on startup, similar to the traditional Java entry point's public static void main(String[] args) parameters. Different BlackBerry devices and software versions may have different limitations on the arguments; however, all devices are guaranteed to support at least 10 arguments with a total of at least 8,192 characters. None of the arguments can be null.

Secondly, you can pass binary data. Invocation.setData() accepts a byte array, which the handling application can interpret however it wants. Binary data might include a custom form of compact parameters, some extra data necessary to complete the request, etc.

The Invocation may provide both arguments and data. However, the device is only required to support a total of 16,384 bytes of parameters. For every character that is included in the arguments, two bytes fewer space is available for binary data. Keep in mind that the server application must serialize and process all parameters, so passing long chunks of data will slow down execution. If you have large pieces of data to provide, such as large images or sound files, it will generally be more efficient for the client application to store that data to a temporary location on the file system and then pass the location in the Invocation, rather than try to stuff all the data within the Invocation itself.

Invocation Life Cycle

An Invocation always exists within a particular state. All states are listed as static fields within the Invocation class.

- INIT: The Invocation has been created.

- WAITING: It has been dispatched to an appropriate handler.

- ACTIVE: The handler has dequeued the request.

- HOLD: The handler must chain the request forward to another handler.

- ERROR: The handler exited without finishing service of the request.

- INITIATED: The handler cannot complete processing the request, but has started doing so.

- CANCELLED: The handler has ceased processing the request, possibly due to a "stop" request.

- OK: The handler has successfully completed the request.

As noted previously, every logical Invocation will occupy two instances, one in the client application and one in the server application. Each follows a slightly different life cycle. Figure 8–3 shows an Invocation initially being created with the status INIT. It remains in this state while the client populates it. Once the Registry receives an Invocation and dispatches it, the status is changed to WAITING. After the server application has finished processing, the status will be one of INITIATED, OK, CANCELLED, or ERROR.

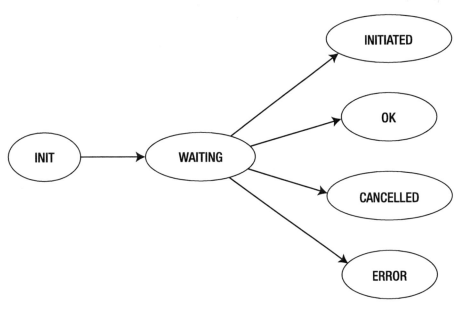

Figure 8–3. *Client Invocation life cycle*

The server application first sees the Invocation after delivery across the process boundary, with an initial status of ACTIVE. The server retains ownership of the Invocation and can keep it in the ACTIVE state as long as it takes to process. Most apps will continue processing until they complete the request, in which case they set an OK value. Certain apps may support cancellation, indicated by going into the CANCELLED state. You should generally avoid using INITIATED. After a request has entered the INITIATED state, you can't later reset it to OK, so you would need out-of-band communication to communicate the final disposition back to the invoking app.

If a server app needs to invoke another app to continue the request, it becomes a client itself. The original request will be set to the HOLD state while the new request is being handled. After that response comes back, the original request re-enters the ACTIVE state.

Note that the server app cannot place an Invocation into the ERROR state; this state is reserved for use by the AMS. However, you can easily imagine many reasons why a request might fail to complete: bad arguments from the client, a network error, running out of filesystem space. How, then, does the server communicate the error back to the client? The simplest way is for the server app to exit without providing a response; this sends the ERROR state back to the client, but provides no additional information about the cause of the error. A better way is to set the state to OK, but provide additional data that the client can read to determine whether the request succeeded or failed. In this sense, "OK" means "I'm done" rather than "Everything went well." Figure 8–4 shows the complete Invocation life cycle within the server app.

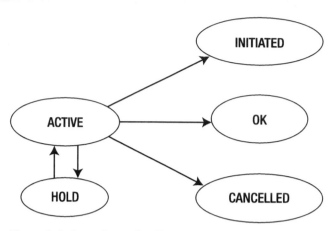

Figure 8–4. *Server Invocation life cycle*

In the same way that the client could set arguments or data in its request, the server can do the same. When it first receives the Invocation, it will see the arguments and data that were included in the request. It can set its own arguments and data using the same methods. After the request is finished, the platform copies those values back over to the client app, which can pull them out for examination. Of course, any changes made to arguments or data after a request is invoked or finished will not be updated in the other app.

There are no standards in place for formatting arguments and data. If you write a content handling app for other developers, you should clearly document any return parameters. If you write a client app, inspect the documentation to make sure you handle all possible return values; if no documentation is available, print out the responses you get back so you can see what they are, and update your code to handle them appropriately. You might see extended status information, such as "Status: ERROR file not found"; returned content, such as "file:///SDCard/BlackBerry/tmp/output.amr"; or tracking data, such as "RequestID=7238497".

Examples

The simplest type of Invocation only has a URL, like so:

```
Invocation request = new Invocation("http://www.eff.org/");
```

If you want to make sure that one particular content handler processes your request, specify it in the ID, along with any other information necessary for it to service the request, like so:

```
Invocation request2 = new Invocation();
request2.setID("com.apress.king.imagestore");
request2.setType("image/tif");
request2.setAction(ContentHandler.ACTION_PRINT);
```

You can provide extended parameters to the server app by setting arguments, data, or both. The following example updates a high score with a new name and player icon.

This presumes that the icon is tiny; if not, you should place the icon on the disk and only pass the file location in the `Invocation`.

```
Invocation request3 = new Invocation("file:///SDCard/BlackBerry/game1.dat");
String[] args = new String[]{"UpdateHighScore", "Chris", "500"};
request3.setArgs(args);
InputStream iconStream = getClass().getResourceAsStream("player.png");
byte[] iconData = null;
try
{
    iconData = new byte[iconStream.available()];
    iconStream.read(iconData);
}
catch (Exception e) {}
request3.setData(iconData);
```

ActionNameMap

If a handler provides a very narrow function, like updating a high-score counter, then choice is not very important: the app only does one thing and can do it without user intervention. Sometimes, though, you may have multiple apps that can all handle the same type of request, such as playing a music file. In other cases, you might have a single handler that provides multiple actions, such as a high-score manager that can update, delete, display, or upload the current high scores. In both situations, the client app may not know exactly which handler or action to use.

The best solution is to present the available options to the user and allow them to select which one to use. Fortunately, CHAPI includes support for internationalization within its framework, and the most successful content handlers will support multiple languages. When apps register as handlers, they can provide locale-specific strings that describe the handler and all their actions.

An `ActionNameMap` instance holds these locale-specific strings. This essentially provides a two-way hashtable that allows you to map between actions (such as "open") and locale-specific action names (such as "Abra"), and between the locale-specific name and the corresponding action. Each `ActionNameMap` contains the mappings for one particular locale.

You can construct an `ActionNameMap` by providing matching arrays of actions and their associated names for a particular locale, as shown:

```
String[] actions = new String[]{"upload", ContentHandler.ACTION_EDIT};
String[] names = new String[]{"Upload to Server", "Update Data"};
ActionNameMap map = new ActionNameMap(actions, names, "en-US");
```

Later, when a program looks for appropriate names to display, it will pass in a desired locale string, such as "en-GB" for Great Britain English. CHAPI will check to see if names have been defined for that locale; if not, it will strip off the characters after and including the last "-" and search again—in this case, for "en". The process repeats until a match is found or all options are exhausted. Because of this, you should provide a basic language code, such as "en", that can provide a default if a client app wants an unavailable country code.

Server applications may create `ActionNameMap` objects to advertise their capabilities. Client applications may obtain them to display available capabilities. Once a client has an `ActionNameMap`, it can look up the corresponding match for each name or action, like so:

```
String localizedName = map.getActionName("upload");
String uploadAction = map.getAction("Update Data");
```

Alternately, an app may choose to iterate through all available actions and expose them all. The next example demonstrates how you could create a set of BlackBerry menu items for all available actions. Each will display a locale-appropriate name in the menu, but use the correct action when selected, as shown:

```
int size = map.size();
for (int i = 0; i < size; ++i)
{
    String name = map.getActionName(i);
    final String action = map.getAction(i);
    MenuItem item = new MenuItem(name, 0, 0){
        public void run()
        {
            // Process "action" here.
        }
    };
}
```

ContentHandler

As discussed in the previous section, client apps will sometimes want to obtain more information about the available options for processing a particular request. If they aren't satisfied with simply firing it off and trusting it will be done, they can obtain more information about available handler apps by querying available `ContentHandler` classes. The `ContentHandler` isn't actually an instance of the servicing application; rather, it holds descriptive information about the app.

- `getAppName()` retrieves the displayable name of the app.

- `getAuthority()` should report what authority has verified the identity of this application. On other MIDP Java ME devices, it will report the subject of the certificate used to sign the app, or `null` if the app is unsigned. For BlackBerry, however, this always returns `null`.

- `getID()` retrieves the handler's unique ID.

- `getVersion()` reports the handler's installed app version number. This can be useful if future versions of the app include more functionality.

You can acquire more detailed information about this handler's capabilities. Actions (such as "open"), suffixes (such as ".mp3"), and types (such as "audio/mpeg") can all be retrieved in two ways:

- By index. You can first find the count, as in `handler.getSuffixCount()`, and then loop through the items, as in `handler.getSuffix(i)`.

- By name. You can quickly determine whether a particular item is supported with a call such as `handler.hasSuffix(".mp3")`.

Finally, each `ContentHandler` contains actions and action names. You have the following options for looking up this information:

- Use `getActionNameMap()` to get the `ActionNameMap` for the current device locale. As noted above, this will search for the best locale match.

- Use `getActionNameMap(String locale)` to retrieve a particular locale's information. This is useful if you allow switching languages within the app. Again, it will retrieve the best match.

- You can retrieve all mappings by calling `getActionNameMapCount()` and then iterating through the index with `getActionNameMap(int)`.

- If you only care about the actions and not the displayable names, use `getActionCount()` and `getAction()`.

> **NOTE:** You can obtain a `ContentHandler` instance from the `Registry`, as described later in this chapter.

The following snippet of code retrieves the name of a handler and then checks whether it supports executing content. If it does, the app will check for all the content types it handles, adding each one as a viewable element on a screen.

```
String appName = handler.getAppName();
if (handler.hasAction(ContentHandler.ACTION_EXECUTE))
{
    int typeCount = handler.getTypeCount();
    for (int i = 0; i < typeCount; ++i)
    {
        screen.add(new LabelField(appName + ":" + handler.getType(i)));
    }
}
```

ContentHandlerServer

`ContentHandler` is a client-facing description of handler capabilities. `ContentHandlerServer` is the server-facing class that can retrieve pending requests, mark the status of completed requests, and query for information about its own capabilities and access restrictions.

A handler app can retrieve pending requests in one of two ways. By calling `ContentHandlerServer.getRequest()`, the handler app directly receives an `Invocation`. This is useful if you know that a request is waiting, or if you prefer to process incoming requests serially within a separate thread. The method takes a `Boolean`: if `true`, the method will block until it receives an `Invocation`; if `false`, the method can return `null` if no `Invocation` is immediately available. The following example shows a handler application first checking to see if an Invocation is present. If not, it will spawn a thread that will continually loop and process all future incoming Invocation objects.

```
public void checkForRequest(final ContentHandlerServer server)
{
    Invocation pendingRequest = server.getRequest(false);
    if (pendingRequest != null)
    {
        // Process this request immediately.
    }
    else
    {
        (new Thread()
        {
            public void run()
            {
                while (true)
                {
                    Invocation incoming = server.getRequest(true);
                    if (incoming != null)
                    {
                        // Process invocation here.
                    }
                }
            }
        }).start();
    }
}
```

If a thread is blocking on getRequest(), another thread can call cancelGetRequest(). This forces the first thread to exit the method with a return value of null, even if it was waiting until an Invocation became available.

CHAPI also offers a non-blocking callback method. ContentHandlerServer.setListener() allows the handler app to register a listener that will be asynchronously notified of any future available requests. Each ContentHandlerServer can only support a single listener at a time. The registered listener will receive all notifications until setListener() is called again with a value of null. This system is useful when you want to handle all incoming requests as they become available. The following example shows how to define and register a simple listener:

```
private class PrintRequestListener implements RequestListener
{
    public void invocationRequestNotify(ContentHandlerServer queue)
    {
        Invocation incoming = queue.getRequest(true);
        // Process request here.
    }
}
public void registerForRequests(ContentHandlerServer server)
{
    server.setListener(new PrintRequestListener());
}
```

A handler might want to restrict access to only a particular set of invoking apps or certain other handlers. ContentHandlerServer provides methods to check whether a particular app ID is allowed access to this app and to check all supported IDs. Access checks are performed by searching for matching prefixes. For example, if I write a handler that grants access to the ID "com.apress.king", then access is also granted to "com.apress.king.mediagrabber" and "com.apress.king.imagestore". If no access IDs are defined, all access is allowed. The following example shows how to verify whether a particular incoming Invocation has appropriate access; if not, it prints out debugging information showing what does have access:

```
public void invocationRequestNotify(ContentHandlerServer queue)
{
    Invocation incoming = queue.getRequest(true);
    String source = incoming.getInvokingID();
    if (queue.isAccessAllowed(source))
    {
        // Process the request
    }
    else
    {
        int count = queue.accessAllowedCount();
        System.out.println("Only the following IDs are allowed:");
        for (int i = 0; i < count; ++i)
        {
            System.out.println(queue.getAccessAllowed(i));
        }
    }
}
```

When a handler has completed all processing, it should first update the Invocation object it received with any return arguments or data, and then call ContentHandlerServer.finish(). It should provide the completed Invocation, along with a final status of OK, CANCELLED, or INITIATED. This method prompts CHAPI to reserialize the Invocation and return it to the requesting app.

> **NOTE:** ContentHandlerServer extends from ContentHandler, so all ContentHandler methods can be called on it as well. This helps a server app introspect itself to check what capabilities it had declared.

Registry

The final and most complex major component in the CHAPI system is the Registry. Registry provides many capabilities to both the client and the server app, including registering handlers, searching for available handlers, and processing requests.

Client Use of Registry

The most important method is Registry.invoke(). This method accepts an Invocation and dispatches it to an appropriate content handler. It can throw a host of errors, including ContentHandlerException if no suitable handler is found; SecurityException if this app is not allowed to access that content; IOException if the content provided in the URL cannot be found; and so on. The method may take a relatively long time to complete; for example, if only an HTTP URL was provided in the Invocation, the Registry will need to open a web connection to determine the content type before it can select an appropriate handler.

This method returns true if the calling app needs to exit in order for the handler to start, and false if it can continue running. All BlackBerry devices support multi-tasking and so always return false; however, if you plan to port your app to non-BlackBerry Java ME platforms in the future, you should check the return value and exit if requested.

The Registry also lets client apps query for ContentHandler objects and otherwise explore available capabilities. Table 8–2 shows the available methods.

Table 8–2. *Client-facing Registry Queries*

Method name	Return type	Description
findHandler(Invocation invocation)	ContentHandler[]	Handlers to consider for this Invocation.
forAction(String action)	ContentHandler[]	All handlers that support this action.
forID(String ID, boolean exact)	ContentHandler	The handler with the requested ID. If "exact" is false, this method can return prefixes; for example, if you request "com.apress.king.mediagrabber", it may return the handler for "com.apress.king".
forSuffix(String suffix)	ContentHandler[]	All handlers that support this suffix.
forType(String type)	ContentHandler[]	All handlers that support this type.
getActions()	String[]	All actions from all registered handlers.
getIDs()	String[]	All IDs from all registered handlers.
getSuffixes()	String[]	All suffixes registered by all handlers.
getTypes()	String[]	All types registered by all handlers.

After initiating an Invocation, the client might simply let it run. If it wishes to learn the result, it can call Registry.setListener() and pass in a ResponseListener. This object will be notified whenever an Invocation has completed, whether successfully or with an error. It will receive notifications of all invocations until setListener() is called again with null.

At any point, the client can call Registry.getResponse() to receive a completed Invocation. Like ContentHandlerServer.getRequest(), you can pass true or false to this method depending on whether you wish to wait until an Invocation is available or not.

You can obtain a `Registry` instance by calling the static method `Registry.getRegistry()` and passing in the classname. The provided classname must be the name of a class in the currently running package.

The next example shows a sample helper method that processes a file selection request. It first checks the `Registry` to see whether a preferred handler is installed. If so, it will specify that handler's ID in the `Invocation` to ensure that it is used; otherwise, it will accept whatever default the `Registry` chooses. The app registers a listener that will be notified when the request succeeds or fails. In a real app, it would continue processing from this point, perhaps by reading in data from the selected file.

```
private void chooseHandler(Invocation toSend) throws ContentHandlerException,
    IOException
{
    Registry registry = Registry.getRegistry(getClass().getName());
    ContentHandler[] candidates = registry.findHandler(toSend);
    for (int i = 0; i < candidates.length; ++i)
    {
        String id = candidates[i].getID();
        if (id.startsWith("com.apress.king"))
        {
            toSend.setID(id);
            break;
        }
    }
    registry.setListener(new FileSelectionListener());
    registry.invoke(toSend);
}
private class FileSelectionListener implements ResponseListener
{
    public void invocationResponseNotify(Registry registry)
    {
        Invocation response = registry.getResponse(true);
        if (response.getStatus() == Invocation.ERROR)
        {
            System.err.println("Invocation failed");
        }
        else if (response.getStatus() == Invocation.OK)
        {
            String fileName = response.getArgs()[0];
            System.out.println("Selected file " + fileName);
        }
    }
}
```

Server Use of Registry

A handler app has access to all the same `Registry` methods that a client has. It will generally ignore these, except in the special case of request chaining. If a handler needs to invoke another handler in order to complete an initial request, it will behave like a client to configure an `Invocation` and optionally select a specific `ContentHandler` ID. The server will then call a special version of `invoke()` that takes two `Invocation` arguments. The first is the new `Invocation` to be dispatched forward; the second is the original

Invocation, which will be set to a status of HOLD until the new Invocation has completed. Alternately, if a handler decides that it doesn't want to handle the provided Invocation, it can call reinvoke(). This tells the Registry to pick another handler to process the request.

In most cases, however, server apps will ignore much of the Registry, and focus on a few particular methods. The static method Registry.getServer() returns an appropriate ContentHandlerServer for the caller. The handler must have previously registered with CHAPI, and the provided classname must be in the current application package.

Finally, the Registry offers a pair of methods to dynamically register and unregister a handler. Registration includes all of the various pieces of information previously listed for a ContentHandler.

- A classname, which must be in the current application package and a main application entry point, such as a MIDlet for a MIDP application, a UiApplication for CLDC UI, or a library class that defines libMain().

- An array of string types, such as "audio/amr".

- An array of string suffixes, such as ".amr".

- An array of string actions, such as "play" or ContentHandler.ACTION_OPEN.

- An array of ActionNameMap objects for locale-specific action name display.

- An application ID, such as "com.apress.king.imagestore".

- An array of strings containing application IDs that are allowed access to this handler, such as "com.apress.king.mediagrabber".

Other than the classname, all arguments are optional; you may pass null for any of them, or an empty array for arrays. A class can choose to register the type ContentHandler.UNIVERSAL_TYPE, which indicates that it can consume any type of content. If you do not specify an ID, the Registry must provide a unique ID that is guaranteed not to collide with any other IDs. A MIDlet will receive an ID such as "Chris_King-Image_Provider-com.apress.king.imageprovider.ImageProvider" while a BlackBerry CLDC handler will receive an ID such as " null-null-com.apress.king.imageprovider.ImageProvider".

Once an ID has been registered, no other app can register with it. Furthermore, no IDs that match a prefix of said ID can be registered. For example, if you register "com.example.food.lunch", no one can register "com.example.food" or "com.example.food.lunch.pizza". Such attempts will fail with a ContentHandlerException.

After an app registers, the registration continues to be valid even after the app exits. If an Invocation is issued for the app, the BlackBerry will automatically start the requested app if it is not already running. Therefore, apps that can register for content requests should check their ContentHandlerServer soon after starting up to see whether they were started specifically to handle a request.

The next example demonstrates a potential server use of the `Registry` class. This will attempt to register an application called `SigningApp` with CHAPI. If this succeeds and no exceptions are thrown, it then retrieves its own `ContentHandlerServer` and spends the rest of this thread's life servicing incoming requests. Note that most of the parameters passed to the `register()` method are null; very few handlers will need to specify all parameters .

```
private void register() throws ContentHandlerException, ClassNotFoundException
{
    String className = SigningApp.class.getName();
    Registry registry = Registry.getRegistry(className);
    String[] types = new String[]{"text/plain", "text/html"};
    String[] actions = new String[]{ContentHandler.ACTION_SAVE, "sign"};
    registry.register(className, types, null, actions, null, null, null);
    ContentHandlerServer handler = registry.getServer(className);
    Invocation next = null;
    do
    {
        next = handler.getRequest(true);
        // Process next request here
    } while (next != null);
}
```

Alternate Entry

The previous example carries a certain risk with it: what happens if this code never executes? If the user installs but doesn't launch the signing app, the next time someone tries to issue a CHAPI request to sign `text/plain`, nothing will happen. To avoid this problem, you can perform registration in an auto-start alternate entry point. You will then have two application entry points: one that automatically executes on start-up with no arguments, and another that executes with an argument when the user selects your icon. This will ensure that you can receive CHAPI requests any time after the user turns on their device. Follow these steps to set up your project appropriately.

1. Open `BlackBerry_App_Descriptor.xml`.

2. Provide a simple but unique string in the box labeled "Application argument", such as "launch". You will use this to distinguish the main entry from the alternate entry.

3. Click the Alternate Entry Points tab.

4. Click "Add..."

5. Provide an application name, such as "MediaGrabberAlternate", and click "OK".

6. Click "Auto-run on startup" and "Do not display the application icon on the BlackBerry home screen".

7. Save.

After you deploy and restart the device or simulator, your application will automatically be called on startup. From now on, you can inspect the args parameter passed to your static void main function. If you receive the "launch" string parameter, you know that this is a normal app launch. If you receive nothing, you are being called on startup. This is the perfect time to perform CHAPI registration or any other initialization tasks for your app.

Installing Handlers

In the course of issuing a request, you may realize that no handlers are available to service the request, but as long as you know where at least one handler is located on the Internet, you can bring it down to the device. Simply create a fresh Invocation with the URL of the JAD file to install, and then execute the Invocation, as in the following example:

```
Invocation install = new Invocation("http://example.com/ImageStore.jad");
Registry.getRegistry(getClass().getName()).invoke(install);
```

Even though you initiate the install, the user will still need to confirm it. Figure 8–5 shows the prompt screen, which is the same form that is used when installing an application from the browser.

Figure 8–5. *Installing a new content handler via CHAPI*

Default Handlers

You saw above how a client app can specify a particular server app to handle its request. If the client does not specify a particular ID and multiple apps have registered to handle that type of request, then the system will automatically select one.

Starting with OS 6, developers can declare their app as the default handler for a combination of types, suffixes, and actions. The following sample shows how to make the SigningApp you previously registered the default handler when signing documents:

```
DefaultContentHandlerRegistry defaultRegistry = DefaultContentHandlerRegistry
        .getDefaultContentHandlerRegistry(registry);
defaultRegistry.setDefaultContentHandler(types, null, actions, registry
        .getID());
```

Multiple apps may try to register as defaults for the same types of invocation. If this occurs, the most recently set version will win. Try to avoid annoying the user by fighting for control of very common content types, and instead only grab the default for types that your app is uniquely able to handle. If you do expect some collision (if, for example, you are writing an alternative viewer for a document format), then respect the user by asking them for permission to become the default.

Built-in Handlers

Every recent BlackBerry device will have at least one content handler available. BlackBerry provides a built-in content handler that can open a huge variety of media types. The specific set will vary depending on the device and software version, but it generally can handle more than 50 content types and nearly 100 content suffixes. It includes support for all types of media, pictures, and even HTML documents.

To directly reference this built-in handler, you can use the ID defined in `BlackBerryContentHandler.ID_MEDIA_CONTENT_HANDLER`. By providing this ID with no other parameters, the `Invocation` will open the native media application.

Starting with device software version 4.7.0, you can also use one of the following arguments to control the initial landing screen when the `Invocation` is handled, all of which are defined in `BlackBerryContentHandler`:

- `MEDIA_ARGUMENT_VIEW_MEDIA`: Opens top-level media screen.
- `MEDIA_ARGUMENT_VIEW_MUSIC`: View music library.
- `MEDIA_ARGUMENT_VIEW_PICTURES`: View the photo library.
- `MEDIA_ARGUMENT_VIEW_PLAYLISTS`: Display the set of playlists.
- `MEDIA_ARGUMENT_VIEW_RINGTONES`: View all installed ringtones.
- `MEDIA_ARGUMENT_VIEW_VIDEOS`: View video library.
- `MEDIA_ARGUMENT_VIEW_VOICENOTES`: View voice notes.

This example will cause the voice notes application to display:

```
Invocation media = new Invocation();
media.setID(BlackBerryContentHandler.ID_MEDIA_CONTENT_HANDLER);
media.setArgs(new String[]{BlackBerryContentHandler.↵
MEDIA_ARGUMENT_VIEW_VOICENOTES});
Registry.getRegistry(getClass().getName()).invoke(media);
```

CHAPI Alternatives

While CHAPI provides a robust and flexible system for invoking apps, you have other options available as well. In Chapter 2, you saw how to use the `Invoke` class to launch several built-in BlackBerry apps such as the camera and phone. To launch third-party applications, you can use the method `ApplicationManager.launch()`. This lets you invoke arbitrary third-party applications, although you will need to have some level of knowledge in order to find them on the device. This sample looks for a particular app and launches it with two parameters:

```
ApplicationManager mgr = ApplicationManager.getApplicationManager();
String url = "ImageProvider&arg1&arg2";
try
{
    mgr.launch(url);
}
catch (ApplicationManagerException ame)
{
    System.err.println(url + " could not start");
}
```

As you can imagine, this approach requires tighter integration between your app and the app you wish to invoke; it does not provide the loose coupling offered through CHAPI. However, using `ApplicationManager` can provide a simpler way to quickly move control between multiple applications, and so it can be useful for demos, testing, or cases where you know what other software will be installed on the device. It also helps if you need to launch a third-party app that does not support CHAPI.

Iconic

Up until now, no matter how cool MediaGrabber is, the icon still looks dull. The default icon varies depending on your BlackBerry model, but it generally looks like a simple blank terminal. The icon is probably the first thing any user will see of your app, so you should make a good first impression—pick something that makes people want to check out your app.

Design Notes

What makes a good icon is a subjective decision, but you should try to think of something that fulfills most of the following criteria:

   ▪ *Legible*: People should instantly recognize the icon.

- *Relevant*: A racecar is a great icon for a racing game, not so great for a word-processing app.

- *Attractive*: BlackBerry devices tend to have high resolutions, so your icon should be as detailed as other icons on the device.

- *Transparent*: Use a transparent background for a nicer look and theme integration.

- *Familiar*: When possible, try to match the visual appearance of native BlackBerry icons so your app integrates cleanly with the device look.

Ultimately, of course, the decision is yours. If you are a great artist, or know someone who is, try coming up with a variety of designs and see which one looks the best.

Technical Notes

BlackBerry devices have historically had widely varying icon size requirements. For OS 6, your icon should have a canvas that is 68x68 pixels large. Within that canvas, center an image that is about 49x49 pixels large. The remaining area is "negative space" and will be used for overlays and effects applied by the OS.

On older versions, your icon size should exactly match the maximum icon size for that device. Unfortunately, icon size depends on the user's current theme, so even if you know what device you are installed on, there may be multiple available sizes. Table 8–3 shows the supported icon sizes for the default themes on some recent BlackBerry models.

Table 8–3. *Default Icon Sizes*

Device Model	Icon Width	Icon Height
Pearl 8100	60	55
Pearl Flip	46	46
Curve 8300	53	48
8350i	52	52
Curve 8520	52	52
8700	53	48
8800	53	48
Curve 8900	80	80
Bold	80	80
Storm	73	73
Tour	80	80

Providing an icon larger than the theme's supported size will have different effects depending on the device software version. On software versions 4.6 or later, if the provided icon is less than 25% smaller than the preferred size, it will be left as is; otherwise, it will be scaled to fit. So, on the Bold, a 75×75 icon will display as 75×75 pixels, while a 40×40 icon will be scaled up to 80×80. Older device software versions follow their own rules for scaling or cropping icons.

When creating an icon, you should generally leave space around the image. For example, the Storm uses a 73x73 canvas size, but the image inside should be about 53x53 pixels with a transparent border of about 10 pixels on all four edges.

Why should you care? Frankly, because scaled icons generally look really bad. There isn't a lot of detail available in an icon anyway, and any sort of distortion can quickly make an icon unattractive or illegible. This isn't a large problem for a personal application, but can have a serious impact on the perceived quality of a commercial app.

You can provide icons in GIF, JPEG, or PNG format; PNG is usually the best choice. Icons have a limited file size; if they exceed the limit, your application will fail to build.

> **CAUTION:** Excessive icon sizes are one of several cases where a deep error may be reported within the BlackBerry Builder Console but does not stop the deployment of the application. If your changes don't seem to be available in the simulator or the device, carefully check the builder output to make sure that everything is building properly.

Providing an Icon

You can set an icon to display on the home screen or the Downloads/Applications folder, along with a second rollover icon that displays when the user focuses your app. Follow these steps to assign the icons:

1. Open `BlackBerry_App_Descriptor.xml`.

2. Find the section labeled "Application Icons" to the right and click "Add External...".

3. Navigate to and select the image you would like to use.

4. Repeat steps 1-3 to select a rollover icon.

5. Save the XML file and relaunch your application.

When you re-deploy your application, you should see the new icon display. If you move your cursor or finger over it, you will see the image change to the rollover icon you specified.

Changing Icons

Sooner or later, you will need to wrestle with a troubling issue: how do you support multiple versions of your app that run on different devices? As you'll see, there are two major schools of thought on this: some people prefer to write a single version of the app that can run on any BlackBerry, while others prefer to create a slightly different version of it for each device. Assume for the moment that you follow the first path. You would want to have a single application that displays the best icon, no matter whether it runs on a Curve, a Torch, or a Bold.

Even if you create a custom version of your application for each of these devices, you still need to deal with the situation where the user has selected a new theme that has a different icon size from the default. Ideally, you would like to update your icon to minimize the effects of scaling.

The HomeScreen class offers additional methods that help with this problem. Specifically, updateIcon() behaves like setRolloverIcon(), but it updates the main nonselected version of your icon instead of the rollover version. Additionally, getPreferredIconWidth() and getPreferredIconHeight() inform you of the best sizes for the current theme. You can even call getActiveThemeName() if you would like to show different icons depending on the selected theme—for example, you might prefer to use different colors to achieve the best contrast with the background.

The following code examines the current preferred icon width, and then selects the best matching icon based on that. You could expand this example to deal with any supported size. As with the previous rollover example, you should place this within the application's main function.

```
Bitmap icon = null;
Bitmap rollover = null;
int width = HomeScreen.getPreferredIconWidth();
if (width <= 46)
{
    icon = Bitmap.getBitmapResource("icon_46x46");
    rollover = Bitmap.getBitmapResource("rollover_46x46");
}
else if (width <= 53)
{
    icon = Bitmap.getBitmapResource("icon_53x48");
    rollover = Bitmap.getBitmapResource("rollover_53x48");
}
else if (width <= 80)
{
    icon = Bitmap.getBitmapResource("icon_80x80");
    rollover = Bitmap.getBitmapResource("rollover_80x80");
}
HomeScreen.setRolloverIcon(rollover);
HomeScreen.updateIcon(icon);
```

Native Menus

You already know how to define a custom menu for your application. What's really cool, though, is adding a new item to an existing BlackBerry menu. You can customize virtually every menu on the device, including the browser, phone, and address book menus.

Defining Native Menu Options

Instead of a standard MenuItem, define these native menu entries with the special ApplicationMenuItem class. To do this, you must provide the following three pieces of information:

- In the constructor, an integer value indicating where this menu item should be located. As with the MenuItem class, lower values indicate higher placement; unlike MenuItem, there are not separate numbers for ordinal and priority.

- A toString() method that provides text to display for this menu item. If you wish to internationalize this string, you must do so yourself.

- A run() method that will execute when the user selects this menu item. Depending on the type of menu, it may receive an object describing the context. For example, a TextMessage would be provided from the SMS editor's menu. You can do whatever you want within the run() method, whether it's starting another application, doing file or network operations, or displaying simple UI.

The next example shows a custom menu item that could be added to the calendar application. When you create, edit, or view a meeting within the native calendar, you can select from the menu to order pizza for that meeting. This example sets a ToDo reminder for yourself; it could also send an e-mail request to your caterer, or start up the phone to call your favorite delivery place.

```
private class PizzaMenuItem extends ApplicationMenuItem
{
    public PizzaMenuItem()
    {
        // Pizza is the most important thing.
        super(0);
    }
    public Object run(Object context)
    {
        if (context == null || !(context instanceof Event))
            return null;
        try
        {
            Event event = (Event) context;
            if (event.countValues(Event.SUMMARY) > 0)
            {
                String name = event.getString(Event.SUMMARY, 0);
                ToDoList todos = (ToDoList) PIM.getInstance().openPIMList(
```

```
                    PIM.TODO_LIST, PIM.WRITE_ONLY);
                ToDo task = todos.createToDo();
                task.addString(ToDo.SUMMARY, PIMItem.ATTR_NONE,↵
                    "Order pizza for " + name);
                task.commit();
                Dialog.alert("Pizza Reminder Created");
                return null;
            }
        }
        catch (Exception e)
        {
            e.printStackTrace();
        }
        Dialog.alert("Couldn't create pizza reminder");
        return null;
    }
    public String toString()
    {
        return "Order Pizza";
    }
}
}
```

Inserting into the Native Menu

BlackBerry offers an almost absurd number of menus that can be modified. Table 8–4 shows everything that is supported, along with the object that is provided as a context when the item executes. All names are defined in the ApplicationMenuItemRepository class.

Table 8–4. *Native Application Menu Items*

Name	Displays In	Context Parameter Type
MENUITEM_ADDRESSBOOK_LIST	Address book in list mode	Contact
MENUITEM_ADDRESSCARD_EDIT	Open address book contact in edit mode	Contact
MENUITEM_ADDRESSCARD_VIEW	Open address book contact in view mode	Contact
MENUITEM_BROWSER	Browser	N/A
MENUITEM_CALENDAR	Calendar in view mode	Event
MENUITEM_CALENDAR_EVENT	Calendar event in view or edit modes	Event
MENUITEM_CAMERA_PREVIEW	Camera preview	String (contains image file location)
MENUITEM_CLOCK	Clock	N/A
MENUITEM_EMAIL_EDIT	E-mail open in edit mode	Message
MENUITEM_EMAIL_VIEW	E-mail open in view mode	Message

Name	Displays In	Context Parameter Type
MENUITEM_FILE_EXPLORER	File Explorer running	String (contains file location)
MENUITEM_FILE_EXPLORER_BROWSE	File Explorer open in browse mode	String (contains file location)
MENUITEM_FILE_EXPLORER_ITEM	Open item in File Explorer	String (contains file location)
MENUITEM_GROUPADDRESS_EDIT	Group address entry in Contacts app open for edit	N/A
MENUITEM_GROUPADDRESS_VIEW	Group address entry in Contacts app open for viewing	N/A
MENUITEM_MAPS	Maps app	MapView
MENUITEM_MEMO_EDIT	Individual memo open for editing	BlackBerryMemo
MENUITEM_MEMO_LIST	List of memos	BlackBerryMemo
MENUITEM_MESSAGE_LIST	List of messages	Message, TextMessage, or MultipartMessage
MENUITEM_MMS_EDIT	MMS open for edit	MultipartMessage
MENUITEM_MMS_VIEW	MMS open for viewing	MultipartMessage
MENUITEM_MUSIC_SERVICE_ITEM	Music section of Media app	N/A
MENUITEM_PHONE	Phone (dialer) app	N/A
MENUITEM_PHONELOG_VIEW	Call log	PhoneLog
MENUITEM_SEARCH	Search window	N/A
MENUITEM_SMS_EDIT	SMS open for edit	TextMessage
MENUITEM_SMS_VIEW	SMS open for view	TextMessage
MENUITEM_SYSTEM	Any menu	Parameter type for this particular menu
MENUITEM_TASK_EDIT	Individual task open for editing	ToDo
MENUITEM_TASK_LIST	List of tasks	ToDo
MENUITEM_VIDEO_RECORDER	Video recorder	String (contains file location)
MENUITEM_VIDEO_SERVICE_ITEM	Video section of Media app	N/A

You may optionally add your app's `ApplicationDescriptor` when adding a custom menu item. This will cause your app to start when the item is selected. The filesystem and maps items require you to provide the `ApplicationDescriptor`. In the case of filesystem menu items, you can optionally pass a `string` context item that defines the MIME type that this menu item handles. For example, if you provide "text/plain", your menu will display if a .txt file is selected but not for any other type of file.

Use `ApplicationMenuItemRepository.addMenuItem()` to insert new items into a native menu, and `ApplicationMenuItemRepository.removeMenuItem()` to remove a previously added item. The following snippet adds our previously defined pizza menu to the calendar app:

```
ApplicationMenuItemRepository repo =↵
    ApplicationMenuItemRepository.getInstance();
repo.addMenuItem(ApplicationMenuItemRepository.MENUITEM_CALENDAR_EVENT,↵
        new PizzaMenuItem());
```

As you learned when looking at rollover icons, the main problem with this system is that you cannot insert this code into a menu until your app executes, whereas what you really want is to add the menu item before it executes. As with icons, the solution is to add the custom menu items within an auto-start application or library so you have a chance to run your code when the device powers on.

App: Enter from Anywhere

Up until now, every time you have run MediaGrabber you have needed to locate the icon first and select it. You will use the tools discussed in this chapter to enable launching MediaGrabber from native device menus or any third-party application. You'll also take this opportunity to add some custom icons for the app.

Adding CHAPI Handling

MediaGrabber mainly focuses on capturing and sending media. For now, let's look at exposing the sending functions to other applications.

Listening for and Handling Requests

You use CHAPI to add new access to MediaGrabber, not to modify its behavior. Therefore, you only need to change `MediaGrabber.java`, the main application entry point. You will do the following:

- Add dynamic registration so you can always accept CHAPI requests.

- Add an alternate entry point to ensure that you register on app boot.

- When you receive a request, grab information about the file to send from the `Invocation`, and then move directly to the `SendingScreen`, skipping past the standard media capture prompts.

To get started, follow the instructions in the Alternate Entry section to change MediaGrabber into an auto-start system application and add a new alternate entry point called MediaGrabberAlternate. If you wish, find and add two icons to MediaGrabber.

Now you are ready to update the main MediaGrabber file. Listing 8–1 contains the new file.

Listing 8–1. *Adding CHAPI Support to MediaGrabber*

```java
package com.apress.king.mediagrabber;

import java.io.InputStream;

import javax.microedition.content.*;
import javax.microedition.io.Connector;
import javax.microedition.io.file.FileConnection;
import javax.microedition.pim.Contact;

import net.rim.blackberry.api.homescreen.HomeScreen;
import net.rim.blackberry.api.menuitem.*;
import net.rim.blackberry.api.pdap.BlackBerryContact;
import net.rim.device.api.system.Bitmap;
import net.rim.device.api.system.RuntimeStore;
import net.rim.device.api.ui.UiApplication;
import net.rim.device.api.ui.component.Dialog;

public class MediaGrabber extends UiApplication implements RequestListener
{
    private Invocation pending;
    private ContentHandlerServer server;

    private static final String CHAPI_ID = "com.apress.king.mediagrabber";
    private static final String[] MIME_TYPES = new String[]
    { "image/png", "image/jpeg", "audio/amr-wb", "audio/amr", "audio/pcm",
        "audio/mpeg" };
    private static final String[] SUFFIXES = new String[]
    { ".png", ".jpg", ".jpeg", ".amr", ".pcm", ".mp3" };

    public MediaGrabber()
    {
        String className = MediaGrabber.class.getName();
        try
        {
            verifyRegistration();
            server = Registry.getServer(className);
            pending = server.getRequest(false);
            server.setListener(this);
        }
        catch (Exception e)
        {
            System.err.println("Error checking CHAPI: " + e.getMessage());
            e.printStackTrace();
        }
    }

    public static void main(String[] args)
    {
```

```java
        MediaGrabber grabber = new MediaGrabber();
        if (args != null && args.length > 0 && args[0].equals("launch"))
        {
            grabber.pushScreen(new ChoicesScreen());
            grabber.enterEventDispatcher();
        }
        else if (grabber.pending != null)
        {
            // Started via CHAPI. Show our UI.
            grabber.processRequest();
            grabber.requestForeground();
            grabber.enterEventDispatcher();
        }
    }

    private void verifyRegistration()
    {
        String className = MediaGrabber.class.getName();
        Registry registry = Registry.getRegistry(className);
        ContentHandler registered = registry.forID(CHAPI_ID, true);
        if (registered != null)
        {
            return;
        }
        // Wasn't registered before, so do it now.
        String[] actions = new String[]
        { ContentHandler.ACTION_SEND };
        String[] actionNames = new String[]
        { "Send Encrypted Via MediaGrabber" };
        ActionNameMap[] maps = new ActionNameMap[]
        { new ActionNameMap(actions, actionNames, "en") };
        try
        {
            registry.register(className, MIME_TYPES, SUFFIXES, actions, maps,
                CHAPI_ID, null);
        }
        catch (Exception e)
        {
            System.err.println("Could not register for " + CHAPI_ID + ": "
                + e.getMessage());
            e.printStackTrace();
        }
    }

    private void processRequest()
    {
        FileConnection file = null;
        InputStream is = null;
        try
        {
            String filename = null;
            String type = null;
            synchronized (this)
            {
                filename = pending.getURL();
                type = pending.getType();
            }
```

```
                if (filename != null && type != null)
                {
                    file = (FileConnection) Connector.open(filename);
                    is = file.openInputStream();
                    byte[] data = new byte[is.available()];
                    is.read(data);
                    SendingScreen sending = new SendingScreen(type, filename
                            .substring(filename.lastIndexOf('/') + 1),
                            "Sent to you by CHAPI", data, true);
                    pushScreen(sending);
                }
                else
                {
                    pushScreen(new ChoicesScreen());
                }
                server.finish(pending, Invocation.OK);
            }
            catch (Exception e)
            {
                System.out.println("Could not send file: " + e.getMessage());
                e.printStackTrace();
            }
            finally
            {
                try
                {
                    if (file != null)
                        file.close();
                    if (is != null)
                        is.close();
                }
                catch (Exception e)
                {
                }
            }
        }

    public synchronized void invocationRequestNotify(
            ContentHandlerServer handler)
    {
        pending = handler.getRequest(false);
        if (pending != null)
        {
            processRequest();
        }
    }
}
```

As you can see, you now support three situations for launching MediaGrabber. The standard case is when the user selects it directly, which you can recognize by the "launch" parameter. The second case is when it is launched via CHAPI, in which case a CHAPI Invocation will be waiting when you start up. Here, the application starts, but does so in the already-configured SendingScreen if provided with a file to send. Finally, it can be started on device boot, in which case you simply create an instance of MediaGrabber, which registers for CHAPI in its constructor if necessary, and then exit. You check and only register for CHAPI if you don't already have a CHAPI entry.

Note that you do register for incoming CHAPI messages. This allows the application to deal with requests if it is already running when a new request comes in. This would occur if, for example, the user backgrounded this app and then issued a request from another app. You use some basic synchronization to make sure that the Invocation doesn't change while you read values from it.

Running with CHAPI

Believe it or not, just by making these changes within MediaGrabber, you may already have modified the capabilities of native applications. Try using the native BlackBerry apps to take a picture or navigate to a media file. Press the Menu key. Scroll around. There's the new command! RIM has rewritten most of its native apps to check for CHAPI registration and add all matches it finds. Figure 8–6 shows what this looks like on the Storm.

Figure 8–6. *Native apps exposing third-party CHAPI apps*

TIP: The simplest way to browse the filesystem is to open the Media app, press the BlackBerry Menu key, and then select Explore.

Once you select the link, MediaGrabber will launch into the sending screen where you can enter a recipient and send as normal.

More Native Menu Integration

On older device software versions, you don't automatically see CHAPI items listed, but you can still add your own items. You are not restricted to CHAPI operations, either: you can run any sort of arbitrary code that you like.

To make something useful for both older and newer phones, add a new option to the Address Book app labeled "Verify Media Shared." This will check the contact to see if it has previously received any media from the MediaGrabber app. If not, it will offer to open MediaGrabber in its normal mode to send some media. Listing 8–2 shows the complete menu option class that you can include within MediaGrabber as an inner class.

Listing 8–2. *A Custom Menu Item to Display in the Contacts Menu*

```
private static class CheckContactMenuItem extends ApplicationMenuItem
{
    private Registry registry;

    public CheckContactMenuItem()
    {
        super(0);
        registry = Registry.getRegistry(getClass().getName());
    }

    public Object run(Object context)
    {
        if (context == null || !(context instanceof Contact))
            return null;
        try
        {
            Contact contact = (Contact) context;
            if (contact.countValues(BlackBerryContact.USER4) > 0)
            {
                // We've sent them media before.
                Dialog.inform("You have shared media with them.");
            }
            else
            {
                // Give a chance to select some media.
                int choice = Dialog.ask(Dialog.D_YES_NO,
                    "No sharing yet. Would you like to send media?");
                if (choice == Dialog.YES)
                {
                    Invocation request = new Invocation();
                    request.setID(CHAPI_ID);
                    registry.invoke(request);
                }
            }
        }
        catch (Exception e)
        {
```

```
            e.printStackTrace();
        }
        return null;
    }

    public String toString()
    {
        return "Verify Media Shared";
    }
}
```

The logical place to add a custom menu item is in your alternate entry point. However, the BlackBerry will occasionally start MediaGrabber even after boot, which could result in the same menu item being added multiple times. To guard against this situation, you use the `RuntimeStore` to check if the item has previously been added to the native menu, and only insert it if it has not. The device clears out the `RuntimeStore` every time the device reboots, which is also when it removes all custom menu items. You can insert the following code below your CHAPI check in `static void main` in order to register the custom menu item:

```
else
{
    // Startup execution.
    try
    {
        RuntimeStore store = RuntimeStore.getRuntimeStore();
        long menuItemID = 0x65fad834642a5345L;
        if (store.get(menuItemID) == null)
        {
            CheckContactMenuItem item = new CheckContactMenuItem();
            ApplicationMenuItemRepository repo = ApplicationMenuItemRepository
                    .getInstance();
            repo
                    .addMenuItem(
                            ApplicationMenuItemRepository.MENUITEM_ADDRESSBOOK_LIST,
                            item);
            store.put(menuItemID, item);
        }
    }
    catch (Throwable t)
    {
        t.printStackTrace();
    }
}
```

The next time you deploy the app, you will see the "Verify Media Shared" option within the address book app. Selecting this option will show the appropriate dialog and allow you to enter the main MediaGrabber screen if you haven't previously shared media.

WANT MORE?

CHAPI offers plenty of possibilities, both as a producer and as a consumer. Consider these options to further enhance MediaGrabber's inter-process cooperation.

- Create multiple entry points into MediaGrabber, such as one for sending unencrypted files.

- Experiment with adding support for multiple languages. Try switching the active language on your device and see if the menu item labels change.

- Use CHAPI to call out from MediaGrabber into other native applications using the BlackBerryContentHandler arguments.

- Create a new, stand-alone application in a new workspace that uses CHAPI to start MediaGrabber. For example, it could download a media file from the Internet, and then use MediaGrabber to send it to your friends.

If you know someone else who is learning BlackBerry development, try splitting these tasks between you. It is great practice to create and expose APIs to other developers, and a more realistic look at how real applications are designed, developed, released, and used.

Excelsior

When two applications share responsibilities and features, the result is more than the sum of its parts. Imagine a world where you couldn't print images you found on the Internet or attach files to your e-mail. The more applications that can touch and share data with one another, the more useful and compelling they become.

In this chapter, you have learned how to take advantage of multiplicative utility in your own apps. You can tap a wealth of features already designed by RIM when you use their hooks to add features to your app. And, in the other direction, you can make your app far more useful to your users if you create an API that allows other developers to use you. If five other apps all use your app, you have just become even more indispensable; you don't even need to write those five new apps.

This level of deep integration blurs the lines between a built-in app and an installed app. When your app is displaying as an option in the Contacts menu, showing a custom rollover icon, and getting opened from other apps, it becomes almost indistinguishable from the apps that came pre-installed on the BlackBerry.

You have now mastered the critical aspects of making powerful, useful, integrated apps. The next goal is to get those apps onto as many devices as possible, operating as smoothly as you can. Part 3 will show you how to make sure your apps can be used by as many people as possible.

Part III

Going Pro

Don't be selfish. Now that you can write an interesting and powerful BlackBerry app, you should share it with as many people as you can. Whether you send it to a few friends for fun, or sell it to hordes of eager consumers, people will appreciate your effort and achievement.

However, there can be a world of difference between writing an app that runs well on your personal phone and one that runs smoothly on everyone's phone. You don't want to deal with frustrated customers, confused managers, or sniping competitors. You especially don't want to take ten times as long making your app run on ten devices as you did on the first one. This final section of the book tackles the tricky problem of scaling up. Anticipate security problems before they arise, port your app to a variety of languages and devices, and make building multiple versions easier than before. These techniques won't just improve your work; they will also let you be more generous with the results.

Chapter 9

RIM Security

Few topics trip up BlackBerry developers more than the RIM security model. Developers often take an app that works perfectly in the simulator and find that it won't even start on a handset; or, worse, it that passes all internal testing, but exhibits strange behavior in the field. Such problems often result from arcane security rules. Some of them you can bend, some you can break, and others you must live with: in all cases, though, just understanding them will allow you to make better decisions. This chapter examines the most important features of BlackBerry device security and how they affect your applications.

The Ownership Question

Who owns your BlackBerry?

At first, that may seem like a foolish question: "I do, of course." After all, you carry it with you, it's got your phone number, and it shows your name on it.

However, actual possession is not quite as straightforward as it may seem at first. If you received your BlackBerry from an employer, then, despite the fact that you carry the device, the company really owns it: the company paid for it, runs the network it connects with, and is responsible for the behavior of the devices. A business has an interest in the ongoing use of BlackBerry devices. They may not want you to upload 3GB of video files onto the corporate intranet, make phone calls to 1-900 numbers, or install malware. When people do these things, they don't only affect their own devices, but they also create financial and administrative headaches for their employers.

Even if you bought your BlackBerry for a personal mobile phone account, the ownership question might not be quite as simple as you might think. If, like most Americans, you got your BlackBerry as part of a two-year contract, you might have only paid $50 or so instead of a list price of $700 or higher. Your mobile carrier will have subsidized the remaining cost to Research in Motion (RIM) to entice you as a customer. In return, the carrier expects you to continue with them as a loyal customer for multiple years. What happens if you renege on your contract after a month and walk away with your new BlackBerry? You could argue that, having violated the contract, the phone company is the one who really "owns" it, having paid for the majority of it and set the terms under which you could have it. The company might not want you to switch to another company and continue using the BlackBerry.

Understanding the intricacies of BlackBerry ownership helps to illuminate many of the topics addressed later in this chapter. As consumers, we tend to feel a certain right to things we own. Once we have paid for something, we expect to continue using it without interference: we should be able to install the software we want, run it when we want for as long as we want, browse to the web sites we want to visit, and so on. Because BlackBerry devices often have complicated ownership, though, your desires might clash with those of other stakeholders. Where there is a dispute, the "real" owner of the device usually comes out on top.

Security Policies: "You Can't Do That!"

The 900lb-gorilla of the security model is the security policy. Inviolate and determined, the policy acts as the ultimate enforcer, providing the final word on what is and is not allowed on a particular device.

Background

BlackBerry devices started life as corporate connectivity devices that were only available to business people who needed them to keep in contact when away from their offices. As discussed in "The Ownership Question" section, despite the fact that each individual person carries a particular BlackBerry, the devices are actually owned by the company, and the company has a strong interest in ensuring that the devices behave appropriately on the network.

Strong, secure IT policies provide one of RIM's strongest selling points. Unlike other smart-phone platforms, RIM devices can be securely locked down with particular rules about their behavior. These rules are contained within a particular file called the security policy, often named `policy.bin`. This file is loaded into the BlackBerry at a very low level: you cannot find it by browsing the filesystem, and you cannot copy over or remove it. The device reads in this policy when first starting up, and, after it loads, nothing can change the rules.

Actual policies will vary tremendously. If you buy a phone through a wireless carrier, it will likely come with a very permissive policy that allows you to do almost anything. After all, the carrier wants you to use your device and be a satisfied customer. Some companies similarly run an open system. Most corporations, however, will place at least some restrictions on the use of their devices, and others will be locked down so tightly that they are completely unusable other than for a few specifically allowed actions.

IT Policy Examples

Administrators have access to a wealth of different IT policy settings. These can be configured differently to apply to individuals, to groups of users, or to an entire organization. For instance, an administrator may grant herself and a handful of power users very open IT policies, provide developers with policies that will not limit their network usage, and send a standard restrictive policy to everyone else. A few of the many available policy settings are listed below, focusing on the settings most likely to interfere with your applications or your development. Many disable or enable particular features, while others allow administrators to configure particular settings such as visible text or URLs.

Device Security Policy Examples

Disable Application Center

Disable App World

Application Restriction List

Category Restriction List for App World

Disable Application Purchasing from App World

Disable BlackBerry Messenger

Disable Forwarding Contacts

Control Bluetooth Power Range

Allow Outgoing Calls on Bluetooth

Allow Application Download via Browser

Allow Wi-Fi Browser

Disable JavaScript in Browser

Enable HTML Tables in Browser

Enable Style Sheets

Disable Photo Camera

Disable Video Camera

Public-Private Key Generation Algorithm

Users Must Confirm Before Sending SMS, MMS, e-mail, or PIN Message

Disable MMS

Enable Simultaneous Phone and Data

Set Owner Information

Enable PIN Messaging

Allow SMS Messaging

Default Browser

Browser Home Page Address

Home Page Address is Read-Only

Automatically Download E-mail Attachments

Display Prompt when Downloading Images

Disable Rich Text/HTML E-mail

Duration to Keep Received Messages

Prepend Disclaimer to Outgoing E-mail Messages

Restrict Incoming Calls

Restrict Outgoing Calls

Allow Geolocation Service

Allow Browser

Allow Phone

Disable BlackBerry Maps

Report GPS Location to Enterprise Server

Force Memory Cleaner

Disable Wireless Synchronization for Calendar, Memos, etc.

Allow External Non-Enterprise Connections

Allow Internal Enterprise Connections

Allow Resetting Idle Timer

Allow Screen Shot Capture

Allow Split Pipe Connections

Allow Apps to Use Persistent Store

Allow Apps to Use Serial, USB, and IrDA Ports

Disable Cut/Copy/Paste

Disable External Memory Media Card

Disable Photo Sharing Apps

Disable Social Networking Apps

Disable USB Mass Storage

Disable Installing Unsigned Apps

Disallow Third Party Application Downloads

External File System Encryption Level

Firewall Block Incoming Messages

Firewall Whitelist Addresses

Password Required for Application Download

Allow Other Browser Services

Allow Other Calendar Services

Allow Public IM Services

Set Local Area Code

TCP APN/Username/Password

TLS Support

Allow VOIP

Enable VPN

VPN Username/Password/DNS

Disallow Rollback to Previous Software Version

Blocked Wi-Fi SSIDs

Disable Wi-Fi

Disable Wi-Fi Access to BES

CAUTION: The split pipe setting often frustrates developers. Most applications will either attempt to connect through an enterprise MDS connection or through a device-side TCP connection. If an application attempts to open both types of connections, it is said to have a split pipe. This can cause security concerns: for example, a malicious app might open a connection to the corporate network, collect data from internal servers, and then open a connection to a hacker's web server and upload sensitive data. The split pipe IT policy forbids this happening: if an app has ever attempted to open an MDS connection before (even if it failed), it is forbidden from attempting to open a public connection. If this happens, you should first change your app to make sure that it only attempts to open either MDS (deviceside=false) or public (deviceside=true) connections. If you use ConnectionFactory, do not mix TransportInfo.TRANSPORT_MDS with other allowed transport types. Wipe the affected device by removing all software via the BlackBerry Desktop Manager and then reload all software.

In addition to these general settings, administrators can also configure a set of application control policy rules. These provide more fine-grained controls that specifically apply to third-party applications that are installed by users. Some of the more important ones are listed below.

Application Control Policy Examples

Allow Internal Network Connections

Allow External Network Connections

Allow Local Connections

Modify Device Settings

Reset Security Timer

Set Applications as Mandatory, Optional, or Forbidden

Access to Browser Filter API

Access to E-mail API

Access to Event Injection

Access to File API

Access to GPS API

Access to Local Key Store (Crypto)

Access to Interprocess Communication API

Access to Media API

Access to Phone API

Access to Module Management API

Access to Media Recording APIs (Microphone, Video, and Screen)

Access to Serial Port/Bluetooth API

Access to Wi-Fi API

List of Domains with Browser Filter Support

List of Permitted External Domains

List of Permitted Internal Domains

Pushing Policies

So how do policies get loaded? A default policy will be in place when you first obtain your device. For most people, this will stay the same for as long as they continue to own the BlackBerry.

If a BlackBerry device connects to a corporate BES network, though, the administrator has the option of pushing down a new IT policy. This will replace whatever policy was previously loaded on the device. Even if you somehow changed the policy, that change will be undone the next time it connects.

Policies can be loaded via the BlackBerry Desktop Manager. You will not see this option in the menu when you connect your device; rather, it will automatically and silently send the policy to the phone. Desktop Manager does not provide any indication when this occurs, but you may notice different behavior later on.

Beware of eBay

This is a good place to comment on one of the common traps that new developers fall into. BlackBerry devices can be expensive, and there is a strong temptation to purchase them second-hand at a substantial discount. Sometimes this leads to good results, but be aware of what you might be getting into.

Many of the devices for sale online, especially those sold by individuals through sites like Craigslist and eBay, were once corporate devices that connected to company networks. The devices might have been replaced with newer models, or an employee might have been allowed to keep her BlackBerry when leaving. These models might be fully functioning and able to make calls, send and receive text messages, and perhaps even be compatible with multiple carriers. However, if they ever were part of a company network, odds are very high that they still have an IT policy installed.

If you get one of these devices, everything might seem fine at first: you will be allowed to use it as you would any other device, and hopefully also load applications. However, you might notice mysterious problems as you use it more. Certain Java API calls might simply fail. You might see annoying security prompts that you are not allowed to permanently dismiss. Maybe an application simply will stop running.

In one sense, this can actually be considered a useful problem to have. After all, there are plenty of real users out there with IT policies on their devices, and if you know how their devices will behave, you can better anticipate the problems they might encounter. Still, having a device with a restrictive security policy can kill your productivity and massively slow down the software development cycle.

What's the solution? If you can afford it, it's safest to buy your BlackBerry devices new. Otherwise, try to contact the seller and get a clearer picture of what this particular device did before. If it was bought new by an individual for a personal wireless account, it will probably be fine. If it has been bought and sold multiple times and was most recently on a corporate network, you might want to avoid it, or at least ask for a return if it proves to carry an IT policy.

Replacing an Old Policy

If you get stuck with a restrictive IT policy, you have a couple of options. If you are on a corporate BES network or have access to one, you can ask the administrator to create an open IT policy for your device to use. Note that this might be a long shot; administrators might not want to have loose policies floating around.

You can also find online tools that claim to remove IT policies. In reality, nothing actually removes a policy; at best, it can replace the existing policy with a more permissive one. Use such tools at your own risk. The updated policy you receive might not be much better than the one you replaced.

Finally, keep in mind that even if you do replace an old policy, updated policies will still be pushed to the device every time you connect to a corporate network. Because of this, you might want to avoid using an individual BlackBerry as both a development device and as part of a secure company network. Getting two devices costs more, but over the long run you will more than make up for the cost with your increased productivity.

What Can You Do?

Your development device aside, you must decide if and how you want to handle devices with security policies that interfere with the running of your app.

In one sense, there's nothing you *can* do. Applications execute in a sandbox, and the security policy is far beyond the reach of that sandbox. Your app cannot replace the IT policy, cannot disable it, and cannot even pre-emptively determine whether or not a restrictive policy is installed.

You should first consider the potential audience for your app, the likelihood that users will have restrictive IT policies, and the impact of those policies on your app. If you are writing an app for yourself or a small group of people, and you know that nobody has special IT policies, you have nothing to worry about.

If you are writing an app for your company's use or for a particular corporation, you should coordinate with the BlackBerry administrator. Define what your app will need to do, focusing on aspects like network usage and data access, and communicate those needs to the administrator. If a policy needs to change, she will have the authority to get it done. If the policy can't change, you need to find out as soon as possible so you can change the scope of your app or get authority from higher levels of management to make the change.

If you are writing an app for general public consumption, you're in a relatively tricky spot. Most commercial apps are sold through BlackBerry App World, carrier stores, or independent smartphone stores. The majority of these buyers will have clean devices and no issues. A minority will be using secondhand phones or devices they got from work, and a subsection of those users will be unable to run all but the simplest apps. You can consider several possible responses.

- *Buyer Beware*: If possible, warn users ahead of time about what your app does. Clearly state that if their device cannot function properly, it's their problem, not yours.

- *Good Neighbor*: If users complain that your app is unusable, appease them by offering a refund. This works best if your app contains a server component so you can track individual users. You won't need to advertise this method, and complaints should be rare enough that this will be the exception.

- *Graceful Degradation*: Depending on your app design and features, you may be able to continue operating even if the security policy blocks some functions. For example, if an offline game connects to a server for a shared high-score counter, your users should still be able to play even if the app cannot connect to the server.

- *Over-communicate*: Include plenty of warnings and help within your application advising the user about what your app is doing and what options they have if the app does not work properly.

Again, at the end of the day, you are powerless to fix any problems that your users encounter that stem from strong IT policies. At best, you can recognize the problem, realize how it may affect your app, evaluate the severity of impact on your users, and plan ahead of time how you wish to handle the problem.

User Permissions: "May I Do This?"

Let's assume that a user's company accepts everything your app does, or that the user does not belong to a company with an IT policy. This removes one significant barrier from your application's proper functioning, but you may still face additional hurdles. In addition to IT policies, which protect the interests of the corporation, BlackBerry devices also support user permissions, which protect the interests of the individual.

Many users share concerns similar to those faced by large corporations. If a user has a data plan that bills them per kilobyte sent or received, she will get quite unhappy if an application uploads several megabytes of data without her knowledge. If a user worries about her privacy, she won't want an application to take photos, record her GPS location, and then e-mail that information to someone.

Therefore, within the confines of the IT policy, each BlackBerry device also offers a flexible set of user permissions that apply to installed applications. These are initially set to certain default values, which can be defined by the organization or the manufacturer. Users can later fine-tune them globally or on a per-app basis.

Setting User Permissions on OTA Installs

When someone installs an application over the air (OTA) by loading a JAD file in his browser, he can choose to set individual application permissions as part of the download, as shown in Figure 9–1. You cannot control what permissions the following screen shows. However, you can include instructions on an HTML landing page describing what the user should do; after they read this, you can direct them to the JAD. For example, you could include a statement such as, "This app must access the Internet in order to function properly. On the following screen, please set application permissions and verify that the Internet permission is set to Allow."

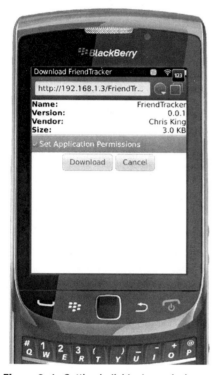

Figure 9–1. *Setting individual permissions*

When the user starts setting application permissions, she will see a variety of settings. The specific choices will vary depending on the device model and the software version loaded. Choices are organized into three broad groups:

1. Connections: These concern data entering or leaving the device.

2. Interactions: These control the app's access to low-level device functions.

3. User Data: These describe the ability to read or write persistent data.

Each group can be set to Allow, Custom, Default, or Deny. If you'd like to modify a group's settings for this app, click the current setting and select a new value from the drop-down menu. This allows you to quickly grant an app all permissions or to turn off broad areas of concern.

In many cases, you will want to exert more fine-grained control. Press the BlackBerry Menu key and select Expand to view all the sub-options under a particular group. This allows you to make more detailed decisions. For instance, you might want to allow an app access to the USB port and Wi-Fi, but forbid access to GPS. You can assign each individual permission to one of three settings:

1. Allow: Always permit the app to do this.

2. Prompt: Display a message each time the app attempts to do this. (You can later permanently dismiss this prompt.)

3. Deny: Never allow the app to do this.

> **NOTE:** Certain low-level permissions, such as Interprocess Communication and Keystroke Injection, only offer the Allow and Deny settings. This is because these actions are usually initiated by libraries, background threads, or other components without a user interface, and so it's awkward to display a prompt when they run.

Figure 9–2 shows a user modifying the default permissions for the MediaGrabber app. This device was configured to disallow recording, which will seriously hinder the usefulness of the app. If changed to Allow, recording will always work; if set to Prompt, the user will still need to click through a message the next time they try to start recording.

Figure 9–2. *Changing a specific permission*

Default Permissions

Every phone comes with a default set of permissions. These apply to applications that you install through a cable. These default settings are also applied to OTA-installed apps if the user doesn't choose to set the application permissions.

To set the global user permissions on your device, follow these steps:

1. Open Options.

2. Open Device.

3. Open Application Management.

4. Press the BlackBerry Menu Key.

5. Select "Edit Default Permissions".

Within this next screen, you can select and modify permissions as you would for an OTA download. The changes that you make will apply to all applications installed in the future. If you'd like to apply them to all previously installed applications, press the BlackBerry menu key and then select "Apply Defaults to All".

Specific Application Settings

If you cable-load or download an application and later realize that it does not have the proper permissions, you can modify the permissions to what you want like so:

1. Open Options.

2. Open Device.

3. Open Application Management.

4. Highlight the application name.

5. Press the BlackBerry Menu Key.

6. Select Edit Permissions.

Once again, you can customize the individual permissions here. Don't forget to save the changes once you are done. You may need to exit and restart the app for the changes to take effect.

Programmatic Control

So far, I have been looking at user permissions from the user's perspective. As you have seen, the person who installs your app can exert a great deal of control over the app's behavior. This can lead to serious problems within your app, though. If you require an Internet connection to run but can't open that connection, then the app is effectively broken.

Older versions of BlackBerry device software had no good solution to this problem. At best, you could detect when a problem occurred and display an error screen to the user describing what they must do to solve the problem. Some people are reluctant to modify their device settings. Others may get lost while navigating the menus. As a result, your app stays broken.

ApplicationPermissions

Fortunately, in more modern devices, RIM has offered developers an API that allows insight into the user's current permissions settings. Since you know what resources your app needs to function, you can inspect the current settings and display a message if they are wrong. Even better, you can ask the user to change them.

RIM does not allow an app to force its permissions preferences upon the user. This would defeat the whole point of user-controlled permissions and allow malicious apps a clear shot at whatever they wanted. RIM offers a fairly elegant solution: your app can describe the specific permissions it wants, and then the BlackBerry will ask the user to confirm the changes.

Of course, the user may decide that she does not want to give you all the permissions you ask for. Your app can examine the permissions again and decide how it wants to proceed. If you simply can't function, you may exit the app or continue asking for permissions. Otherwise, continue running normally, perhaps warning the user about what degradation she will see.

Table 9–1 shows the permissions that are available to query and change. All are defined in the ApplicationPermissions class.

Table 9–1. *Application Permissions*

Name	Allows	Added	Deprecated
PERMISSION_APPLICATION_MANAGEMENT	Install or delete other applications.	4.6	
PERMISSION_BLUETOOTH	Send and receive data via Bluetooth and access Bluetooth profiles.	4.2.1	
PERMISSION_BROWSER_FILTER	Register a filter with the web browser.	4.2.1	
PERMISSION_CHANGE_DEVICE_SETTINGS	Change configuration and user settings.	4.2.1	4.6, use PERMISSION_DEVICE_SETTINGS
PERMISSION_CODE_MODULE_MANAGEMENT	Install or delete other applications.	4.2.1	4.6, use PERMISSION_APPLICATION_MANAGEMENT
PERMISSION_CROSS_APPLICATION_COMMUNICATION	Share data and messages with other apps.	4.6	
PERMISSION_DEVICE_SETTINGS	Change configuration and user settings.	4.6	
PERMISSION_DISPLAY_LOCKED	Draw on top of the device lock screen.	5.0	
PERMISSION_EMAIL	Send and read e-mail.	4.2.1	
PERMISSION_EVENT_INJECTOR	Simulate user events.	4.2.1	4.6, use PERMISSION_INPUT_SIMULATION
PERMISSION_EXTERNAL_CONNECTIONS	Connect to the Internet.	4.2.1	4.6, use PERMISSION_INTERNET
PERMISSION_FILE_API	Read and write files.	4.2.1	
PERMISSION_HANDHELD_KEYSTORE	Access locally stored crypto keys.	4.2.1	4.6, use PERMISSION_SECURITY_DATA
PERMISSION_IDLE_TIMER	Reset security timer to prevent the device from locking.	4.2.1	

Name	Allows	Added	Deprecated
PERMISSION_INPUT_SIMULATION	Simulate user events.	4.6	
PERMISSION_INTER_PROCESS_ COMMUNICATION	Share data and messages with other apps.	4.3	4.6, use PERMISSION_ CROSS_APPLICATION_ COMMUNICATION
PERMISSION_INTERNAL_CONNECTIONS	Connect to corporate MDS network.	4.2.1	4.6, use PERMISSION_SERVER_ NETWORK
PERMISSION_INTERNET	Connect to the Internet.	4.6	
PERMISSION_KEYSTORE_MEDIUM_ SECURITY	Access locally stored medium-strength crypto keys.	4.2.1	4.6, no replacement
PERMISSION_LOCAL_CONNECTIONS	Connect through USB or the serial port.	4.2.1	4.6, use PERMISSION_USB
PERMISSION_LOCATION_API	Access GPS and other LBS resources.	4.2.1	4.6, use PERMISSION_LOCATION _ DATA
PERMISSION_MEDIA	Access and modify media files.	4.3	
PERMISSION_ORGANIZER_DATA	Access data from calendar, contacts, tasks, and memos.	4.6	
PERMISSION_PHONE	Make voice calls, receive voice calls, read phone logs.	4.2.1	
PERMISSION_PIM	Access data from calendar, contacts, tasks, and memos.	4.2.1	4.6, use PERMISSION_ORGANI ZER_ DATA
PERMISSION_RECORDING	Access microphone, camera, or screen capture.	4.6	
PERMISSION_SCREEN_CAPTURE	Capture screenshots.	4.3	4.6, use PERMISSION_RECOR DING
PERMISSION_SECURITY_DATA	Access locally stored crypto keys.	4.6	
PERMISSION_SERVER_NETWORK	Connect to corporate MDS network.	4.6	

Name	Allows	Added	Deprecated
PERMISSION_THEME_DATA	Provide themes.	4.2.1	4.6, use PERMISSION_THEMES
PERMISSION_THEMES	Provide themes.	4.6	
PERMISSION_USB	Connect through USB.	4.6	
PERMISSION_WIFI	Make Wi-Fi connections and collect data about Wi-Fi configuration.	4.3	

ApplicationPermissionsManager

ApplicationPermissions contains information about the permissions set on an application. ApplicationPermissionsManager allows you to retrieve the current permissions, query the setting of a particular permission, or ask for more permissions.

Checking Permissions

If you want to find out whether a particular permission is set, use one of the versions of ApplicationPermissionsManager.getPermission() shown below. You must provide one of the permissions from Table 9–1. You will get back the current setting.

- ApplicationPermissions.VALUE_ALLOW means access is granted.

- ApplicationPermissions.VALUE_PROMPT means access will be permitted if the user confirms.

- ApplicationPermissions.VALUE_DENY means access is forbidden.

The following snippet demonstrates how you can check to see whether a permission is properly set before starting a potentially restricted operation:

```
ApplicationPermissionsManager permissions = ⏎
    ApplicationPermissionsManager.getInstance();
int currentSetting = permissions.getPermission(⏎
    ApplicationPermissions.PERMISSION_FILE_API);
if (currentSetting == ApplicationPermissions.VALUE_ALLOW)
{
    // We can access the file here.
}
```

You can optionally provide two extra arguments to getPermission(). If the permission deals with accessing a network, like ApplicationPermissions.PERMISSION_INTERNET, it's possible that a domain-specific permission may be in effect. For example, a user might ordinarily set connections to Prompt but allow all connections to www.google.com. You can pass in the domain you plan to connect to learn its setting, as shown here:

```
int domainSpecificSetting = permissions.getPermission(⏎
    ApplicationPermissions.PERMISSION_SERVER_NETWORK, "securesite.example.com");
```

To retrieve all the permissions set for an app, use getApplicationPermissions(). This allows you to more compactly check multiple permissions settings at once, as you can see here:

```
ApplicationPermissions current = permissions.getApplicationPermissions();
if (current.getPermission(ApplicationPermissions.PERMISSION_INPUT_SIMULATION)
        != ApplicationPermissions.VALUE_ALLOW || current.getPermission(
            ApplicationPermissions.PERMISSION_IDLE_TIMER) !=
                ApplicationPermissions.VALUE_ALLOW)
{
    // Deal with lack of permissions.
}
```

Changing Permissions

To request greater permissions, first construct an ApplicationPermissions object that contains your desired settings. The user will see a prompt that describes which additional permissions they need to grant. All requested permissions will be requested as VALUE_ALLOW; you cannot request the user to grant you VALUE_PROMPT or VALUE_DENY permissions.

After configuring your ApplicationPermissions, issue a request to ApplicationPermissionsManager.invokePermissionsRequest(). This is a synchronous blocking call: your app will suspend while the user reviews your request. By the time it returns, the user has completed his selections. You can inspect the return value to see what he chose: true means all your requests were granted, false means at least one was set to Prompt or Deny. This example requests a set of necessary permissions for a particular app:

```
ApplicationPermissions requested = new ApplicationPermissions();
requested.addPermission(ApplicationPermissions.PERMISSION_LOCATION_DATA);
requested.addPermission(ApplicationPermissions.PERMISSION_INTERNET);
requested.addPermission(ApplicationPermissions.PERMISSION_FILE_API);
if (permissions.invokePermissionsRequest(requested))
{
    // Granted, continue running the app.
}
else
{
    // Denied, show an error and exit.
}
```

> **NOTE:** The permissions dialog is generated by the operating system, not your app, so you can invoke a permissions request from a library or other invisible component.

Keep in mind that, even when your app really wants certain permissions, the user may not be able to grant them if his IT policy forbids it. Avoid haranguing users for things beyond their control. You can check ApplicationPermissionsManager.getMaxAllowable() to find the most permissive possible setting for a particular permission. It might be that the IT policy demands a setting of at least Prompt for Internet connections, so if it's already set to Prompt, you can't get anything better.

Give Me a Reason

As a strange sort of parallel to application permissions, a particular set of APIs generate their own warning when accessed. If you call certain methods, the user will see a message such as, "The application MyFlashlight is attempting to change device settings." RIM does not document all the instances where this occurs, but it happens for when invoking `EventInjector.invokeEvent()`, as well as the following APIs if Device Settings permission is set to Prompt.

APIs with Customized Prompts

ApplicationDescriptor.setPowerOnBehavior

ApplicationManager.lockSystem

ApplicationManager.requestForeground

ApplicationManager.requestForegroundForConsole

ApplicationManager.setCurrentPowerOnBehavior

ApplicationManager.unlockSystem

Backlight.enable

Backlight.setBrightness

Backlight.setTimeout

Device.requestPowerOff

Device.requestStorageMode

Display.setContrast

Device.setDateTime

EventLogger.clearLog

EventLogger.setMinimumLevel

Keypad.setMode

Locale.setDefaultInputForSystem

MIMETypeAssociations.registerMIMETypeMapping

MIMETypeAssociations.registerType

Radio.activateWAFs

Radio.deactivateWAFs

The user can allow or deny this access; she also has the option of suppressing future requests. What's especially unusual about this set of APIs is that you can provide some custom text that will display as part of the permissions prompt. You do this by implementing the ReasonProvider method and invoking ApplicationPermissionsManager. addReasonProvider()as shown:

```
ApplicationPermissionsManager mgr = ApplicationPermissionsManager.getInstance();
mgr.addReasonProvider(ApplicationDescriptor.currentApplicationDescriptor(),
        new ReasonProvider(){
    public String getMessage(int permissionID)
    {
        if (permissionID ==
            ApplicationPermissions.PERMISSION_CHANGE_DEVICE_SETTINGS)
        {
            return "I need to change device settings to keep the screen on.";
        }
        return "Please allow this access for full app functionality";
    }});
Backlight.setTimeout(255);
```

After you set a reason provider and invoke one of the restricted methods, the user will see a link labeled "Details from the vendor. . ." as part of the application permissions window. If she clicks this link, she will see your custom message.

As you can see, the system passes the specific permission ID as a parameter to your ReasonProvider, and you can select an appropriate message depending on the permission. This would make much more sense if BlackBerry invoked ReasonProvider for other permissions requests. Instead, this class has very limited utility. In practice, you should simply ask for permissions to be granted prior to invoking sensitive APIs rather than display some custom text buried within a prompt. If you'd like to communicate with the user, do it before invoking the permissions request.

Firewall: "Don't Go There!"

You are probably already familiar with the concept of a firewall from your own personal computer or company network. A firewall is a piece of software, often integrated with the operating system, that applies a set of rules to all incoming and outgoing connections. Figure 9–3 illustrates some typical behavior from an active BlackBerry firewall.

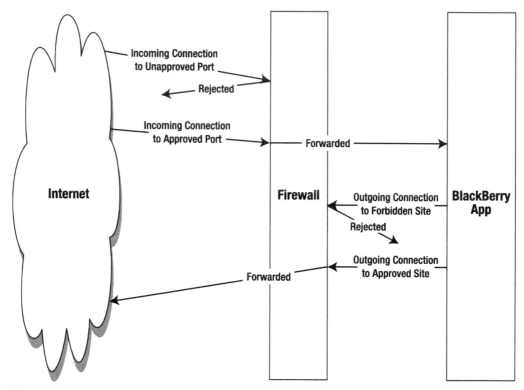

Figure 9-3. *A BlackBerry firewall*

Firewall Actions

Any time the device receives an incoming request, it checks to see whether that request is permitted. The rules might call for blocking certain ports, or only permitting connections from certain approved IP addresses, ranges, or domains. If the device approves the request and an application is listening on that port, the application will receive the incoming data. If the request is denied, the data will not be provided. In both cases, the firewall is invisible to the application: if you get data, it looks just the same whether it passed through a firewall or not; if you don't get data, it's as though it was never sent.

Similar rules apply on outgoing connections, although here your app does get a little more visibility into the presence of a firewall. At the moment the app tries to open a connection, the firewall will check to see whether to permit the connection. It makes this decision based on a combination of factors: the permissions granted to the requesting app, the domain being accessed, the port number used, and the transport protocol type. The request will either succeed or fail.

On BlackBerry devices, the firewall can have more subtle effects as well. The firewall might prevent certain file operations, prevent certain dialogs from displaying, or interfere with app installation.

Firewall Settings

To view and modify your firewall, follow these steps:

1. Open Options.

2. Select Security.

3. Select Firewall.

You can enable or disable the firewall from this screen. If your IT policy mandates use of a firewall, you may see a lock icon here, which indicates that it can't be modified. Otherwise, simply select the current Status setting to switch between Enabled and Disabled.

The firewall also allows you to block certain types of incoming messages, such as SMS text messages or PIN messages. You can choose to allow messages from everyone in your contacts or only specific addresses. If you select specific addresses, you can press the BlackBerry Menu key to configure the exceptions; this takes you to a new screen where you can enter the approved senders.

Firewall Effects

Many users don't realize that they have a firewall. The firewall silently grants or denies permissions. If the firewall is disabled, it doesn't even interfere with any operations.

However, firewalls do often warn users about app actions. The standard firewall prompt will show a message such as, "The application SearchCrawler has requested an HTTP connection to www.google.com." Users can allow or deny the request. They also can check options like "Do not ask for HTTP." or "Do not ask for HTTP to www.google.com."

While the prompt displays, app execution will freeze. Once the user has dealt with the prompt, the operation will return or an exception will be thrown. You cannot influence the text that displays in this firewall prompt or provide a default setting.

If the user selects an option like "Do not ask again," they will never again see the prompt in this app unless they later reinstall the application or modify the firewall settings. If the prompt is for accessing a particular domain, they may need to reapprove accesses to later domains.

> **TIP:** If the firewall is set to Prompt, your app's execution will cease at the moment it attempts to open a connection. This allows the BlackBerry to display a modal security prompt that allows the user to grant or deny permission. However, if the connection was made from the app's main UI thread, the BlackBerry might not be able to draw the modal dialog and the app will freeze. To avoid this problem, follow the best practice of always making connections from another thread.

Even if the firewall is disabled, firewall-style prompts will still display for unsigned applications. Such applications are presumed to be less trusted than signed apps, so they are held to a higher level of scrutiny.

Dealing with the Firewall

Unfortunately, the BlackBerry API does not offer developers a good way to deal with the firewall. You can't query it to determine whether it is enabled, and you can't request it to be disabled for your app or globally. If you wish to influence the firewall setting, your best option is to provide the user with instructions on how to manually modify the firewall.

> **TIP:** If your app runs on a corporate network, you can ask the administrator to push a new firewall setting to your app's users.

Firewalls can be frustrating for users and developers, as they require extra clicking that interrupts the flow of the app. You can't do anything about this, so just advise your users of the situation and describe what steps they can take to mitigate it. On the plus side, most BlackBerry users who do have firewalls grow very accustomed to seeing these prompts, and after a while start automatically granting new apps safe passage through the firewall.

Application Signing: "Do I Know You?"

What's the deal with signing? Unlike several other phone platforms, signing a BlackBerry application is quite cheap, and you can sign an effectively limitless number of apps. You might wonder why RIM supports app signing.

Identity Establishment

The most important factor in application signing is to establish authorship. Every set of code signing keys is unique, and every code signing request verifies that you are the person who originally ordered the keys.

Unlike some other certificate-style operations, RIM doesn't actually perform a background check or physically verify your identity. Still, it does recognize you as an individual entity, and, because your apps are signed with your keys, it knows who wrote a given app.

Code Signing Impacts

Almost nobody will ever have a serious problem with application signing. Still, by setting up the system the way they have, RIM has gained certain abilities.

- They can monitor the APIs used by individuals. This allows them to deny cryptographic API use to people in certain geographic regions, for example.

- Because signatures come from a remote server, in extreme cases, RIM could revoke a set of code signing keys if a developer was discovered writing virus software, for example.

If an app is not signed, it is missing this audit trail. As a result, devices trust this application less and will treat it differently from signed apps.

- All restricted APIs will fail to execute. This includes items like the application manager, e-mail messages, the persistent object store, and many more.

- Certain operations will always result in a user prompt requiring their approval before proceeding. These operations include network I/O and filesystem access.

Signing only has an impact when running on an actual BlackBerry device; the simulator does not need signatures and will not behave any differently if an app has been signed.

App: Ask for Permissions

MediaGrabber exercises a wide range of functions. This also means it crosses a lot of boundaries and requires a large set of permissions to function properly. You won't notice any problems while running in the emulator. However, once you start running it on devices, you may run across some things that don't work properly: maybe the audio recording doesn't start, or the file isn't saved, or you can't invoke it via CHAPI.

Fortunately, by using knowledge from this chapter, you can help mitigate these problems. When the app starts up, check if you have the permissions necessary to run. If so, proceed as normal. If not, ask the user to grant you the proper permission, and refuse to start unless you get them.

Checking and Requesting Permissions

Listing 9–1 shows a helper method that checks the current application permissions. If it sees that any of them are not set to Allow, it will ask the user to grant those permissions. This method uses APIs and fields added in OS version 4.6; if you need to support earlier versions, check table 9–1 to find the substitutions.

Listing 9–1. *Checking and Requesting Required MediaGrabber Permissions*

```
private boolean checkPermissions()
{
    ApplicationPermissionsManager manager = ApplicationPermissionsManager
            .getInstance();
    ApplicationPermissions current = manager.getApplicationPermissions();

    int email = ApplicationPermissions.PERMISSION_EMAIL;
    int interProcess = ↩
        ApplicationPermissions.PERMISSION_CROSS_APPLICATION_COMMUNICATION;
    int file = ApplicationPermissions.PERMISSION_FILE_API;
    int media = ApplicationPermissions.PERMISSION_MEDIA;
    int pim = ApplicationPermissions.PERMISSION_ORGANIZER_DATA;
    int screenCapture = ApplicationPermissions.PERMISSION_RECORDING;
    int allow = ApplicationPermissions.VALUE_ALLOW;
    if (current.getPermission(email) != allow
            || current.getPermission(interProcess) != allow
            || current.getPermission(file) != allow
            || current.getPermission(media) != allow
            || current.getPermission(pim) != allow
            || current.getPermission(screenCapture) != allow)
    {
        ApplicationPermissions updated = new ApplicationPermissions();
        updated.addPermission(email);
        updated.addPermission(interProcess);
        updated.addPermission(file);
        updated.addPermission(media);
        updated.addPermission(pim);
        updated.addPermission(screenCapture);
        return manager.invokePermissionsRequest(updated);
    }
    return true;
}
```

> **NOTE:** I assigned the permission names to local variables simply to make the code more legible on the printed page. In a real app, you would likely just refer to the `ApplicationPermissions` fields directly.

This just shows one of a few potential ways to make the request. You could check for and request each permission individually; this would be annoying, but possibly more elegant to code. An even better solution would be to check all permissions but only ask for the permissions that are not already granted. This is less likely to intimidate the user, who may be more likely to accept the change if he sees that you're only asking for permission to record than he would be if you ask for a half-dozen permissions at once.

Plugging In

Where do you want to invoke your `checkPermissions()` method? This is a tough call. The best place to locate it is within your constructor; because MediaGrabber checks for CHAPI registration right away, and CHAPI is guarded by an application permission, it would be nice to check that you have permissions before doing anything else. However, because MediaGrabber is an auto-start application, it will start running automatically on boot-up, as well as whenever it receives CHAPI requests. Users may get confused or annoyed if they see permissions windows popping up, seemingly without any cause.

As a compromise, I have decided to call the method after the user directly launches MediaGrabber from the icon, as shown in the following code. At this point, the user knows what app is running and is more likely to grant permissions. In practice, most users will run the app directly shortly after installing it. And, once you get the permissions you want, they will remain set that way even after the device reboots.

```
public static void main(String[] args)
{
    MediaGrabber grabber = new MediaGrabber();
    if (args != null && args.length > 0 && args[0].equals("launch"))
    {
        if (grabber.checkPermissions())
        {
            grabber.pushScreen(new ChoicesScreen());
            grabber.enterEventDispatcher();
        }
    }
    // Remaining startup cases handled below.
}
```

Because MediaGrabber is ultimately an entertainment application, this approach makes sense. If your app is designed to provide more low-level capabilities or doesn't contain a UI component, you'll probably want to ask for permissions almost immediately.

Running the App

Adding permissions checks won't have any impact at all on the simulator, which always permits everything. The impact on the device may vary based on the particular handset you use. If you have previously always been able to run MediaGrabber with no problems or annoyances, you probably already had all the permissions you need, so the permissions request will never display. For most developers, though, you will see the prompt display the first time you launch the new version of MediaGrabber on the device.

Experiment with granting or denying permissions to see how it affects the app's behavior. If you have previously set all permissions, you can continue testing by changing some back to Deny or Prompt, as previously described in the "Application Permissions" section of this chapter.

WANT MORE?

As you have seen, there is only a limited amount of code available to control security features. However, your use of that code and accurate information about application and device security will make your app look truly professional. Consider making these additional enhancements:

- Delay permissions requests until they are necessary. You may never need to ask for e-mail permission if the user never sends the media they record.

- Check the highest level of permission that a user can grant instead of always requiring Allow. If corporate users install MediaGrabber and have a restrictive IT policy, they may not be able to change permissions no matter how often you ask.

- Consider allowing the user to continue running even without the requested permissions. This may cause problems later on, so display a warning.

Requesting permissions is a little like a dance between yourself, the user, and BlackBerry. Like any dance with three partners, it is a little awkward. Applications that handle themselves with grace stand out from the field.

Excelsior

You probably now know more than you ever wanted to know about how application security works on RIM. Although the details occasionally seem arcane, they are absolutely critical to creating smoothly functioning apps and developing an app distribution strategy. You wouldn't want to embarrass yourself with a huge release, only to find out that the app doesn't even run for many of your users.

The fundamental point to keep in mind when thinking about device security is that your needs as an application developer are subordinate to other stakeholders' needs. The carrier wants the network to function smoothly, the company wants their information to remain secure, the user wants their privacy protected, governments want to control the export of security software, and so on. Navigating these often conflicting desires can feel like a negotiation. Simply recognizing the complexity of the situation places you ahead of the curve.

Fortunately, you can do more than just complain about tight security. APIs do exist that allow you to query most permissions settings, and you can use these to try to free your app from some of its constraints. Even when the app is on a device that simply refuses to run, at least you can communicate the reason to the user and describe what they could do to fix it, even if that solution involves buying a new phone.

In this chapter, you saw how some security APIs have changed through different software versions. This is only the tip of the iceberg: if you are a successful developer who wants to release your app across the widest possible range of devices, software versions, countries, and languages, you will need to come to grips with the challenges of porting. The next chapter will introduce you to these challenges and discuss ways to help resolve them.

Chapter 10

Porting Your App

Developers tend to make assumptions when they start programming for BlackBerry. You probably have a single device for initial development, and any time you have questions about how BlackBerry devices handle something, you can simply check to see what the device does. The picture grows far more complicated after you have written your app and start making it available to other BlackBerry devices. Suddenly, you must deal with different keyboards, varying screen sizes, unavailable APIs, different carrier Internet settings, and more. Navigating this can become a nightmare. Or it can feel exhilarating.

This chapter will discuss the major items to keep in mind as you write and port your app to other models. By considering them early, you can cut down on the grindwork of rewrites and focus on the joy of bringing your app to everyone.

Understanding Hardware Differences

It's sometimes hard to believe that BlackBerry smartphones first arrived in 2002. Since that time, the sheer number of devices has exploded, along with the set of capabilities they offer. To a large degree, this has been driven by RIM's increasing push from the business market into the consumer market. Most companies give all their employees the same device, but when it comes to private wireless subscribers, everyone seems to want a phone that is uniquely theirs.

Processors

Mobile phones have more detailed CPU requirements than computers or other devices. In order to minimize costs and power consumption, modern phones usually combine general-purpose computing and cellular operations onto a single chip. RIM uses specialized chips from a variety of manufacturers to achieve their goals for performance and costs. Depending on the device model, the chip may come from Intel, ARM, or Qualcomm. Qualcomm chips are most common on CDMA devices such as those used in the United States on the Verizon and Sprint networks.

Each chip has its own MHz clock speed. The latest devices are capable of over 600MHz, while older devices operate at far slower speeds. As with PC chips, though, the megahertz tell only part of the story. Your app's speed will vary a great deal depending on how it uses the display, the filesystem, and the network; a processor that efficiently does these things may run your app more quickly even if it has a lower MHz rating.

> **CAUTION:** Don't assume that MHz always refers to clock speed. MHz is also used to describe wireless frequency ranges. A 800/1900 MHz device describes the radio bands at which it can operate, not two different processor speeds.

Processor speeds matter most for games and for computationally complex applications, particularly scientific and graphical apps. Because apps are written in Java, you do not have access to as many tricks as you might have when compiling native code such as C. It's a good idea to create an early, rough version of your app and then try to run it on all the devices you are considering in order to judge whether the processor speeds will cause an issue. If an app runs a little slowly, you can probably find ways to make it acceptable. If it runs unbearably slowly, you may need to skip that device, drastically rewrite the app, or consider profiling and dropping features that slow it down.

Radios

Different BlackBerry devices are designed to work with different wireless technologies. These technologies restrict the carriers that a phone can use and can also create subtle differences in seemingly unrelated behavior.

GSM

Worldwide, Global System for Mobile (GSM) is a dominant technology. GSM phones are distinctive for including Subscriber Identity Module (SIM) cards. A SIM card carries your information as a wireless subscriber, independent of the phone you are using. You can freely move a SIM card between multiple GSM devices and continue to make calls on your wireless account.

In the US, carriers often lock GSM devices. A locked device will only connect to that particular carrier; you can give it to another subscriber, but not to the customer of a competing carrier.

GSM devices generally have very good battery life.

GSM generally describes the voice-calling features of a mobile network. Data networks are also available to GSM users, and include the following types.

- General Packet Radio Service (GPRS) offers fairly slow speeds of roughly 50–100 kilobits per second.

- Enhanced Data rates for GSM Evolution (EDGE), a superset of GPRS, has been widely deployed. Many different versions of EDGE are available with widely varying speeds as fast as 200 kbit/s.

- Universal Mobile Telephone System (UMTS) is a third-generation protocol. Like EDGE, UMTS has many flavors, and ongoing work will continue improving it. UMTS requires different radio and tower technologies than standard GSM. It is available to 3G subscribers in most major cities and will likely continue spreading.

- High Speed Downlink Packet Access (HSDPA) and Evolved HSPA (HSPA+) expand UMTS to support even faster download speeds, with theoretical maximums of over 40 mbit/s.

CDMA

Code Division Multiple Access (CDMA) is common in North America. CDMA describes an alternate algorithm for supporting a large number of simultaneous conversations within a relatively narrow frequency spectrum. CDMA was developed by Qualcomm and the company has continued advancing it through multiple iterations.

Unlike GSM devices, CDMA devices are usually tied to a particular subscriber. If you wish to trade devices, you will need to contact your wireless carrier to do so.

CDMA devices often offer slightly better voice quality and fewer dropped calls at a cost of shorter battery life.

As with GSM, several data networks have evolved in parallel with CDMA as the technology matures:

- 1xRTT usually has a maximum transfer speed of about 144 kbit/s.

- Evolution Data Optimized (EV-DO) offers faster speeds with maximums above 3 mbit/s.

- Long Term Evolution (LTE) and WiMAX are competing 4G standards with far faster data transfer rates of 40 mbit/s or higher.

A related technology, WCDMA, also shares some characteristics with GSM and is most common in Japan.

CDMA devices run on top of different chipsets from GSM devices, and so they actually require a different operating system. This can lead to some nonintuitive situations; for example, a Curve 8320 and Curve 8330 look identical, but they run at different speeds and handle SMS messages differently.

Dual Band

In recent years, interest in so-called `world phones` has increased. These phones tackle the challenges met by people who travel overseas and find that they can no longer make calls.

As a solution, these BlackBerry devices actually contain multiple radios: one that operates within GSM networks and another that uses CDMA. Each radio has the characteristics that you would expect from a phone that only supported that radio.

In the United States, BlackBerry world phones are sometimes locked so they will only connect to CDMA networks in the United States and to GSM elsewhere.

iDEN

iDEN was developed by Motorola and is best known in the United States for its use by Sprint/Nextel. iDEN supports the Push-to-Talk feature that makes mobile phones behave more like walkie-talkies. It has borrowed several features from GSM, including the use of SIM cards.

Again, iDEN phones use a different chipset with different capabilities, and so they behave differently from similar GSM or CDMA models. The most striking difference is their different treatment of BES networks. As you may know, you can specify that a connection should be made using the client-side TCP stack by appending ";deviceside=true" to the end of a URL, and specify an MDS network connection by appending ";deviceside=false". On most models, if you do not specify either option, the BlackBerry will first try to make the connection with MDS; if MDS is unavailable, it will fall back to TCP. However, on iDEN devices, the device will attempt to open a TCP connection by default. If you use ConnectionManager, you can provide your own preferred order for connection.

Wi-Fi

Many modern BlackBerry devices include a Wi-Fi antenna in addition to a standard mobile antenna. This allows users to connect to a Wi-Fi access point instead of or in addition to a cellular tower.

Wi-Fi is a completely separate interface from the mobile interface, so if you are not using ConnectionManager and wish to make a connection over Wi-Fi you must explicitly do so by specifying ";interface=wifi" in a URL connection string. You can use APIs to determine whether a particular device has Wi-Fi and is connected to a network.

External Memory Storage

All recent BlackBerry models include support for MicroSD cards, and some of the newest support MicroSDHC. By inserting these cards, users can drastically expand the amount of storage available on the device. If your application will store large files, it should definitely place them on the SD card if available.

Most newly purchased devices come with a card, and users can later purchase replacements with larger capacity if desired. The maximum capacity varies depending on the device model and the operating system version.

Memory storage should have a minimal effect on your porting efforts, but remember that very old devices do not have external storage available, and users might have removed their cards from newer devices. Try to avoid blindly writing out to the SD card: a more polished app will first check if the card is available by checking `FileSystemRegistry.listRoots()`. If unavailable, the app should fall back on writing to internal storage or display a friendly error message asking the user to run the app again with a valid card inserted.

Keyboard

In order to support different form factors, RIM has created several different types of keyboards for use in its phones.

Keyboard Profiles

BlackBerry devices made their reputation by offering full QWERTY keyboards, similar to those found in Figure 10–1, at a time when other phones almost universally used awkward 12-key multi-tap text entry. The QWERTY keyboard lets you directly enter every letter of the alphabet by pressing a single key and allows access to common special characters through use of an ALT key. A hardware SYM key offers more unusual characters. Slightly different QWERTY keyboards can be found on different models, adding or removing particular nonletter keys.

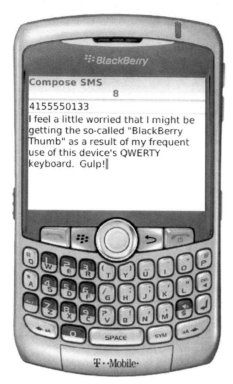

Figure 10–1. A BlackBerry with a QWERTY keyboard

Later, RIM released a new keyboard technology dubbed SureType. A SureType keyboard is more compressed than a full QWERTY keyboard; it displays multiple letters on each key, as shown in Figure 10–2. The SureType software examines the letters you have pressed and tries to guess what word you meant to enter. For example, if you type 112318, it will assume you mean to type "return", since that is the only English word that can be constructed out of the possible letters. SureType will enter the text "return" and will also display a pop-up window that lists other possible words; you can select one of these by scrolling and clicking the one you want. This technology resembles those found on phones with traditional 12-key pads, such as iTap and T9.

Figure 10–2. A BlackBerry with a SureType keyboard

When using a SureType keyboard, you can also enable Multitap mode. This makes the keyboard behave more like a traditional multi-tap phone keypad that cycles through the available letters when you press each key. To enter an "e" you would press 1 once; to enter "r" press 1 twice. To type "return" in Multitap mode, you would type "11 (pause) 1231188".

Touch-screen BlackBerry devices such as the Storm might not have a physical keyboard at all. Instead, they can display one of several virtual "soft" keyboards. This can allow more flexibility and comfort to a user. For example, a full QWERTY keyboard might display when the phone is in landscape mode (held horizontally), but a SureType keyboard might display when the phone is in portrait mode (held vertically). A number-only version can display when dialing a phone number or entering a PIN. Users generally have the option to show or hide the keyboard in order to manage the amount of visible space shown.

Detecting Keyboards

The Keypad API allows you to detect at runtime what keyboard is present on the device. Call Keypad.getHardwareLayout() to return one of the enumerations found in Table 10–1.

Table 10–1. BlackBerry Keyboards

Name	Description	Mode	Hardware Series	OS availability	Physical?
`HW_LAYOUT_32`	38-key keyboard	QWERTY	87xx	4.1	Yes
`HW_LAYOUT_39`	39-key keyboard	QWERTY	88xx	4.3	Yes
`HW_LAYOUT_HANDW_RECOGNITION`	Handwriting recognition	N/A	N/A	6.0	No
`HW_LAYOUT_ITUT`	12-key dial pad keyboard	Numeric	N/A	6.0	Yes
`HW_LAYOUT_LEGACY`	30-key keyboard	QWERTY	57xx, 58xx	4.1	Yes
`HW_LAYOUT_PHONE`	34 keys with phone keyboard layout	QWERTY	65xx, 67xx, 72xx, 75xx, and 77xx	4.1	Yes
`HW_LAYOUT_REDUCED`	23-key keyboard	SureType	71xx	4.1	Yes
`HW_LAYOUT_REDUCED_24`	24-key keyboard	SureType	81xx	4.2	Yes
`HW_LAYOUT_TOUCHSCREEN_12`	12-key phone-style keyboard	Dial pad	95xx	4.7	No
`HW_LAYOUT_TOUCHSCREEN_24`	24-key keyboard	SureType	95xx	4.7	No
`HW_LAYOUT_TOUCHSCREEN_20N`	20-key keyboard	Numeric and hex	95xx	5.0	No
`HW_LAYOUT_TOUCHSCREEN_29`	29-key keyboard	QWERTY	95xx	4.7	No

> **NOTE:** Starting with device software version 5.0, many of the HW_LAYOUT_TOUCHSCREEN keyboards also have special versions for particular languages, such as HW_LAYOUT_TOUCHSCREEN_12A for 12-key Arabic and HW_LAYOUT_TOUCHSCREEN_35J for Kana Japanese.

For most physical keyboards, the hardware layout directly corresponds to the physical device. On touch-screen devices, this allows you to determine which virtual keyboard is currently displaying.

In some cases, you won't care which specific keyboard is being used, but rather whether a specific key is available. You can use the following static Keypad methods to make this determination (note that not all APIs are available on all software versions):

- hasCurrencyKey() shows whether there is a dedicated key for entering currency symbols.

- hasMediaKeys() indicates whether the device has one or more keys for media operations, such as start, pause, rewind, and skip.

- hasMuteKey() describes whether there is a dedicated mute key.

- hasSendEndKeys() indicates whether the device has dedicated keys for starting and ending phone calls.

- isOnKeypad(char ch) allows you to check whether a specific character is available on this keyboard.

- isValidKeyCode(int code) checks if the provided key code exists for this keyboard.

Changing Keyboards

On touch-screen devices, you can use the VirtualKeyboard class to determine whether the keyboard is displaying, and also to force it to hide or show.

isSupported() returns a boolean that describes whether the device supports virtual keyboards. If not, the other methods will have no effect.

setVisibility() allows you to specify whether the keyboard should display when this application's context has focus. VirtualKeyboard supports the following modes:

- HIDE: The keyboard should be hidden at the next opportunity. Afterward, it will automatically be shown or hidden as normal.

- HIDE_FORCE: The keyboard should always be hidden.

- IGNORE: Keep track of keyboard visibility, but do not automatically show or hide it.

- RESTORE: Return keyboard to its previously saved state.

- SHOW: Display the keyboard at the next opportunity. Afterward, it will automatically be shown or hidden as normal.

- SHOW_FORCE: Always show the keyboard.

getVisibility() will return the currently set keyboard visibility state.

VirtualKeyboard can only be used by BlackBerry CLDC applications. If developing a MIDlet, you have access to VirtualKeyboardControl, which provides similar methods for querying, showing, and hiding the virtual keyboard. You can obtain a VirtualKeyboardControl by creating a BlackBerryCanvas or BlackBerryGameCanvas and retrieving the virtual keyboard from getControl() or getControls().

Porting Impact

If you are developing business or productivity apps that mainly involve text entry, you may be able to ignore the keyboard issue altogether. The native BlackBerry text entry fields are well integrated with keyboard behavior, automatically handling QWERTY or SureType keys, so no extra effort is necessary on your part.

However, if you are developing a game or have a highly customized non-BlackBerry user interface, keyboards will likely cause issues. For example, you might control a game by pressing four buttons, but those four buttons might not exist on all devices.

You can use the methods described in this section to dynamically query the phone and determine what the keyboard layout is like, and then make an appropriate decision about how to handle incoming key events. Setting up such a system can take some effort, but in the long run it will be much more efficient than creating a new version of your app for every keyboard type.

If you support touch-screen devices, carefully consider the user experience. If you write a game that is entirely touch-based, you might want to forcibly hide the keyboard so the full screen always displays. If your game supports a high-score name entry, you might want to show the keyboard on that screen while hiding it everywhere else.

If your apps will only run on OS version 6.0 or higher, you should consider using the new InputSettings class and the related methods in UiEngineInstance and Screen. These allow you to query and set input modes on an application-wide or per-screen basis, which can let you easily construct powerful interfaces within your app. InputSettings follows the same principles discussed above, just in a simplified manner.

Hardware Features

Every device has some sort of CPU, radio, and keyboard. However, only some devices have cameras and/or GPS. If your app requires these features, or optionally supports them, you will need to determine whether they are present on the device.

Determining by Model Number

Even before you install the app, you should be able to determine the phone's capabilities by looking at the device model number. This can be very useful if you have a web page that allows users to identify their phone before they download your app.

BlackBerry devices have four-digit model numbers, such as 8120 or 9530. The first two digits are the series number. These identify broad families of devices, which often share a similar marketing name. For example, the 8300, 8310, 8320, 8330, and 8350i are all part of the 8300 series and are known as BlackBerry Curve. All devices in a particular series share the same form factor and physical characteristics. For example, all BlackBerry Curve devices have a QWERTY keyboard, a trackball, and a 2-megapixel camera.

The final two digits for modern BlackBerry devices complete the model number, and they identify what radio technologies are available on the device. Radios include both the cellular technology and also Wi-Fi and GPS. For example, the 8120, 8320, and 8820 all look different, but each is a GSM-compatible device with Wi-Fi capabilities. The following is a list of model numbers and radio technologies:

- xx00: GSM
- xx10: GSM with GPS
- xx20: GSM with Wi-Fi
- xx30: CDMA
- xx50: CDMA with Wi-Fi
- xx50i: iDEN

The model-number naming scheme can be inconsistent at times, particularly on older models, so you should verify with your particular device early in a project if you depend on the presence of certain capabilities.

Determining by API

You can use the following methods to determine a device's identity or capabilities at runtime:

- `DeviceInfo.getDeviceName()` reports the model number of the device, with an optional suffix describing the radio type.
- `DeviceInfo.hasCamera()` reports whether a camera is physically present on the device. This does not necessarily mean that your app will have access to it.
- `DeviceInfo.getTotalFlashSizeEx()` reports the maximum storage capacity of the flash filesystem.
- `WLANInfo.getWLANState()` reports whether the device is connected to Wi-Fi.

- `RadioInfo.getNetworkType()` reports the cellular network technology, which may be `NETWORK_802_11`, `NETWORK_CDMA`, `NETWORK_GPRS`, `NETWORK_IDEN`, or `NETWORK_UMTS`.

- `RadioInfo.isDataServiceOperational()` describes whether any data interfaces are available for use.

- `LocationProvider.getState()` reports the GPS state, which will be `OUT_OF_SERVICE` if GPS is not present, and either `AVAILABLE` or `TEMPORARILY_UNAVAILABLE` if the phone has GPS.

Porting Impact

If your app requires certain hardware capabilities to function, you should start communicating this fact well before the user downloads the app. Users get frustrated when they find that something doesn't work—and far more so if they paid for it.

You might consider releasing different versions of your app for different devices, based on whether or not they support particular features. For example, you might make a version of MediaGrabber that omits camera support for devices like the 8800 that do not include a camera. This would slightly decrease the size of the app and could prevent confusion if you clearly state that the app does not support taking pictures.

To some extent, though, MediaGrabber already does a good job of examining device capabilities by checking the presence of recording options when building its options menu. Many developers will prefer to go this route. In such cases, the best strategy is usually to check for supported device statistics when the app first starts. Depending on what you find, you can enable or disable particular app features and display messages to users if you want to advise them of what they may be missing out on.

Screen Sizes

Possibly the most important difference between BlackBerry devices, the screen resolution will determine what art assets to use, what size of sprites to create, how much text you can fit on a screen without wrapping, and so on.

You can generally reuse an application's design between two different BlackBerry devices that share the same screen resolution. If the resolutions differ, you should decide whether a redesign is necessary. The BlackBerry CLDC UI components generally adjust well to multiple screen sizes so long as you stick to simple organizations like the VerticalFieldManager. However, elaborate user interfaces that look great on one screen size may be illegible on another.

In addition, touch-screen devices can rotate into either portrait or landscape mode. Here, too, so long as you stick to common UI designs, your app will probably function well in both orientations. Otherwise, you have the following options:

- Lock the screen into a particular orientation. You can do this by calling `Ui.getUiEngineInstance().setAcceptableDirections()`, passing in one of the direction orientations from the `net.rim.device.api.system.Display` class, such as `Display.DIRECTION_LANDSCAPE` or `Display.DIRECTION_PORTRAIT`.

- Detect the device orientation by calling `Display.getOrientation()`. This will return one of the enumerated direction values listed above. Then, display an appropriate UI for that orientation. You might need to switch to another UI if the user rotates while on the same screen.

Some common BlackBerry devices and their screen resolutions are shown in Table 10–2.

Table 10–2. Screen Resolutions

Device Series	Horizontal Pixels	Vertical Pixels	Rotates?
71xx/81xx	240	260	No
82xx	240	320	No
83xx/87xx/88xx	320	240	No
89xx/96xx/97xx	480	360	No
90xx	480	320	No
91xx	360	400	No
95xx	360	480	Yes
98xx	360	480	Yes

Understanding OS Differences

Hardware capabilities are locked in stone. If your device doesn't have a camera, it won't ever have a camera. The OS, though, is much more fluid and can evolve over time. Because your software runs on top of the OS, you must carefully note the OS availability and features as you port to different phones.

OS Availability and Updates

The gift of BlackBerry keeps on giving. RIM has traditionally released updated versions for every BlackBerry device. Sometimes these are patches that fix bugs and improve performances; other times, they add significant new features.

RIM releases the updates, but the wireless carrier or enterprise needs to approve the update prior to making it available to end-users. Updates from wireless carriers are optional and can either be installed through the BlackBerry Desktop Manager or over the air. Enterprises have the option of pushing out forced updates to newer software versions.

BlackBerry has a higher proportion of power users than most phones, and people sometimes seek out and install unapproved device updates in hopes of getting better features or performance. The BlackBerry toolset allows a user to later downgrade to a previous software version, so there is little risk in trying new things.

Determining the Version

You can find a device's current software version by clicking Options, Device, and then About Device Version. The current OS software version will display towards the top, followed by the Platform version. Both these versions can change as part of an update.

At runtime, you can find the version by calling `DeviceInfo.getSoftwareVersion()`. When parsing this string, remember the four-part format of the version number; you cannot simply cast it to a double and compare to a desired version. Instead, examine each numbered section individually to find the version.

If you are hosting application downloads or help on your own web server, you can inspect the HTTP headers to see what version a phone is using. This is typically contained in the `User-Agent` header, which generally will have a value similar to `"BlackBerry9530/4.7.0.148 Profile/MIDP-2.0 Configuration/CLDC-1.1 VendorID/105"`.

> **CAUTION:** The BlackBerry browser includes options to masquerade as Firefox or Internet Explorer. If the user has selected one of these options, the User-Agent string will be replaced with a fake version. Also, users may use a third-party browser such as Opera Mini.

Version Effects

OS versions have a four-part version number. The first two parts describe the major feature set, the third number is the minor feature set, and the final number describes the patch version. For example, an upgrade from 6.0.0.278 to 6.0.0.695 will fix bugs but not change behavior. However, an upgrade from 5.0.0.1014 to 6.0.0.324 will significantly affect the device's capabilities.

The OS version has a direct correlation to API availability. Throughout this book, I have occasionally made note of certain features becoming available in particular OS versions. The terms *operating system* and *device software* are often used interchangeably. Patch numbers have no impact on API behavior.

As described in Chapter 9, the OS version can also impact the default permissions. Certain operations that worked in prior versions of the OS may not initially function due to more restrictive permissions settings.

Porting Impact

From your perspective, the single most important impact of the OS version is program compatibility. RIM devices are backwards compatible; that is, a program that runs on the 4.2 version of software will also run on the 4.5 version. However, they are not forwards compatible. You can't run a program designed for newer software on older software.

> **NOTE:** Compatibility is generally determined by API usage, not the actual compiler. If you compile an app using the 4.5 version of the BlackBerry JDE, but only use APIs from version 4.2, the app can run on a 4.2 handset.

This leads to a quandary in writing portable software. You can't write something like the following pseudocode; the mere existence of an API is what makes a program incompatible, not the moment you call it.

```
if (softwareVersion >= requiredVersion)
{
    callFutureAPI();
}
```

You have a few strategies available to deal with this problem.

The Lowest Common Denominator

Early on, determine the oldest BlackBerry software version that you must support. Write the app using this version of the BlackBerry Java SDK, only using APIs from this version or earlier.

You will still need to test your app on multiple versions; even though your app will run on all future devices, certain aspects may behave differently. If you find discrepancies, you can test the device software version at run-time and make your app behave appropriately depending on the version.

- Pros: This is the simplest approach. At the end of the project, you will have a single version of the app that runs on everything you want.

- Cons: Your app may lack useful features from future versions. This could lead to a disadvantage if your app has competitors.

Multiple Builds

Suppose you have an app that uses the network a lot. It would be really nice to use the ConnectionManager if it's available. Coding good Wi-Fi support is more complicated in OS versions prior to 5.0. However, many of your users never upgraded to 5.0.

In this scenario, you might consider making two different versions of your app, one with ConnectionManager support and one without. This will ensure that your app gets the widest possible usage and that each user can get the most out of their app.

If you take this approach, I highly recommend putting all OS-specific code in a few particular files or packages, rather than scattering them throughout your app. This will make it much easier to maintain two versions of the software in parallel, since you can share the majority of the code between both versions.

- Pros: This offers a high reach and a high level of performance.

- Cons: This is the most complicated approach. If you support multiple OS levels, the complexity of your source control and build systems can rapidly explode.

Mandate Change

Your app simply might not run properly if a particular API feature is not available. Or perhaps the app will run on a previous OS version but offers a very poor experience. As long as you are willing to accept the consequences, you can mandate a particular OS version and require users to have at least that version installed in order to use your app.

As mentioned previously, BlackBerry users have an easier job than most phone owners when it comes to upgrading their operating system. If a newer version of device software is available, odds are that many users have already upgraded to it. If your app is sufficiently compelling, you may convince the remainder to take the plunge.

- Pros: You only need to maintain a single version of your app. It offers a superior product.

- Cons: Provides the smallest potential user base. It may alienate users who can't upgrade their devices or don't wish to do so. The latest operating systems do not run on older devices.

Understanding Language Differences

Once you write a great app, you can get a large audience. In order to get the largest audience, though, you can't confine yourself to one particular language or one particular country. BlackBerry has a significant global presence, and only a fraction of those users live in your nation.

If you try to add multi-language support to multi-device and multi-OS support, you can enter a nightmare where any little change needs to be copied and tested on dozens or even hundreds of possible combinations. Fortunately, RIM offers a set of tools to support localizing your app for different markets.

Localization Overview

The terms *localization*, *internationalization*, and *i18n* are often used interchangeably to describe the process of translating a product into a different form for different markets. Translation is an important part of this process—you probably would not choose to use a Greek-language app if you could not read Greek. Likewise a Greek speaker would probably not choose to use an English-language app if they couldn't read English.

Localization goes deeper than simple translation. Different cultural groups have different associations with images and sounds that you should keep in mind as you develop your app. For example, many Americans would look at a red octagon and assume that it means "Stop." However, many Chinese users would not have that same association, which could lead to confusion and frustration. Part of localization is to make appropriate substitutions, or, even better, to avoid ambiguity in the first place.

As noted previously in this book, a locale is described as a two-character language code combined with an optional country code. English words can be spelled differently in the United States than they are in Great Britain, so you can choose to provide different words for the "en-US" locale than you would for "en-GB". In some cases, you might only offer a single "en" locale that would be applied to all English-speaking users. Similarly, English and French are both official languages in Canada, so a Canadian user might select between "en-CA" and "fr-CA".

Adding Multi-Language Support

A fair amount of effort is required to internationalize your app, but it will save you far more time and grief later on.

Defining Resource Files

Follow these steps to add support for internationalized text to your app:

1. Click File, New, Other…, BlackBerry Projects, BlackBerry Resource File.

2. Navigate to the package where your app is located. If your app uses multiple packages, I recommend selecting the highest-level common package.

3. Give the file the same name as your app, with an extension of .rrh. For example, if your app is named BonjourWorld, name it BonjourWorld.rrh.

> **NOTE:** rrh stands for Resource Header. This header file is similar to a header file in C or C++.

4. Observe that two files were created in your selected package with extensions .rrh and .rrc. Note that *rrc* stands for Resource Content.

5. If you'd like to add support for other languages now, repeat steps 1–3, but this time append the language code to the app name and add the .rrc extension. For example, to create a US English language file, create BonjourWorld_en_US.rrc; to create a generic English language file, create BonjourWorld_en.rrc.

6. Double-click the .rrh file to open it. You should see a grid similar to that shown in Figure 10–3.

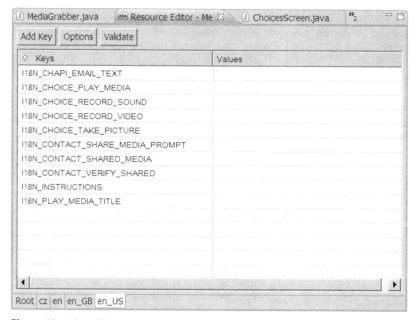

Figure 10–3. Localizing an application

7. Click Add Key. Enter the name of your localized resource.

> **TIP:** I prefer to prefix my keys with the string "I18N_" to make them easier to find with Eclipse's auto-complete feature. Try to pick descriptive key names that indicate the meaning or role of the text instead of its default value. For example, use I18N_INITIAL_GREETING rather than I18N_WELCOME_TO_MY_APP.

8. Repeat step 7 for all the text you wish to internationalize in your app.

9. Provide a default translation for every key listed. You will probably use your native language for this, or text provided by a designer.

10. For each language that you added previously, a tab will display at the bottom of your translation window. You can provide translations for all of these now, or leave them alone until later on.

11. Save the resource file. If you have not configured Eclipse to build automatically, right-click on your BlackBerry application project and select Build Project.

Behind the scenes, the BlackBerry Plug-in will generate a Java interface file that contains all the keys you defined. You can now add this text into your source files instead of using hard-coded literal strings.

Understanding Bundles

A set of resource files define a resource bundle. The bundle collects together a set of localizable resources. The bundle contains all possible values to be translated, identified by their key, and all of the supplied translations.

The locales within a bundle are hierarchical, as shown in Figure 10–4. At the root level are the default translations that will be shown for any unknown locale or for locales that do not override the key. In the Figure 10–4 example, "Goodbye!" would be provided as the "Exit" translation for "fr", "en", and "en_GB". If a user's locale is not present or does not contain a desired key, Java will search up the hierarchy until it finds a match. Therefore, the "Title" for "en_US" will translate as "Airplane for Me". Likewise, the "Exit" for "cs_CZ" will translate as "Sbohem!" since "cs" is above where "cs_CZ" would be.

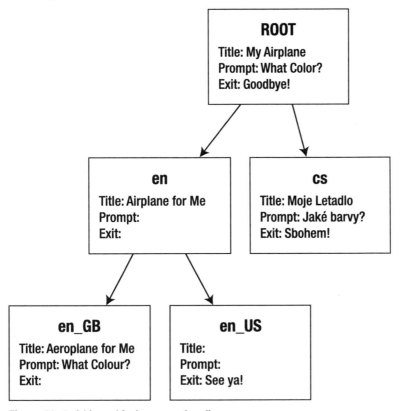

Figure 10–4. A hierarchical resource bundle

This system has the advantage of reducing the total amount of data required for complete translations. For example, most US and UK translations will probably be the same. Rather than duplicate the same texts for both locales, you can define all the common elements in "en", and only override the cases where you need to use a variant spelling.

Adding Resources to Java Classes

Modify your class declaration to implement the generated resource file. The file will have the same name as your app with the word Resource added to the end, as in the following example:

```
public class BonjourWorld extends UiApplication implements BonjourWorldResource
```

To make it more convenient to access translated text, include a `static ResourceBundle` member in your class that loads the bundle. By implementing the resource file, you gain access to the `BUNDLE_ID` and the `BUNDLE_NAME` that uniquely identify this resource bundle. I like to use a short name here, as shown below, since it cuts down on typing when translating a lot of text:

```
static ResourceBundleFamily r =
    ResourceBundle.getBundle(BUNDLE_ID, BUNDLE_NAME);
```

Now, all that's left is the actual translation. Any place where you would ordinarily use a `String`, you can look up the proper translation from the `ResourceBundle`. Your resource interface provides all the keys you added as integer enumerations. If you follow a consistent naming scheme, you can type the prefix (like "I18N") and then select the proper key from the drop-down selection box. The following is a sample localization:

```
add(new LabelField(r.getString(I18N_PROMPT)));
```

When this line executes, Java will check to see what the current locale is. It will then check the bundle for a match, walking up the hierarchy tree if necessary. Once it finds the best match, it returns the `String`, which is then handled by the program as though you entered it literally.

RIM has also created alternate convenience constructors that let you directly supply the resource bundle information for common UI elements. The following sample produces the same results as the one above:

```
add(new LabelField(r, I18N_PROMPT));
```

Similarly, you can directly provide resource gets to most methods that modify textual UI content, like so:

```
private void updateText(LabelField label)
{
    label.setText(r, I18N_PROMPT);
}
```

Testing Languages

The BlackBerry device simulators tend to skimp on language support. Depending on your device, you may only have access to US English and UK English. You can still use these languages to verify the correct functioning of your localization effort.

To switch your language, open Options, Typing and Input, and then the Language menu. Of course, these may have different names depending on the current language setting of the device. UK English uses "Localisation" instead of "Language." In the Language screen, you can select the language or dialect you wish to use from the drop-down menu.

> **NOTE:** You may need to close and restart your application in order to test a new language setting. You can completely close the application by pressing Menu and then Close.

A device usually has many more languages available, although it requires a little effort to get them. Each language has its own dictionary, menus, and other resources, so the initial Setup Wizard typically removes unnecessary languages. You can check for available languages following the same steps you took on the simulator. To load additional languages, follow these steps:

1. Download a recent version of BlackBerry device software from your wireless provider or your enterprise and install it on your PC.

2. Open the BlackBerry Desktop Manager.

3. Select Application Loader and then Add/Remove Applications.

4. Select the checkboxes for languages you wish to load. You may also choose to remove languages.

5. Select Next and follow the prompts to load the languages.

After your phone reboots, the new languages will be available for testing.

Managing Resource Bundles

Using a single resource bundle is a no-brainer for a simple app with a single class file. Most real-world apps, though, will contain substantially more. Depending on your needs, you might consider several strategies.

One Bundle, Many Implementors

You can follow the steps given above, changing all your class files that contain localizable resources so that they each implement the same generated bundle interface.

- Pros: This approach simplifies translation efforts: because all your strings are located in a single .rrc file, none will be overlooked. This approach also requires the smallest amount of typing, since you can directly reference all the resource keys within each class.

- Cons: If you have a large number of resource keys, it can grow confusing to keep them all straight. This approach will increase the size of your final executable slightly, especially if you have a large number of class files.

One Bundle, Single Implementor

You can follow the steps given above to implement the generated bundle in a single class. Give the `ResourceBundle` member `public`, `protected`, or package visibility. Other classes can then access translations through the implementing class, as in this example:

```
String translated = BonjourWorld.r.getString(BonjourWorld.I18N_HELP);
```

This approach has the same pros and cons listed above, except that the size of the final executable will be slightly smaller, and a bit more typing is required.

Multiple Bundles

If you prefer, you can create multiple .rrh files, each of which will generate its own bundle. Each class can then choose which bundle class to implement, or it can implement multiple bundles.

- Pros: You can easily group together the localizable resources for a particular screen or area of the program. Implementation is usually easy, as you have only a small set of key options for each class and little extra typing.

- Cons: It can be difficult to track the resource files, making it easier to overlook particular translations. This approach will generally create larger executables than the previous two.

Other Localization Concerns

Once you understand the basics of translation, you will be well prepared to handle other localization needs that your app may require.

Dealing with Images

Although the resource files focus on text translation of words and phrases, you can also use them for images and other non-text resources. Imagine creating a key called `I18N_IMAGE_ALERT_ICON`. The default English value for this key might be `"/YellowExclamation.png"`, while the Chinese value might be `"/ChAlert.png"`. You can then use code like the following to display the proper image for the user's locale:

```
String alertPath = r.getString(I18N_IMAGE_ALERT_ICON);
Bitmap alert = Bitmap.getBitmapResource(alertPath);
```

This approach works best if your app only has a few images and all are relatively small. Otherwise, supporting multiple images for many locales can quickly increase your app's size. In those cases, you might consider the following options:

- Place the resources in separate library COD files for each language. Users can choose to load the languages that they need, and thus not take up space with unnecessary languages.

- Don't place images in your app at all. Instead, store them on a server and have the app download them as needed. This will make the app a bit slower and use more network resources, but it also gives you more flexibility if you later decide to change images.

Locale-aware Formatting

Different languages and countries have more differences than just their words. They also use different conventions for displaying dates (such as 5/30/10 or 30/5/10), numbers (such as 13,500.42 or 13.500,42), plural forms, and subject-verb-object placement. If your app programmatically generates such text, translating words will not suffice when localizing to a new country.

Java ME has traditionally lacked good support for such localization, forcing developers to create their own solutions or build custom versions of their apps for each locale. More recently, JSR 238 with the javax.microedition.global package has begun to offer a more standard way to treat some of these tasks. However, BlackBerry has ported many familiar classes from Java SE and Java EE that provide powerful and fairly simple tools for flexible localization. These classes, which were originally located in java.text or java.util, can all be found in net.rim.device.api.i18n. Some of the most useful are listed here:

- SimpleDateFormat lets you format and parse an abstract time representation, provided by Calendar, into a natural style for a given locale. Despite the name, it is very flexible, offering strings of varying length (such as "6/10/10" as opposed to "June 10th, 2010") and structure (such as "15:00" as opposed to "3 o'clock PM").

- MessageFormat allows you to define flexible string constructions that can be dynamically built with varying data at a later time. For example, a MessageFormat for a particular locale might have the pattern "Only {0} more shopping {1} until Guy Fawkes Day!" You could then format this pattern with the variables 1 and "day", or with 10 and "days". In another language, the order of the words would likely change, but the appropriate variables would be inserted into the {0} and {1} fields.

Dynamic Localization

In almost all cases, your app should use the current device locale setting. However, certain apps might allow the user to choose their own locale. For example, a city travel guide might include an option to switch languages so you could hand your phone to a native speaker and have them pick out a restaurant for you. Switching locales within the app can also make it easier to test the display of different languages without needing to exit the app and switch device languages. To change the locale, retrieve the `Locale` you want to use, and then pass it to `setDefault()`. Locales can be retrieved by name or from an enumeration. The two examples here are equivalent:

```
Locale.setDefault(Locale.get("cs"));
Locale.setDefault(Locale.get(Locale.LOCALE_cs));
```

Porting Impact

You should think early on about whether your app will require localization. If you're confident that its use will be so narrow that localization is unnecessary, ignore it. Otherwise, the earlier you start addressing localization, the more easily it will go.

If you are working from a specification, you might know before you start coding exactly what text the app will use. This is the best situation: you can define all your strings even before you start writing code, inserting the keys in the app as you write it.

If you don't know the text up front, create a blank resource bundle at the start of your project. As you write your app, create keys for any user-visible text you create. Provide a default translation in your native language; don't worry about other languages for now. After finishing the app, you can pass off the keys to a translator to get the necessary translations. More likely, your app will initially be released with only your native language supported, but once you have demand from other countries or languages, you'll be able to meet their needs almost instantly.

In practice, most programs (including MediaGrabber) start off with hard-coded String literals. Towards the end of the project, or even after release, someone will go through the source code to find all visible text and convert it to using resource bundles. This approach requires the greatest total effort, but it does mean that the initial stages of the project can have more legible source code than they would with resource keys.

While designing the visual look of your app, keep localization needs in mind. The length of text will probably change drastically depending on the language used; going from English to German will greatly increase the text length, while going from English to Japanese may shrink it. As such, text might flow to multiple lines or be cut off. Design your UI flexibly so you can accommodate these changes.

Avoid including text within your images: for example, don't include the word "Stop" in a stop-sign graphic. Doing this would force you to create a new image for every language, which takes up much more space than creating new text. Instead, consider creating blank versions of your images, and then drawing text on top of the images at run-time. Even better, pick images that are self-explanatory, or place labels outside the image.

Try to be culturally sensitive. Images, sounds, and phrases that are innocent or funny in one culture might be very offensive in another. Avoid using casual speech, idiomatic phrases, and dialect. This doesn't mean that your app shouldn't have personality, but if your app uses language too narrowly, it won't make a good impression on foreign users.

Understanding Platform Differences

Apps used to be a sideshow; now they can take center stage. Consumers and businesses increasingly base their phone purchase decisions on applications. If you write a great app, people will hear about it, and you may soon hear a clamor from other users to support them. Other smartphone platforms such as Android, Windows Mobile, and iPhone should have the power to run any app that would run on BlackBerry; feature phone platforms like Java ME and BREW may require evaluation to determine whether they can handle your app.

Porting to another platform is an order of magnitude more difficult than porting to another BlackBerry. However, by following some basic tips, you can make this process less painful.

Forget Porting the UI

Each phone platform has its own UI toolkit, and each is incompatible with everything else. Good programmers have learned the importance of reusing code and so attempt to take advantage of the UI code they have already written. Don't. The effort involved in translating between platforms is usually greater than that required to rewrite the UI from scratch. Additionally, by using a phone's native UI, your application is more likely to look and feel like the native apps to which the users are accustomed.

Functionally Divide the App

Taking a chunk of code and translating it to a new platform can be an overwhelming, frustrating process. Instead, follow good object-oriented design techniques. Divide your application into components. Where possible, cleanly separate concerns through strategies like the Model-View-Controller paradigm. Diagram your app's structure, and ensure it makes sense.

You can then port individual components, a far simpler task. You should test each individual component prior to finishing the entire app. For example, if your app contains networking operations, pull those operations into a separate networking component and write unit tests to verify that you receive the same data on each platform.

Some components, like those that contain pure business logic, should be fairly straightforward to port; you will just need to translate them into a new programming language. On the other hand, components that contain a lot of platform-specific functionality such as user interface or persistent storage will require more substantial changes. Be prepared to spend extra time making these changes and testing to ensure they work.

Identify Language Reuse Opportunities

Java ME and Android both use versions of Java. You may be able to reuse non-UI code between these platforms. If so, consider creating a separate JAR project that contains your application engine, business logic, or other generic Java code.

Be aware, though, that many Java APIs are not shared between these platforms. For example, none of the `javax.microedition` packages is available on Android. Conversely, Android is based on a later version of Java, so many of its basic Java APIs are not available for BlackBerry.

Back to the Drawing Board

Many developers porting to multiple platforms fall into the trap of the lowest common denominator. If you only support the features present on every platform, you miss out on many opportunities for taking advantage of the unique advantages each phone has to offer.

You shouldn't re-create your app for every individual phone—that would take far too much effort for far too little return. But do take a fresh look whenever you consider moving to a new platform. It may provide an opportunity to do something new, fun, and interesting, instead of the drudgery of a boring port.

App: Localized Text

MediaGrabber's simple UI can run on a wide variety of devices without requiring changes to the code. By using the CLDC UI framework, the same code works fine on touch-screen and QWERTY devices. Throughout the book, I have been careful to test for feature support within the app, so no extra work is required to support the presence or absence of a camera or other piece of hardware.

Also throughout this book, I have been happily putting hard-coded strings into the MediaGrabber source. This makes the samples easier to read and understand (assuming English is your native language), but, as you have seen in this chapter, it also limits the potential audience for the app. Fortunately, you can add internationalization with only a few extra classes. While a fair amount of code is required to internationalize the app, the actual process is very simple.

Create the Resource Files

Following the steps given in the section "Adding Multi-Language Support," create a new resource header file called `MediaGrabber.rrh`. Provide .rrc files for each language you would like to support. I have chosen to use "_en", "_en_US", "_en_GB", and "_cs", but you can include any other language you would like to see.

Create keys for all visible strings in MediaGrabber and copy the existing string values into the default MediaGrabber.rrc file. You can either do this in the Eclipse grid editing window, or directly edit the .rrc file by hand if you prefer. If you edit the .rrc file outside of Eclipse, you might need to refresh or restart Eclipse for it to recognize the changes.

Listing 10–1 shows a partial set of the English translations, covering the main MediaGrabber class file as well as the initial UI from ChoicesScreen.

Listing 10–1. *Initial Default Translations for MediaGrabber*

```
I18N_CHAPI_EMAIL_TEXT#0="Sent to you by CHAPI";
I18N_CHOICE_PLAY_MEDIA#0="Play Media";
I18N_CHOICE_RECORD_SOUND#0="Record Sound";
I18N_CHOICE_RECORD_VIDEO#0="Record Video";
I18N_CHOICE_TAKE_PICTURE#0="Take a Picture";
I18N_CONTACT_SHARED_MEDIA#0="You have shared media with them.";
I18N_CONTACT_SHARE_MEDIA_PROMPT#0="No sharing yet. ⏎
Would you like to send media?";
I18N_CONTACT_VERIFY_SHARED#0="Verify Media Shared";
I18N_INSTRUCTIONS#0="Please enter a location, ⏎
then select a choice from the menu.";
I18N_PLAY_MEDIA_TITLE#0="Playing {0}";
I18N_PROMPT_LOCATION#0="Location:";
```

Notice the {0} towards the bottom. This indicates a place where you will dynamically construct the final displayable string based on other variables.

Provide any translations you like at this point. The initial Czech translations are shown in Listing 10–2. Notice that Unicode characters are supported by simply entering "\uXXXX". You can also copy and paste Unicode characters directly into the Eclipse editing window. Unicode support allows you to port to any locale, including traditionally difficult ones like Chinese and Arabic.

Listing 10–2. Initial Czech Translations for MediaGrabber

```
I18N_CHAPI_EMAIL_TEXT#0="Zasláno na Vá\u0161 CHAPI";
I18N_CHOICE_RECORD_SOUND#0="Záznam zvuku";
I18N_CHOICE_RECORD_VIDEO#0="Video záznam";
I18N_CHOICE_TAKE_PICTURE#0="Vyfotografovat";
I18N_CONTACT_SHARED_MEDIA#0="Máte sdílená média.";
I18N_CONTACT_SHARE_MEDIA_PROMPT#0="Dosud \u017Eádné sdílení. Chcete poslat média?";
I18N_CONTACT_VERIFY_SHARED#0="Ov\u011B\u0159te Media Sdílená";
I18N_INSTRUCTIONS#0="Prosím, zadejte umíst\u011Bní, vyberte volbu z menu.";
I18N_PLAY_MEDIA_TITLE#0="Hra {0}";
I18N_PROMPT_LOCATION#0="Poloha:";
```

TIP: Most of the above translations come from Google Translate. However, translations by native speakers are always superior to those generated by a machine, which can have a difficult time capturing nuances or determining different parts of speech. If you are creating a commercial app, hire a professional translator. If you are releasing a free or open-source app, you can often find volunteers who will do a good job. When using volunteers, try to get input from multiple sources so you can determine the best and most common translations.

Modify Source

For the most part, the changes to MediaGrabber are very straightforward. Simply follow the instructions in "Adding Multi-Language Support" to make each file implement `MediaGrabberResource`, obtain a `ResourceBundle`, and look up strings dynamically.

One wrinkle occurs when it comes to building up strings that include variables. Here, you want to define a pattern in your translation file, with placeholders defined with a numbered sequence like {0}, {1}, and so on. Then, instead of manually concatenating strings, use the `MessageFormat` class to apply the variables to your translated pattern. Listing 10–3 contains the complete internationalized class for ChoicesScreen. Note the new code in LaunchPlayer near the bottom, which will create a string like "Playing file:///SDCard/BlackBerry/Music/captured.amr" that is localized for the user's language.

Listing 10–3. Localized Version of ChoicesScreen

```
package com.apress.king.mediagrabber;

import net.rim.device.api.i18n.*;
import net.rim.device.api.ui.*;
import net.rim.device.api.ui.component.*;
import net.rim.device.api.ui.container.MainScreen;

public class ChoicesScreen extends MainScreen implements MediaGrabberResource
{
    private static ResourceBundleFamily r = ResourceBundle.getBundle(BUNDLE_ID,
            BUNDLE_NAME);

    private BasicEditField location = new BasicEditField(r
            .getString(I18N_PROMPT_LOCATION), "file:///SDCard/BlackBerry", 100,
            Field.FIELD_VCENTER | BasicEditField.FILTER_URL);
    private MenuItem audioItem = new MenuItem(r,
            MediaGrabber.I18N_CHOICE_RECORD_SOUND, 0, 0)
    {
        public void run()
        {
            launchRecorder(RecordingScreen.RECORD_AUDIO);
        }
    };
    private MenuItem pictureItem = new MenuItem(r,
            MediaGrabber.I18N_CHOICE_TAKE_PICTURE, 0, 0)
    {
```

```java
        public void run()
        {
            launchRecorder(RecordingScreen.RECORD_PICTURE);
        }
    };
    private MenuItem videoItem = new MenuItem(r,
            MediaGrabber.I18N_CHOICE_RECORD_VIDEO, 0, 0)
    {
        public void run()
        {
            launchRecorder(RecordingScreen.RECORD_VIDEO);
        }
    };
    private MenuItem launchVideoItem = new MenuItem(r,
            MediaGrabber.I18N_CHOICE_PLAY_MEDIA, 0, 0)
    {
        public void run()
        {
            launchPlayer();
        }
    };

    public ChoicesScreen()
    {
        setTitle("MediaGrabber");
        add(new LabelField(r, MediaGrabber.I18N_INSTRUCTIONS));
        add(location);
    }

    public void close()
    {
        location.setDirty(false);
        super.close();
    }

    public void makeMenu(Menu menu, int instance)
    {
        if (instance == Menu.INSTANCE_DEFAULT)
        {
            String property = System.getProperty("supports.audio.capture");
            if (property != null && property.equals("true"))
            {
                menu.add(audioItem);
            }
            property = System.getProperty("video.snapshot.encodings");
            if (property != null && property.length() > 0)
            {
                menu.add(pictureItem);
            }
            property = System.getProperty("supports.video.capture");
            if (property != null && property.equals("true"))
            {
                menu.add(videoItem);
            }
            menu.add(launchVideoItem);
        }
```

```
        super.makeMenu(menu, instance);
    }

    private void launchRecorder(int type)
    {
        String directory = location.getText();
        RecordingScreen screen = new RecordingScreen(type, directory);
        UiApplication.getUiApplication().pushScreen(screen);
    }

    private void launchPlayer()
    {
        String url = location.getText();
        String pattern = r.getString(MediaGrabber.I18N_PLAY_MEDIA_TITLE);
        MessageFormat format = new MessageFormat("");
        format.setLocale(Locale.getDefaultForSystem());
        Object[] arguments = new String[]
        { url };
        format.applyPattern(pattern);
        String formatted = format.format(arguments);
        PlayingScreen screen = new PlayingScreen(url, formatted);
        UiApplication.getUiApplication().pushScreen(screen);
    }

    public boolean onSavePrompt()
    {
        return true;
    }

}
```

You can find the other localized classes online. They follow the same technique shown here. If your app includes a large number of dynamically constructed strings, you should create a helper method that manages the MessageFormat operations to cut down on repeated code.

Testing Localization

Depending on your simulator, you can probably switch between US English and UK English, or two other language variants. As such, it's good to define at least these languages so you can verify that you are localizing correctly in the simulator.

When you are ready to test on the device, load MediaGrabber and start changing languages. Try to keep track of what the Language menu is called in each new language so you can find it again. Navigating the native BlackBerry menus can be tricky—for example, the permissions prompt will display in the new language, so you may need to hunt a bit for the Save option. You should see your localized text display in the new languages you have defined.

If possible, you should send the translated version to a native speaker. They will let you know if any of the text needs to change. They can also quickly identify problems that might not be obvious to you, such as text being truncated or diacritical marks missing.

Porting can be a pain, but it's a good pain. If you're interested in porting, it means that you have made a good impression on your initial target market and are looking to expand. Here are some other things you can try with MediaGrabber to get more practice:

- Include still more languages. If you know a native speaker for a language you do not speak, work with them to translate the app. This is very valuable experience and will help you learn how to manage translation efforts.
- Include menu options on the Choices screen for switching between supported languages within the app.
- If you have a BlackBerry with older software on it, try creating a new version of MediaGrabber that will run on it.
- Try running MediaGrabber on a variety of BlackBerry form factors, including QWERTY devices, touch-screen devices, and SureType devices. Are you happy with the experience? If not, think about ways you could change the app so that it performs better on those devices.

Fortunately, after your first couple of experiences with porting, you will start automatically thinking about it when you start a new project. Making smart decisions about your program's structure early on will ease the development process and turn the porting process into a pleasant afterthought rather than a chaotic scramble.

Excelsior

Porting gets too little respect. Without porting, each app would only run on a tiny fraction of phones. Without efficient porting, the amount of time spent getting an app to run on a new phone can approach the amount of time writing the app in the first place.

As you have seen in this chapter, the secret is to start thinking about porting before you write your first line of code. Early decisions can make an app far more difficult to port later on. Spend some time with a sheet of paper or a whiteboard and ask some fundamental questions. On what devices does the app need to run? Will it need to run on other devices later? Can I force people to use a particular phone or OS version? Do I only want English-speaking Americans to use my app? Get input from your management or users if possible.

Then, as you construct your app, always keep the future in mind. Even if you are just writing for a particular device and language now, write flexibly so that the same code can support other types of users. Try testing with different configurations as you develop so you can verify that your code does adapt as planned.

If all goes well, your app will be a roaring success. Then you can spend an afternoon translating text and dropping in new image files, rather than weeks or months struggling with a labyrinth of hard-coded values. You will reach every market while your competitors are still lacing up their boots.

Once you're reaching a market this big, it's time to make sure you can satisfy it. Sooner or later, you'll want to consider how to best run your engineering process, including generating builds, delivering updates, and managing multiple versions. The next chapter will look at how to best build apps.

Chapter 11

Advanced Build Techniques

Whether you run a one-person programming shop or work for a multinational corporation, your BlackBerry experience will depend on building and maintaining software. In Chapter 10 you saw how applications can grow more complicated as you increase the number and variety of users you target. This chapter looks at the other side of the problem: how to manage your project and run it efficiently.

Techniques that worked very well when you first started, such as using Eclipse to build and test an app, become unfeasible once your app starts to run on a dozen different phone models. You will learn the techniques to scale up your development so you can handle the trials that come with success.

Moving Beyond Eclipse

I love Eclipse. I've used every major IDE, as well as old-school Unix editors and tools, and I feel more productive in Eclipse than I do anywhere else. That said, while Eclipse is a great resource for initially writing your application, it's not a great tool for managing a large number of builds. You really want a way to automatically build your application for many different devices—and possibly incorporate other steps such as automatically deploying to a distribution server. For these kinds of capabilities, you will need to move beyond the human-driven Eclipse and embrace the machine-driven command line.

The Command Line

Behind the scenes, the BlackBerry Java Plug-in for Eclipse wraps some existing tools that have been around for much longer. Like RIM's proprietary JDE, a stand-alone IDE, the plug-in calls out to these tools to handle the real work of building your app.

rapc

rapc is the core compiler that transforms your Java source files and other resources into a BlackBerry executable. rapc has an executable, `rapc.exe`, that internally invokes its associated JAR, `rapc.jar`.

Operations

You can study the use of rapc by examining the Eclipse build output window. Typically, it will run on all source files under a particular tree. This process runs through several operations.

- *Initialization* checks to make sure that the passed arguments are correct and all required files have been provided.

- *Compilation*: All source files are run through a compatible Java compiler. If you provide a compiled JAR file, it skips this stage.

- *Verification* inspects the resulting bytecode and reports any warnings or errors.

- *Optimization* removes any unused classes or methods.

- *Create CODs*: BlackBerry phones actually deal with small sections of code, referred to as sibling COD modules, which are typically 64kb or smaller in size. rapc will divide the application among all the sibling CODs (such as MyApp.cod, MyApp-1.cod, MyApp-2.cod, etc.) and then zip them up into MyApp.cod.

- *Create or modify JAD*: The compiler adds BlackBerry-specific fields to the JAD file. These include descriptions of the sibling COD modules, SHA1 checksums, and other fields. If no JAD file exists yet, rapc will generate a minimal file with all required fields, populating items such as the publisher name from your project settings.

Arguments

You can directly call rapc.exe yourself. The command has the following form:

```
rapc.exe {parameters} {Source files, compiled .class files, or compiled JAR file}
```

> **NOTE:** Unfortunately, rapc does not support wildcards. If you wish to supply multiple files, you must list each one.

rapc isn't very well documented. The most important parameters are shown here:

- `import={paths}` specifies the location of `net_rim_api.jar` and any other required libraries.

- `codename={name}` provides the application name.

- ■ -midlet indicates that this application is a MIDlet.

- ■ -quiet suppresses some messages.

- ■ -verbose shows all messages.

- ■ jad={file} provides the input JAD file to use. This same file will be modified with the final JAD contents.

A typical use of rapc may look like the following:

```
C:\dev\ide\eclipse_35_32bit\plugins\net.rim.ejde.componentpack6.0.0_6.0.0.29\components\
bin -\rapc.exe
import="C:\dev\ide\eclipse_35_32bit\plugins\net.rim.ejde.componentpack6.0.0_6.0.0.29\com
ponents\lib\net_rim_api.jar"↵
    BonjourWorld.java BonjourWorld.rrh BonjourWorld.rrc
```

SignatureTool

Eclipse also wraps the important SignatureTool program, which contacts the BlackBerry signing servers and applies signatures to your compiled program. As with rapc, you can directly interact with SignatureTool through the command line.

> **NOTE:** Refer to Chapter 1 for more information on using SignatureTool and how to install signing keys.

You can run SignatureTool on a compiled BlackBerry program with the following command line:

```
{Path to JDE installation directory}\bin\SignatureTool.jar {Cod Name}.cod
```

The parameters include the following options:

- ■ -r {Directory} recursively searches a directory for COD files to sign.

- ■ -f {File} reads the COD files to sign from the provided file.

- ■ -d deletes the file passed with the −f command.

- ■ -a automatically requests signatures.

- ■ -p {Password}password for code signing requests.

- ■ -s shows statistics about signatures requested and received.

- ■ -c closes the window after successfully requesting signatures.

- ■ -C always closes window after requesting signatures.

Build Environments

Armed with knowledge of how the BlackBerry toolchain works, you can set up automated builds. These will greatly increase your productivity. Instead of opening

Eclipse, navigating to a particular project workspace, and clicking on the options to package and sign, you can simply double-click a build file or wait for an automated build server to incorporate your changes.

Build Options

You can use any tool that supports running a command-line argument and passing parameters: that is to say, pretty much any build tool ever. If you belong to an organization that already has a build system in place, it will be worth the effort to adapt the BlackBerry build process to fit that system. If you are starting from a blank slate, you can consider the options in the following sections.

Batch Files

A build script simply defines a series of executable commands. You could type those commands into a .bat file, place it in the folder with your source code, then double-click it any time you wanted to do a build. The batch file might look like the following:

```
set FILES=BonjourWorld.java BonjourWorld.rrh BonjourWorld.rrc
set
JDE_PATH=C:\dev\ide\eclipse_35_32bit\plugins\net.rim.ejde.componentpack6.0.0_6.0.0.29\co
mponents\
%JDE_PATH%\bin\rapc.exe -import="%JDE_PATH%\lib\net_rim_api.jar" %FILES%
%JDE_PATH%\bin\SignatureTool.jar BonjourWorld.cod
```

> **CAUTION:** Whenever you use automated builds, be careful about what JDE version you reference. Remember Chapter 10's rules about forward and backward compatibility.

Ant Scripts

Today, most Java programmers prefer to use Ant for build scripts. A full description of Ant is beyond the scope of this book; essentially, it divides a build into a set of targets and tasks, each with parameters that can control their behavior. Therefore, you can write a generic Ant build file to compile any of your projects and use different parameters to control the specific project to build.

You can directly call out to the rapc tool by using Ant's <exec> task. However, consider looking at the useful and free BlackBerry Ant Tools package, also known as bb-ant-tools. This set of Ant tasks is not officially sanctioned by RIM but has nevertheless been widely adopted by developers. Prior to the release of the BlackBerry Java plug-in for Eclipse, many people used bb-ant-tools to develop BlackBerry programs within Eclipse.

bb-ant-tools contains tools for nearly every BlackBerry-specific task you can imagine.

- ▪ <rapc> will run rapc to generate your executable. It has a large number of options, including choices for setting the application location, icon, etc.

- ■   `<sigtool>` will start the signature request process. This supports all command line arguments, including the option to automatically supply a password.

- ■   `<alx>` packages a release with a valid ALX file and all the associated COD files. This is useful when creating a cable-load version of your app.

- ■   `<jadtool>` will patch up a JAD file by adding information for all the COD files. This is useful when preparing an OTA version.

bb-ant-tools excels in its cross-platform support. You will still need a Windows machine to install the tools, but you can copy the JDE installation to a Linux or Mac machine and then use bb-ant-tools to perform the actual builds.

Makefiles

Many in-house build systems rely on makefiles. While not as elegant as Ant, make has a long history and supports powerful command-line expressions.

If you plan to use makefiles, consider defining a BlackBerry rule to build the .cod target. This rule can then use other rules for running rapc, signing, and performing any other required build steps. Your standard build cycle can invoke the BlackBerry rule, alongside other steps such as generating documentation, publishing artifacts, or performing other important tasks.

Versioning Strategies

One of the most important BlackBerry properties you can define is the version number of the app. The BlackBerry uses the version number to determine whether a user needs an upgrade. However, versioning goes far beyond picking a unique version number. Before you decide your app needs a new version, you will need to decide how to make that version available to your users.

Version Numbers

Like Java MIDlets, BlackBerry applications come with a three-part version number: you can define two or three version numbers, each separated by a dot, each with a value between 0 and 99. Thus 1.0.3, 4.2, and 0.99.0 are all valid numbers but 2, 1.125, and 4.1.3.2 are not.

The first two numbers are known as the major and the minor version numbers. The optional third number is called the patch version. By convention, a version with a different patch number contains bug fixes but no new features; a minor version change signifies the addition of new features; and a major version number change indicates significant changes that include a break in program compatibility.

For example, imagine that you release an app that lets college students register for their courses. Your first version might be 1.0. Later, you let students add their reviews of professors and classes. This change would be released as version 1.1. You might find that some reviews aren't formatted properly; you fix this bug and issue an update as version 1.1.1. Then the college changes its course scheduling software, meaning your app no longer works with the new system. You make the necessary changes and release version 2.0.

A switch from a lower version to a higher version number is called an *upgrade*. BlackBerry also supports switching from a higher version to a lower version, which is a *downgrade*. You may also choose to install a new copy with the same version number. This is useful during development when it may not be practical to create a new version number with every build change, but it could confuse your users. Any time you release a new version of your app, it should have a higher version number.

> **NOTE:** If you change the application name or the vendor name, it will be considered a different application and won't replace the previous version. So, if the name changes from CollegeBuddy to MyRegistrar, a user who upgraded to MyRegistrar will actually have both apps. As long as the name and vendor remain the same, installing a new version will replace the older version.

Distribution Options

Once you have built a new version of the app with a new version number, you must decide how to make it available to your users. You can choose between several options.

- *Cable load*: Send the updated app to the user's PC. You can do this through any mechanism you like: send them an e-mail with the new version attached, instruct them to visit a web site where they can download it, and so on. If the downloaded .alx file is placed in the same location as the original .alx, the user will automatically be prompted to install the updated version the next time they view the applications within BlackBerry Desktop Manager. Otherwise, they can browse to the updated file within the desktop manager and select it. In general, your update must have a higher version number or the Desktop Manager will resist installing the update.

- *OTA*: Place the JAD file and the sibling COD modules on a web server. Configure the JAD files to have a MIME type of `text/vnd.sun.j2me.app-descriptor` and the COD files to a MIME type of `application/vnd.rim.cod`. Direct the user to visit the JAD file with their BlackBerry web browser. They will be prompted to download and install the new app.

- *Store*: Recent versions of BlackBerry App World will notify users within the store if a previously purchased application has a new version available. Other stores may offer this feature as well.

- *In-app updates*: BlackBerry's CodeModuleManager API allows one application to install another application. If you have a suite of applications, you could have one app check for updates for another application, then download and install them. This approach allows you to provide your own user interface on the device to manage updates, rather than relying on the BlackBerry browser.

- *Push*: If your app runs in a BES environment, the administrator can forcibly send a new version of the app to all affected phones.

You also must decide how to let users know when a new version is available. Even if you use an application store to deliver your updates, keep in mind that some people may frequently use your app but only rarely launch the store, so they may not see your updates.

- *Poll*: Your app can connect to a server you control to check for the latest version number. If it finds an update, it will alert the user within the app. This works best when the user can complete the update on the device, either OTA through the browser or within the app.

- *Push*: If you have access to the user's e-mail address or similar information, you can send him notifications when new versions are available. This approach works best if the update must be completed on the desktop.

You will generally have the most successful upgrades if you deliver updates through the same channel that originally installed the app. If you initially distributed the app OTA, use OTA for updates; if you used a PC-based application to download the app, use that same app to download the latest versions.

Where's My Data?

Nearly every interesting app will make some use of persistent storage. Whether saving games, user preferences, or downloaded art, persistent storage enhances apps by providing more convenience and increasing speed.

Persistence also leads to potential problems. Different versions of the app may store data in different formats, leading to potential problems if the user updates.

Files

BlackBerry does not have any logic that associates files to applications. Your app can write to any directory and read from any directory that it wants. When the app is deleted or upgraded, all the files it created will remain in place.

This has a few ramifications. First, if you store your program's data in files, you will be responsible for maintaining your own versioning system. For example, you might tag the start of each file with the version number of the file format. This way, when future versions of the app try to read those files, they can quickly determine whether the files are compatible and either translate or delete them if the file format has changed. Second, if you store media files like images or sounds, you can keep them in place and safely reuse on newer app versions. However, if you have a larger number of media files, they will still take up space after the user deletes your app; this may annoy some people. To be a good citizen, offer a choice within your app to clean up any such files. Users can run this option before deleting your app and return to a blank slate.

RMS

BlackBerry supports the Record Management System from Java ME. This provides a convenient way to store sets of records, such as recent news headlines or restaurant details. Records are stored as raw byte streams without any version number or ordering.

Unlike files, RMS records are tied to a particular application. If you delete an app, the phone will automatically remove all its RMS records. When you install an upgraded version, the RMS records will remain in place and the new version can read the old data. If a user updates OTA through the web browser, she will be able to choose whether or not to retain the old RMS data.

Few applications actually want to deal with raw bytes, so typically an app will serialize and deserialize to translate between the RMS record data and some sort of object. For example, you might define plain Java classes like NewsStory or RestaurantInfo and define methods to create these objects from byte arrays. So long as the class structure remains exactly the same, you can reuse the data across different app versions. However, the record format will likely need to change at some point to support later application features. In order to future-proof your record storage, you should always tag the beginning of an RMS record with the version number. Future versions of the app can inspect this value first and decide how to handle the data that follows.

> **TIP:** The version number of your record can be different from the version of your app. Maybe app versions 1.0, 1.3, and 2.0 all use the same record structure; if so, the records can share version number 1. If you later change the structure, such as adding a Byline field to the NewsStory class as part of your changes to app version 2.1, you would increase the RMS record version number to 2.

BlackBerry Persistent Storage

The PersistentStore and PersistentObject classes provide the capability to save application data. Unlike RMS, BlackBerry persistent storage is object-based rather than byte-based. This allows for more flexible and elegant coding.

You store persistent objects based on a provided key. However, BlackBerry also tracks persisted objects by the application that created them. If the user later deletes an application, BlackBerry automatically deletes all of its persistent objects that are no longer accessible on the device.

BlackBerry tries to detect the compatibility of persisted objects. If you load a new version of the application that has the exact same class structure for the persisted objects, the previous data will probably remain. On the other hand, if the data in a class changes or its structure is significantly altered (for example, by adding, removing, or reordering many methods), the device will automatically remove old data when installing the new version. Therefore, you should avoid relying on BlackBerry persistent storage for data that you will need to access in future versions of the app. Look at this as a convenience to speed program operation, not as a reliable storage system.

Debugging and Logging

Applications have bugs. Pretending that your app is perfect won't make the problem go away—it makes the bugs more difficult to squash. In order to quickly detect bugs and determine the root cause, developers often rely upon logging and debug information placed within their apps.

This leads to a quandary. Ideally, you would like to place debugging features in your app so you can quickly and conveniently debug any problems that come up. However, you probably don't want end-users to have access to the program's inner workings. This often leads developers to create separate "debug" and "release" versions of their application. This, in turn, creates additional problems because it means that the version a developer runs for testing isn't exactly the same as the version that people are actually using. Few things are more frustrating than finding a bug in the release version (which you cannot debug) that does not appear in the debug version.

Capturing Logging

The most primitive method of debugging is to make your program print out information about what it's doing. While low-tech, it can also provide exactly what you need. If the phone isn't able to connect to the network, you can hook it up to the logger and see the message "ERROR: Permission not set to open connection." You've just cut an hour-long debugging session down to a few minutes!

BlackBerry makes it easy to get logging information. Simply connect the device to your PC with a USB cable, start Eclipse, and then click Run ➤ Debug As ➤ BlackBerry Device. Even if you do not have access to the source code or .debug files for the app, you will be able to watch the output window to view all the messages that are generated by the BlackBerry. These include messages from the running application, as well as more inscrutable messages from the BlackBerry operating system.

The BlackBerry logger reports anything that you send to System.out or System.err. You should include plenty of logging information as you write your app, particularly for areas that you suspect might fail at some point.

> **TIP:** Stack trace information also gets printed to the log. However, most exceptions will not produce a useful stack trace. If you want to see the full trace information in the log, you must catch the `Throwable` instead of an `Exception` subclass. Don't blame me; I didn't create this system.

Visual Logging

Sometimes it's nice to actually see what's happening on the device itself—without needing to hook it up to a PC. This is especially useful if someone else is testing the app and you want more information about a problem that occurred. You can capture relevant information yourself, and then direct that information to an onscreen element. You have used this approach with `StatusUpdater` in MediaGrabber to get more detailed information about exceptions that occurred.

You can take this idea one step further and create a full-blown logging screen within your app. Rather than directing logging information to `System.out`, store it within your app or in a log file. Your debugging screen can then read through this information on demand and display a detailed log of everything the app has done.

On or Off?

You can follow several strategies to address the problem of providing a useful debugging environment without giving users or competitors overly detailed looks into the app's functions.

- *Bifurcate*: Create two versions of the application, one with debugging compiled in and another without. If you use a preprocessor as part of your build process, you can use it to automatically strip out logging calls. Alternately, you could create a proxy logging method like `Log.writeLog()`, then provide different versions of the `Log` class for debug and release builds. The debug build would write to standard out or your internal log, while the release build does nothing.

- *App property*: You can include a special JAD property in your application that controls whether or not to display the log. If this property is set, `Log.writeLog()` would create logging information; if the property is unset, it would do nothing. The advantage of this approach is that you only need to build the application binary once, and the same code is loaded OTA on both testing and user devices; the only difference is the run-time check for whether logging is enabled.

- *Secret code*: Similar to the previous strategy, you can have a flag within your application that controls whether or not to display debugging information. You can toggle this flag by entering a secret code, following a particular sequence, or otherwise performing some unusual action within the app. What's really nice about this approach is that even if a bug occurs on an actual released version, you can ask the affected user to enter the code and report the logging information to you. The disadvantage is that the secret code will eventually leak out and then your competitors will have access to your logging information.

Data Collection

Even if you can look at logging information, it may be awkward and difficult to parse. It's much easier to deal with detailed log files on the PC than it is on a handset.

Therefore, consider including some error reporting capabilities within your app. For example, you might include a menu option that reads "Send report to developer." If a user selects this item, the app will collect all the current logging information, place it in an e-mail, and send it to you. This way, if a user runs into a problem with their application, they can help you solve it by providing more insight into what the app is doing.

Consider combining this approach with the secret code strategy. You might not want to receive reports from thousands of curious users, but it's nice to have the option for cases where things have gone seriously wrong.

> **NOTE:** Other Smartphone platforms have started adding the capability of automatically collecting crash reports from devices, which are then forwarded on to the responsible developers. RIM has not yet added this capability, but it may come in the future. In the meantime, writing your own reporting framework gives you more flexibility plus the capability to gather data on problems other than crashes.

Other Build Issues

No two people or organizations will settle on the exact same process for building and releasing their applications. You may encounter several other issues and ideas when preparing your own builds.

Obfuscation

Java ME developers often rely on obfuscators such as Proguard to optimize their code. Obfuscators have several effects. First, true to their name, they conceal the workings of an application by renaming classes, variables, and method names; therefore, even if someone decompiles an application, he will find it difficult to understand. More importantly, obfuscators also remove unused sections of code. If an obfuscator determines that an application can never call a particular method or never tries to instantiate a certain class, it will strip out the affected code. For mobile platforms with limited space available for applications, such savings can prove crucial.

As noted earlier, `rapc` includes an optimization stage that will strip out unused code. In addition, because the COD file format is proprietary and unique to RIM devices, it can't be reverse-engineered with the same ease that Java ME JAR files can. You have previously seen that you can open a COD file in a hex editor to view program information, but, currently, no true decompiler exists for the COD format.

Because of these aspects, you can generally omit obfuscation from your build process. However, sometimes Proguard offers more aggressive obfuscation settings or more fine-tuning than the automatic behavior you get from `rapc`. If you feel that your application is still too large, you may choose to add a third-party obfuscator to your process. In this case, you would probably follow these steps:

1. Compile your source using the RIM tools; a JAR file will be produced as part of this process.

2. Extract the JAR contents to another directory.

3. Run an obfuscator on the resulting files.

4. Run RIM's preverify.exe command (found in the bin directory) on the obfuscated files.

5. Pass the preverified files to `rapc` for the final transformation into a COD.

> **CAUTION:** If you do not use `rapc` to preverify and compile your source files, you can encounter unusual and frustrating errors such as the dreaded Stack Map message when launching your app. Pay careful attention to your Java compiler version, obfuscation settings, and especially any messages generated by `rapc`. You may need to tweak your settings to get the right results.

Packaging OTA Installs

You have already seen how to configure a web server to deliver BlackBerry applications directly to a phone via its web browser. This approach works well for simple applications with a single module. However, if an application contains multiple parts, such as related applications in a suite or a set of libraries, the user must individually download and install each module. This is a tedious and error-prone approach.

Fortunately, you can short-circuit this problem by referencing all required COD modules within the JAD file. The user then sees a single application to download, but behind the scenes, all other required apps will be installed as well.

If you use bb-ant-tools to generate OTA deployments, you can easily get this behavior by using the `<jadtool>` task with multiple COD files. Otherwise, you might need to collate the JAD information yourself. First, build each project separately. Open the JAD files. You'll notice that the COD information inside includes text like the following:

```
RIM-COD-Module-Dependencies: net_rim_cldc,net_rim_os,net_rim_bb_framework_api,↵
    net_rim_bbapi_menuitem,net_rim_pdap,net_rim_crypto_1,net_rim_crypto_3,↵
    net_rim_bbapi_mailv2
RIM-MIDlet-Flags-1: 1
RIM-MIDlet-Flags-2: 0
RIM-COD-URL-9: MediaGrabber-9.cod
RIM-COD-Size-9: 49972
RIM-COD-SHA1-9: a4 75 3d 10 c9 93 e6 49 b0 05 80 96 39 03 42 0f 12 ff 69 9d
RIM-COD-URL-10: MediaGrabber-10.cod
RIM-COD-Size-10: 49976
RIM-COD-SHA1-10: 87 b5 20 cb c5 7e 29 10 4c 8e c6 2a 4d fa 90 11 8f 1d 70 87
```

Take all the `RIM-COD-*` lines in the other JAD files and merge them into the first JAD file. You will need to increment the COD file numbers. For example, if the first JAD file goes up to `RIM-COD-URL-13`, then you would import the next JAD file's `RIM-COD-URL-1` as `RIM-COD-URL-14`. You might also need to edit the `RIM-COD-Module-Dependencies` so it contains the dependencies of each individual project. Finally, any `RIM-MIDlet-Flags` or `RIM-Library-Flags` must be moved over into the main JAD file. Again, renumber so that the imported modules start one number higher than the highest number.

You can edit a JAD file by hand, and this approach will work fine if you create OTA releases very infrequently. Otherwise, look into creating a basic script to handle the JAD file collation process. Python, Perl, and sed are all good candidates. If you don't know any text processing scripting languages, this is a great excuse to learn.

Packaging ALX Installs

As with OTA installation, a cable load install will more likely succeed if you deliver all the required code modules as part of a single operation. You can use bb-ant-tools to easily generate an ALX file that contains multiple COD components. Or you can simply edit the ALX file yourself. The following code shows a basic ALX file that includes both an application and a library as part of the install:

```
<loader version="1.0">
    <application id="MediaGrabber">
        <name>MediaGrabber</name>
        <description>All media everywhere</description>
        <version>1.0.0</version>
        <vendor>Apress</vendor>
        <copyright>Copyright (c) 2009 Apress</copyright>
        <fileset Java="1.39">
            <directory ></directory>
            <files >
                MediaGrabber.cod
                FriendTracker.cod
            </files>
        </fileset>
    </application>
</loader>
```

App: Logging, Building, and Updating

You will make a trio of changes to MediaGrabber: two for your own convenience, and one for your users' convenience. These don't require advanced APIs or esoteric techniques and will lead to smoother development and use.

Adding a Logger

You already collect information about almost everything interesting that occurs in your app within the StatusUpdater class. You can easily extend this class to hold that logging information in memory and provide a way to access it. This can be useful if you see that something has gone wrong but the onscreen messages have already been replaced.

Listing 11–1 shows the changes to StatusUpdater. To maintain a single unified log that captures the use of all individual instances, use a single static instance of a Vector that holds the old log messages.

Listing 11–1. *StatusUpdater with Stored Logging*

```
package com.apress.king.mediagrabber;

import java.util.*;

import net.rim.device.api.ui.UiApplication;
import net.rim.device.api.ui.component.LabelField;

public class StatusUpdater implements Runnable
{
    private LabelField status;
    private String message;
    private UiApplication app;
    private static Vector messages = new Vector();

    public StatusUpdater(LabelField status)
    {
        this.status = status;
        app = UiApplication.getUiApplication();
    }

    public void sendDelayedMessage(String message)
    {
        messages.addElement(message);
        this.message = message;
        app.invokeLater(this);
    }

    public static String getLog()
    {
        StringBuffer result = new StringBuffer();
        Enumeration lines = messages.elements();
        while (lines.hasMoreElements())
        {
            String line = (String) lines.nextElement();
            result.append(line);
```

```
            result.append("\n");
        }
        return result.toString();
    }

    public void run()
    {
        status.setText(message);
    }
}
```

You'll invoke this code soon. For now, recognize that this captures almost every Throwable that can occur within the program because of the way you have already set up your error handling. On a successful run of the application, very little logging information will be generated. Failures will be retained until the application unloads. Of course, you could enhance this to support multiple log severity levels and other useful items.

Build Script

Even if you don't have GNU make or Apache Ant installed, you can whip together a quick and dirty build script using Notepad or another basic text editing program. Use the build script in Listing 11–2 to generate a new application without requiring Eclipse to be open. You can modify the variables at the top of the script with the location of your BlackBerry component package, signing password, and so on.

Listing 11–2. *Build Batch File*

```
set JDE_PATH= C:\dev\ide\eclipse_35_32bit\plugins\↵
        net.rim.ejde.componentpack6.0.0_6.0.0.29\components\
set PASSWORD=swordfish
set FILES=MediaGrabber.java ChoicesScreen.java PlayingScreen.java↵
    RecordingScreen.java SendingScreen.java StatusUpdater.java MediaGrabber.rrh↵
    MediaGrabber.rrc MediaGrabber_cs.rrc MediaGrabber_en.rrc↵
    MediaGrabber_en_GB.rrc MediaGrabber_en_US.rrc
set SOURCEPATH=src\com\apress\king\mediagrabber
set STARTDIR="%CD%"
cd %SOURCEPATH%
%JDE_PATH%\bin\rapc.exe -import="%JDE_PATH%\lib\net_rim_api.jar" %FILES%
%JDE_PATH%\bin\SignatureTool.jar -a -p %PASSWORD% -c MediaGrabber.cod
copy MediaGrabber.cod %STARTDIR%
cd %STARTDIR%
```

Updates

If you have access to a web server, you can place the MediaGrabber JAD file and the unzipped sibling COD files on a publicly accessible directory. Then, direct MediaGrabber to open a browser to the JAD location to check for an update. You can do this using the Browser. Listing 11–3 shows the changes to ChoicesScreen that add a new menu item to perform the update. You can also create a menu item that captures information from the logger and then sends it via e-mail using your existing SendingScreen class.

Listing 11–3. *Adding Logging and Updates to MediaGrabber Choices*

```java
public class ChoicesScreen extends MainScreen implements MediaGrabberResource
{
// ...
    private MenuItem sendLogItem = new MenuItem("Send Log", 0x10000, 0)
    {
        public void run()
        {
            String message = StatusUpdater.getLog();
            SendingScreen sending = new SendingScreen("text/plain", "log.txt",
                    "Log attached", message.getBytes(), false);
            UiApplication.getUiApplication().pushScreen(sending);
        }
    };
    private MenuItem updateItem = new MenuItem("Get Latest Version", 0x20000, 0)
    {
        public void run()
        {
            String url = "http://www.example.com/MediaGrabber.jad";
            Browser.getDefaultSession().displayPage(url);
        }
    };
// ...
    public void makeMenu(Menu menu, int instance)
    {
        if (instance == Menu.INSTANCE_DEFAULT)
        {
            String property = System.getProperty("supports.audio.capture");
            if (property != null && property.equals("true"))
            {
                menu.add(audioItem);
            }
            property = System.getProperty("video.snapshot.encodings");
            if (property != null && property.length() > 0)
            {
                menu.add(pictureItem);
            }
            property = System.getProperty("supports.video.capture");
            if (property != null && property.equals("true"))
            {
                menu.add(videoItem);
            }
            menu.add(launchVideoItem);
            menu.add(sendLogItem);
            menu.add(updateItem);
        }

        super.makeMenu(menu, instance);
    }
// ...
}
```

WANT MORE?

You can endlessly tinker with your build configuration. Any time you find yourself doing something repetitive or inefficient, consider what you could do to reduce the monotony. Here are a few things you could try in MediaGrabber:

- When your application starts, check the web server's JAD file and extract the version number. Only show the update option if this number is more recent than the current version.

- Modify StatusUpdater to persist information to a log file or other persistent storage. Include an option to clear the log information as well as upload it.

- Download a recent version of Ant and the bb-ant-tools add-on. Create a build script that allows you to create versions of MediaGrabber for different versions of the JDE.

Creating new build options doesn't let you add new bullet points to your app's feature list, but it helps every aspect of development become easier and faster. The time you invest here will be well spent.

Excelsior

Even the smallest developer will appreciate the convenience of a powerful build system when she starts releasing multiple versions of her application. You will probably spend some time tweaking your builds to find a process that works well for you. Once you understand how the tools work and the implications of upgrading, you can mix and match techniques until you find the best possible fit.

You have now encountered the tools and strategies that you can use to elevate your app from a good idea up to a professional piece of software. If you haven't entered the enterprise yet, you may receive an invitation soon. Enterprise applications have several differences from regular consumer applications; push technology is one of the most exciting. The next chapter will show how to create an application that responds to remote activity and plugs the user into their enterprise.

Part IV

The New Frontier

RIM continues to evolve the BlackBerry platform. As its hardware grows more powerful, its competition more fierce, and its customers more demanding, RIM has focused on releasing new versions of its device software that unlock new capabilities for developers. This final part of the book will look at the latest set of APIs and services that RIM has released. We will leverage the push API, which takes a device capability that has been around since the beginning, and finally makes it available to the masses. We will look at the latest UI features for making modern, attractive screens. We'll round out the book by examining a variety of useful and interesting cross-platform libraries, such as barcode scanning and OpenGL.

Making the most compelling applications requires you to stay ahead of the curve. Mastering the latest APIs means that you can create the best-looking and most useful apps around.

Chapter 12

Push Services

Much of this book focused on making apps as indispensible as possible. You've seen how to make powerful apps that tie in with the operating system at a low level and display as options throughout the phone. Apps can become fully indispensible by adding *push*, which allows them to automatically present themselves to the user when something interesting happens. Push technology proactively does something useful to benefit the user, rather than passively waiting for them to initiate an action. In other words, rather than wait for the user to open your app, you tell them what they need to know now.

In this chapter, I will survey the options available for push. You'll learn about push technology's benefits and drawbacks, the different cases where you should use it, and how it fits into RIM's ecosystem. You'll examine the components that make up an end-to-end push solution, and you'll update `MediaGrabber` to add push capability so you can remotely push media onto the device. By the end of the chapter, you'll have the tools necessary to start adding push to your apps and the knowledge to identify what areas will benefit most.

Why Push?

Let's be honest: push is hard. It requires many moving parts that all must be created in synch and coordinated with one another. Debugging a push system can be maddening, as any one of multiple components may cause failures. Before embarking on this process, you should identify the reasons why push will benefit your app.

Right Here, Right Now

All mobile phones rely on push technology. When someone calls you, your phone immediately rings. You don't need to launch a phone application and press a button to see whether you have an incoming call. Similarly, when you receive a text message or a message from BlackBerry Messenger, your phone lets you know about it right away.

Users demand this kind of push availability from their phones, but they typically do not get it from their apps. Most apps simply wait in the background, quietly passing time until the user deigns to select their icon. These apps may do cool things, but users won't think about them often because the app remains idle.

By adding push features to your app, you gain the same kind of immediacy that people associate with their phone and e-mail. When something really remarkable happens, you can let people know about it immediately. Push is the best way to get your message out right away, no matter where people are and no matter what they are doing.

> **CAUTION:** Of course, you shouldn't abuse this power. Users will quickly uninstall your app if you constantly pester them about unimportant information.

A Few Examples

Consider the following use cases. If your app plays a similar role or has similar needs, you should strongly consider adding push.

Medical Emergencies

Emergency medical technicians typically receive dispatches through radio, but a mobile app could provide significant additional resources, including map directions to the emergency address, medical history for the patient, and the status of other nearby EMTs. When the dispatcher sends out an alert, he could also push the relevant data to the EMTs' devices. Without needing to switch applications, hunt for an icon, or even freeing their hands, technicians could immediately see the relevant data on their screen.

This scenario illustrates the most extreme example of push technology value. By moving critical data to the device as quickly as possible, you gain extra time in a situation where seconds can save lives.

Going Fast

When tickets went on sale for the band Wilco's 2010 concert in Durham, they went fast. After just 17 minutes, not a single ticket remained. If you were a Wilco fan and didn't buy your ticket in that 17 minute window, you were extremely disappointed.

Push technology can provide time-sensitive information when it's most important and useful. Which would you rather do: check a web site every day to see whether your favorite band has started to tour yet, or have your phone automatically notify you on the rare occasions when your band is coming to town? A simple but useful push app could remain quiet almost all the time, only grabbing your attention when you need to take some action.

Speedy Delivery

Many large vehicle fleets already use BlackBerry devices to coordinate drivers with their headquarters. With push, management can deliver new job instructions to their workers; depending on the industry, this may involve passenger pickup, flower delivery, or a sales call location. Push can also proactively warn drivers about traffic problems in the area, recall a previously ordered job, and prepare them for the upcoming task.

By using an app for assignments, you could construct an almost completely automated dispatch operation: a server-side app could process service requests entered via the web, then generate pushes to the driver in the area with the fewest assignments. Because BlackBerry Push optionally supports delivery acknowledgments, the service can know when a driver has received the job, which may trigger a billing event; if it does not receive an acknowledgment, it can automatically send the job to the next available worker.

Faster and Easier

Non-push solutions generally involve polling, as shown in Figure 12–1. Your application must check in with a server to see whether it has new information. From the user's perspective, this might seem like the same behavior as a push app: you can do your checks in the background, without the user needing to make a selection, and only pop up when new content is available. However, this approach requires a difficult tradeoff between efficiency and timeliness. The more frequently you poll, the more quickly you can notify the user of changes, but you also take more processor time, use the network, and drain the battery.

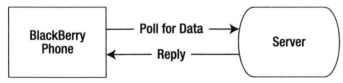

Figure 12–1. *Polling for new data*

In contrast, a push only occurs when something of interest happens, as shown in Figure 12–2. It may be a minute since the last push or it may be several months, but your app won't have performed any checks in the interim. Once you do receive the push, you may simply process the data in the push, assuming it provides all you need or you may just notify the user and let them initiate an action or you may retrieve additional data on your own.

Figure 12–2. *Receiving a push*

By only running when required, you put no extra overhead on the device's other operations. This architecture helps the BlackBerry's battery last longer, makes your users happier, and keeps your app installed.

How Does It Work?

The diagrams above are deceptively simple; there's actually a lot hidden in those arrows. In this section, I will dive deeper into the mechanism of push.

Old BES Model

BlackBerry has had push technology from the beginning, but in the past, only enterprises could take advantage of it. This makes sense if you consider how difficult it is to actually find a phone. You may have run into this problem if you have ever tried to connect to a server socket running on a device: you can't know ahead of time what IP address the device will use, and even if you do find out (for example, by having the device report in to a server), it will often be hidden behind a NAT, and in any case will change when the user moves around or switches networks.

In contrast, users on a BES always connect through the enterprise server, which keeps track of the connected devices. Each device has a unique PIN that identifies it. Push applications can leverage the same technology as push e-mail. The downside, of course, is that your push application can only push to users who belong to this BES.

Traditional pushes start on an application server, typically located within the corporate network, which has access to the BlackBerry MDS Connection Service. Your application will send the request to the MDS, including the data to send and the recipients who should receive it. The MDS will then attempt to deliver the push. You can optionally request to receive delivery notification when the push reaches each target device.

New BIS Model

All BlackBerry devices support push. Now that the devices are increasingly used by consumers in addition to businesses, more people are taking advantage of these capabilities. Most BlackBerry consumers have a BlackBerry Internet Service (BIS) account, which provides the same sort of push support that business users receive from their BES. A BIS has the same overall design as a BES, with a BlackBerry infrastructure that mediates between the device and the rest of the network; however, it comes with far fewer restrictions than most BES servers.

NOTE: While most BlackBerry consumers are required to get a BIS account when buying their BlackBerry phone, not 100% of users will have one; for example, if you buy a used BlackBerry from eBay and use a SIM card from a non-BlackBerry phone, you will not get BIS service. You can still make phone calls and browse the Web through WiFi, but you won't receive push e-mails or other push services. Make sure you have a BIS account on devices you will use for testing. Also, note that BlackBerry App World requires a BIS or BES account, so if you plan to distribute exclusively through AppWorld, you can assume that the users can receive pushes.

RIM has rebranded their push technology as BlackBerry Push Service and opened it up for third-party developers and consumers. The low-level push technology remains the same, but for the first time, you can push to all of your users regardless of their status or network.

Push System Overview

RIM still needed to solve the problem described above: how to find devices. Rather than require each individual developer to hunt down or track individual users, their new model keeps all the subscriber information in their own push data servers. Your client application will register with that push data server, which afterwards will keep track of how to find the device. Your server application will issue requests to the push server, which then forwards them on to the appropriate device.

RIM offers two levels of push support. The first, Push Service Essentials, offers the following features"

- Free to use.
- Unlimited pushes allowed.
- Up to 8kb data payload.
- No delivery acknowledgement.

Figure 12–3 shows how Push Service Essentials works. Your message gets delivered through the BlackBerry infrastructure in a straight shot. If it cannot reach the target (for example, if the user has turned off their phone), then the push service will continue trying for a while before eventually giving up. The push completes once the data reaches the target; note that, at this point, the device could open a connection back to the server to send an application-level acknowledgment or to retrieve additional data beyond the 8kb limit.

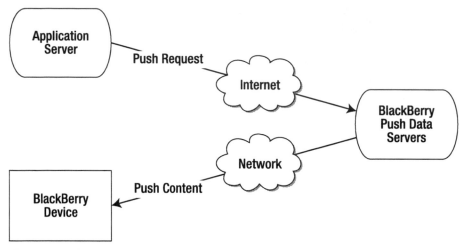

Figure 12–3. *BlackBerry Push Service Essentials operation*

Essentials works best for non-critical information, like games or lifestyle applications. If your application relies on the delivery of push messages, you may want to consider Push Service Plus. The Plus version provides the following features:

- Support for delivery acknowledgments.

- Configurable quality of service notifications.

- Checks the status of outstanding pushes.

- Fee based on volume of pushes; free below a threshold.

Adding delivery notifications results in additional communication between the client, the push server, and your own server. Figure 12–4 shows a full delivery flow for a single push. Depending on your application's needs, you can choose what kind of delivery acknowledgement you want to receive. You may only need to know that the push reached the device successfully, or you may want to ensure that your application actually read the data provided. Note that device-level acknowledgements will require an extra network call back to your server.

Figure 12–4. *BlackBerry Push Service Plus delivery and acknowledgements*

Keep in mind that your server will need to handle all acknowledgements that you request. BlackBerry Push Service scales well, but your own server will need to scale, too. A single broadcast request from the server may result in millions of acknowledgements, so think carefully about what data you need and whether you can handle it.

Tooling Up

Later in this chapter, you will look at the support for push that's built into the RIM SDK. To use BIS push services, though, you will need to acquire a separate component, the BlackBerry Push Service SDK. You can find a link to the download from the BlackBerry Developer web site. Unlike most RIM downloads, you don't need to register before downloading the SDK.

The SDK comes in two types, a Windows and a Linux version. Download the one for the server you expect to send pushes from. The install package will present you with several options.

- *Install set*: When first evaluating the Push SDK, you may want to choose the Distribution+Tomcat option, which automatically installs and configures a Tomcat server running some useful tools and samples. For later installs, you might just choose the Distribution set, which comes with the SDK alone.

- *Tomcat*: If you chose to install a server, you can set some basic parameters, such as the HTTP ports used. Be sure to pick available ports.

- *Database*: The Push SDK requires a MySQL or Oracle database. You will need to have already installed the database program, set up an administrative account, and created a separate database for the push SDK. If you provide the proper information, the install program can automatically configure the database for push services.

- *Gateway*: Your server will communicate with RIM's gateway when sending pushes. You must specify whether you will send to BIS or to BES users. You must also enter your server URL; you can use any URL you like while evaluating, but you'll need to provide an actual server before RIM will accept your push application.

- *Application ID*: While evaluating, you probably won't know your application ID. Once you have registered your app with RIM, you can provide the ID so the gateway will recognize your application.

Inside the Push SDK, you will find several library JAR files, Javadoc documentation, and both client and server sample applications. With these tools, you can practice building push applications and evaluate whether push makes sense for your own application. Testing is difficult at this stage, but you can get started developing your application and invoking the push APIs.

> **NOTE:** Remember, this process specifically applies to the BlackBerry Push Service, which mainly targets BIS users and also supports delivery to BES customers. If your push application will only send to a BES, you do not need to use the SDK; you can find further information later in this chapter.

Once you decide on your strategy, register with RIM to evaluate the Push Service. You will need to provide some details about your expected volume of use, your server URL, and contact data. In return, you will gain access to a test environment that lets you experiment with sending pushes. Once you are satisfied with the quality of your application, you can register to launch the app in production. At this stage, RIM will review your application, negotiate any fees, and then allow you to start sending real pushes to BIS consumers.

Server in Depth

Whether you write a traditional BES push application or a new BIS push, all pushes will start on your server. From the application's perspective, the most critical part of the push is the payload—that is, the data that will be sent to the device. Additionally, you will need to provide sufficient information to the infrastructure so it can find your intended targets.

Directing the Push

Pushes will work slightly differently depending on whether your app runs in a BES or a BIS environment.

Sending a BES Push

A traditional BES push uses an HTTP POST request to the BlackBerry MDS for your BES. You will need to know the server URL and the MDS port number; contact your BES system administrator if you need this information. She can also configure the system to accept connections from your application server.

BES pushes support two formats of push request.

- A PAP request is based on the WAP PAP 2.0 standard for pushing content. This format uses the multipart MIME standard for composing requests. It is more verbose and so has a bit more overhead, but it also supports some additional features like request cancelation and status query.

- In contrast, a RIM HTTP request uses a proprietary byte stream format; this tends to be shorter, but can only be used in BlackBerry environments and does not support cancelation or querying.

Sending a BIS Push

All BIS push applications use BlackBerry's push gateway, so you do not need to specify a URL. Use the classes found in the net.rim.pushsdk.push package, included in the BlackBerry Push SDK download. Internally, these will generate a request based on WAP PAP 2.2 and send it to the gateway. To initiate a push, you will first configure a

PushParameters object with the details of your push request, and then pass that object to PushService.push(). Behind the scenes, the SDK will work with your web server configuration and deliver the request appropriately.

Configuring the Push

You can provide several parameters that describe how the server and clients should handle your push request. These choices will vary based on your type of push.

BES PAP Push Attributes

If you send a BES PAP push, you supply a <pap> control entity that describes how to send your message. This contains a single element called <push-message> that defines the following attributes:

- push-id: A globally unique identifier for this push request.

- deliver-before-timestamp: Instructs the MDS to stop trying to transmit the push after a certain time. Use this if the information in the push ceases to be useful beyond a certain point; for example, don't send a concert notice after the concert has finished. If you do not specify this, the MDS will continue to retry delivery until its configured expiration time elapses.

- deliver-after-timestamp: This optional attribute allows you to send push messages in advance; the MDS will hold on to them and only start delivery after the timestamp passes. You could use this to push out birthday greetings ahead of time and deliver them on the proper days.

- ppg-notify-requested- to: If you wish to get delivery notifications, you must supply a URL to receive these messages.

<push-message> also can hold an optional child element, <quality-of-service>. This contains a single required attribute, delivery-method, which can have the following values.

- confirmed: Send application-level acknowledgements.

- unconfirmed: Send transport-level acknowledgements.

> **NOTE:** delivery-method also accepts the values preferconfirmed and notspecified, but it treats them the same as unconfirmed.

BES RIM Push Attributes

A BES RIM-formatted push can provide similar configuration, which it sets through HTTP headers instead of through XML. Table 12–1 shows the possible configuration settings.

Table 12–1. *BES RIM Push HTTP Headers*

Name	Required?	Description	Value	Example
X-RIM-Push-Deliver-After	No	Wait until specified time to push.	HTTP formatted date	Sat, 16 Apr 2011 14:00:00 GMT
X-RIM-Push-Deliver-Before	No	Do not push after specified time.	HTTP formatted date	Fri, 15 Apr 2011 12:30:00 GMT
X-Rim-Push-Description	No	Describes the push.	Any string	Monday sale alert to preferred subscribers.
X-Rim-Push-Id	Yes	Globally unique identifier for this push.	String	1234567890@example.com
X-Rim-Push-NotifyURL	Only if X-Rim-Push-Reliability set	Server to receive delivery notifications.	URL	http://www.example.com/pushAcks
X-Rim-Push-Reliability	No	Delivery acknowledgement desired	transport, application, or application -preferred	transport

NOTE: Very old BlackBerry devices do not support application-level acknowledgements. If your organization includes devices with software versions older than 3.8, using `application-preferred` will provide application-level acknowledgements for devices that support it and transport-level acknowledgements for older devices.

BIS Push Attributes

BIS pushes can set equivalent parameters through method calls on the `PushParameters` class, as shown in Table 12–2.

Table 12–2. *BIS Push Service PushParameters Options*

Method name	Type	Description
setApplicationId	String	Your application's ID.
setApplicationReliable	Boolean	Boolean.TRUE for application-level acks, Boolean.FALSE to disable application-level acks, null to use the default for the application.
setDeliverBeforeTimestamp	Date	The time after which this message should not be delivered.
setPushId	String	A unique identifier for this push, or null to have the SDK generate a random unique value.

NOTE: BIS pushes do not support a "deliver after" setting. You define other settings, like the notification URL and transport-level ack configuration, when you register with RIM; these apply globally to all pushes you send.

Finding Your Audience

In a traditional BES push, you can specify your recipients in several ways.

- One or more PIN numbers.

- One or more e-mail addresses.

- One or more BlackBerry user group names. These must already exist on the server; for example, you can push to all managers in the company or to all members of a particular project.

You should keep a few things in mind when deciding how to address your pushes.

- *Overhead*: Pushing to a large number of users will require a very large push request message, which may be more than the server can handle. If you run into this problem, you can switch to user group names or you can send multiple push requests that each have a smaller number of recipients.

- *Acknowledgement feedback*: You get a less granular view of delivery status if you request acknowledgement for a push to a user group instead of individual users.

A BES PAP push will append additional XML elements as children of the <push-message> element. Each recipient or group will be listed separately, as in the following examples:

```
<address address-value="WAPPUSH=name%40example.com%3A4242/TYPE=USER@rim.com"/>
<address address-value="WAPPUSH=2100000A%3A4242/TYPE=USER@rim.com"/>
<address address-value="WAPPUSH=%24Managers/TYPE=USER@rim.com"/>
```

Note that the above examples include URL-encode special characters, such as the @ in the e-mail address name@example.com, and the $ in the group name $Managers. The port number for the client application is specified after the %3A separator: in this case, it's 4242.

A BES RIM formatted push will append the recipients into the HTTP URL, as in the following example:

```
http://mds-url:8080/push?DESTINATION=name@example.com&DESTINATION=2100000A&↵
    DESTINATION=$Managers&PORT=4242&REQUESTURI=/
```

The BIS push system offers several different ways to address your push.

- *Broadcast*: Delivers the push to all users of your application.

- *Multicast*: Delivers to a set of specified users identified by PIN.

- *Targeted*: Delivers to one particular user identified by PIN.

As noted earlier, use caution when pushing to a large group of users if you have requested delivery acknowledgments, as this may put a strain on your server.

You specify BIS push recipients by passing a single address or a list of addresses to the PushParameters constructor. Alternately, you can call setAddresses() on an existing PushParameters object. The following snippet shows how to send content to a particular recipient:

```
private void sendContent(String appID, Content content)
{
    PushParameters params = new PushParameters(appID, "2100000A", content);
    // Finish sending push here.
}
```

Using "push_all" as the recipient address will instruct the gateway to send this content to all registered subscribers.

Infrastructure in Depth

As a developer, you will not have any direct control over what happens to your push request between your application server and the device. However, you should understand this aspect, as it critically affects your application.

BES MDS

In general, you shouldn't need to make any extra changes within the MDS for a BES push application. The organization already has all subscribers configured, and anyone belonging to the BES can receive your pushes.

You should check the following as part of your deployment within the BES:

- *Firewalls*: Make sure your application server can reach the MDS Content Server.

- *Configuration*: Check with your BES administrator about current settings for push expiration, reliability, and payload size. If your application requires changes, start negotiating them early.

- *Deployment:* If everyone in the organization will need to get your app, the BES administrator can deploy it. Otherwise, you'll need to distribute it yourself. In the latter case, you may want to maintain a record of current users; otherwise, your server may push to clients that do not have an application listening for the pushes.

BIS Push Proxy Gateway

Working with the BIS requires a bit more work. RIM doesn't want to let arbitrary companies spam users and overwhelm their push servers, so they have put in place a system to make sure that only authorized applications can send pushes and only registered users can receive them.

Earlier in this chapter, I discussed the process by which you register your application with RIM. This allows them to uniquely track your application's push usage and lets them identify all of your pushes as coming from a particular registered server. They will also evaluate your client application and verify that it meets certain criteria, such as the following:

- Notifies users that the application uses data services, which may result in charges from the wireless carrier.

- Provides an option to disable push functions.

- Lets users uninstall the application or change to another device.

Registering the Client

For both BES and BIS applications, after you have passed registration, you can distribute your app and send pushes from your application server. However, your users must also register before they will be able to receive pushes. Starting with device OS version 5.0, clients gain access to the push API located in the package `net.rim.blackberry.api.push`. Registering simply requires calling `PushApplicationRegistry.registerApplication()`. You pass this method a `PushApplicationDescriptor` that tells the platform which application to invoke for incoming pushes and what port number to use. The following sample shows how to register an application to receive pushes:

```
ApplicationDescriptor descriptor = ApplicationDescriptor.
    currentApplicationDescriptor();
ApplicationDescriptor pushDescriptor = new ApplicationDescriptor(descriptor,
    new String[]{"push"});
PushApplicationDescriptor registeredDescriptor = new
```

```
    PushApplicationDescriptor(4242, pushDescriptor);
PushApplicationRegistry.registerApplication(registeredDescriptor);
```

In this example, you retrieve the descriptor for the currently running application. You create a new descriptor that instructs the platform to launch this application with the extra argument "push"; you can use this argument later to distinguish the push launch case from other pushes. You then create a `PushApplicationDescriptor` that associates this launch point with incoming pushes on port 4242 and then registers. From now on, the platform will invoke you on incoming pushes.

> **Note** Only BlackBerry CLDC applications can accept arguments. If your push application is a MIDlet, the platform will invoke it for incoming pushes but it won't receive launch parameters.

You can also query the client to find its registration status. Do this by calling `PushApplicationRegistry.getStatus()`, which returns one of the statuses listed in `PushApplicationStatus`. Note that `STATUS_ACTIVE` indicates that your registration is active and you do not need to re-register; other statuses include unregistered, pending, and failed registrations.

You should note that client registration with the gateway or MDS is separate from registration with your application server. In most applications, you will want the user to authenticate with your server, perhaps by logging in with a username and password; you will then have sufficient information to uniquely identify the user and their PIN, which you can use to send them appropriate pushes. If your client just registers with the push application registry, your server will never hear about it.

Client in Depth

After all the work is done to set up your push server and register your clients, actually receiving a push is incredibly simple. You only need to implement an interface, listen for incoming pushes, and then respond to them.

Your main application, which can be an `Application` or a `MIDlet`, should implement `PushApplication`. This requires implementing two methods.

`onMessage()` provides the key entry point into your application. You will receive the push here in the form of a `PushInputStream`. This RIM-specific class extends `DataInputStream`, and so you can access convenience methods to directly read off primitive types or raw bytes of data. You can also choose whether to `accept()` or `decline()` the push; this may get reported back to the application server, depending on the acknowledgements requested. Most apps will always accept pushes, but you may choose to decline for your own reasons, such as if the device is busy with another task. `PushInputStream` also supports querying the sender and source of the push, but these should always be the same for your push application. The following example accepts a push, reads in a list of sales sent from the server, and prints them out:

```
public void onMessage(PushInputStream inputStream, StreamConnection conn)
{
    try
    {
        inputStream.accept();
        int count = inputStream.readInt();
        for (int i = 0; i < count; ++i)
        {
            String sale = inputStream.readUTF();
            System.out.println(sale);
        }
    }
    catch (IOException ioe)
    {
        System.err.println("Problems reading push: " + ioe.getMessage());
    }
}
```

Your application should also implement the onStatusChange() method. The platform will invoke this method when your application is registered, if the network fails, if the SIM card changes, and so on. Your application doesn't need to perform any action in response, but this information can provide critical debugging information. You may wish to show appropriate messages to the user based on the status events you receive here. You'll see an example of using this method to perform logging in the app sample at the end of this chapter.

App: Media Pusher

You've already expanded Media Grabber to support moving your captured content off the device. Now, let's look at the opposite behavior: taking incoming pushes of media. Because you already added support for displaying media in Chapter 3, you can hook in this capability with just a little added code.

A Simple Pushing Server

As you've seen, you have many options for pushing content: BES PAP, BES RIM, or BIS. For the sake of brevity, I'll illustrate sending pushes using BES RIM, which takes the least code and can be easily tested in the simulator; however, you can adapt this example to send other types of pushes as well.

Before you get started, locate the rimpublic.property MDS configuration file for your BlackBerry Java Plug-in component pack; this should be located in a directory like C:\eclipse\plugins\net.rim.ejde.componentpack6.0.0_6.0.0.29\components\MDS\conf ig. Append the following line to the bottom of this file:

```
push.application.reliable.ports=4242
```

This change tells your simulated MDS to support delivery acknowledgements to your chosen push port of 4242. Save and exit the file.

Next, you'll build a simple command-line Java utility, shown in Listing 12–1. This is a Java SE application that will run on the same machine as your simulator. It accepts two command-line arguments, a MIME type for the data you wish to send and a filename that contains the actual file. It then reads in that data and communicates with your simulated MDS to send a BES RIM push message. For simplicity's sake, you omit the acknowledgement; if you wanted one, you could provide a notify URL in the push request and open a server socket to listen for the acknowledgement.

Listing 12–1. *A Utility for Pushing Media Files*

```java
import java.io.*;
import java.net.*;

public class MediaPusher
{

    public static void main(String[] args)
    {
        if (args.length < 2)
        {
            System.err.println("Must provide a MIME type and a filename.");
            return;
        }
        String mime = args[0];
        String filename = args[1];
        String pushId = "MediaGrabber" + System.currentTimeMillis();
        try
        {
            // Read in media to send.
            FileInputStream fis = new FileInputStream(filename);
            int length = fis.available();
            byte[] data = new byte[length];
            fis.read(data);

            // Configure push
            URL url = new URL("http", "localhost", 8080,
                    "/push?DESTINATION=2100000A&PORT=4242&REQUESTURI=/");
            HttpURLConnection conn = (HttpURLConnection) url.openConnection();
            conn.setDoOutput(true);
            conn.setRequestMethod("POST");
            conn.setRequestProperty("X-RIM-PUSH-ID", pushId);

            // Send push payload
            OutputStream out = conn.getOutputStream();
            DataOutputStream dos = new DataOutputStream(out);
            dos.writeUTF(mime);
            dos.write(data, 0, length);
            dos.close();
            out.close();
            conn.getResponseCode();
            conn.disconnect();
        }
        catch (IOException e)
        {
            System.err.println(e);
        }
```

```
        }
}
```

Some configurations of the BlackBerry Java Plug-in for Eclipse will misbehave if you run this from an Eclipse project while debugging your BlackBerry project, so to be safe, you should save this file to another directory. You can compile it with the following command:

```
javac MediaPusher.java
```

Place one or more media files in the same directory. Because of limits on push data sizes, I recommend using small audio files such as .amr audio.

A Listening Client

Open MediaGrabber.java and change the declaration to also implement PushApplication. Add the methods in Listing 12–2 to the bottom of MediaGrabber.

Listing 12–2. *PushApplication Implementation for MediaGrabber*

```
public void onMessage(PushInputStream inputStream, StreamConnection conn)
{
    try
    {
        String mimeType = inputStream.readUTF();
        PlayingScreen screen = new PlayingScreen(inputStream, mimeType,
                "This just in!");
        pushScreen(screen);
        requestForeground();
    }
    catch (Exception e)
    {
        e.printStackTrace();
    }
}

public void onStatusChange(PushApplicationStatus status)
{
    System.out.println("New status " + status.getStatus() + ": "
            + status.getReason() + ": " + status.getError());
}
```

As you can see, the client application matches up with the server application you just wrote. You first read a Java string out of the stream that describes the MIME type of the content. You then take the rest of the data in the stream and pass it directly off to the PlayingScreen. It already can play any type of media based on the MIME and the media content, so no further work here is necessary. When an incoming push arrives, the platform will automatically create an instance of MediaGrabber, so you push the screen onto the stack for the user to see. UiApplication.requestForeground() will bring this application in front of whatever the user was doing before, allowing them to see the new media. When the user closes the PlayingScreen, the application will automatically exit.

You don't do much with onStatusChange() here, just log some information that may help debugging. You could check for particular status codes and respond to them if you wanted.

Finally, you need to make some changes to MediaGrabber.main(), which are shown in bold in Listing 12–3. First, you handle the new entry point for push invocation. All you do here is enter the event dispatcher; the platform will call onMessage() after calling main(), so you will let onMessage() do the rest of the work. You'll do the actual push registration at the same place where you register for listing in the contacts application menu; this code will only run once (each time the phone powers on), so you can always be sure that the registration is active.

Listing 12–3. *Entry Points for MediaGrabber*

```
public static void main(String[] args)
{
    MediaGrabber grabber = new MediaGrabber();
    if (args != null && args.length > 0 && args[0].equals("launch"))
    {
        if (grabber.checkPermissions())
        {
            grabber.pushScreen(new ChoicesScreen());
            grabber.enterEventDispatcher();
        }
    }
    if (args != null && args.length > 0 && args[0].equals("push"))
    {
        grabber.enterEventDispatcher();
    }
    else if (grabber.pending != null)
    {
        // Started via CHAPI. Show our UI.
        grabber.processRequest();
        grabber.requestForeground();
        grabber.enterEventDispatcher();
    }
    else
    {
        // Startup execution.
        try
        {
            RuntimeStore store = RuntimeStore.getRuntimeStore();
            long menuItemID = 0x65fad834642a5345L;
            if (store.get(menuItemID) == null)
            {
                CheckContactMenuItem item = new CheckContactMenuItem();
                ApplicationMenuItemRepository repo =
                    ApplicationMenuItemRepository.getInstance();
                repo.addMenuItem(ApplicationMenuItemRepository.
                    MENUITEM_ADDRESSBOOK_LIST, item);
                store.put(menuItemID, item);
                ApplicationDescriptor descriptor = ApplicationDescriptor
                    .currentApplicationDescriptor();
                ApplicationDescriptor pushDescriptor = new ApplicationDescriptor(
                    descriptor, new String[] { "push" });
                PushApplicationDescriptor registeredDescriptor = new
```

```
                    PushApplicationDescriptor(4242, pushDescriptor);
              PushApplicationRegistry
                    .registerApplication(registeredDescriptor);
          }
      }
      catch (Throwable t)
      {
          t.printStackTrace();
      }
    }
}
```

Testing Pushing

Because you are delivering pushes through the MDS, some extra steps are necessary to test on the simulator.

1. Modify your Eclipse debug configuration. Check the option for "Launch Mobile Data System Connection Service (MDS-CS) with simulator", as shown in Figure 12–5.

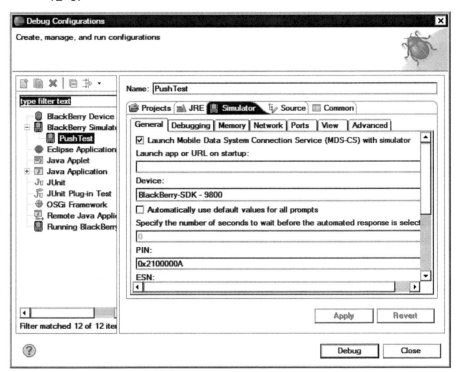

Figure 12–5. *Configuring Eclipse to launch the MDS-CS simulator*

2. Start debugging. Make sure that you see a separate DOS-style window appear that includes MDS-CS messages, as shown in Figure 12–6.

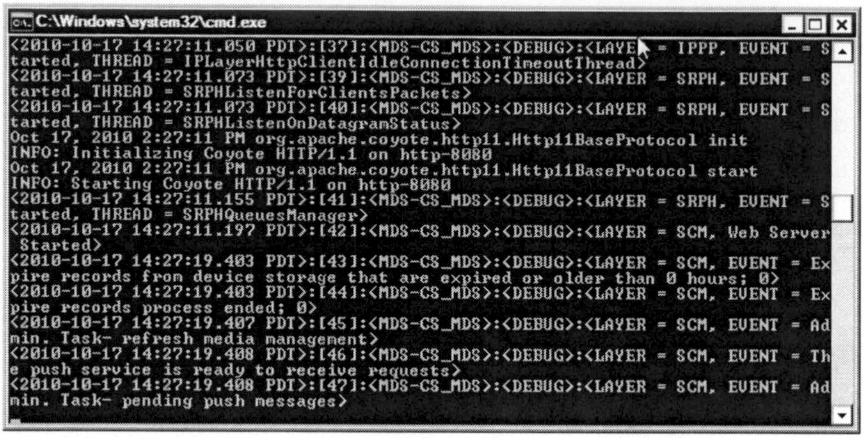

Figure 12–6. *The MDS-CS simulator running*

3. Once the simulator launches, open the browser and browse to a URL. You should see activity in the MDS-CS window; if not, exit the simulator, clean the simulator, and then try debugging again.

4. On your PC, run your MediaPusher utility, providing parameters for a media file, such as java `MediaPusher audio/amr clip.amr`.

5. MediaGrabber should pop open in the simulator, displaying the media playback screen, ready to play the media you just pushed. You can start the playback, after which the application will play and automatically close. You can repeat the pushes as many times as you like, providing different content with each push.

By observing the output in the MDS-CS window, you can see how push architecture helps minimize network usage. Absolutely nothing will happen while your application is idle, and a burst of activity will occur once you push new media. In contrast, a polling app would regularly access the network.

If you set breakpoints in your main() and onMessage() methods, you can observe how the platform creates your application when it receives a push and lets you exit when done. Again, this helps minimize resource utilization: since your app doesn't need to constantly run and listen on a socket, the device will have more memory and CPU cycles free for running other applications.

As you've seen, push applications require a great deal of advance work, but the actual client application only needs minimal modifications to accept pushes. You can try some other changes to further enhance the MediaGrabber push experience.

- Add support for pushing media URLs. This will allow you to push larger content than a single push can carry. PlayerScreen already supports playing from a URL, so you will just need to modify the push message to describe whether it holds binary data or a URL.

- Create a BES PAP push that has the same payload as the BES RIM push.

- Request delivery acknowledgements, and keep track of when each push was delivered.

Even though push does not require many changes to your client code, it can have a drastic impact on the overall user experience. Keep experimenting with the possibilities and see what else you can add.

Excelsior

Push technology can radically alter the feel and purpose of an application. It takes the user out of the driver's seat and lets you steer for a while. This is a very powerful position, and many users will appreciate the things you can show them through push.

BES and BIS push applications differ from one another. BIS push applications ultimately focus on the consumer, and you should keep their wishes in mind. BIS push apps must communicate what they are doing and give consumers the option to disable push features. In contrast, BES push applications ultimately serve the purposes of the business; in many cases, they should constantly remain active, not necessarily informing the user about what they are doing. When moving between the BIS and the BES worlds, keep these different standards in mind.

Depending on your role, you may have responsibility for only the client piece of a push application, or you may need to design the entire end-to-end system. The latter certainly requires the most work, but also gives you the most insight into how the system works and allows you to test, debug, and make modifications at both ends. If you only need to write the client piece, you should still keep the overall push system design in mind, as it will help you determine where errors occur.

Push has served critical needs of BlackBerry users since the beginning. With the latest push API and services, more developers than ever before can take advantage of it. In the next chapter, you'll look at other sets of APIs recently released by RIM that help you create better-looking applications that will further entice your users.

Chapter 13

BlackBerry 6 UI

Throughout this book, I have primarily focused on the underlying APIs and features of BlackBerry devices, sticking to simple user interfaces that just exercise the features you're using. In commercial applications, though, user interfaces matter critically. No matter how elegant your software, if the app looks horrible, people will not want to use it.

In this chapter, you will look at some of the latest user interface tools to arrive for BlackBerry. You will learn how to give feedback to users via progress indicators, present complex overlapping elements via a new type of field manager, attractively organize and present large sets of data, and let users easily browse for content. You'll learn how to use these components, and, more importantly, when to include each one. Not every app will benefit from all of these, but all apps should use the best tools available.

Progress Indicators

Any decently interesting app will eventually make users wait. It may need to pause while it downloads data over the network or reads in resources from a file or solves a complex math equation. One of the best known principles of interaction design is that you can reduce perceived latency by simply providing visual feedback to the user. If the user presses a button and nothing happens within one second, they will perceive the app as broken and will start pressing other buttons or quit. On the other hand, if you acknowledge the press and indicate that you are working on the request, they will gladly wait for an extended period of time.

In the past, developers have generally cobbled together their own custom progress indicators. This satisfied users, but it required a great deal of duplicated effort between developers. It also led to visual fragmentation for users' BlackBerry experiences. Starting with version 6.0 of the BlackBerry OS, developers can use the Activity and Progress Indicator UI, defined in package `net.rim.device.api.ui.component.progressindicator`, to create consistent and reusable progress components.

Progress Indicator Design

The progress indicator API follows the Model-View-Controller design pattern. It contains the components discussed in the following sections.

AbstractProgressIndicatorModel

This class represents the underlying data behind the progress activity: that is, the thing that is not yet done. Depending on your specific case, this might be a file downloading from the network, a scan for an available Wi-Fi access point, or some other ongoing activity. Apps will primarily use the following methods:

- isComplete() is the method subclasses must override in order to indicate whether their activity has finished.

- cancel() stops the underlying progress operation and notifies associated UI to cease showing progress.

- resume() picks up from where a cancel() left off.

- setNonProgrammaticValue() directly sets a new value of the underlying operation. This typically indicates a value set by the user as opposed to by your program; for example, if they choose to skip through part of an operation.

The class also offers methods to add, set, and get the classes I will discuss below.

AbstractProgressIndicatorView

This specialized Manager class presents progress in the user interface. Subclasses can describe exactly how to display progress; this class defines the hooks that connect with the model and the controller so the components communicate smoothly. It also offers some convenient methods for common progress-related designs, described below:

- cancelled() stops the progress animation.

- resumed() continues the progress animation.

- setLabel() provides a textual description of the progress, such as "Downloading..." or "Processing..."

If you wish to allow users to interact with your progress animation, you can override key- and click-related methods either in this class or in AbstractProgressIndicatorController. As with the model, the view has methods for assigning and retrieving companion classes.

> **CAUTION:** Pay attention to the order in which you configure your `AbstractProgress IndicatorView` and its subclasses, as certain operations might undo earlier actions. For example, you might assume that you could call `setModel()` and `setLabel()` in any order, but setting the model will reset other changes you have made. Therefore, you should always set the model on the view prior to modifying the view.

AbstractProgressIndicatorController

The controller accepts input from the user to provide custom handling. In general, most progress operations are purely informative and do not support interaction; as such, the abstract controller does not do anything by default. If you wish to add special behavior, such as displaying more verbose feedback if the user clicks the progress animation, you can override the controller to define your specialized actions. The controller has the same user interface methods that are defined in `Field`, including `keyDown()`, `navigationClick()`, and `touchEvent()`.

ProgressIndicatorListener

The listener interface lets other components observe changes in the progress of the operation. Listeners will learn when the underlying value changes, as well as when progress is `cancelled()` or `resumed()`. You add listeners to the model, after which they will automatically receive their notifications.

Adjustment

This class, defined in the `net.rim.device.api.ui` package, lets you adjust underlying data values to fit a desired set of values. For example, you can use `Adjustment` to restrict values to a particular range, such as treating negative values as 0 and values over 100 as 100. Adjustments support the following properties, which you can set, get, and increment up or down:

- *Step size*: The smallest granularity that you wish to support in your user interface. For example, you may only want to show 5% increments and ignore interim values.

- *Page size*: A larger chunk of movement. This is rarely used in progress indicators.

- *Upper*: The maximum allowable value.

- *Lower*: The minimum allowable value.

Adjustments only apply to progress animations that represent a range of progress, not those whose progress is indeterminate. You can add `Adjustment` objects to your model, after which they will apply to future value changes.

Activity Indicator

Most progress indicators fall into one of two categories: determinate or indeterminate. Determinate progress can be measured, as in the number of bytes downloaded for a file of known length. Indeterminate progress represents a task of unknown duration, such as waiting for a server response. RIM has provided a specialization of their abstract progress classes that you can use to show that some activity is taking place.

ActivityIndicatorModel

Because an activity has no known duration, the model class is quite simple. It implements the isComplete() method to report whether the activity has finished. Activities do not have underlying values, so you cannot associate Adjustment objects with them.

ActivityImageField

This class, associated with the view, shows indication of an ongoing activity with a Field. Examples include hourglasses, stopwatches, and spinning circles. The field internally holds a bitmap that contains multiple frames of an animation; ActivityImageField will handle slicing the image into multiple frames and animating them. You create an ActivityImageField by providing a bitmap and specifying the number of frames and the Field style; you can also specify whether the animation should loop and how quickly to display each frame. You can invoke the following methods to further control your ActivityImageField:

- setAnimate(): Start or stop the animation.

- setCurrentFrameIndex(): Advance to a specified animation frame.

ActivityIndicatorView

This view represents an ongoing indeterminate activity. It may or may not contain an ActivityImageField; if you like, you may choose just to display text or some static image to describe the activity, although animations are certainly better. In addition to the methods from AbstractProgressIndicatorView, you can invoke the following options:

- createActivityImageField(): A convenience method that automatically creates and initializes an ActivityImageField and inserts it into this view.

- getAnimation(): Returns the current ActivityImageField.

ActivityIndicatorController

This class does nothing by default. As before, you can override this class if you wish to allow users to interact with your activity indicator.

An Example

Listing 13–1 shows how to create a simple activity indicator and add it to a Screen.

Listing 13–1. *Building an Activity Indicator*

```
ActivityIndicatorView view = new ActivityIndicatorView(FIELD_HCENTER,
        new HorizontalFieldManager());
Bitmap bitmap = Bitmap.getBitmapResource("waiting.png");
view.createActivityImageField(bitmap, 12, 0);
ActivityImageField animation = view.getAnimation();
animation.setPadding(0, 5, 0, 0);
view.setLabel("Please wait...");
add(view);
```

You can see the results in Figure 13–1. Because you want to show both the busy indicator and a label on the same line, you create a HorizontalFieldManager that will manage your ActivityIndicatorView; without specifying this, the label and the animation would lay out vertically instead. The file waiting.png contains twelve frames, which you specify when creating the image field. After creating it, you retrieve the ActivityImageField so you can manipulate it. Here, you just add a bit of padding to clearly separate the label from the indicator.

Figure 13–1. *A spinning activity indicator*

Progress Indicator

A non-abstract progress indicator represents, well, progress: steady advancement towards a goal. You'll commonly use progress indicators for tasks whose duration you can measure, like loading data from file resources. However, you can also use progress indicators for any sort of measurement, including progress through a game or a song. Once again, RIM provides concrete MVC implementations to streamline the process of showing progress.

ProgressIndicatorModel

This class describes the current status of the operation and the total amount of work to do, and it allows you to advance that progress. Use the following methods to control progress:

- setValue() provides an integer description of the quantity of work complete; for example, if you have downloaded 400 of 1200 files, you can set 400 here.

- setValueMax() describes the total amount of work to do; in the above example, you would set a max of 1200.

- setValueMin() describes the initial amount of work. This defaults to 0, but in certain cases, it may be simpler to describe a non-zero value, such as if you need to process dates in the years from 1970 through 2020.

- step() advances by one step, as defined in an associated Adjustment.

- page() advances by one page, as defined in an associated Adjustment. Pages should encompass multiple steps.

- initialize() and reset() allow you to define the current value, the max and min values, and optionally a step and page size.

- isComplete() reports whether the task has finished; typically this equates to having reached the maximum value, although in some cases you may still need to do some final processing.

ProgressBarField

Like ActivityImageField, this is a Field that displays a graphic showing ongoing activity. Unlike ActivityImageField, though, a ProgressBarField is represented as a bar that grows from left to right; this convention is familiar to all phone and computer users. You can specify the following styles when creating the object:

- `NO_TEXT` displays the bar with no characters.

- `CURRENT_WITH_MAX` displays text with the associated model's current progress and maximum value; for example, if you have downloaded 300 of 1200 bytes, this will display as "300/1200".

- `PERCENT` shows text with the progress as a percentage; in the above example, this would display as "25%".

Default: If you do not select one of the above styles, the current value will display without the maximum; in your example, this would be "300".

For any style other than `NO_TEXT`, you can describe where the text should display via the following styles:

- `PROGRESS_TEXT_LEADING`: Left-align text within the bar.

- `PROGRESS_TEXT_HCENTER`: Horizontally align text in the center of the bar. This also happens if you do not specify one of the other styles.

- `PROGRESS_TEXT_TRAILING`: Right-align text within the bar.

You create a `ProgressBarField` by providing the style along with a min/max range of values and an initial value. Set the progress by calling `updateValue()`; `ProgressBarField` will internally manage updating the bar graphic and the displayed text. If you wish to reuse the progress bar later, you can call `changeConfiguration()` with new values for maximum, minimum, and initial values.

ProgressIndicatorView

A `ProgressIndicatorView` displays the amount of progress to the user. This is a composite `Field` that uses an associated `Manager` to display its components.

In addition to the methods from `AbstractProgressIndicatorView`, this class adds convenience methods for creating and retrieving the progress bar through the methods `createProgressBar()` and `getProgressBar()`. `createProgressBar()` accepts the style flags described above and will automatically insert the bar into this view.

ProgressIndicatorController

As with the activity indicator's controller, by default the progress indicator controller does nothing. You can override it if you wish to specify special user interaction behavior.

An Example

Let's build a more complex progress bar. Listing 13–1 showed how you could simply display an indicator without worrying about the model or controller. Listing 13–2 shows a progress indicator where you do retain the model and use it to update your view. This example shows the device's progress as it downloads a large text file.

Listing 13–2. *Using a Progress Indicator to Display Download Status*

```
ProgressIndicatorView progress = new ProgressIndicatorView(0);
final ProgressIndicatorModel model = new ProgressIndicatorModel(0, 1, 0);
progress.setModel(model);
progress.createLabel("Downloading...", Field.FIELD_HCENTER);
progress.createProgressBar(ProgressBarField.PROGRESS_TEXT_TRAILING
        | ProgressBarField.PERCENT);
add(progress);
(new Thread()
{
    public void run()
    {
        HttpConnection conn = null;
        InputStream is = null;
        try
        {
            conn = (HttpConnection) (new ConnectionFactory())
                    .getConnection(
                            "http://www.gutenberg.org/cache/epub/4300/pg4300.txt")
                    .getConnection();
            is = conn.openInputStream();
            long total = conn.getLength();
            model.setValueMax((int) (total));
            long read = 0;
            long totalRead = 0;
            do
            {
                model.setValue((int) (totalRead));
                read = is.skip(1024);
                totalRead += read;
            } while (read > 0);
        }
        catch (Exception e)
        {
            e.printStackTrace();
        }
        finally
        {
            try
            {
                if (is != null)
                    is.close();
                if (conn != null)
                    conn.close();
            }
            catch (Exception e)
            {
            }
        }
    }
}).start();
```

As you can see, actually creating the progress indicator takes only a few lines of code. When you first create the model, you don't yet know how many bytes are in the file to download, so you set a current value of 0 and a maximum of 1 so 0% will initially display in the bar. You then create the label and the progress bar; because the view adds them in the order you call these methods, the label will display on top of the bar. You have now finished initializing the view. You made the model `final` so you could access it in the anonymous inner class for downloading; you could also have stored it in an instance variable. The anonymous thread grabs the complete text of Ulysses from Project Gutenberg in one-kilobyte chunks. You cast the `long` file size to the `int` a model expects; this should work fine in practice, but if you anticipated transferring files larger than 2GB, you could scale the maximum and current values down by some factor to remain in the `int` range. As you update the model, the view learns of the change and prompts the progress bar to redraw its image and text, as shown in Figure 13–2.

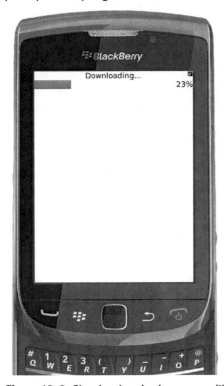

Figure 13–2. *Showing download progress with a progress indicator*

You may notice one other advantage of the MVC architecture shown here. Because the model class isn't a `Field`, you can safely update it from a non-UI thread. Internally, the progress indicator classes will prompt the view to redraw on the main UI thread. This saves you from the overhead of passing control between two threads to do work and to update the screen.

Overlapping Fields

Historically, BlackBerry has made it surprisingly difficult to perform a seemingly simple task: to draw one thing over two other things. All primitive UI toolkits allow designers to do this, but it has never fit in well with the RIM CLDC UI design. All `Field` objects must be contained within a `Manager`, and each `Manager` is responsible for laying out its children within its own area. `Manager`s tend to place their children based on each `Field` object's extent, spacing and wrapping them when necessary. Because the same `Field` can't belong to multiple `Manager` objects, you have not been able to create two fields that overlap one another.

Overall, this decision has proved beneficial; the constraints of the `Field`/`Manager` system have generally encouraged developers to design nicely compartmentalized, clean-looking user interfaces. Still, in some instances you might want to break these design rules. Such cases have grown more common since RIM introduced touch-screen phones; users often want to select one element and drag it around the entire screen, even if they cannot drop that object in certain locations.

And so, starting with OS version 6, RIM added a new type of manager: the `AbsoluteFieldManager`. This counters current mobile SDK trends, as other mobile toolkits have increasingly discouraged developers from using just this type of layout. Still, with cautious use, it can be a valuable resource; just make it your last choice instead of your first one, as the `AbsoluteFieldManager` does a much poorer job of scaling to other screen sizes and orientations.

Usage

As with all other `Manager` classes, you can use `AbsoluteFieldManager` as-is or you can override it for more specialized behavior. Use the following methods to control the default implementation:

- `add()`: This key method lets you add a `Field` at the specified (x, y) coordinate. This will place the newly added `Field` on top of all items that you previously added. Note that the coordinates are relative to this `AbsoluteFieldManager`'s position, not coordinates on the screen.
- `setPosChild()`: Move a previously added `Field` to a new location.

If you choose to override this class, you may wish to add support for controlling the Z-order of overlapping children.

Example

You can use the `AbsoluteFieldManager` with little code. Listing 13–3 shows how you can create multiple types of `Field` (in this case, two `BitmapField` objects and one `EditField`) and specify their location within the manager.

Listing 13–3. *Inserting Field Objects at Absolute Coordinates*

```
AbsoluteFieldManager absolute = new AbsoluteFieldManager();
BitmapField lake = new BitmapField(Bitmap.getBitmapResource("CathedralLake.jpg"));
BitmapField peak = new BitmapField(Bitmap.getBitmapResource("TuolumnePeak.jpg"));
EditField title = new EditField();
absolute.add(lake, 50, 50);
```

```
absolute.add(peak, 220, 200);
absolute.add(title, 200, 190);
add(absolute);
```

You can see the results in Figure 13–3. Each item you added displays on top of the one below. This layout looks unusual, and for good reason: BlackBerry applications very rarely display fields on top of one another. It behaves as you would expect, though, and the `EditText` control even draws with nice transparency on top of the images.

Figure 13–3. *Overlapping items on the same screen*

Tables and Lists

BlackBerry 6 added another new UI package called `net.rim.device.api.ui.component.table` that provides a powerful collection of classes for generating attractive and well-integrated lists and tables. Because business applications are so popular on BlackBerry devices, these should see a wide adoption.

People are very familiar and comfortable with reading lists and tables to collect information; you have encountered many examples of both throughout this book. You should consider using lists when you wish to group together a set of related ideas. Tables work better for more complex data presentations and when you wish to describe multiple aspects of a group of ideas. From a technical perspective, you can treat a list as a one-dimensional table that has multiple rows but only one column.

Table Design

As with the progress indicator, the Table UI explicitly follows the MVC design pattern. People who have built web pages with tables in HTML will recognize the usefulness of this pattern. Good web design seeks to separate information's structure (represented in HTML) from its presentation (defined in CSS). Similarly, RIM allows you to define a table's structure by using the model and its presentation by configuring the view. This decouples your data from the rendering and allows you to switch around the user interface without needing to touch the underling data.

Models

RIM provides multiple model classes that can hold different organizations of data. You can also choose to extend one of the abstract classes if you wish to define your own structured data. Figure 13–4 shows the hierarchy of model classes; abstract classes are in italics and concrete classes are in a regular style.

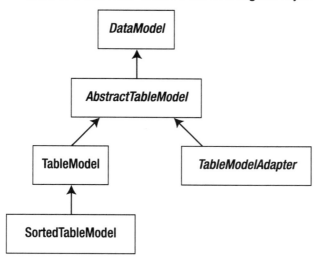

Figure 13–4. *Data models for lists and tables*

DataModel

The most generic type of model, a DataModel simply allows you to register, unregister, and notify DataModelListener objects. These will learn of changes to the model, which may prompt them to redraw UI components or perform other actions. The modelReset() method will notify all listeners about a significant change in the model.

AbstractTableModel

This class drastically extends its parent to provide a description of a structured table. You can add, insert, get, and remove rows and columns. Use columns to describe additional aspects of data; for an employee table, your columns may include ID numbers, birthdays, anniversaries, and salaries. Use rows to describe entities; in an employee table, each employee should receive her own row.

Each add and insert method takes an object, which goes into in the corresponding row or column. If the other dimension has been defined, then you will need to provide an array with that number of elements. For example, if you have added four columns to the table, then when you add a row, you must provide an array of four objects.

> **NOTE:** Unlike a printed table, there is no header in an AbstractTableModel. In other words, the first row should describe the first data entry, not the names of each column.

Once you have defined the dimensions of a table by adding or inserting rows and columns, you can update individual items within that table by calling setElement(). This will replace the previously added member.

Each of the mutator methods delegates to an implementing method; for example, addRow() will call doAddRow(). Subclasses of AbstractTableModel will override the corresponding do methods for the table mutators and define how to store the added data. Classes may keep their table data in memory or persist it in a database or proprietary file format. This gives a great deal of flexibility, which allows developers to support both very small and very large tables.

TableModelAdapter

This class provides default implementations for almost all of the abstract methods defined in AbstractTableModel. You still must override getNumberOfColumns() and getNumberOfRows(). By extending this class instead of AbstractTableModel, you can more quickly create your own data store for a table; in practice, this is useful if you do not anticipate needing to support all of the operations that a table can theoretically handle. For example, if you will never remove data from a table, you do not need to implement those methods.

TableModel

This is the first concrete model class in the package, and it provides a sensible default in-memory storage of table cells. It has two constructors, one for creating an empty table and another that takes a two-dimensional array of objects for initialization. It does not add any new methods but does provide implementations for all the abstract methods defined in AbstractTableModel.

SortedTableModel

This useful model allows you to sort all the data in a table based on a sorting column and a Comparator you define. For example, you could sort a list of employees by their salary.

The SortedTableModel constructor takes two additional parameters, a Comparator instance and an int for the column to sort. You can define your own Comparator for comparing custom data types or providing arbitrary sorting logic. You can also use StringComparator.getInstance() to retrieve a Comparator that sorts alphabetically, either case-sensitive or case-insensitive; to do a reverse alphabetical sort, wrap the StringComparator in an InvertedOrderComparator.

SortedTableModel automatically sorts rows as you insert them, based on the criteria you defined; you do not need to call a method to perform the sort. Unfortunately, the class does not support changing sort criteria, so if you wish to re-order a table by other criteria, you must rebuild a new SortedTableModel.

View Supporters

The Table API does not include many view classes, but it does have a collection of helper classes that assist in defining the look of a particular table. Properties describe how to present rows and columns, while templates describe the layout of a complete table.

TemplateColumnProperties

This class describes how a particular column should look. You define the width available to the column. By default, this class has the style PIXEL_WIDTH, meaning that it interprets the width as a number of pixels; providing a width of 40 means that it will display 40 pixels wide. You can specify the alternative style called PERCENT_WIDTH that interprets the width as a percentage of the entire screen; if you specify 40, then this column would display with 128 pixels on a Curve device and 192 pixels on a landscape-mode Storm.

TemplateRowProperties

This class exactly mirrors TemplateColumnProperties, but it applies to a row's height instead of a column's width.

RegionStyles

A region in a table can span an area that encompasses multiple rows and columns. Similarly to the properties classes, RegionStyles lets you describe the visual properties of a section of the table, but you have many more options at your disposal, including the following:

- *Font*: The text to use for cells within this region; you might use bold, italic, underlined, etc.

- *Border*: Box drawn around the edges of the region. You can style this to be solid, dotted, etc.

- *Margin*: Extra spacing outside the border.

- *Padding*: Extra spacing inside the border.

- *Horizontal and vertical alignment*: RegionStyles accepts the standard choices of top, middle, bottom, left, center, and right. By default, it will align to the top left.

If you choose not to specify region style properties, they will default to the settings used by the current theme.

Regions group together multiple table cells into logical collections. For example, a logical table row may internally contain multiple rows and columns, such as two vertical cells for an image and four horizontal cells for a long block of text. Simple tables will usually have one region per column, but you can experiment with more elaborate layouts by defining other regions.

DataTemplate

A DataTemplate works with a DataView to describe how rows and columns in a table are presented. It defines several useful operations.

You can set a TemplateColumnProperties for each column and a TemplateRowProperties for each row in the table. You will often want to customize column widths so they are appropriate for the data to display in those cells; for example, a column that displays names should be wider than a column that displays birthdays.

You can call useFixedHeight() to define whether rows should grow and shrink based on the data inside. A very long name like "Christopher Charles Horatio Xavier King III, Esq." will not fit on a single line. If rows have a fixed height, long strings like this will be truncated; if heights are not fixed, a row's height can automatically expand to hold the entire wrapped string.

createRegion() allows you to define a RegionStyles object that will apply over a provided range of cells. You can choose to omit the RegionStyles; this will return the number of the new region you have created, which you can use later when manipulating the view.

The abstract method getField() will return an array of Field objects; each Field is a single cell in a row. Implementing classes will define exactly what type of Field to use.

SimpleListDataTemplate

This class gives a basic, concrete implementation of DataTemplate that you can use when building a list. A list is a one-dimensional table, so each cell is a LabelField that fill the table's width. This template only accepts String objects from the associated model, tossing any other class types.

RichListDataTemplate

Unlike the simple list, a rich list can include Bitmap objects as well, which will display as images in their cells. This template also accepts Field objects in the model; these will be presented as-is in their own cells.

SimpleList

A SimpleList provides a convenient way to insert lists of text into your app. It internally handles the MVC connections, so you do not need to explicitly create any other list objects. It uses a SimpleListDataTemplate to convert each String object that you provide into a list entry.

When you create a SimpleList, you provide a Manager. From then on, the SimpleList will directly insert or remove list rows from that Manager. You can add() a new String, optionally specifying the index into the list where it should be inserted; remove() with an index to take a row out; get() to look up the String at an index; or set() to replace an indexed row with a new String. The SimpleList supports focus and allows the user to scroll through the list; call getFocusRow() to find which item currently has the highlight. Finally, if you wish to allow the user to take action on a list row, call setCommand() to specify what should happen when they click on an item.

RichList

RichList behaves similarly to SimpleList, but since it internally uses RichListDataTemplate, you can also provide Bitmap objects. The RichList is rather tightly specified; each row accepts a single optional Bitmap image that will display on the top left; a collection of String objects that will be vertically stacked in the top right; and a collection of String objects that will be vertically stacked at the bottom. In other words, even though it is a list, each row in the list will look a bit like a table. Because of this strong structure, most developers will choose to create their own custom list or table rather than reuse RichList.

Views

The view hierarchy for tables is much simpler than the model hierarchy. There's a single abstract class that you can override to create a customized view and a single concrete class that provides a good default implementation.

CAUTION: You currently can't add the table view classes into scrolling managers. Specify Manager.NO_VERTICAL_SCROLL on your screen or add the view into another Manager that can't scroll.

DataView

This class defines a Manager capable of displaying a structured collection of data. It internally uses a DataModel, which you can provide in the constructor or in a mutator. You can also associate a DataTemplate and a TableController.

TableView

A TableView displays a table's data to the user. You can choose to override this to provide a custom look for the view, but the default implementation should work well for most developers, and it provides some useful hooks for customization. This class adds the following methods:

- addDockedHeader(): This allows you to attach a Field to the table; the TableView will ensure that it always remains visible on the top of the rows below. You will often use this to provide the names for your table columns; that way, even if a user scrolls through hundreds of rows, they will be able to see the column names without scrolling back up. You may also choose to use the header to give a name for the table or to provide branding information.

- setDataTemplateFocus(): You provide a background, which you can obtain from the BackgroundFactory. The view will display this background behind the currently focused row. For example, your table might usually have white backgrounds but draw a darker gray to show that a particular row is highlighted. Even if table rows do not accept input, you still want to show focus so the user can see where they are in a table and how to scroll longer tables up or down.

- getDataTemplateFocus() returns the previously-set focus background.

- getRowNumberWithFocus() describes how far into the table the user has gone.

- getRegionNumberWithFocus() indicates which of the regions, which you previously defined in a DataTemplate, has focus.

> **CAUTION:** TableView requires you to provide a DataTemplate with TemplateColumn Properties and TemplateRowProperties; it can't create a default, since it doesn't know how to interpret the DataModel. If you fail to supply a required object, you will get a NullPointerException at runtime.

Controllers

Table controllers allow you to observe and respond to user input when navigating a table.

DataController

This generic type of controller defines the common user interaction methods found in Field, such as keyChar(), touchEvent(), and navigationClick(). It has a special version of moveFocus() that describes the direction and amount of movement to advance. This class also has its own makeMenu() method that creates menus for this table.

TableController

A TableController adds some extra methods that you may want to take advantage of when building an interactive table. This class is concrete, so you can use it as-is or selectively extend it.

- setFocusPolicy() specifies how the focus moves as the user scrolls through a table. FIELD_FOCUS will focus individual cells and allows horizontal as well as vertical scrolling. ROW_FOCUS will highlight individual records, while REGION_FOCUS gives focus to groups of cells that you defined earlier in the table model.

- moveFocus() moves to a specific x and y coordinate, along with status flags for the trackwheel and time information.

- navigationMovement() resembles moveFocus() but provides x and y values relative to the currently focused position.

- setCommand() allows you to provide a CommandHandler to execute when the user makes a selection from the table.

If you only intend the user to view tables, you can usually omit providing a controller. However, if you want to let them take actions on a table, like updating cell values or follow a link to more information, controllers offer the cleanest way to provide that ability.

Examples

Let's start with a simple use of a list. Listing 13–4 shows how you can take advantage of the Table API without explicitly creating models, views, or controllers.

Listing 13–4. *Adding a Simple List to the Screen*

```
VerticalFieldManager manager = new VerticalFieldManager();
SimpleList list = new SimpleList(manager);
list.add("Eggs");
list.add("Flour");
list.add("Sugar");
list.add("Butter");
add(new LabelField("Shopping List"));
add(manager);
```

This basic shopping list will display as shown in Figure 13–5. It already allows users to scroll through and highlight individual items, which will be perfectly sufficient for many apps.

Figure 13–5. *A simple list*

Next, let's consider a more complex example: building a table that will display all of your contacts and even dial the contact you select. To get started, you will create a custom `DataTemplate`, as shown in Listing 13–5.

Listing 13–5. *A Template for Showing Contact Names and Phone Numbers*

```
private class PhoneDataTemplate extends DataTemplate
{
    public PhoneDataTemplate(TableView view)
    {
        super(view, 1, 3);
    }

    public Field[] getDataFields(int modelRowIndex)
    {
        Object[] data = (Object[])((TableModel)getView().getModel()).
            getRow(modelRowIndex);
        Field[] fields = new Field[3];
        fields[0] = new LabelField(data[0], DrawStyle.ELLIPSIS);
        fields[1] = new LabelField(data[1], DrawStyle.ELLIPSIS);
        fields[2] = new LabelField(data[2], DrawStyle.ELLIPSIS);
        return fields;
    }
}
```

Each entry will consist of a single row that contains three column fields: one each for the contact's first name, last name, and phone number. Whenever the system prompts you for the fields to display, you retrieve the model from your view and then create LabelField objects to hold each component. Since some names and numbers may be longer than the screen allows, you specify that you wish to truncate long labels with ellipses.

Next, you define the command to execute when the user clicks on a contact. Listing 13–6 shows how you retrieve the selected item from the TableView, then once again index into the model to find your data. Because you built the model yourself, you know the exact type of each object and the index that will hold the number. Once you get the number, you invoke the native BlackBerry dialer app.

Listing 13–6. *Calling the Chosen Contact from the Table*

```
private class CallCommand extends CommandHandler
{
    public void execute(ReadOnlyCommandMetadata metadata, Object context)
    {
        TableView view = (TableView)context;
        int focused = view.getRowNumberWithFocus();
        if (focused >= 0)
        {
            String number = (String)((Object[])
                    ((TableModel)view.getModel()).getRow(focused))[2];
            if (number != null && number.length() > 0)
            {
                PhoneArguments args =
                    new PhoneArguments(PhoneArguments.ARG_CALL, number);
                Invoke.invokeApplication(Invoke.APP_TYPE_PHONE, args);
            }
        }
    }
}
```

With those custom classes in place, you can build the actual table. You will create the table MVC objects and then populate the model with your data, as shown in Listing 13–7.

Listing 13–7. *Creating and Initializing a Table*

```
TableModel model = new TableModel();
TableView view = new TableView(model);
PhoneDataTemplate template = new PhoneDataTemplate(view);
template.createRegion(new XYRect(0, 0, 1, 1));
template.createRegion(new XYRect(1, 0, 1, 1));
template.createRegion(new XYRect(2, 0, 1, 1));
template.setColumnProperties(0, new TemplateColumnProperties(30,
        TemplateColumnProperties.PERCENTAGE_WIDTH));
template.setColumnProperties(1, new TemplateColumnProperties(30,
        TemplateColumnProperties.PERCENTAGE_WIDTH));
template.setColumnProperties(2, new TemplateColumnProperties(40,
        TemplateColumnProperties.PERCENTAGE_WIDTH));
template.setRowProperties(0, new TemplateRowProperties(20));
template.useFixedHeight(true);
view.setDataTemplate(template);
TableController controller = new TableController(model, view);
controller.setFocusPolicy(TableController.ROW_FOCUS);
view.setController(controller);
controller.setCommand(new CallCommand(), null, view);
add(new LabelField("Who you gonna call?"));
add(view);

PIM pim = PIM.getInstance();
ContactList list = (ContactList)pim.openPIMList(PIM.CONTACT_LIST,
        PIM.READ_ONLY);
Enumeration contacts = list.items();
String[] rowHolder = new String[3];
while (contacts.hasMoreElements())
{
    try
    {
        Contact person = (Contact)contacts.nextElement();
        String[] names = person.getStringArray(Contact.NAME, 0);
        String number = person.getString(Contact.TEL, 0);
        rowHolder[0] = names[Contact.NAME_GIVEN];
        rowHolder[1] = names[Contact.NAME_FAMILY];
        rowHolder[2] = number;
        model.addRow(new Object[] {names[Contact.NAME_GIVEN],
                names[Contact.NAME_FAMILY], number});
    }
    catch (Exception e) {
        e.printStackTrace();
    }
}
```

You define three regions, each covering a single column, and describe how to present them. First and last names both get 30% of the available width, while the number gets the remaining 40%. Each row is 20 pixels tall and is not allowed to grow taller. You tell the controller to give focus to whole rows; if you displayed multiple numbers for each contact, you might prefer to give field focus and let users select either field, but with a single number it's a better user experience to just select vertically. After associating all the objects with one another, you insert the TableView into the screen.

The contacts operations should look familiar from the Personal Information chapter. You scan through all entries in the user's address book, and pull out each one's names and first number listed. If any items are missing, an exception will be thrown and you'll continue to the next Contact. You add each contact as a new row in the model.

When you run this example, you'll see a screen similar to Figure 13–6. As with the SimpleList example, movement within the table automatically works as expected: you can scroll through using the trackwheel or click on touch-enabled devices. After you make a selection, the phone will place a call on the contact you selected.

Figure 13–6. *A custom table*

With this framework in place, you can easily make additional customizations: change the colors, add other fields, change the layout of the table, and so on. Tables require a bit more up-front work to get the design right, but they are extremely powerful at showing a consistent look for large amounts of data.

Pick Me Up

Starting with OS version 5, RIM has introduced several pickers that help provide a standard and clean-looking interface for common selection tasks. You can find these pickers in the `net.rim.device.api.ui.picker` package. They have further expanded the selection in OS version 6 with additional useful choices.

FilePicker

Many apps will allow users to save data to persistent storage and later to open that data again. Other apps allow users to import files that may have been created elsewhere. In both cases, you will need some way to present the user with a choice between multiple records of data. In the past, developers have been able to easily traverse and manipulate the filesystem through the FileConnection API, but each developer has needed to create their own custom UI to present the filesystem to the user.

Now, you can use the powerful `FilePicker` class to take care of this task. `FilePicker` supports many configurable options; you can set the root path for the picker to initially display (for example, a private directory created by your application or the phone's shared SD card), as well as a filter that limits the filetypes that display as options (for example, you can choose to only show `.doc` files).

The picker also supports several options for visual customization. `setTitle()` allows you to present your own description of the picking operation, such as "Choose Theme Music." `setView()` will present the same interface as the native media applications; your choices include `VIEW_MUSIC`, `VIEW_PICTURES`, `VIEW_RINGTONES`, `VIEW_VIDEO`, `VIEW_VOICE_NOTES`, or `VIEW_ALL`. Switching to a media view will restrict the picker to only show media that's stored in the default BlackBerry locations, so do not use one of these if you wish to let the user browse through other directories.

You can acquire a `FilePicker` by calling `FilePicker.getInstance()`. After configuring it, call `show()` to display the picker dialog. This operation blocks; it will return with a `string` describing the full path to the file, or `null` if the user canceled. A separate thread can call `cancel()` on the `FilePicker` to abort the picking operation; this might be useful if some other activity in the app has taken higher precedence and requires the user's attention.

If you prefer, you can create a class that implements `FilePicker.Listener` and set it as the listener on a `FilePicker`. Your listener will then receive a notification from the `FilePicker` after the user has made or canceled a selection. This is equivalent to the return value from the `show()` method, but may better fit your design.

The example below shows how to display a picker that only allows the user to select `.amr` files. It starts in the root of the SD card and allows the user to navigate anywhere when making a selection.

```
FilePicker picker = FilePicker.getInstance();
picker.setFilter(".amr");
picker.setPath("file:///SDCard/");
```

```
String chosen = picker.show();
if (chosen != null)
{
    // Act on the chosen file here.
}
```

Figure 13–7 shows this FilePicker in action. You would get a different look if you called setView() and would see different files if you set a different filter.

Figure 13–7. A FilePicker limited to displaying .amr files

HomeScreenLocationPicker

This class is rather specialized but also quite useful. It allows users to select the location for a shortcut on the home screen or in a device folder. Unlike FilePicker, this is a non-modal Field that you integrate into your own Screen. You instantiate a HomeScreenLocationPicker by calling its static create() method.

Once you have a Location object, you can pass it to HomeScreen.addShortcut(). This method also takes a shortcut, which you can retrieve from ShortcutProvider. This allows you to create shortcuts on the home screen that bring the user into particular places within your app. The example in Listing 13–8 creates a shortcut that could be used to start playing a particular song in a music app.

Listing 13–8. *Working with HomeScreenLocationPicker to Create a Custom Shortcut*

```
add(new LabelField("Where would you like to put your favorite song?"));
final HomeScreenLocationPicker picker =
    HomeScreenLocationPicker.create();
add(picker);
ButtonField button = new ButtonField();
button.setRunnable(new Runnable()
{
    public void run()
    {
        Location location = picker.getLocation();
        Shortcut shortcut = ShortcutProvider.createShortcut("Play Tunes",
            "playMusic:///SDCard/BlackBerry/Music/WorldLeaderPretend.mp3", 1);
        shortcut.setIsFavourite(picker.getIsFavourite());
        HomeScreen.addShortcut(shortcut, location);
        close();
    }
});
button.setLabel("Create Shortcut");
add(button);
```

This example adds the picker directly into the Screen. When it displays, the picker will show the default location and a checkbox for favorites; selecting the location will open up a menu to choose the shortcut location, as shown in Figure 13–8. Your application isn't notified when the user makes a choice in the menu; instead, you add a ButtonField that will create a shortcut based on the user's selection, add it to the device's main menu, and then close this screen. "Play Tunes" describes the label that the user will see; the second parameter is the shortcut ID that will be provided to the application's launchShortcut() method; and the third parameter specifies that the platform should use the second entry point if the application isn't already running.

Figure 13–8. *User making a selection from the HomeScreenLocationPicker*

If you run this example, you'll create a shortcut that will display like the one shown in Figure 13–9. Tapping this shortcut will re-launch the application and call launchShortcut(). In a full application, you could parse the filename out of the shortcut ID, switch to the appropriate screen, and immediately start playing.

Figure 13–9. *A custom shortcut added to the Media location*

DateTimePicker

This picker behaves like FilePicker in that it displays a modal, blocking pop-up dialog and allows the user to make a selection. In this case, the user will choose a date, time, or combination. You can customize the pop-up to display the type of information you wish to collect.

Obtain a DateTimePicker by calling one of the static createInstance() methods. You can optionally specify the format you wish to present. Find the enumerations in the DateFormat class; for example, DateFormat.DATE_SHORT will present abbreviated dates, and DateFormat.TIME_FULL will display all available time fields. You can also provide your desired format by passing strings; for example, "MM/dd/yy" will display dates as "07/05/11" and "HH:mm:ss" will display times as "20:30:00".

> **CAUTION:** DateTimePicker does not guarantee that your selected format will fit on your device's display. You should experiment on your target devices to ensure that the end of any long date/time dialogs is not clipped off. If you encounter problems, try switching to a shorter format; you can apply this globally or just to affected devices.

By default, the picker will initially display the current date and time. You can modify this by constructing and passing a `Calendar` object that holds your desired initial date and/or time. You can also pass additional `Calendar` objects to `setMaximumDate()` and `setMinimumDate()`, which set limits on the range of dates or times that the user can select. `DateTimePicker` offers convenience methods called `cloneCalendar()` that create copies of `Calendar` objects, which you can manipulate while not affecting the original `Calendar`; this is useful if, for example, you wanted to start on one particular date and allow the user to choose a time up to one week earlier or one week later.

To actually display the `DateTimePicker`, call `doModal()`. You can pass in the field that you wish to initially have focus, such as `DateFormat.HOUR_FIELD` or pass `-1` for the default focus. You can optionally specify an `XYRect` describing where you wish the modal screen to display; for example, you might want it to display on top of the screen or in the center. The device may choose not to place the pop-up exactly where you requested, depending on the dimensions of the pop-up and your screen. `doModal()` will return `true` if the user made a selection or `false` if they canceled. Afterwards, you can call `getDateTime()` to retrieve the `calendar` describing the user's selection.

Suppose that you want to have the user select a date for an appointment. Listing 13–9 shows how to configure a `DateTimePicker` that will only display dates. The choice defaults to one year from today; the user cannot select a day earlier than today or later than five years from now.

Listing 13–9. *Creating a Picker for Choosing Dates*

```
Calendar initial = Calendar.getInstance();
initial.set(Calendar.YEAR, initial.get(Calendar.YEAR) + 1);
Calendar max = Calendar.getInstance();
max.set(Calendar.YEAR, max.get(Calendar.YEAR) + 5);
DateTimePicker picker = DateTimePicker.createInstance(initial,
    DateFormat.DATE_LONG, 0);
picker.setMinimumDate(Calendar.getInstance());
picker.setMaximumDate(max);
if (picker.doModal())
{
    Calendar chosen = picker.getDateTime();
}
```

Running this will display a large date picker similar to Figure 13–10. Once you retrieve the chosen date, you could use it to create an event on the user's calendar, communicate it to a server back-end, or take whatever action is appropriate.

Figure 13–10. *A DateTimePicker set to display long date format*

App: Screen Bling

You'll use some of the new UI tools to enhance your media grabbing app. The current system for playing back media is rather unwieldy, as it requires you to know where your files are located; let's switch to using the FilePicker instead. Also, the sending screen does not provide much feedback while you send a file, so you'll add an activity indicator to show the user that you're still working.

Picking Files

Your existing MediaGrabber application has supported playing back local media files since Chapter 3, but doing so has been cumbersome: you need to memorize the path to the media file, then type in the entire absolute filename. You can significantly speed up this process and make the app more usable by switching to FilePicker. Listing 13–10 shows an updated version of the ChoicesScreen constructor that adds a new button for bringing up the file location picker; the added portions are shown in bold.

Listing 13–10. *Using a FilePicker to Select Media Files for Playback*

```
public ChoicesScreen()
{
    setTitle("MediaGrabber");
    add(new LabelField(r, MediaGrabber.I18N_INSTRUCTIONS));
    add(location);
    ButtonField button = ButtonFieldFactory.getInstance().create(
            new Command(new CommandHandler()
            {
                public void execute(ReadOnlyCommandMetadata metadata,
                        Object context)
                {
                    FilePicker picker = FilePicker.getInstance();
                    picker.setPath("file:///SDCard/BlackBerry/");
                    picker.setTitle("Choose media");
                    String file = picker.show();
                    if (file != null)
                    {
                        location.setText(file);
                    }
                }
            }));
    button.setLabel("Choose media");
    add(button);
}
```

When you run this example, you'll see that you can much more quickly browse to your previously recorded files. By default, you start in the same location where you save captured media. A custom title on this picker helps keep users oriented.

Wait For It....

If you send a very large media file, users may get antsy. The screen just says "Sending. Please wait." They may worry that the application has frozen. You can provide soothing encouragement by using an `ActivityIndicatorView`. First, define a model that you will use to turn the spinner on and off. Open `SendingScreen.java` and add the instance variable as shown:

```
private ActivityIndicatorModel sendingModel;
```

Next, modify the constructor to create the model and view, and initialize both. You will add the spinner to the top of the screen and initially keep it stationary. Listing 13–11 shows the updated constructor with additions in bold. You can find the 12-frame `waiting.png` image in the code downloads for this chapter on the Apress web site or you can create your own animating image.

Listing 13–11. *Creating an Activity Indicator for Sending Media*

```
public SendingScreen(String contentType, String filename, String message,
        byte[] data, boolean encrypt)
{
    this.contentType = contentType;
    this.filename = filename;
```

```
    this.message = message;
    this.data = data;
    this.encrypt = encrypt;
    status = new LabelField(r, I18N_PROMPT_EMAIL);
    receiver = new BasicEditField(r.getString(I18N_LABEL_RECIPIENT), "",
            100, BasicEditField.FILTER_EMAIL | Field.USE_ALL_WIDTH);
    ActivityIndicatorView busy = new ActivityIndicatorView(0);
    Bitmap bitmap = Bitmap.getBitmapResource("waiting.png");
    busy.createActivityImageField(bitmap, 12, 0);
    sendingModel = new ActivityIndicatorModel();
    busy.setModel(sendingModel);
    sendingModel.cancel();
    add(busy);
    add(status);
    add(receiver);
    updater = new StatusUpdater(status);
}
```

Finally, update the inner class MessageSender as shown in Listing 13–12. It will prompt the activity indicator to begin spinning right before you start sending and stop it after you finish.

Listing 13–12. *Updating MessageSender to Report Activity*

```
private class MessageSender implements Runnable
{
    public void run()
    {
        String address = receiver.getText();
        sendingModel.resume();
        try
        {
            Message outgoing = createMessage(address, contentType,
                    filename, message);
            Transport.send(outgoing);
            updateContact(address);
            updater.sendDelayedMessage(r.getString(I18N_STATUS_SENT));
            state = STATE_SENT;
        }
        catch (Exception e)
        {
            updater.sendDelayedMessage(r.getString(I18N_ERROR_SENDING)
                    + e.getMessage());
            e.printStackTrace();
        }
        sendingModel.cancel();
    }
}
```

When you run the updated version of MediaGrabber, you will now see the busy indicator spinning while it sends your media.

WANT MORE?

You may have already made several visual enhancements of your own to MediaGrabber. Here are some other options you might consider.

- Create a new screen that supports creating shortcuts. Experiment with different types of shortcuts that automatically open to different screens within the app; for example, you could let the user create a shortcut that immediately plays the media they just recorded.

- Use the Table API and your custom PIM information to create a table that shows all the contacts a user has shared media with and the number of times they have shared with each one.

- Create a `ProgressBar` in `PlayingScreen` that shows how much of the media has played so far.

Of course, you can also add any other styling that you want to the app. Drop in some new colors, play with the fonts, maybe move items around on the screen. Have some fun with it!

Excelsior

Good-looking apps rule. Try to impress your users right away, giving them enough incentive to keep using your app and get to know all its great features. Too many developers put too much time into optimizing esoteric aspects of their apps that people never get to see, while giving short shrift to the interface that everyone needs to use.

Fortunately, you're now in a good position to join the ranks of the elite. A great-looking BlackBerry app will integrate with the native UI and provide the look and feel that users have grown comfortable with. In this chapter, you've learned how to take advantage of the latest UI features RIM has added to their SDK when crafting your app. You should still follow good design practices, including user experience testing and iterative feedback cycles. Knowing all of the tools at your disposal will help you and your designers come up with the best solutions: apps that are feasible to create, fit cleanly into the phone's experience, and look as good as possible.

You're approaching the end of your journey through BlackBerry 6 development. The final chapter will cover a variety of useful cross-platform libraries that RIM has recently incorporated into their platform. Learning these technologies will further round out your collection of useful BlackBerry skills.

Chapter 14

Cross-Platform Libraries

Each major revision of the BlackBerry OS has added a slew of interesting features. This chapter explores several of the new additions to the SDK in OS versions 5 and 6. RIM has incorporated several powerful and useful standardized libraries that can provide impressive benefits to your application. You will learn how to turn a BlackBerry into a portable handheld scanner that can read barcodes and connect users to associated information. You will also learn about SQLite, which offers a powerful mobile-optimized relational database, and the advanced graphics packages OpenGL and OpenVG. These various APIs will let your app offer the latest, most modern features to your users.

A Scanner, Darkly

While BlackBerry devices tend to have great keyboards, they still remain phones, and people will generally prefer to avoid typing. You can significantly cut down on the amount of time a user needs to look up information, and increase accuracy, by having the user scan a barcode instead of type in information. You can scan existing barcodes to look up product information; or, you can create your own custom barcodes for any purpose that you want, such as navigating people through a building or making a treasure-hunt contest. Users will generally scan barcodes by using their phone's camera, but current libraries also support interpreting a barcode from an image file. Scanning barcodes is a complicated task, especially with phones that may not have ideal lighting conditions, but the BlackBerry API encapsulates the bulk of the effort and simplifies the process. BlackBerry's scanning API builds on top of the open source ZXing library, also known as Zebra Crossing.

Barcode Basics

When most Americans think of barcodes, they think of UPC labels, that collection of thick and thin vertical bars that shops scan to ring up purchases. More recently, two-dimensional barcodes such as QR codes (shown in Figure 14–2) have gained in popularity. All barcodes accomplish the same task: to encode a set of numbers or letters into a visual image. By converting that image back into the original string, you can look up the associated information.

Types of Barcodes

Barcodes have gradually evolved as their demand has increased and the available supply has shrunk. The earliest could encode only a few numeric digits, while the latest can hold long URLs. Barcodes can have several different properties.

- Dimensions: Traditional one-dimensional barcodes, also known as linear barcodes, consist of several vertical bands separated by white space. Figure 14–1 shows a UPC barcode. Newer two-dimensional barcodes, also known as matrix codes, consist of boxes or circles scattered across white space and can encode much more data than a one-dimensional barcode occupying the same space. See Figure 14–2 for a sample QR code barcode.

Figure 14–1. *A linear UPC barcode*

Figure 14–2. *A matrix QR code*

- *Widths*: One-dimensional barcodes may have only two widths, or multiple widths, for each bar or space. More widths will support more data in a smaller space; however, scanners have more difficulty reading codes with varying widths if the barcode is warped.

- *Separation*: One-dimensional barcodes may be either discrete or continuous. A discrete code spaces out each individual encoded character; this means that you can read an individual item from the middle of the barcode. A continuous barcode runs all the characters together; you must read a continuous barcode in sequence, since you cannot know otherwise where one character begins and another ends. Continuous barcodes require less space, but have less tolerance for poor scanning conditions than discrete barcodes.

- *Encoding*: The earliest barcodes could encode only digits. More recent ones support ASCII characters, while the newest also support Unicode and special control characters.

Currently, the ZXing library offered through BlackBerry supports the following types of barcodes.

- `CODE_128`: A linear, continuous code of varying widths. It switches between three modes that collectively support the ASCII character set, plus a compact form of digit encoding.

- `CODE_39`: A linear, discrete code with two widths. It has a much more limited character set than `CODE_128`, supporting only upper-case letters A-Z, numbers, and a few special characters like arithmetic operators.

- `DATAMATRIX`: A two-dimensional code of varying size that can encode characters or binary data.

- `EAN_13`: Originally known as European Article Number 13, this linear, continuous barcode uses varying widths and expands the original UPC coding.

- `EAN_8`: A much smaller barcode derived from EAN 13. Manufacturers often place this code on very small packages.

- `ITF`: Also known as Interleaved Two of Five, this linear code uses continuous markings of varying widths. The most common implementation, ITF-14, encodes exactly 14 digits.

- `PDF417`: A two-dimensional code that prints codewords in clusters. You can find PDF417 on postage and identity cards, among other applications.

- `QR_CODE`: This two-dimensional code is the most popular format for mobile phones. QR codes often encode URLs that can direct users to web sites.

- *UPC_A*: UPC was the first widely used barcode, and UPC-A is the most common variation. This linear code uses continuous bars of varying width. It can encode 12 digits of data.

- *UPC_E*: This variation of UPC uses a compressed format that holds only six digits.

In practice, most apps will know ahead of time what type of barcode they will decode. You can consider the various supported codes' strengths if you have control over which barcode format your project will use. Most mobile apps will gravitate toward QR code due to its large payload, relatively compact size, and widespread existing scanning support in mobile platforms; however, UPC and related linear codes are very interesting for apps that deal with shopping, packaging, books, media, and other existing products.

Mobile Scanner

A barcode decoder tries to convert the barcode image into a set of black and white areas, and then run an algorithm to decode the image. Because it uses the phone's camera in the real world, it will never receive a perfect picture: the scanner always needs to adjust the image to reach the format it wants. You can help the user get a successful scan by offering the following advice.

- Try to fill the phone's viewfinder with the code.

- Take a picture with bright light, but avoid glare on the code.

- Hold the device steadily.

- If an object has multiple barcodes, try covering up all but one.

Google's ZXing

The open source ZXing library, developed by Google, is natively available on Android phones, free for download in various iPhone apps, and now an option for developers on BlackBerry. ZXing collects free algorithms that encode and decode the most popular barcode formats. The library includes an overwhelming 17 packages and dozens of classes; fortunately, you will need to directly work with only a few in the com.google.zxing package.

BarcodeFormat

This simply contains the available barcode formats in static fields.

DecodeHintType

This contains available hints that you can provide to a decoder in order to make it faster or more accurate. It has several options, but you'll most often use the following fields.

- *POSSIBLE_FORMATS*: Use this in conjunction with the definitions in BarcodeFormat to restrict a decoder to search only for particular types of barcodes. This can drastically decrease the time to determine whether an image holds a barcode; in most cases, you can safely limit the format to a particular type that you expect to find.

- *PURE_BARCODE*: This indicates that the provided image has already been converted into a pure barcode: a monochromatic black-and-white image. Do not use this for images captured from the camera, which will likely have varying shades of gray and other picture elements outside the barcode, but you can use this for other situations such as interpreting a barcode image downloaded from a web site.

- *TRY_HARDER*: This instructs the decoder to spend more time trying to convert the provided image into a pure barcode. Most applications will enable this in order to get more accurate results, at the cost of slightly slower operation.

If you want to, you can explore the remaining packages and classes. Most applications won't have much use for this, but they can provide lower-level information about barcodes or help influence the scanning process.

RIM's Wrappers

Most of your work with barcodes will use the net.rim.device.api.barcodelib package. This contains a much more manageable number of classes.

BarcodeDecoder

This class hooks into the ZXing library to decode provided images. By default it will try to match an image against every possible barcode format, which will take a long time. To speed this up, you should specify the format of barcode to scan for. You can provide this information and other hints by building a Hashtable and passing it to the BarcodeDecoder constructor. Use values from DecodeHintType as the keys. The following example will scan for both short and long UPC codes.

```
Vector supported  = new Vector();
supported.addElement(BarcodeFormat.UPC_A);
supported.addElement(BarcodeFormat.UPC_E);
Hashtable hints = new Hashtable();
hints.put(DecodeHintType.POSSIBLE_FORMATS, supported);
hints.put(DecodeHintType.TRY_HARDER, Boolean.TRUE);
BarcodeDecoder decoder = new BarcodeDecoder(hints);
```

BarcodeDecoderListener

This interface defines a single method, barcodeDecoded(). After the scanner successfully decodes a barcode, it will invoke this method, passing it a String that contains the characters or numbers represented by the code.

BarcodeBitmap and BitmapLuminanceSource

Few third-party applications will use these classes. They support in-memory Bitmap objects that can represent barcode images, but unless you intend to do more low-level processing, you can safely ignore them.

Return of Media Players

Scanning a barcode requires using the camera, so it shouldn't surprise you that this means bringing back the viewfinder from Chapter 2. The BlackBerry classes conveniently wrap the viewfinder and related elements together, so you can move from barcode scanning to barcode processing with little work. BarcodeScanner will be your main class for scanning. You provide a BarcodeDecoder and a BarcodeDecoderListener instance.

The scanner provides three levels for acquiring a viewfinder. getPlayer() is the most primitive; it provides a Player object like one you would create for a camera. It accepts all standard Player methods, including retrieving the VideoControl and creating a Field as described in Chapter 2. For convenience, BarcodeScanner also offers a getVideoControl() and a getViewfinder() method that retrieve those elements for you; most applications will call getViewfinder() and insert the Field it returns into their Screen, or will retrieve the VideoControl and call setDisplayFullScreen().

Once your app is ready, call startScan() to begin looking for barcodes. The phone will continue processing camera images until it finds a match or until you call stopScan(). If it finds an image, it will call your listener with the barcode's payload; it will stop searching for additional images until you call startScan() again.

> **CAUTION:** If the viewfinder Field goes away while a scan is in progress, either by removing the Field or by closing your whole Screen, the scanner may not clean up the camera resources. This could mean that future attempts at scanning will fail. To be safe, call stopScan() or make sure you've found a barcode before the viewfinder goes away.

An Example

Listing 14–1 searches for UPC codes. This sample updates an onscreen label once it detects a barcode.

Listing 14–1. *A Barcode Scanner*

```
public class ScanScreen extends MainScreen implements BarcodeDecoderListener
{
    private LabelField match;
    private BarcodeScanner scanner;

    public ScanScreen()
    {
        match = new LabelField("Scanning...");
        add(match);
        Vector supported = new Vector();
        supported.addElement(BarcodeFormat.UPC_A);
        supported.addElement(BarcodeFormat.UPC_E);
        Hashtable hints = new Hashtable();
        hints.put(DecodeHintType.POSSIBLE_FORMATS, supported);
        hints.put(DecodeHintType.TRY_HARDER, Boolean.TRUE);
        BarcodeDecoder decoder = new BarcodeDecoder(hints);
        try
        {
            scanner = new BarcodeScanner(decoder, this);
            add(scanner.getViewfinder());
            scanner.startScan();
        }
        catch (Exception e)
        {
            e.printStackTrace();
        }
    }

    public void barcodeDecoded(String rawText)
    {
        match.setText("Found: " + rawText);
    }

    public void close()
    {
        try
        {
            scanner.stopScan();
        }
        catch (Exception e)
        {
            e.printStackTrace();
        }

        super.close();
    }
}
```

SQLite

You have already learned about many forms of data storage offered on BlackBerry.

■ The FileConnection API writes files to internal memory or a removable media card.

■ RMS stores simple byte records that are private to a suite of apps.

■ The PersistentObject API serializes objects to persistent storage.

These systems work well for storing media files and simple data structures. However, more complex collections of data benefit from a full relational database, which can hold large numbers of structured records and support complex operations for insertion and querying.

SQLite and SQL are large topics. If you are not already familiar with SQL, you may want to consult a book such as *Sams Teach Yourself SQL in 10 Minutes* (Sams, 2004) or a web tutorial such as www.w3schools.com/sql/. This section of the book gives a brief overview of the major APIs that allow you to execute SQL commands and interpret the results.

Database Overview

SQLite builds on the Structured Query Language, or SQL (pronounced "Sequel"). A given database consists of multiple tables, each with their own separate structure. Each table defines a set of columns; for example, a table of employees might have columns including the employee name, identification number, and date of hire. Each table can contain an arbitrary number of rows, also known as records. If an organization has ten employees, it will have ten rows in the employee table. Figure 14–3 shows a sample database.

Employees		
ID	Name	Hire
1	Speedy	8/7/04
2	Henchman #21	4/15/95
3	Henchman #24	6/10/99

Assignments	
Employee	Project
2	1
2	2
3	2

Projects			
ID	Name	Start	Budget
1	Cocoon Maintenance	8/7/04	500
2	Spider Skull Island Raid	10/30/04	250000

Figure 14–3. *A database with three tables*

SQL defines operations for creating tables and performing operations such as inserting and deleting records. The real power of SQL, though, comes from combining data from multiple tables. With a database like that shown in Figure 14–3, you can add projects and employees by simply adding rows to their respective tables. Using the Assignments table as shown here allows us to decouple workers from their assignments, which lets us define complex relationships such as multiple-employee projects without polluting either table with unnecessary information. You can then query the database to find out things like the average level of experience for all workers on a particular project, or which employee works on the most projects, and so on.

SQL has been around for a long time, and powers the vast majority of corporate databases and Internet web sites. SQLite has more recently come onto the scene to provide a lot of SQL's features to mobile devices. Android has included SQLite for several years, and now that RIM has adopted it as well, developers should find it easier to unify data storage across multiple platforms.

Initializing a Database

RIM has created classes that wrap and control access to SQLite. You can find these classes in the `net.rim.device.api.database` package. Inside that package, the `DatabaseFactory` class allows you to create, open, or delete a database.

> **NOTE:** An application can create and use multiple databases. However, keep in mind that each database is separate; you cannot execute statements that span multiple databases. Most applications will want to create a single database that contains multiple tables.

You may need to use only a single method from this class: openOrCreate(), which returns a Database if it already exists and creates it otherwise. You provide the database's name, which will be created in a default location in the device's memory. This usually is in file:///SDCard/databases/[Application Name]/.

More complex applications that need finer control over database creation and access may want to use other methods offered by DatabaseFactory, including the following.

- *create()*: Makes a new database.
- *open()*: Returns an existing database.
- *exists()*: Checks to see whether a database already exists.
- *delete()*: Removes an existing database.
- *decrypt()*: Converts a previously encrypted database into a plain-text format that can be exported from the device.

These methods all are overloaded, and accept additional parameters instead of or in addition to the database name.

- *URI*: Instead of naming the database, this takes a full path. You can use this if you wish to store the database in your application's private folder.
- *DatabaseOptions*: Specify whether the database should check that tables' foreign keys are valid.
- *DatabaseSecurityOptions*: Encrypt the database and restrict the applications that can access it.

You can create a Database with the following command.

```
Database db = DatabaseFactory.openOrCreate("com.apress.king.Business");
```

> **NOTE:** Most SQLite methods can throw a DatabaseException or a subclass of that exception. The samples in this chapter omit error handling for brevity, but a full application must catch and respond to these errors.

Creating Tables

Most SQLite operations require the use of two classes: a Database object that you retrieved from the DatabaseFactory, and a Statement that contains the literal SQL to execute. All SQLite operations within a given database operate on the Statement class. You obtain a Statement by calling createStatement() on an open Database, passing in the SQL command to execute, as shown here.

```
String command;
Statement s = db.createStatement(command);
```

You must prepare() the Statement, which makes it ready for execution. For commands like table creation that do not return results, you call execute() to perform the command. Finally, you should close() the Statement after you have finished to release its resources back to the system.

> **TIP:** SQLite also supports binding formal parameters by calling bind() on the Statement. This lets you generate one Statement and then re-use it multiple times with different arguments.

To create a table, build the SQL statement that defines the table name, column names and types, and any other supported aspects. The following fragment constructs the three sample tables we discussed earlier in the chapter.

```
Database db = DatabaseFactory.openOrCreate("com.apress.king.Business");
String[] commands = new String[]
{
    "CREATE TABLE 'Employees' ('ID' INTEGER, 'Name' TEXT, 'Hire' TEXT)",
    "CREATE TABLE 'Projects' ('ID' INTEGER, 'Name' TEXT, " +
        "'Start' TEXT, 'Budget' INTEGER)",
    "CREATE TABLE 'Assignments' ('Employee' INTEGER, 'Project' INTEGER)"
};
for (int i = 0; i < commands.length; ++i)
{
    Statement s = db.createStatement(commands[i]);
    s.prepare();
    s.execute();
    s.close();
}
```

> **TIP:** SQLite commands like CREATE TABLE are case-insensitive, but are capitalized by convention.

Inserting Data

You can add records in the exact same way you create a table; simply update your SQL command to use the INSERT command, as shown in the following example.

```
Statement s = db.createStatement(
    "INSERT INTO Projects(ID,Name,Start,Budget) " +
    "VALUES (4242,'TPS',date('now'),1000000)");
s.prepare();
s.execute();
s.close();
```

Querying

To extract information from the database, you first prepare a Statement as described previously. However, instead of calling execute(), call getCursor(). This returns a Cursor object that you can use to walk through the results set, using the following commands.

- *first()*: Moves the cursor to the first row of results. Returns false if your query returned no results.

- *isEmpty()*: Describes whether the cursor has results. This will always return true until you move the cursor, such as by calling first(), so you cannot use it to test for results ahead of time.

- *getPosition()*: Returns your current row's index, or -1 if you have not moved the cursor.

- *getColumnIndex()*: Given a name, returns the index for that column.

- *getColumnName()*: Given an index, returns the name for that column.

- *next()*: Advances the Cursor by one row.

- *prev()*: Returns the Cursor to the previous row.

- *position()*: Moves the Cursor to the specified row index.

- *last()*: Jumps to the last row of results.

> **TIP:** The standard Cursor supports only forward navigation, so calls to prev() will fail. If you wish to navigate both forward and backward, create a BufferedCursor. This wraps a Cursor and implements all of its methods.

Once you have placed the Cursor correctly, call getRow() to retrieve a Row object. You will use this to pull data out of this row. Row has a set of methods, like getInteger() and getString(), that will retrieve the data for a given column index. Since you created the statement, you should know which index has the value you want, but you can also use getColumnIndex() to look up the proper index.

The following example shows how to execute a query and iterate over the results Cursor. This prints to system out, but you could use the data to create a table or populate a network request.

```
String operation = "SELECT Employees.Name, Projects.Name FROM "
    + "Projects,Employees,Assignments WHERE Assignments.Employee=Employees.ID "
    + "AND Assignments.Project=Projects.ID";
Statement statement = db.createStatement(operation);
statement.prepare();
Cursor results = statement.getCursor();
System.out.println("Current assignments:");
if (results.first())
{
```

```
    do
    {
        Row match = results.getRow();
        System.out.println(match.getString(0) + "->" + match.getString(1));
    } while (results.next());
}
results.close();
statement.close();
db.close();
```

Running this will print out all of the employee assignments that you have previously inserted into the database, and will look like the following:

```
Current assignments:
Henchman #21->Cocoon Maintenance
Henchman #21->Spider Skull Island Raid
Henchman #24->Spider Skull Island Raid
```

Other SQL Commands

SQLite supports most of the major standardized SQL commands. If you run into problems with your statements, you can probably find another way to craft the operation you want. Keep in mind that for operations that return results, you should call getCursor(), while all other operations should call execute().

OpenGL

The latest BlackBerry devices have impressive graphics hardware, and if you want to take full advantage of what they offer, you will need to use OpenGL ES and OpenVG. These powerful, standardized libraries give you direct access to graphic acceleration hardware and let you create impressive visual effects. OpenGL ES defines a language for creating and manipulating three-dimensional graphics, ranging from first-person shooting games to architectural renderings. OpenVG provides a similarly rich library for defining two-dimensional scenes, which you can use to create side-scrolling games, compelling animated menus, and other attractive screens.

Acceleration Overview

RIM first added APIs for OpenGL ES 1.0 and OpenVG with OS version 5.0. OS 6 has added support for OpenGL ES 1.1. However, not all phones with these OS versions support the acceleration APIs; currently, only CDMA devices such as the Style 9670, Storm 2 9550, Bold 9650, and Curve 8530 offer these libraries. This is because acceleration relies on particular hardware that currently is present in these devices and not others.

You can still run your app on all other devices, but you will not be able to exercise accelerated graphics functions. Similarly, a device that supports only OpenGL ES 1.0 will not be able to perform functions defined in OpenGL ES 1.1. If your app depends on hardware acceleration, you should distribute it only to phones capable of running the app. If you use acceleration only to add visual flair to your app, then you may want to detect its presence at runtime and gracefully fall back to standard BlackBerry UI if the device does not support acceleration.

OpenGL ES 1.0 corresponds to OpenGL 1.3, and OpenGL ES 1.1 is equivalent to OpenGL 1.5. Developers with existing games that target these versions of OpenGL should find it relatively easy to port to the BlackBerry, although they will still need to account for the different form factor and mobile limitations. OpenVG provides 2D acceleration that can support much more impressive user interfaces than non-accelerated versions.

> **CAUTION:** While OpenGL ES 1.1 builds on OpenGL ES 1.0, OpenGL ES 2.0 is a radically different language that is not compatible with the 1.x versions of OpenGL ES. OpenGL ES 2.0 is not currently available on BlackBerry devices, but is supported on the most recent iPhone and Android devices. If you plan to port between these devices, keep compatibility in mind.

Both OpenGL ES and OpenVG work on top of a portable graphics layer called EGL, as shown in Figure 14–4. Having a shared context allows you to mix together 2D and 3D effects on the same screen.

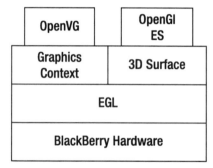

Figure 14–4. *Accelerated graphics architecture*

APIs

As with SQLite, exhaustive coverage of OpenGL ES and OpenVG is beyond the scope of this book. Instead, we will give an overview of how to gain access to these features and will work through a brief sample. For additional information, consult a book such as *Mobile 3D Graphics: with OpenGL ES and M3G* (Morgan Kaufmann, 2007) or a web site like www.khronos.org/developers/resources/opengles/. Be sure to refer to OpenGL ES 1.x and not to OpenGL ES 2.0.

BlackBerry has incorporated support for OpenGL ES through JSR 239, a Java binding created for Java ME devices. The APIs come from the Khronos Group, a nonprofit consortium that oversees the development of standards-based, royalty-free APIs.

The EGL layer is provided in the javax.microedition.khronos.egl package. You can obtain a reference to the device's EGL by calling EGLContext.getEGL(). This will return an object that implements EGL10, and possibly EGL11 if the underlying implementation supports it.

> **CAUTION:** Do not confuse EGL 1.0 and 1.1 with OpenGL ES 1.0 and 1.1. Although the two libraries work together, they are not the same.

You can find the low-level OpenGL ES interfaces in the javax.microedition.khronos.opengles package. Again, you will find interfaces named for the level of support offered, such as GL10 and GL11.

BlackBerry offers useful higher-level classes in its two packages net.rim.device.api.opengles and net.rim.device.api.openvg, which provide support for OpenGL ES and OpenVG respectively. Both packages include a Field subclass and a Utils class that help you more easily incorporate graphical features into your application. Using the Field subclasses will automatically manage EGL resources for you, and allows you to more easily integrate with native BlackBerry UI elements such as menus and popups. The Utils classes provide some convenient utility functions, most usefully methods that convert BlackBerry Bitmap objects into images compatible with OpenGL ES and OpenVG.

An Example

We will build a simple OpenVG field that demonstrates drawing images, text, and shapes on the same surface. Listing 14–2 shows a screen with a custom Field that initializes the OpenVG surface, and then renders our content in a custom drawing method.

Listing 14–2. *Drawing OpenVG Content*

```
public class OpenVGScreen extends MainScreen
{

    public OpenVGScreen()
    {
        add(new LabelField("Rendered content below...", Field.FIELD_HCENTER));
        add(new DemoField(VGField.VERSION_1_1, Field.FIELD_HCENTER));
        add(new LabelField("That's all, folks!", Field.FIELD_HCENTER));
    }

    private class DemoField extends VGField
    {
        protected DemoField(int version, long style)
        {
            super(version, style);
        }

        private final float[] BACKGROUND = new float[]
        { 0.0f, 0.0f, 1.0f, 1.0f };
```

```
protected void layout(int width, int height)
{
    setExtent(75, 75);
}

protected void initialize(VG vg)
{
    ((VG11) vg).vgSetfv(VG10.VG_CLEAR_COLOR, 4, BACKGROUND, 0);
}

protected void render(VG vg)
{
    VG11 vg11 = (VG11) vg;
    vg11.vgClear(0, 0, getWidth(), getHeight());
    int pathHandle = vg11.vgCreatePath(VG10.VG_PATH_FORMAT_STANDARD,
            VG10.VG_PATH_DATATYPE_F, 1, 0, 0, 0,
            VG10.VG_PATH_CAPABILITY_ALL);
    VGUtils.vguEllipse(vg, pathHandle, 45, 45, 30, 20);
    vg11.vgDrawPath(pathHandle, VG11.VG_FILL_PATH);
    vg11.vgDestroyPath(pathHandle);
    Bitmap hourglass = Bitmap.getPredefinedBitmap(Bitmap.HOURGLASS);
    int imageHandle = VGUtils.vgCreateImage(vg11, hourglass, false,
            VG10.VG_IMAGE_QUALITY_FASTER);
    vg11.vgDrawImage(imageHandle);
    vg11.vgDestroyImage(imageHandle);
    String text = "Hello";
    VGUtils.vgDrawText(vg, getFont(), text, 0, text.length(), null, null);
}
    }
}
```

As you can see, you can externally treat the custom VGField like any other Field: it has
an extent, accepts styling parameters, and so on. Internally, the render() method
replaces a Field's paint() method. In our example, the platform will call render() once.
We mix low-level OpenVG calls defined in the VG10 and VG11 interfaces with higher-level
methods defined in VGUtils; most applications will similarly combine operations, but you
can also work entirely with the low-level methods.

When you run this example, you will see a screen like that in Figure 14–5. You can
experiment with modifying the sizes and positions of the elements. Remember that you
must use a device or simulator that supports OpenGL ES.

Figure 14–5. Simple OpenVG drawing

The foregoing structure works well for static OpenVG constructions, which suffice if you just want to use OpenVG's utilities for rendering and manipulating graphics. However, if you wish to use animated drawing, such as for a game or an interactive menu, then you can specify a target frame rate on your VGField. From then on, the platform will try to call your drawing functions as frequently as you specified. You can override the update() method to prepare your scene, and use render() to draw out the scene. Listing 14–3 updates our previous example to bounce the ellipse back and forth within the Field.

Listing 14–3. *Animating an OpenVG* Field

```
public class OpenVGScreen extends MainScreen
{

    public OpenVGScreen()
    {
        add(new LabelField("Let's move!", Field.FIELD_HCENTER));
        DemoField demo = new DemoField(VGField.VERSION_1_1, Field.FIELD_HCENTER);
        demo.setTargetFrameRate(25);
        add(demo);
        add(new LabelField("That's all, folks!", Field.FIELD_HCENTER));
    }
```

```java
    private class DemoField extends VGField
    {
        private float direction = 1;
        private float ellipseX = 45;
        protected DemoField(int version, long style)
        {
            super(version, style);
        }

        private final float[] BACKGROUND = new float[]
        { 0.0f, 0.0f, 1.0f, 1.0f };

        protected void layout(int width, int height)
        {
            setExtent(75, 75);
        }

        protected void initialize(VG vg)
        {
            ((VG11) vg).vgSetfv(VG10.VG_CLEAR_COLOR, 4, BACKGROUND, 0);
        }

        protected void update()
        {
            ellipseX += direction;
            if (ellipseX <= 15)
                direction = 1;
            else if (ellipseX >= 60)
                direction = -1;
        }

        protected void render(VG vg)
        {
            VG11 vg11 = (VG11) vg;
            vg11.vgClear(0, 0, getWidth(), getHeight());
            int pathHandle = vg11.vgCreatePath(VG10.VG_PATH_FORMAT_STANDARD,
                    VG10.VG_PATH_DATATYPE_F, 1, 0, 0, 0,
                    VG10.VG_PATH_CAPABILITY_ALL);
            VGUtils.vguEllipse(vg, pathHandle, ellipseX, 45, 30, 20);
            vg11.vgDrawPath(pathHandle, VG11.VG_FILL_PATH);
            vg11.vgDestroyPath(pathHandle);
            Bitmap hourglass = Bitmap.getPredefinedBitmap(Bitmap.HOURGLASS);
            int imageHandle = VGUtils.vgCreateImage(vg11, hourglass, false,
                    VG10.VG_IMAGE_QUALITY_FASTER);
            vg11.vgDrawImage(imageHandle);
            vg11.vgDestroyImage(imageHandle);
            String text = "Whoa";
            VGUtils.vgDrawText(vg, getFont(), text, 0, 5, null, null);
        }
    }
}
```

OpenGL ES behaves very similarly from BlackBerry's perspective: instead of a VGField, you'll extend a GLField, and instead of using VGUtils, you'll use GLUtils. In practice, most OpenGL games will contain very little BlackBerry code—just a few basic wrappers around a lot of OpenGL ES–specific calls.

App: Selection Memory

Let's continue making enhancements that make it easier for users to select media files to play. Adding a file picker dialog as we did in the last chapter simplifies navigation to a file. We can further improve this by modifying our app to remember the most recent files a user has played, and present those in an auto-complete field. This way users can quickly browse and select previously chosen files without even needing to navigate to them.

In order to keep track of previously played files, we will use a simple database with a single table. Listing 14–4 shows the method we can add to `MediaGrabber.java` that will check to see whether the database already exists, and initialize it if not. We'll just keep track of each file's name and the time it was accessed; we'll use the first piece of data when presenting choices to the user, and the second piece of data so we can sort and show only the most recent selections.

Listing 14–4. *Creating a Database*

```
static private void initDatabase()
{
    try
    {
        if (!DatabaseFactory.exists(DATABASE))
        {
            Database db = DatabaseFactory.create(DATABASE);
            Statement creation = db.createStatement
                ("CREATE TABLE 'Playlist' ('Path' TEXT, 'Timestamp' INTEGER)");
            creation.prepare();
            creation.execute();
            db.close();
        }
    }
    catch (DatabaseException de)
    {
    }
}
```

We can call this method from `main()`, prior to pushing the `ChoicesScreen`. This will ensure that the database is ready for use at the start of the application.

Next, we will modify `ChoicesScreen` to create a new method for entering file names. We'll replace the old `EditField` with a new `BasicEditField` and add a `Database` to the instance variables.

```
private Database db;
private BasicEditField location;
```

We will query our database for the five most recently selected names, and if we find any, we'll populate them as choices. Listing 14–5 shows our additions to the ChoicesScreen constructor.

Listing 14–5. *Accessing a Database*

```
public ChoicesScreen()
{
    setTitle("MediaGrabber");
    add(new LabelField(r, MediaGrabber.I18N_INSTRUCTIONS));
    BasicFilteredList previous = new BasicFilteredList();
    try
    {
        db = DatabaseFactory.open(MediaGrabber.DATABASE);
        Statement query = db.createStatement("SELECT Path FROM 'Playlist' ORDER BY
Timestamp DESC LIMIT 10");
        query.prepare();
        BufferedCursor results = new BufferedCursor(query.getCursor());
        if (results.last())
        {
            String[] previousQueries = new String[results.getPosition() + 1];
            do
            {
                Row row = results.getRow();
                String debug = row.toString();
                previousQueries[results.getPosition()] = row.getString(0);
            } while (results.prev());
            previous.addDataSet(0, previousQueries, "History");
        }
        query.close();
        results.close();
    }
    catch (Exception de)
    {
        de.printStackTrace();
        de.toString();
        // Fall back on the empty autocomplete field if there were any problems.
    }
    AutoCompleteField autoComplete = new AutoCompleteField(previous);
    autoComplete.setHintText("file:///SDCard/BlackBerry");
    add(autoComplete);
    location = autoComplete.getEditField();
    // Remainder of constructor stays the same.
}
```

To avoid leaking database connections, we'll modify close() in Listing 14–6 to explicitly release our database handle.

Listing 14–6. *Cleaning up database resources.*

```
public void close()
{
    location.setDirty(false);
    if (db != null)
    {
```

```
    try
    {
        db.close();
    }
    catch (DatabaseException de) {}
}
super.close();
}
```

Finally, we will record every file that the user plays. Listing 14–7 shows code we can insert into ChoicesScreen.launchPlayer() that inserts a new record each time the user makes a selection.

Listing 14–7. *Modifying a Database*

```
if (db != null)
{
    try
    {
        Statement save = db
                .createStatement("INSERT INTO 'Playlist' VALUES ('"
                        + url + "',datetime('now'))");
        save.prepare();
        save.execute();
        save.close();
    }
    catch (DatabaseException de)
    {
    }
}
```

When you run this example, you'll initially see text input similar to the old screen. After playing several files, though, this will look something like Figure 14–6. As you continue to perform more playbacks, you'll notice that older items get cycled out of the list of choices.

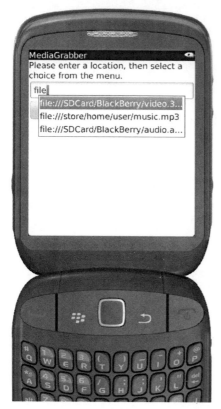

Figure 14–6. *An* `AutoCompleteField` *with recently played media files*

WANT MORE?

Databases add powerful capabilities to applications. You might consider the following ideas to further improve MediaGrabber and take advantage of their features.

- Remove duplicates from the list of recent files. You can do this when building the UI, but a better approach is to enforce uniqueness within the database table.

- Populate the database with files the user has recorded to for easier playback later.

- Refresh the `AutoCompleteField` when the user returns to `ChoicesScreen` from playing or recording media.

If you feel adventurous, you can also experiment with building a new version of `ChoicesScreen` using OpenVG. Replace the menu options and button with animated selections. This may take some time, but can lead to impressive results.

Additional Resources

The single most valuable skill you can learn is how to find additional information. I've found the following resources especially useful. When you're facing an unusual BlackBerry bug or want to learn how to do something new, check these first.

- *The BlackBerry Technical Solution Center* (www.blackberry.com/btsc/): The Developer Knowledge Base articles at the Developer Resource Center are particularly useful. These articles provide very specific information while describing how something works or how to accomplish a particular task. RIM updates articles when it releases new versions of software, so check back periodically for more information.

- *The official BlackBerry Java Development forums*: A sub-forum found at http://supportforums.blackberry.com/rim/. RIM employees frequent the boards and offer authoritative answers on particular issues and questions. Many talented private contributors also gain kudos with their helpful input. If you run across a problem, someone else has probably already stumbled across it and solved it on these forums.

- *Unofficial BlackBerry developer forum* (www.blackberryforums.com/developer-forum/): Prior to the launch of the official RIM forums, this was the main go-to place for technical questions. They have grown much quieter since the official forums launched, but a good amount of historical information about prior software versions can be found here.

- *Sample code*: Unfortunately, the BlackBerry Java Plug-in for Eclipse does not come with program samples. However, the RIM JDE and the JDE Component Package both include samples along with development tools. You can download and install these from RIM's web site. Look for the samples folder under the installation directory. The samples cover many APIs, are well organized, and provide good insight into how to successfully use particular technologies.

- *BlackBerry Developer Newsletter*: You can sign up for this newsletter at any time. While it lacks in-depth technical information, it's a great way to keep abreast of ongoing changes with the platform.

> **NOTE:** URLs can change, but the names tend to stay constant, so a quick search on RIM's web site or your favorite search engine will help locate these if the foregoing addresses do not work for you.

Summit

Have fun! Write code! The more you practice and the more you build, the more you will learn. Every new project brings new opportunities with it, and you will learn the most from hands-on experience.

Feel free to continue tweaking MediaGrabber; you may have some new ideas about how to make it more powerful or useful to you. If so, go for it! Or, while reading this book, you might have come up with a cool app idea on your own. Great! BlackBerry development combines a powerful platform, low barrier to entry, and immediate impact. If you write a good app and put it out where everyone can see it, you will be noticed.

Keep in mind that everything changes. OS versions 7 and 8 will eventually come along, offering still more features and capabilities. Keep your eyes open, find out what's new, and decide what would be useful. At the same time, hold on to the essentials. Now that you have mastered the key aspects of BlackBerry software development, you should be able to incorporate new information without losing sight of the critical elements of an application.

The journey never stops. Keep climbing a little higher—you never know what sight awaits you over the crest.

Appendix

Codec Support

Chapter 3 discussed how BlackBerry devices offer a range of codecs to play back audio and video content. This appendix provides some more details on codec support for a range of popular BlackBerry devices. Please see Table A–1 for this information. Notes applying to each device/codec combination follow the table.

Table A–1. Devices and Their Supported Codecs

Device Model	Container	Codecs	Notes
Torch 9800	MP4/M4A/M4V/3GP/MOV	H.264	(1) (2) (6)
		H.263	(3)
		MPEG4	(2) (22)
		AAC-LC/AAC+/eAAC+	(2) (6)
		AMR-NB	(2)
	AVI	MPEG4	(2)(22)
		MP3	
	ASF/WMA/WMV	Windows Media Video 9	(5)
		Windows Media Audio 9 Standard/Professional	
		Windows Media 10 Standard/Professional	
	MP3	MP3	
	FLAC	Flac / Ogg Vorbis	

Device Model	Container	Codecs	Notes
	OGG	Flac / Ogg Vorbis	
	AMR	AMR-NB	(2)
	AAC	AAC-LC/AAC+/eAAC+	(2) (26)
	WAV	PCM/G.711(A)/G.711(U)/GSM 610	(23)
	MID	MIDI	(24)
Bold 9700	MP4/M4A/3GP/MOV	H.264	(1)(2)
		H.263	(2)(8)
		MPEG4	(2)(6)(22)
		AAC-LC/AAC+/eAAC+	(2)(6)
		AMR-NB	(2)
	AVI	MPEG4	(2)(22)
		MP3	
	ASF/WMA/WMV	Windows Media Video 9	(5)
		Windows Media Audio 9 Standard/Professional	(2)
		Windows Media 10 Standard/Professional	(2)
	MP3	MP3	
Style 9670	MP4/M4A/M4V/MOV/3GP/3GP2	H.264	(1)(2)
		H.263	(2)(3)
		MPEG4	(2)(4)
		AAC-LC/AAC+/eAAC+	(2)
		AMR-NB	(2)
		QCELP EVRC	

Device Model	Container	Codecs	Notes
	AVI	MPEG4	(2)(4)
		MP3	
	ASF/WMA/WMV	Windows Media Video 9	(2) (5)
		Windows Media Audio 9 Standard/Professional	(2)
		Windows Media 10 Standard/Professional	(2)
	MP3	MP3	
	FLAC	Flac	
	OGG	Flac / Ogg Vorbis	
	AMR	AMR-NB	
	AAC	AAC-LC/AAC+/eAAC+	(2) (25) (26)
	WAV	PCM/G.711(A)/G.711(U) /GSM 610	(23)
	MID	MIDI	(27)
	QCP	QCELP EVRC	
Tour 9630, Storm 2 9520, Storm 2 9550	MP4/M4A/3GP/3GP2	H.264	(1)(2)(6)
		H.263	(2)(3)
		MPEG4	(2)(4)
		AAC-LC/AAC+/eAAC+	(2)(6)
		AMR-NB	(2)
		QCELP EVRC	
	AVI	MPEG4	(2)(4)
		MP3	

Device Model	Container	Codecs	Notes
	ASF/WMA/WMV	Windows Media Video 9	(5)
		Windows Media Audio 9	(2)
		Windows Media 10 Standard/Professional	(2)
	MP3	MP3	
Storm 9500/9530	MP4/M4A/3GP/3GP2	H.264	(1)(2)(6)
		H.263	(2)(3)
		MPEG4	(2)(4)
		AAC-LC/AAC+/eAAC+	(2)(6)
		AMR-NB	(2)
		QCELP EVRC	
	AVI	MPEG4	(2)(4)
		MP3	
	ASF/WMA/WMV	Windows Media Video 9	(5)
		Windows Media Audio 9	(2)
		Windows Media 10 Standard/Professional	(2)
	MP3	MP3	
Bold 9000	MP4/M4A/3GP/MOV	H.264	(2) (11)
		H.263	(2)(8)
		MPEG4	(2)(6)(12)
		AAC-LC/AAC+/eAAC+	(2)(6)
		AMR-NB	(2)
	AVI	MPEG4	(2)(11)

Device Model	Container	Codecs	Notes
		MP3	
	ASF/WMA/WMV	Windows Media Video 9	(13)
		Windows Media Audio 9 Standard/Professional	
		Windows Media 10 Standard/Professional	
	MP3	MP3	
Curve 8900, 8520	MP4/M4A/3GP/MOV	H.264	(2) (7)
		H.263	(2)(8)
		MPEG4	(2)(6)(9)
		AAC-LC/AAC+/eAAC+	(2)(6)
		AMR-NB	(2)
	AVI	MPEG4	(2)(9)
		MP3	
	ASF/WMA/WMV	Windows Media Video 9	(10)
		Windows Media Audio 9	
		Windows Media 10 Standard/Professional	
	MP3	MP3	
Curve 8330, 8830	MP4/M4A/3GP/MOV	H.263	(2) (8)
		MPEG4	(2) (6) (19)
		AAC-LC/AAC+/eAAC+	(2)(6)
		AMR-NB	(2)
	ASF/WMA/WMV	Windows Media Video 9	(21)

Device Model	Container	Codecs	Notes
		Windows Media Audio 9 Standard/Professional	
		Windows Media 10 Standard/Professional	
	MP3	MP3	
Curve 8300, 8310, 8320, 8350i, 8800, 8820	MP4/M4A/3GP/MOV	H.263	(2) (8)
		MPEG4	(2) (15) (19)
		AAC-LC/AAC+/eAAC+	(2)(15)
		AMR-NB	(2)
	AVI	MPEG4	(2)(18)(20)
		MP3	(16)(18)
	ASF/WMA/WMV	Windows Media Video 9	(21)
		Windows Media Audio 9 Standard/Professional	
		Windows Media 10 Standard/Professional	
	MP3	MP3	
Pearl 8130	MP4/3GP	H.263	(2) (8)
		MPEG4	(2) (6) (14)
		AAC-LC/AAC+/eAAC+	(2)(6)
		AMR-NB	(2)
	ASF/WMA/WMV	Windows Media Video 9	(17)
		Windows Media Audio 9 Standard/Professional	

Device Model	Container	Codecs	Notes
		Windows Media 10 Standard/Professional	
	MP3	MP3	
Pearl 8100, 8110, 8120, 8220	MP4/M4A/3GP/MOV	H.263	(2) (8)
		MPEG4	(2)(14)(15)
		AAC-LC/AAC+/eAAC+	(2)(15)
		AMR-NB	(2)
	AVI	MPEG4	(2)(16)(18)
		MP3	(18)
	ASF/WMA/WMV	Windows Media Video 9	(17)
		Windows Media Audio 9 Standard/Professional	
		Windows Media 10 Standard/Professional	
	MP3	MP3	

Notes

(1) Baseline Profile. 480×360 resolution. Up to 2Mbps, 30fps.

(2) Supports RTSP streaming with device software 4.3 or later.

(3) Profile 0 and 3, Level 30. 480×360 resolution. Up to 2Mbps, 30fps.

(4) Simple Profile, Level 3. 480×360 resolution. Up to 2Mbps, 30fps.

(5) WMV3 Simple Profile. 480×360 resolution. 30fps.

(6) Recommended format for local playback.

(7) Baseline Profile. 480×360 resolution. Up to 1.5Mbps, 24fps.

(8) Profile 0 and 3, Level 45.

(9) Simple/Advance Simple Profiles. 480×360 resolution. Up to 1.5Mbps, 24fps.

(10) WMV3 Simple Profile, Main Profile. 480×360 resolution. 24fps.

(11) Baseline Profile. 480×320 resolution. Up to 1.5Mbps, 24fps.

(12) Simple/Advance Simple Profiles. 480×320 resolution. Up to 1.5Mbps, 24fps.

(13) WMV3 Simple Profile, Main Profile. 480×320 resolution. 24fps.

(14) Simple Profile. 240x320 resolution. Up to 768kbps, 24fps.

(15) Recommended format for local playback for device software version 4.5 or higher.

(16) Simple/Advance Simple Profiles. 240×320 resolution. Up to 768kbps, 24fps.

(17) WMV3 Simple Profile. 240×320 resolution. 24fps.

(18) Recommended format for local playback for device software version 4.2 or 4.3.

(19) Simple Profile. 320×240 resolution. Up to 768kbps, 24fps.

(20) Simple/Advance Simple Profiles. 320×240 resolution. Up to 768kbps, 24fps.

(21) WMV3 Simple Profile. 320×240 resolution. 24fps.

(22) Simple/Advance Simple Profiles. 480×360 resolution. Up to 2Mbps, 30fps.

(23) Stereo

(24) Supports SMF formats 0 and 1

(25) Supports Audio Data Interchange Format (ADIF) format

(26) Supports Audio Data Transport Stream (ADTS) format

(27) 128 polyphony

Index

H

■X, Y

■Z

Breinigsville, PA USA
15 February 2011
255649BV00002B/57-318/P